1006213217

D1121587

MASTER CURRENCY
SUSTAINABLE ECONOMIC
SYSTEM

VOLUME 1, 2, & 3

RODNEY A. FISHER

LIBRARY
GRANT MacEWAN
COLLEGE

Master Currency Sustainable Economic System

Volumes 1, 2 & 3

Copyright: Rodney A. Fisher 2007

All Rights Reserved

No part of this book may be reproduced in any form,
by photocopying or by any electronic or mechanical means,
including information storage or retrieval systems,
without permission in writing from both the copyright owner
and publisher of this book.

ISBN 978-1-906045-03-6

First published February 2007 by

RODNEY A. FISHER

Gofynach Fawr,
Llanarth,
Ceredigion, SA47 OPD.
Wales

Printed in Wales by Cambrian Printers Aberystwyth

MASTER CURRENCY
SUSTAINABLE ECONOMIC SYSTEM

FOREWORD

The purpose of the economic system is to provide powerful economic tools for developing the whole world into a fully sustainable economy, working in harmony with the environment.

The human race has reshaped the environment to improve their standard of living, using their knowledge and skills developed over thousands of years. Since the industrial revolution the process of development has accelerated to present day levels. This has enabled many people to enjoy a high standard of living, security and considerable time for leisure, but not necessarily happiness! However, what we have not yet achieved is a world economy that is free from all major conflicts, and one that functions fairly and honestly, that serves people properly throughout the world, without exploitation and all the financial distortions presently taking place. The world also lacks the infrastructure to guide people onto a sustainable economic path for their families, free as possible from manmade problems.

The Master Currency Economic System takes all matters into account to deal with all events of our lives, so as to guide world economies onto a sustainable path that is humanly possible. The system is used as an economic tool to explain to people, politicians, specialists, businesses, governments and all other institutions their roles in the economy, and how it should be integrated, maintained and developed. It explains how the components of the economy interact and what our duties should be, and stresses that the right form of education at the right time is essential.

The author, (a professional consulting civil engineer and businessman with a wide range of skills and international experience), by the time he reached half way through his career, was very aware present market force led to economies failing badly, creating national and international problems. Since that time he took every opportunity to carry out research into economies, and started the creation of his economic system, a development process over thirty years. In this period he checked and rechecked his models and ideas to see whether the sustainable concept was right. This enabled him to complete the skeleton for the world's first sustainable system, taking all matters into account, including how the development process operates. His book on the system can only give the methodology, strategy, skeleton for the system and its key trading rules. To complete his work for the full structure of the system is a collective task for thousands of professional and skilled persons. Very few economists, like himself have had the opportunity in their working life to be involved with all the key processes forming the economy. It is this form of experience that has permitted the Master Plan to take the world economies forward to be developed, following a natural structure in harmony with the environment.

Many people and government bodies, including central banks, and private institutions have helped the author with all sorts of information, and many have wished him success. Very many years of carefully thought through work have shaped the economic structure and the tools to develop it.

The author did not want to make the book too long, and accordingly has concentrated on key structures and information issues. He is aware, that however long the book, there would always be information that some persons would wish for. In due course this sort of extra information would become available in other books, or obtained in workshops on the author's system, to explain other details people would wish to have or discuss.

The proposed new economic system will create many new skills and products worldwide that are needed to develop sustainable economies. All values for products, studies and estimates would be carried out in Master Currency Units, so that accurate comparisons can be made worldwide. Some of the products and information required as soon as possible are:

1. Translation of the author's books into each national language.
2. The building of the structure for the new modern world information system.
3. The conversion factors for each national currency into Master Currency Units, until currencies can be pegged to the MCU.
4. An international organisation to co-ordinate and manage all the activities required to run a sustainable form of economic development worldwide.
5. Banking products and accounts based on the Master Currency.
6. Business advisors on setting up sustainable economies and providing specialist courses as needed.
7. A continuous series of television programs informing the public of what is required to create sustainable economies and protect the environment, and why.

Until governments take up their tasks, it will need to be carried out and managed by the private sector.

The author will naturally have to be available to assist with the above tasks and also to explain to governments how his system is used to rid the world of major conflicts, and solve national and international problems peacefully.

INTRODUCTION

The Master Currency Sustainable Economic System, the title of this book, is based on the MH System. MH is the abbreviation for man-hour. This unit is a productivity unit for hours of work done by the workforce, and is the unit that the author has employed to study economies and how they function, and the unit used to model and develop the world economies. It is also the unit that industry uses to study and plan its activities. The Master Currency is a productivity unit based on general, or basic education that we all need when living in modern economies.

The MH System is a sustainable form of economic system designed to maintain and develop a sustainable environment and world economy. The book is in three volumes and explains and describes how economies should function to follow a logical and natural path. It follows the aspirations of 'The Earth Charter' and is a tool and methodology that can make it reality. The three volumes taken together outline the skeleton of the MH System and explain how it should be built and managed as the world moves forward.

Volume 1 forms the basis of knowledge that we should all need to understand during our individual life span: it informs people of what is needed to achieve the best possible existence during our lives, and how we need to work together in harmony to support an achievable standard of living, as free as possible from human conflicts, which requires respecting our human rights, being honest and moral.

Volume 2 is concerned with the economic sector that provides all the goods and services producing the world's standard of living: it includes key models for the overall economy and for its productive elements, the businesses and institutions. It explains how the monetary and financial system should operate and how sustainable economies function.

Volume 3 deals with the government sector of the economy and their duties. Using data in volumes 1 and 2 and other information it guides governments and politicians in understanding how sustainable economies are managed and developed.

Chapter 29 Volume 3, the concluding chapter, is like an overview of the MH System, and could also be read first.

VOLUME 1

Contents

VOLUME 1 TABLE INDEX

VOLUME 2

Contents

Page

VOLUME 2 TABLE INDEX

VOLUME 3

Contents

Page

VOLUME 3 TABLE INDEX

MASTER CURRENCY SUSTAINABLE ECONOMIC SYSTEM

VOLUME 1

FAMILY SECTOR

CHAPTER 1

THE NATURAL ECONOMY

The natural economy that supports our lives commences with the family unit. A family can consist of one, or more persons, where they jointly run their home economy in the manner they decide. Their home is normally run using their own skills wherever possible. Where their skills are insufficient a member/s works outside the home economy to earn money, purely to buy in the needs and wants the family cannot themselves provide.

The needs and wants bought in the outside economy create the business, government and other bodies and institutions to supply families with goods and services they require. These organisations are the servants of the families and not the reverse. In a modern economy these organisations are substantial, and form a very large part of our overall national wealth.

We now go into greater detail of the key elements of the natural economy that support us. This then gives a sound basis on which we can later make comparisons.

Family Unit

The family unit includes single persons, married couples and married couples with one or more children, or say any group living in a family type unit.

Under normal conditions families support themselves, and decide on the standard of living they wish to achieve, or the one they consider to be acceptable.

Each family would decide their individual duties to support their home activities: cooking, cleaning, shopping, developing the economy of the home, and the amount of do-it-yourself activities. Some persons may remain at home the whole time to manage it, and it could be anyone in the family unit. Maybe children would help to run the home and later in life contribute to the financial costs. Who does what in the home is a family decision and all families are likely to be different, nowadays in a modern industrial economy. It is no more a woman's job than a man's to look after the home – they decide for themselves who does what. It makes sense to use the person who is best for running and managing the home, so that it can be done quickly and efficiently, and at the same time result in a good standard. No longer in a modern world can we be completely self-sufficient, as in a modern society taxes have to be paid to support the nation's infrastructure. We also demand a wide range of goods and services to supply our needs and wants, and no longer can a family make and provide them using entirely their own resources. Many of the tasks of running a home they would be able to carry out themselves without outside help, and some families would even be able to supply some of their own goods and services, which other families cannot..

Preparing meals, cleaning and shopping can create several hours work daily for one person and it could vary between 2 to 10 hours per day depending on the size of the home and the family. If the home also has a garden further hours of work would be required to keep it in order. The garden can also be used to produce food. Looking after a home and garden can involve the husband and wife, or family in more hours of work than they actually need to work for others, to earn money for the needs and wants they cannot provide for themselves.

Most families do not build their own homes or provide the goods and services to support it. Businesses and government bodies can usually supply these more economically than they could themselves, i.e. for far less human hours of productivity, the reason being that the people producing them in industry have the right skills, equipment, machines and other resources to do so. Families will never be able to learn the millions of skills or find the money to buy the equipment, and machines, that are used in the general economy.

If one does not have one's own transport, the family would need to use other people's transport when travelling distances too far to walk. Holidays, which are not spent at home, with relatives or friends, would have to be paid for, as also many forms of entertainment. All these we cannot provide for ourselves.

In a modern society we expect schools for our children, and protection for ourselves, homes and country, complete with an economic system to support us. We are not always able to work, and in these periods could need financial support and, later in life, a pension when we are retired. When ill, we need medical services. Government bodies and businesses should fulfil these needs.

There is no doubt that the needs and wants of the family units create the need for businesses and government services, whose sole purpose it is to provide these on behalf of the families.

One or more members of each family need to be able to work full-time, part-time or sometimes over-time to earn money (to exchange their hours of labour) using the skills they have available (or others they are able to learn). These persons normally only do so in the general economy.

We can conclude by stating we must have work (other than at home), so that we are able to support our family economies. We can say quite fairly that to have work in the general economy is a human right and, therefore, that any sound economy should allow for it to be achievable, although it may not always be the type of work we may desire.

Throughout our lives we spend time making comparisons against standards and various objects. We also need to keep our economies and lives in balance with our resources. These lead to achieving our various levels of development. Comparisons, standards, balance and levels form very important elements in our lives, as they are needed in making our decisions.

Comparisons

Consciously and subconsciously we are using comparisons every day of our lives. Our physical movements are gauged all the time to ensure they are correct. When they are not, we do not make the right movements, and need to correct them. We judge these correct movements by making comparisons. Mentally we are comparing our own knowledge and those of others (written and spoken) so we can make decisions that we believe to be correct, or to the best advantage, whatever that might be.

We frequently compare prices of goods and services, quality of products, and other people's productivity, often in comparison with our own, to consider whether we are properly paid, or have done an honest day's work for the money we are paid. When we are working, or buying we frequently compare what we require against standard measures – weight, length, volume, time and money, the ones we all need to use. For many of us there are many other standards we need to compare against, some being specialised products and services.

By making comparisons we develop our economy. People that are engaged in it make comparisons with existing and previous things – quality, quickness, strength, resistance, ease of use, heaviness, price, efficiency and methods of production are some of the items of comparisons made. People, by making certain modifications, or alterations, from the experience of their careful observations, can make improvements that would raise the quality of the product, or service, in some way that will give rise to a better and perhaps more secure human economy. To achieve some of these improvements, many people need to specialise in just one small element of the economy, because they need to absorb a substantial number of facts (knowledge) on their particular speciality, before any real improvements or progress can be made.

Standards

As mentioned above, standards are required so that many comparisons can be made. For most of us the most important ones are the measures of length, volume, weight, time and money. Money can be a constant or a variable in value. The natural economy needs money that remains a constant value, which is a properly defined standard. Money should not vary in value and this can be achieved by linking it to average human productivity based on time. What money buys does vary, resulting from changes in development and economic conditions. Sometimes this gives more for our units of money, and for others less.

By using well-known standards on which we can make comparisons we can judge quality, and when improvements or deteriorations occur. When planning our economies, whether they are at family, business or national level, we can work out the cost of our needs and wants in stable prices (a natural money), and decide what is too expensive and what should be improved next, by making it less expensive, or better quality. With sound budgets we are able to determine how much money is available for improvements and decide how many can be made, and which ones would give the optimum benefits (this forms part of the development process).

Balance

Everything in an economy should be kept in balance. Family, business and national budgets, must be what we can afford. The family must not spend all its money on food, clothing and luxuries, but must also leave sufficient money in the budget for housing. A business should not spend most of its money on the head office and not leave enough money for the factory. A government must not spend so much on its prisons that there is little left for research and rehabilitation of the prisoners. If our nation has insufficient money for education, health and pensions, its people must not only work longer hours to provide them, but also in the right skills, which might mean some retraining for some people, to restore the balance of the economy. Alternatively, we must make savings in time, in making goods and providing services, by using modern inventions, so we do not have to work longer hours. Finally the balance could also be achieved by lowering our standard of living, to what we can afford.

Our skills must satisfy our needs and not only our wants. For example we need to maintain our skills in the right balance so that we can always earn an income. Our skills must not only be the ones we like, but must be the ones business and governments want.

The demand of our economies on the natural resources must be kept within the resources that can be abstracted, without upsetting the natural balances of the environment.

Levels

From the previous paragraph it is clear that the level of our economy is dependent on the degree of our nation's development, i.e. the level of our education: the range of skills we possess, the nature of our production process, how advanced the technology in them are and how long we are prepared to work. The standard of living, or its level, is determined by what the citizens seek. When planning and maintaining an economy one must know the levels of development that are wanted. For a business it would be the demand for its products, or services. For government the level of its services would be dependent on what the people can afford to pay in taxes.

The development of our lives in family economies, in businesses and government services are dependent on the use of these comparative elements of the economy, and the proper use of them. We must all understand how to make comparisons, how to use standards, how to keep the economy in balance, particularly our own, and how to select the right level for our economy.

Our economy will only be sustainable so long as we steer it on the correct path. As the world is continuously changing we will have to re-adjust our economies accordingly. It will not happen on its own, but only under our influence.

Work and Basic Productivity

Work is a human right and we must have work in the general economy so that we can support ourselves, and our families. We work for other people, businesses, or government, to earn units of productivity, for our hours of labour. For most of us this is all we have to offer to be able to earn money, that we need to buy the goods and services to support our individual economy, and pay taxes to support the government and the services it supplies.

How many hours we have to work depends on the quantity of our needs and wants, and the amount of taxes we have to pay. We need to keep our economy in balance, and must therefore earn money to support it, but we do not have to work more hours than necessary, if we do not want to. Those of us that do work more hours than we need to support our economy, create savings with the money not spent, which they can spend at a later date. The money is capital, our units of productivity that have been invested in goods and services we have made, or supported by working. From what has just been said, it is important to know the cost of the goods and services, so we can work out how much money we will need for ourselves, or the family budget, as we need this to calculate how many hours we need to work. It is also important to know how many units of money we should receive for an hour's work.

Everything we collect, make and provide for the economy is only available because we have worked the necessary hours to create them. Without work we would not survive. The goods and services we cannot provide for ourselves are provided by other people's hours of work. By working for others, outside our family economies, and earning units of human productivity we can exchange them through the medium of money we have earned. How this exchange happens is explained later.

The human productivity unit must be clearly a standard, as if it is not, how can we value our goods and services so that we can estimate the cost of our economies, and decide how many hours of work are needed to support them? Human productivity varies from person to person, depending on our ability and experience. Businesses need to know what the productivity of their workforce is, in every skill, so that they can estimate the number of hours of work that are needed for each task to be carried out. They consequently need the average rate of productivity. If everybody works on average human productivity as a standard, we can then all exchange our hours of work on this basis, as every skill has an average rate. If we then link the value of our money to this human productivity unit, we have money that remains stable in relation to our productiveness. By working on this basis, all goods and services can be priced in these stable standard units, which means that the price would not change once established, unless there is a change in the way products are produced, that causes more or less hours of average human labour to be used. A natural economic system, therefore, is founded on this basis, as this will allow prices to remain stable (no inflation). Working on this basis on a set standard for comparison we can all trade with each other fairly and honestly. Rates of productivity are discussed in Chapter 3.

So far we are all aware we must work for others to earn our wages, but what sort of work? From our own point of view we wish to work at what we like to do and probably what we are best at, so we can gain the highest possible wages. Many of us are able to achieve this for much of our lives; unfortunately some may not, and would have to seek their second, third, or even less favourable choice for some parts of their lives. The reason for this is that we are in a world where changes are taking place quickly, due to the pace of our inventions and improvements, which produce them. As this process takes place, many old skills can become obsolete, and many more new ones are created, some requiring quite long periods of retraining. With so many millions of skills now needed in a modern world, it is so easy for too many people to train in some skills that seem very desirable (or which they think would earn the most money). This then means that some people will be disappointed. Many professional skills take years to learn and then, having been learnt, perhaps a few years later are no longer required.

Nowadays it is sound advice to plan one's life to be skilful in more than one vocation, and certainly one or more of these should be simple skills (often called unskilled work, but quite wrongly). We should count on having periods of retraining. Because of the changes taking place, skilled workers (those who have taken special skills requiring long periods of training) are more likely to find their investment in themselves at risk, like businesses are when markets change, reducing the balance in the number of the skills required. With unskilled work one can fairly soon retrain and it is usually paid for by the employer. Skilled workers, when they have to retrain, usually do so partly at their own cost.

The rate of productivity for unskilled work is negotiated around the trade's average rate of productivity. That of skilled workers is also negotiated similarly, but the rate is increased to take into account the period of further education and training. This can be calculated in different ways, depending on the economic system in use. Wage differentials are described in Chapter 3.

Improvements in production, gradually reducing the human element of productivity, do not take place at a constant rate; and it can happen that more existing jobs are shed than new ones created, or the reverse could happen. This would cause a shortage of jobs, or insufficient workers. It has been mentioned that work is a human right, as without it people cannot support themselves. An economy, therefore, needs to monitor development improvements very carefully so that arrangements can be made to keep people in 'full' employment. Without careful management and understanding of the economic system, high unemployment rates can arise. Properly trained managers can prevent this situation from occurring. Maintaining full employment is a government duty. Full employment is not a self-balancing operation and, therefore, must be managed.

Businesses

Businesses are created to supply all the needs and wants we cannot, or do not want to supply for ourselves, and our families. Businesses also supply other businesses and government with their requirements. Businesses are usually privately owned, but governments can also own them: the numbers and type, depending on the political policies. Most businesses specialise in a particular type of work or service, and most of us are well aware of this, particularly for the domestic goods and services. What most people know very little about are all the industries that support the key industries, like the retail shops, farming, transportation, construction, water and electricity supply, education and health. There are probably millions of supporting industries, so no attempt is made to list them in this book. However, consider a hardware and ironmongery shop business fully stocked with a complete range of goods. The business only sells the goods and, therefore, buys in the thousands of lines from manufacturers. Take nuts, bolts and screws from the largest to the smallest, different metals, different strengths and qualities. These would not all come from one manufacturer. So let us think about the factory. Each group of sizes would require different sizes of machine. Each thread size would require its own cutting tool and each type of metal would again require perhaps other special tools. Next, the various sizes of product would each need suitable packaging. By following through for all the lines in just an ironmongery shop, then all the other businesses involved to produce the goods, and all their supporting industries that make their tools and equipment, and the ones that supply them etc., it is not surprising that millions of skills are required.

The number of people in a business can range from one person to thousands as it all depends on the type of the business and the demand for their product.

Businesses use tools and equipment from small to very large. They allow the businesses to produce their product more efficiently, to a better standard, and for less human hours of productivity. By this process goods and services become less expensive, and in consequence we can all have more of them to improve the quality of our lives. Factories with modern production lines can make goods very inexpensively, compared with manual methods using simple tools. The tools and equipment, including computer software, that industry uses run into millions of items, and operators have to know exactly how to use each of the ones in their control.

The markets for the many very specialised industries are international, and need to be, as the demand for their special product could be small, but very important to every national economy.

Most of our domestic needs are created by businesses using mass production methods and labour intensive services. Probably 80% of us work in these industries. In say a large village, or small town, of 1000 families about 60% of all needs and wants could actually be supplied by their own skills. If the inhabitants wish to be in a sustainable economy, it would appear that they must be able to trade at least nationally (so that the majority of the human skills are available)

Sound businesses usually give a good service and quality products, because the people there have well trained skills to suit their vocation. In a small town, a small group of people may have skills that cannot be used to support domestic requirements, but are only suitable for industrial purposes. To enable these persons to work in their area all types of business become necessary, so that these specialists can earn their living. By this process the country has the benefits of industries best methods, and quality goods and services at their disposal; and everyone can gain from this. Each town or community only provides some of the specialised goods and services needed in the overall economy, for example, prams, bicycles and toys in a town and garden tools and sheds in a large village.

In many districts of our country there are perhaps just one, or a few major businesses mainly making goods for domestic requirements, which are supported by a whole range of small, specialised companies. Some of these, because of overseas competition, and an unstable economic system, could be on the point of having to close. If the main businesses collapse, probably many of the others supporting them would too. It is important that a natural economic system is used that would protect them from any unfair overseas competition, that can be caused by an improper monetary economic system and unsound trading rules.

There is little point in businesses buying from other nations goods and services that can be produced to the same standards in their own country. Unnecessary transportation wastes the world's resources and adds to pollution.

Many people believe businesses' sole objective is to make huge profits from their venture, and all the proprietors running them have this sole motive. Although this is true for a few greedy proprietors, the majority do not have this attitude. Many are run for the proprietor's achievement in creating his product, of which he could be very proud. Probably most firms' annual profits are below 10% of the value of their product turnover, which is quite acceptable and necessary for a business to remain sustainable. Businesses should not make excessive profits, but only reasonable ones for their particular industry. If they overcharge, the balance of the economy is distorted, and this would not be fair or correct in a sustainable form of economy.

There is no doubt that to satisfy domestic demand there are millions of products created, and a nation's citizens rely on businesses to supply them. If people did not specialise in millions of different skills we could not support our present day standard of living. Businesses rely on human skills and cannot survive without a properly trained workforce.

Exchange of Labour for Goods and Services

To illustrate how goods and services can be exchanged fairly using money, a very simple model is used in the following tables.

The wages earned by a hundred people in Tables 1 and 2 assume they all have average productivity and work the same hours, making their wages all the same; but where their productivities vary, the figures given in the example would average out.

Table 1 shows how the weekly wage to support a family of four could be spent. This too indicates what businesses must supply to cover our needs and wants. The hours of productivity are the average required to produce the needs and wants in each section, and assume a standard education, without special study. This unit is chosen, because it is the only one that we can all exchange (it is common to all persons, skilled and unskilled). The table shows how a person's weekly wage could be spent and also for a hundred people. It should be noted that skilled persons' wages would be increased by a wage differential, so they would work less hours for the same average wage.

Table 1

How wages of £219.00 are spent in an average week.
(Based on families of four persons.)

	Food	Clothing	Shelter		Luxuries	All Taxes (Government Services)
			Contents	Buildings		
Percentage spent on needs and wants	16	6	9	22	21	26
= hours of average human productivity.	5.84	2.19	3.285	8.03	7.665	9.49
£s spent.	35.04	13.14	19.71	48.18	45.99	56.94
100 people's wages spent in £.	3504.00	1314.00	1971.00	4818.00	4599.00	5694.00

Table 2

How money is earned
(Among businesses, organisations and 100 families of four.)

	Food	Clothing	Shelter		Luxuries	All Taxes (Government Services)
			Contents	Buildings		
Persons working in businesses.	16	6	9	22	21	26
100 person's wages earned in £.	3504.00	1314.00	1971.00	4818.00	4599.00	5694.00

Note: Tables 1 and 2 are based on the assumption that the people work 1900 hours per year. This would average out at 36.5 hours in each of the 52 weeks of the year, however holidays must be allowed for: so if we work a 40 hour week we would have to work for 47.5 weeks in the example.

In the tables the £ is based on 6 per hour (of average human productivity, a natural standard unit of work). One minute of work, therefore, would be worth 10 pence. Each week's wage for 36.5 hours worked (over 52 weeks) at £6 per hour = £219.00.

Table 2 shows the number of people that would have to work in each of the 6 sections of the economy shown in order to make and provide all the services the families demand in Table 1 (to obtain the right proportions of people working in the business, say food, one multiplies the 100 people by the percentage of the wages spent on food as shown in Table 1, i.e. 100 x 16% = 16 employees). The wages also represent the turnover of the businesses to keep the economy for 100 people in balance. The 100 people form their own economy in the tables and, therefore they represent the business owners, government employees and the businesses employees. In the example one could say that there are 5 businesses and one government body. These supply all the needs and wants of the families of the 100 persons working (total population 400 people in the example). The food business would produce all the food and have its own shop for selling it. The other sections would be similar. For example the building business would gather all the materials, manufacture the articles wanted and build the buildings. The government would provide the education, health services, pensions, roads, laws etc.

Normal barter is usually between two parties (or persons) and everyone understands this. However, how money circulates to create an exchange does cause confusion. So let us go through the motions of what happens. First we work for an employer, say for a week's wages. The 100 people doing this in the community create the goods and services we need. Our employer then pays us at the end of the week with a cheque. This cheque is not the goods or service we want, but just the promise of the number of units of work converted into £s, in the example given. These units are then exchanged with businesses and government to buy what we want for the family for the week ahead. If we buy from all sections we need to write six cheques. When the employers have received the cheques, and the people the goods and services they wanted, the transaction (or monetary barter) is complete and the employer has fulfilled his promise. The cheques that each business or government wrote are all balanced by the cheques they received for their sales. Six people could represent these six sections of the economy and carry out the exchange as explained to prove that it works, i.e. the persons representing the food business would write out 16 cheques to pay his business wages (16 x £219.00 = £3504.00) – hundred people would then write cheques out to him for food (100 x £35.04 = £3504 – the amount of the cheques he wrote balances with the amount he has received. From this explanation it can be understood that the cheques are no more than a means of exchange of our human labour. The £ in the example is fixed to human productivity: therefore it is not subject to inflation. The £ sterling is no more than a means of exchange, and it is only a promise to pay that value (whatever it may be at the time, as it is subject to inflation). If the £ sterling should fall before the goods are bought the goods would go up in value, and the exchange would no longer balance. Most currencies are subject to this problem, which in a natural economic system does not happen. The monetary exchange system just described is natural and sustainable.

Cheques, in whatever currency they are issued, are like money, but with one difference: they may not be honoured if a person runs out of finance, or is dishonest. Legal tender (money issued by government) is backed by national assets, provided they are notes and coins issued by the government. Unlike cheques, which are not normally passed around from person to person, cash continues in circulation for years, being passed from person to person. It is therefore important that this money does not devalue as it represents people's savings, particularly when people keep savings in cash, sometimes for years. Money represents goods and services we have created. To keep money in balance, it should be noted that governments should not use tax money they converted into notes and coins, unless of course they have actually sold them to the banks and they are truly in circulation. If they do, the money would not be backed by assets (goods and services). If it wished to, the government could back the money with gold reserves, instead of goods and services that are held by businesses. The value of gold however, does vary, whereas average human productivity is constant.

Money in circulation is money that has been sold to banks, which they pay for by cheque (or money transferred electronically) and then, in turn, sell to the public. When the money is not held by the government, but by people, it is still backed by goods and services, because money represents goods and services ready for use. Money represents savings and is like a credit balance on our bank statements or other savings held by financial institutions holding our savings.

When we earn money we create new goods and services. Money, therefore, represents goods and services in a new condition completely ready for use. People who borrow money are the ones that hold goods or services we have made. In order to keep the money in 'as new' condition borrowers must maintain assets (goods and services) in 'as new' condition, and in a form that is wanted (out-dated stock would not be wanted).

One can conclude from this explanation that money is only a means of exchange for our hours of human labour working for others (businesses, institutions and government). One cannot really avoid savings and debts from occurring in the economy: to do so would make fair distribution of goods and services very difficult, and could make people very wasteful. Money should never vary in value, but be a fixed measure, representing in the natural economy our hours of human productivity.

Prices and what they represent.

When we spend money each unit could represent the elements of the economy shown in Table 3. It should be noted that the percentages in the table would be different for every item or service bought. Many people may be surprised to see how little an actual item bought ex-factory might cost, and how selling, advertising etc. can cost a great deal as Table 3 indicates. Some of us, although not very skilled, might find it cheaper to provide some items for ourselves, like growing vegetables. In practice, a whole chain of businesses could be involved in providing a product or service.

Much of items 9, 11, 12 and 13 in Table 3 could be spent in other businesses that support the final business in the chain of businesses that supply the final goods or service. Some of those other businesses could be very specialised, using people's skills that would be of little use in our domestic economy.

Table 3 also represents how the prices of goods can be established. There is another very important element of the price 'net rent' items Nos. 10, 12 15 and 16 in Table 3, and this is a new term for economists. 'Net rent' is the proportion of any sale price of a product we buy, on which no human effort has been expended (no work done for it), not even the cost of collection. It is like a gift. Net rent is usually found in the following: wages, interest rates, business net profits, rents, royalties, currencies which are overvalued and any overcharging, which gives unjustifiable net profits.   Net rents are given to take risk and give incentive to set up and run businesses, to learn skills requiring further education and apprenticeships, to loan money and create new products, which is normally paid in royalties.

Table 3

Some of the elements of spent money.

Elements of the economy	Possible percentage of monetary unit spending power.
1 Actual goods or service the customer buys	38
2 Cost of selling	17
3 Storage while awaiting sale	2
4 Packaging	1
5 Transporting goods	1
6 Wastages	5
7 Rent for premises	2
8 Interest on loans	1
9 Royalties	1
10 Cost of development (net rent)	2
11 Writing off outdated stocks	3
12 Net rents in wage differentials	8
13 Maintenance of business assets (buildings and machines)	6
14 General expenses in running the business	5
15 Retained profit to be used later in business (net rent)	3
16 Profit for proprietors (net rent)	5
Total of all elements	100

The overall net rents as given to Table 3 could amount to 18% when taking into account rent interest and royalty payments. Although not shown, the prices in Tables 1 and 2 include for net rents, not exceeding 25% of the real value of the goods. Suppose all the employees and the businesses were greedy and all charged 50% more than they should have, the total net rents would then be 75%. The 25% has been carefully worked out and is affordable, and allows for sustainable development. The 50% extra when added to the 25% would amount to 75% (three quarters of the earnings), clearly not affordable or sustainable. Generally speaking a large proportion of the workforce would then only be able to afford one third of the goods and services they actually need. Such a redistribution of wealth is unacceptable. To prevent this from happening in a natural economy trading rules are introduced, so that the trading exchange process remains fair, honest and sustainable. Trading rules create sound wage earnings and prices for goods and services, and inflation disappears. If a monetary system allows money that has not been earned to enter into the wage, goods and service exchange system, it would become distorted and out of balance; and the greater the amount the higher inflation would be. Therefore, trading rules must never be broken. Prices must represent realistic costs, because everything we buy and sell has an element of human productivity, and it is that productivity we rely on to support our family economies.

Existing Assets

So far the simple models have shown the exchange process for new goods and services. However, the economy exchanges second-hand goods and other assets, like houses, land, industrial buildings, businesses and shares. These, like new goods and services, must also be bought and sold to comply with the trading rules. They must not be overvalued, and where appropriate must take into consideration their condition and be discounted for wear and tear. If they are bought and sold for too much, the balance of the economy would be distorted and become unsustainable.

Existing assets in developed nations can be worth many years of national human productivity, the useful assets probably between 5 and 10 years work. Part of our collective daily tasks is in maintaining these in sound useable condition, and there is a limit to how much time we can spend on this large element of the economy without affecting the overall sustainability of the economy.

Royalties

Many goods and services sold contain a royalty element. At the time the amount of royalty is agreed, the quantity that may be sold can only be estimated. This can give rise to a popular product making the owner of a copyright, or patent, very rich. Clearly, to ensure a sustainable balance of the economy, there must be a cut-off point where the payment should cease, and this point would also form part of the trading rules.

Development

The development process needs many tools for real success. To commence any project sound information is essential. Information has to be gathered and this, for many projects, can frequently be a very costly process. Ideally, in a modern world economy, the information system needs to be organised to follow the natural sequence on which we actually need to collect information; and then, be recorded in the right key sectors of the economy that exist. Such an information system can then be so arranged that each element of the economy can have its own coding. This structural system can then be used in many ways, for example:

- locating skills,
- used to see the overall shape of our industrial economy,
- used to locate the framework of the local, regional and national models of a country's economy,
- to obtain physical information of a local district and obtain local statistics
- locating the right businesses and visit their website
- locating products and assets new, old, or second-hand
- locating typical business models
- locating places for development
- locating any other information that is required that is actually available
- for projects planned and ready for development.

The commercial information system would be the only one world wide, and eventually the most complete and efficiently compiled information system. Many thousands of organisational resources can be linked together to set information out in a format that is international, and in the chosen international trading language.

The next tools required for planning are the ones needed for the development process. A universal productivity/monetary unit, on which sustainable economies can be studied, developed and built: the unit as described earlier in this chapter. The other new tools required are the models of existing forms of business laid out on a special format, which records standard monetary and labour statistics of every type of business. These would be used to develop any economy. All economic modelling would be based on a natural set of trading rules appropriate for developing sustainable forms of economy.

In general terms, the development process involves observation, facts, research, innovation, economic levels of development, comparisons, balance, efficiency, selection planning and affordable prices. The process must also take into account what is achievable. The development process is often a 'trial and error one', where various models and concepts are studied to achieve the set objectives, and sometimes pilot projects. Objectives can involve small development projects to exceptionally large ones. The author has been working on his study to develop truly sustainable economies since 1976. It involves understanding all the natural elements that are needed and that are important in building sound economies, which really serve everyone fairly, properly and on a basis that is achievable.

Sound development makes good use of existing resources and considers the short to long-term affects of the development. It needs to take all sorts of matters into consideration, like health and safety, ease of use, pollution, efficiency, sustainability, and affordability. Complicated projects can involve many disciplines and need to be well managed, perhaps with many innovators. Development also takes into account what has been learnt from past failures and from what nature has developed.

Often development is governed by two important factors, the skills and finance available. Money alone does not ensure that a project will progress, as this can only finance it, but not necessarily supply all the other resources needed. Any project must have the right balance so that all the components required are available.

In conclusion the development process is a most important element in our economy, which we rely on to improve it and solve many of our problems. It is a vast subject and other aspects of it will follow in other chapters of this book and in the other volumes on the sustainable economy.

Planning

One cannot go through life, run a business, or a country without planning or any organising, and expect a satisfactory life. By planning we can make sure that the things we want are there when we want them. There is little point working hard only to find one has produced the wrong goods and services. Producing luxury items for pleasure does not produce the needs for survival, and producing all needs does not produce the items for relaxation and enjoyment. Clearly we must create the right balance in the economy. We can only achieve this by planning.

Families are the prime movers of the economy, so their demands and plans for their lives will form the basis for the products, which should be supplied by the economy. The cost of the goods and services, and how much they earn, determines the quantities the economy needs to provide. The products and services generated by the family demands sets the shape for the form of economy that businesses and government should plan. Businesses and other institutions also need to supply the services and products required by the government.

Businesses need to plan their activities to supply the market with the products required now or in the foreseeable future. They have also been set up to provide employment, or income for the proprietors. They would plan to remain in business to be as successful as possible so as to continue in business. They would not plan to create a sustainable economy and likewise nor do the families, but only to serve their own aspirations. Governments, therefore, need to provide all the other requirements to ensure that the economy fulfils the objectives of a natural economy, a sustainable one.

Governments have to plan their operations in conjunction with the rest of the economy to remain sustainable. Without planning and understanding how economies need to function in a natural world, the economies will never be in balance or give people the security they desire, and deserve.

The Moral Aspect

Few people seem to realise how important morals are in ensuring stable economies. Natural economies need to be guided by trading rules to ensure the economy remains stable, and so that people enjoy a secure existence. Without morals the rules would be broken. Morals in a sound economy are concerned with:

- right and wrong,
- give and take,
- fairness,
- honesty and,
- trust.

If these are respected by society the economy not only becomes stable, but it also gives the feeling of security and freedom. However, because there are constraints in a natural world, that we must all accept, freedom would not be 100%.

Sound education concerning morals and how important they are to our well-being is the only route for success; and it is well worth everyone's effort to thoroughly understand the price the world would have to pay, if the moral aspect of the economy is ignored. The economies become very unstable and insecure when people ignore them, so indeed leading to many of the problems in the world we have at present.

The World Environment

Human habitation in the world is naturally managed at different levels:

- Family,
- Local Districts,
- Regions,
- National and
- International.

Families manage their own level 1 economy, and economies levels 2 to 5 are managed by government.

Local Districts serve rural areas and small towns. Their population, which can be properly managed with an intimate knowledge of their environment, would serve about 100.000 persons.

Regions would be responsible for large populations that could run into many millions. The land area would probably follow natural boundaries, like an island or a river basin.

Countries would include a few to many regions, with perhaps a language or natural boundaries forming their borders.

The last category is at international level and this also includes the EU.

How all these areas are managed is very important. They should follow a logical sequence that can produce sustainable forms of economy. In Volume 3, the management of the environment and the human economy is discussed in much greater detail. However, for the family the Local District Authority is the one they would all need to rely upon, and it would co-ordinate with other local districts and their region.

The role of Government

In the general economy people live alone, in groups and families; manage their own affairs to sustain them, and work in the general economy. Businesses and other institutions supporting the economy sustain their organisations and are loyal to their objectives. However, the family units and business institution sector, without government is not a complete economy. It does not provide all the goods and services needed to make it sustainable. Families manage their home economies and businesses their organisations, but if government did not exist there would be no one responsible to manage the balance of the overall general economy. This is why the world has governments, of some form, to take on this leadership and management role.

In this chapter the natural sequences taking place in our work economy have been described: where the work is done and how we need to exchange our hours of labour. Taking our human nature into account, it is clear that the majority of people wish to have an economy that is just, fair, and as honest and as moral as is possible, as these are essential components for a sustainable economy. Trading rules and sound measurements are essential to achieve this objective. Further, people also need the right to work and be properly paid. The government's first role is to establish the right conditions for trade, so that all objectives can be achieved, including managing the economy to remain sustainable.

So that the economy can run smoothly, and efficiently, governments need to monitor the economy to check that it is running on a sustainable path. They must provide all the missing elements required to form a complete economy. Governments also need to network with other governments so the world economy functions correctly for the sustainable objectives.

The family and private sector of the economy are not responsible for ensuring people are given the right education to understand their duties in it, which includes collectively the right proportion of skills for the economy. Clearly, government must have highly skilled specialists, who thoroughly understand how economies function, and are guided and developed to meet conditions as the world moves forward.

Generally speaking governments are responsible for establishing the national and international trading rules, security services, laws, appropriate education, monitoring and guiding the economy, and setting a level of taxation that is affordable. The local and regional governments would be responsible for maintaining their sectors in a sustainable form in conjunction with the inhabitants.

The following chapter outlines the economic tools and system for building sustainable economies that should satisfy the majority. The methodology is designed to reshape any economy and also to converge economies with the minimum of disruption and in pace with people's abilities.

CHAPTER 2

THE MH SYSTEM

The MH System is based on the natural occurrences that take place in human economies and life, as has been explained in Chapter 1. Any economic system to be successful must not oppose the natural forces and take into account human nature, strengths and weaknesses. The system must be compatible not only with a modern industrial world, but with economies at any level of development. An economic system cannot create and maintain a sustainable world, as it is only a tool on which it can be built. The economy must always be managed to be sustainable, by properly trained experts in the use of the system.

The key elements and factors of the MH system are:

- A master currency for money, based on average human productivity, to which all national currencies would be fixed.
- A set of trading rules based on a sound understanding of our natural economy.
- People understanding what money represents and how to use it as a measure to plan their family and work economies.
- People understanding why sound morals in any form of economy are essential for it to function smoothly.
- An education system that takes account of the natural human economy and our individual roles in it.
- Natural resources are not priced in monetary terms (as they are priceless); only the added value in collecting or extracting them is used to calculate their sale value.
- That the country's balance of payments is kept in general equilibrium; probably using import/export agencies, whose duty would be to keep the trade in proper balance
- A common international commercial language, probably English, being the most widely used already.
- A sound insurance system to cover major losses.
- A proper control on 'net rent', money that is paid for no human effort, not even the cost of collection
- A banking system for the monetary exchange (current accounts) where money remains in the customer's ownership.
- A banking system where money can only be used for loans by the bank when deposited by the customer for that purpose, and such money must only be lent against security.
- A banking system where the depositor's money lent without security must be insured.
- How these key elements and factors concerning the economy are used is crucial.

MH System trading rules

To establish trading rules involves modelling to establish the right equilibrium for sustainable economies. This is a trial and error process (using the master currency as an economic tool), which was carried out by the author to obtain a set of realistic criteria, now listed below:

1 Money shall be fixed to a productivity unit, which is based on skills gained in a general education, as can be achieved by the age of 15 years. The more developed an economy the longer the period of general education.

2 Interest paid on deposits to loan institutions shall not exceed 4% APR.

3 Business profit shall not exceed more than 4% of the capital employed and not more than 10% on the added value of the workforce's labour (wages), including working directors' hours of work in running the business.

4 Shareholders' profit should not exceed 4% of the par value of their shares (or original capital and further external capital) plus, and not exceeding half the business profit (5% of the added value, maximum). If, say, the business profit is only 2% of the added value, the shareholder's profit would not exceed 1% plus 4% of the par value of the share, giving a total of 5%. However, if there is no profit on the added value, where funds are available, they would at least be paid up to 4% interest on the par value of the shares.

5 Wage differentials are used to compensate for the time spent in education after completion of the general education. Further education can also include later periods of retraining, where investment costs are involved at the individual's expense (not paid for by the employer or state) to gain special skills (tradesman, clerk, technician, professional and specialist). The employer only pays for the skills he has engaged the worker for, or later skills that he uses.

Time spent in further education is like paying one's own wages (or self-employed, but investing in one's own further skills). If education is free and living costs are subsidised, say worth 30% of average wage earnings, the person is then assumed to have invested 70% of his wage in further education for every full year (part years are pro-rata). Interest on the investment is based on the maximum permitted, of 4% APR. At the end of the period of further education the total investment sum is calculated, including the interest. The average wage differential is then 1 plus 10% of the investment based on 1900 hours per annum.

Actual wages paid are based on the productivity and quality agreed by the employer and employee. The final wage rate is equal to 1 x wage differential x productivity/quality rate x the value of the productivity unit (master currency) valued in the national currency.

Productivity normally varies between 50% and 200%. It becomes difficult to justify any wage beyond 1000% or 10 times the average basic wage received by persons who have not taken further education. A fuller explanation on wages and salaries is in Chapter 3, 'Wage Negotiations'.

6 Copyrights and patents shall allow the owners to recover all their costs and an adequate profit, to ensure an incentive to invest in new concepts and products. However, a cut off point may become necessary where profits from inventions are enormous.

Businesses should not charge royalties on copyrights and patents they have developed and use in their own business, as their costs have already been covered in the price they charge for the products they sell, and the sale prices include an element of permissible profits. However, when they use a copyright, or patent, they are entitled to include the cost of the royalty they pay the owner in the cost of their product.

7 Employees pay the taxes and not the businesses, once a sustainable economy has been built. The reason for this is that the economy is created to serve the citizens, not the businesses. This creates a level basis for business competition, because their taxation would be zero in all nations.

8 Each nation shall keep its balance of payments in general equilibrium from year to year. This does not prevent aid being given to nations, or substantial loans, within the capacity of a nation to repay. It should be noted that all monetary gifts or loans made to another country, are backed by the goods and services of the donor country. The gifts and loans could be made by individuals, organisations, or business.

9 All exchanges of assets (new or used) shall be properly valued in the master currency (including tools, devices, machines). The exceptions may be the exchange of rare items like antiques. If products are exchanged at inflated prices (not complying with the trading rules), the economy becomes distorted and the distribution of wealth becomes out of balance.

10 The only money supply created (in the monetary system described in the author's solution for sustainable economies) is that created by wages paid for human productivity. Money supply shall not be increased by money not earned, or selling overvalued products (new or old). This results in unjustified redistribution of wealth.

It should be noted that families often create assets within the family unit, which at that time are only for use by the family. Later they may decide to sell one or more of the products they have made. The sale of these goods should be properly valued when sold, but do not form part of the money supply.

11 Insurance policies shall have no exclusions for major cover; whatever may be the cause. However, cover for minor losses would be a matter for the parties involved.

The eleven trading rules given are crucial in creating sustainable economies and sound models to analyse and develop them. The rules have been made and chosen for specific reasons, particularly for stability and to allow sound, well planned developments to take place.

The MH monetary/ productivity unit is a fixed measure. Like weight and measures and length, allowing proper comparisons to be made. This allows savings to be protected, as inflation has been eliminated. It also creates an economic tool that allows economies to be analysed to discover why they are unstable and unsustainable; to develop long-term plans; and to develop solutions to solve economic problems. It gives a basis on which citizens can be correctly paid for their production, thereby allowing wages that would support their families without subsidies, under normal conditions.

The control of net rents to low levels, and consistent in all transactions requiring incentive, takes account of human nature. It restricts any greed, but gives adequate incentive to innovate, to become skilled, to take business risks, and loan our surplus funds.

Money as explained is only a means of exchanging our hours of work for goods and services. Money only represents the value of our labour in creating the goods and services. These, the moment they are created, have to be maintained by their owners. Maintenance costs money (and can also include the cost of storage). The very minimum could cost 2% per annum of the original purchase price of the products. So it is like paying interest. When money is lent, it is the borrower that owns the product/s, that balance with the value of the loan made to them, and it is they that have to maintain them. If the lender of the money had the product/s instead of savings, he would then have the expense of maintaining the products. Some goods deteriorate quickly, or become obsolete, and owners of them may also have to set aside money to cover the cost of depreciation, and this can be quite costly. It is clear that one could save a lot of money by lending one's savings, rather than storing our wealth in goods. Because of the expense of maintaining products (which costs money) interest rates must be kept at a very low level (a maximum 4% APR is set under the system, excluding bank charges).

An advantage of the MH banking system is that the savings are not placed at risk by the bank. The bank does not lend the depositors savings, if they cannot be lent safely. However, under these circumstances, if they could not loan the funds, interest rates could fall to zero, and under these circumstances, the money could then be returned to the person's current account. When the interest rate falls to zero, it indicates there is no demand for money to be borrowed, which is an unlikely event.

Master Currency

The MH unit is a master currency and although it can be used as money for international exchanges, its main purpose would be for establishing the value of other currencies. For example, in 1995 currencies were 'floating', due to inflation and market forces: see Table 5 in Chapter 3. From the table it can be observed that, using national statistics, the £ sterling is being re-valued every quarter. Where a county's legal tender is 'floating' it is very difficult to carry out long term budgeting and planning, as is necessary for many projects. This is overcome by using the MH currency by converting prices for goods and services into MH units in each country, so true comparisons can be made and proper costs established.

Insurance

Insurance for major losses and catastrophes should fully cover any loss of material wealth, and consequences of injury and death. The whole object of insurance is to give security and allow recovery from unfortunate events. However, minor losses should not really be insured, where for example they could be comfortably allowed for from the family, or business budget contingency. For a small claim insurance is costly and really uneconomic. Insurance premiums can be raised and lowered as necessary to maintain the funds in balance with the claims.

Should major catastrophes occur government could share the compensation costs with the insurance companies.

Education

The education system is essential for any stable economy and involves education bodies, and everyone should help to pass on sound knowledge to others, particularly to children. They would need to have the economy explained as they grow up, on how it supports them and what they are expected to do in it for their satisfactory survival. Reasons must be given for the need of sound morals, and for the constraints needed to protect our rights, and on how give and take applies. If the right effort is not put into the economy, people cannot expect a sound, secure and sustainable economy. Everyone's effort is required, and we all need to understand the basic principles of the natural events supporting the economy.

Natural Resources

Natural resources are not priced in the MH system. The value of the natural resources used involves the added value when we put in hours of work to mine, gather, and fashion them into the products we want. Resources are not spread evenly through the world, and few countries have all the resources they need to support their economy. Consequently natural resources should be shared.

Some resources are scarce, so these must be used sparingly, and alternatives for them should be sought. Other resources, like various living species, need protection to prevent their loss. The whole balance of the environment needs to be properly understood and cared for to ensure sustainability.

For the reasons given, the MH system advocates that only the human added value is priced (plus normal business profit). Goods and services should not be rationed by price, as this distorts the economy and is not fair. Distribution by other methods should be applied: waiting lists, rationing and chance methods, whatever is appropriate and does not distort the monetary exchange balance of the economy.

Prices of goods and services shall also take into account the safe disposal of waste created in their production. However, the pollution and waste caused by past events needs to be gradually removed by the joint resources of governments, particularly the developed nations.

Standard of living

The MH system takes into account that in material terms the standard of living would never become equal, but only similar. There are sound reasons for this, which commence at the individual and family level. We all have different objectives in life. We do not necessarily wish to have the same value or quantity of material goods. They depend on the nature of our hobbies and our life-style. Some people would wish for homes needing the minimum of upkeep and they could have low cost hobbies, like hiking in their local countryside, whilst others may desire large homes full of expensive leisure facilities.

Our habitats vary considerably depending on where they are situated in the world. Some areas are very cold whilst others are temperate or hot. Rainfall and snow vary. The ground varies from soil to rock. Some areas are bleak, whilst others are lush. The country could be flat, hilly or mountainous. Water resources and minerals could be scarce, or plentiful. These and many other conditions, such as living in the city or country, would all affect how much it would cost to live in the area we chose, or decide to remain in for whatever reason.

Another very important factor that influences our standard of living, apart from the natural conditions just related, are our nation's human skills and wealth of technology. This creates a vast difference in material wealth in those countries where very advanced stages of industrial development have been reached in comparison with countries in earlier stages of development. The highly computerised and mechanical production lines used on farms, in factories and in offices have allowed numerous products and services to be made at very low cost in terms of hours of human labour per product.

The MH master currency and trading system rules allow for these different natural economic levels to exist and find their own levels. It also allows people to trade and exchange their skills on the MH systems basis anywhere in the world, provided the system is not opposed by governments. It allows developing nations to buy developed country's goods and services at the lowest rates possible when they make an exchange. Presently, 'floating' currencies, distorted by market forces, make developed nation's products very expensive, and third world goods and services in some of the poorest countries undervalued by as much as 50 times.

Management of Economies

Whatever type economy, (family, business or country) it must be managed to ensure it remains sustainable. What we need and want must be produced by us expending our human labour. The more complicated the economy the better we need to organise and manage our economies. For success we must have sufficient skilled personnel that understand exactly how our economies function, are developed and are maintained. It is an art and requires its own technology. The author provides this written material, such as presented in this series of 3 volumes. New technology needs to be taught and transferred to others.

We all understand that, if we do not work and organise our family economies, we soon start to suffer in all sorts of ways. To meet our requirements we have to organise our activities, plan and work both at home, and in the general economy for others, to produce income and save for our future pension. Businesses and governments must act similarly, and the larger they are the grander the scale of their activities. However, governments throughout the world do not operate in the manner that businesses and families need to in supporting themselves. Families and businesses serve their own needs and neither of them is trained to manage the overall economy. Governments have the duty to manage the overall economy, as the private sector and families are not responsible for this operation and, therefore, the MH system includes models and tools to help governments with their duty to manage the overall economy. But, to make the change needs more than a system: it needs governments to fulfil what the changes require in their present management of their countries. If they do not make the change voluntarily and correct the errors, the people and businesses have the natural right to do so, as in a natural economy businesses and government are the servants of the people and not the contrary.

The MH system is one that has been designed to engineer economies to the shape desired, or as far as possible within the resources available to maintain a sustainable economy. Defining money as a fixed measure of productivity makes it possible to create long term plans for economies and guide the public and industry on what is needed to create the economy to fulfil what is required. This is very necessary for planners of industries and economies. In Volume 1 we will only go into further detail of family economies, as they generate the demands of the overall economy. Being able to price all goods and services in stable monetary units, allows models to be created for families over a lifetime. Once one can see the overall picture of the economy, it is possible by arrangement to produce the optimum solution, and appreciate where problems lie. The manner in which the family economy can be studied, shaped and applied would also be similar for business and government; but the number of models they would require would be very extensive in comparison with those needed by individuals and families.

Sources of information are extremely important for designers and developers (at family, business and government levels). Millions of skills and products are available, but they are very difficult to find quickly, unless a very good system is available. The MH system visualises a proper co-ordination of all information into one system that is comprehensive and is complete as possible. Present information is often repeated many times as it is in many directories, but none are very complete. Seeking information is therefore a time consuming task as many lists have to be examined and often with the result of not finding what is required in any of them, as it is not recorded. The actual information can be in businesses or government organisations, or both. It does not matter who has them, as long as the information can be co-ordinated into one system, without duplication of information. This is a massive task that can be taken up by government, or the private sector. However, it is a government task to sort the problem out.

Industries and government services supply the needs and wants. These cover all the goods, services, machines, equipment and skills we require. As the economy reshapes, the skills pattern changes creating job losses and new jobs and different demands on businesses and government industries and services. The MH system foresees an information service that makes available information on new demands well in advance of requirements, wherever this is possible. In this manner industry can prepare the stocks and services to meet the increase, or reduction, in demand. Governments and business training centres, with the help of advance information, would seek to produce the skills desired to meet demands. Where problems can be foreseen concerning lack of employment, future plans can be examined to advance, or retard schemes, ensuring full employment conditions can be maintained: actually producing what is really needed, with optimum results. Future development projects need finance. One way of increasing savings is to encourage people to work longer hours in the parts of the economy that will be expanded, and also to save the additional money they earn. Only sound planning can allow economies to develop smoothly.

In the MH system governments and businesses need to operate in unison as they both serve the demands of families and their own requirements. However, government must manage all the tasks to fulfil a sound sustainable economy that cannot, or should not be the task of families and private enterprise.

Finally the MH system properly used would help to solve all the economic problems in running sustainable economies, subject to its rules being adhered to and having properly trained managers, (with a thorough understanding on how economies are engineered and developed to meet requirements), throughout the various levels of the economy wherever they should be employed.

CHAPTER 3

WAGE NEGOTIATIONS

Skills and Knowledge

There are millions of human skills in use in a modern world. Some skills can be easily learned and quite quickly, whilst others can take years to learn.

Every tool, machine or piece of equipment (including every model or variation of it) requires a separate skill to be learnt. Each musical instrument, and many games require an appropriate skill. Every language, method and human technology also requires skill in applying it. One can summarise by saying each little element of the economy, whether for domestic pleasure or business use requires human skills. No one person has the capacity to learn every skill, but only a small proportion of the skills, and only a few really well.

The skills we have and the hours we are prepared to use them, together with human aids and machines, determine our standard of living (the goods and services we have produced to serve our requirements). Everybody's standard of living varies and probably always will, as people have different objectives in their life. This can determine how many hours they wish to work to earn money to exchange for (to buy) goods and services. Skills for the same type of work should be paid for at the same rates, whichever industry the people are working in.

As development takes place skills can become of no further use. When and where this will happen is difficult to forecast. It can happen in any occupation. The development process changes the nature of the skills we need. In a modern world in certain industries changes can be very rapid, whilst in others they can be quite slow, and they are unlikely to be at a similar pace. Often, when development takes place, the amount of human labour required to carry out the work is reduced. The development process often alters the skills required, and introduces new skills adding to all the others we have, and it also creates fresh employment. This process is perfectly natural and has been going on for centuries, and is not the cause for unemployment, but it is the process that has increased our standard of living from those of prehistoric times. Other factors cause unemployment, like the way we manage change as developments take place, which requires new skills and a redistribution of people in existing and new businesses. No longer in a modern world can we expect to use the same skills for our vocation throughout our lives.

It is usually inventors and businesses that create the new skills required for their product, perhaps created by their own technology. They are the only ones that can forecast what their requirements will be, and in may cases the only ones with the knowledge to teach it in the early stages of its use. It will be the businesses that decide where the new training should take place. Schools, colleges and universities for example would be expected to teach all the general knowledge required, but much of the special knowledge sometimes can only be learnt while at work in a business. The skills people have must be in balance with the demands of industry, and it is up to industry to indicate the skills they require.

Knowledge can be said to embrace our skills and facts that we have remembered. Much of what we memorise does not need a lot of practice, so normally not too much time is taken in learning to remember each element. Some people can memorise facts more easily than others. As human beings we seem to have different qualities, those that are better at memorising and those that are quicker at learning other skills.

Skilled and Unskilled – what it means

Skills can be physical, mental, or a combination of the two. Skills that are usually easy to learn are frequently called unskilled, although some require a considerable amount of skill and can take a long time to perfect. Skills needing further education, apprenticeships and long periods of learning are called skilled.

Many of our skills for a vocation can be updated by refresher courses. Simple skills do not normally take long to learn; many of them can be learnt in a few hours, or up to a week. More complicated skills may take up to a month to acquire. Where businesses want these skills, probably most of them could be taught in the place of work. Where the employee has been paid a wage while being trained by the employer, it would not be unreasonable for him to expect the employee to stay at least six months with the employer after completion of training before moving to another business, which does not have to pay for the training. For more complicated special skills, periods of up to six months may have to be paid for by the employer. Skilled workers, who need at least one year of further education, cannot learn a new skilled vocation quickly and would probably need financial support while doing so.

It should be noted that many skills people use for their hobbies can be greater and more complicated than they use in employment. Sometimes these skills can be used for a vocation, or adapted to do so.

Work skills of one's first choice cannot always be found where one is living, and one may need to commute, sometimes long distances, or even have to move to another area. Many skills make it imperative to live in the area in which they are required, which may even be in another country.

Nowadays it would be prudent to be skilled in more than just one type of work, particularly if continuity of work is necessary in one's desired living location. Everyone should be prepared to accept unskilled work to support themselves. With millions of skills available, it can take quite a while to choose a preferred vocation. Professional and skilled careers need to be carefully chosen owing to the time required to learn the skill. Modern technology is making many previous skilled vocations obsolete, or reducing the number of people needed for them, and one needs to take care not to study something not going to be required soon.

Skilled Vocations

In many skilled vocations the persons working in them are specialising in just a small part of the industry. This gives them a very sound knowledge of that element of the industry. Being experienced in its activity, they know how long it will take, and how much work they need to do to fulfil each task they are given. This, therefore, gives them an intimate knowledge, including their rate of productivity in all the various tasks they perform. If they are asked how much time they would need to carry out each task, they would be able to give it; or give it in the form of minimum time, expected time and maximum time, to cover any errors, or contingencies in their judgement. Persons supervising specialist teams would also have a sound knowledge of their teams, including individual rates of productivity, which allows them to plan the work to be done. This knowledge allows work to be completed when required, or to say how long they would need to complete the various tasks in hand.

Technicians, clerical persons and tradesmen normally specialise in a fairly narrow range of skills, and the rates of productivity for these should not be too difficult to establish. Many professions are also highly specialised in a narrow field of work, and they also would not have too much difficulty in agreeing rates of productivity. However, there are skilled vocations that cover a much wider range of skilled operations. Many of those operations that they carry out are the same as those skilled in a narrow field of work tasks, and these are used to establish proper rates of productivity/quality for those using a wide range of skills.

Many of the skilled, working in a wide range of tasks in their trade or profession, are sometimes also highly specialised in some narrow field of it. As they work up to management levels in their chosen vocation, they need to have a wider knowledge of other skills and to become experienced in many more, although they are unlikely to become expert in all of them, but only in the ones they use the most. Understanding and using a wide range of skills can only be developed by longer and longer years of practical experience. These persons can often justify higher wage differentials for the further hours of study, where it has taken place in their own time. For some management positions, a considerable amount of experience is essential and can normally only be attained by middle age.

A C.V. is very important, and necessary to assess a person's skill and suitability for required tasks. They should be detailed to ensure there are no misunderstandings concerning a person's abilities and degree of expertise.

Wage Differentials and Productivity

Wage Differentials

We all receive a general education in developed nations, which normally finishes between the ages of 15 to 18 years, depending on the country we are living in. In due course it is anticipated that children's education in developing countries would not finish before the age of 15, as there is so much for them to learn. On completion of a general education, one can commence working in the general economy, or take further education for a skilled vocation, or just for the pleasure of further learning to meet a personal objective, provided the latter option is affordable.

In a fair and sustainable world economy one needs to assume that further education is an investment in ourselves, partly or wholly at our own expense. Just like businesses charging for its investment and making a modest profit, people taking further education for their vocation can make similar charges for their investment in themselves. The charge is based on a wage differential, which can be justified by calculation.

Skilled persons could well find that their special skill cannot be used throughout their working lives and, like a business, is at risk. Their investment in themselves could be lost, just as an investment in a business that was no longer in demand, because its product, or service had been superseded in another business with a better, or more up-to-date product. Also, unlike the unskilled worker, whose retraining is paid for by the employer, the skilled person has to pay for his own retraining into another skilled occupation (unless the person should decide to change to unskilled work).

Wage differentials can be calculated in different ways. In this book a capitalist form of wage differential is now described. Table 4 illustrates calculations for typical occupations. The table is fairly self-explanatory. However, the pay under training, which is to cover the basic cost of living normally covered by a government grant, could alternatively be a grant received from a business. Governments, to ensure fair and sustainable economic conditions, can vary the figures for the grants and interest rates shown in table 4. For the U.K. the figures used are recommended, and everyone in the country should use the same basis to ensure fair trade. The total years of wage investment (as at the bottom of Table 4) are used to calculate the wage differential, which amounts to 1 + 10% of the investment (where '1' represents the average productivity of an unskilled person) as follows:

Tradesman,
Clerical &
Technician $1 + (2.372 \times 10\%) = 1.2372$

Professional $1 + (6.551 \times 10\%) = 1.6551$

Specialist $1 + (10.273 \times 10\% = 2.0273$

The calculations given assume the cost of the training courses for the further education is paid for by the government and/or businesses. It should be noted that the 10% added is similar to the anticipated profit made by a business. Graph 1 indicates how these wage differentials would be applied in practice. On completion of studies or apprenticeships, the pay does not suddenly jump to the wage differential as calculated, but wages gradually rise as the person gains practical experience, although in certain special cases it could do so where further practical experience is not required. The graph also shows the approximate number or years of average wage that could be earned (if one remains average throughout the period) on the assumption of full employment throughout one's working life (shown to end at 65). This calculation fits quite well with wages actually paid.

A communist country, (such as China) would not need a wage differential for skilled people, if a full average wage (pay under training = 1) were paid while studying.

In wage negotiations employers and employees would establish the correct wage differential for the appropriate skill, calculated as explained.

Productivity

The basis for wages so far described assume average productivity, but the productivity of many human skills varies from low to high rates. Figure 1 shows how these rates could vary. The graph will vary in shape depending on the skill and operation. In practice it is unlikely that a person would produce at less than half (50%) the average rate, and the majority are likely to achieve rates varying between 70% and 140%. For many skills it would be possible to work at rates up to double (200%) the average rate, and a few at even higher rates.

Every skill for every element of the economy has a rate of productivity and/or quality median that can be based on the hour. Most skills have an average rate of productivity. This unit is ideal for industry to calculate the labour force it will require for its tasks. It also helps to create plans that will allow it to complete projects on time (using a critical path technology).

Many businesses and professions already have records of rates of productivity and are used to determining new ones; but for many other businesses this has not been their practice. Sometimes rates of productivity have been agreed with the workforce, or trade unions. Some industries have published books on rates of productivity for labour, equipment and machinery used in it, which any member of the public can purchase. As new business aids are invented, rates of productivity can be established. Some people's livelihood is gained from making time and motion studies.

Productivity is not only judged on the rate of productivity, but also on the quality where this is achieved by human skills. The quality of work should also be judged on the average, where this is applicable to the occupation. If a high quality is required, the average rate of quality must also be established and, if a low rate is acceptable, a figure must also be established for this.

Often productivity rates are not only for one type of work, or operation, but many different ones involving a number of skills by the same person. This mixed operation would be repeated many times. As an example, maybe all the operations take an average time of 2 hours 23 minutes. A mixed work operation is sometimes carried out by a gang, or team.

Productivity should be based on the time one is actually working, and normally would exclude tea breaks and travelling, even around the office or premises, where this would be appropriate. However, if travelling normally forms part of the work operation it would be included.

The average productivity unit and Currencies

The basic productivity unit is also a 'Master Currency' as all other currencies can be compared with it and valued in its unit. However, national wage statistics, and details of hours spent by those persons who had further education in colleges and apprenticeships are required to calculate the value of existing currencies, based on the master currency unit. When a product can be valued in master currency units quick comparisons can be made on the total human element of a product and/or service (whether carried out in the past, or in a different country).

It should be noted that the basic productivity unit is based on each person having had a general education. The other skills requiring further education are multiplied by the respective wage differentials, which take into account the time spent in their training and hence can be valued in the master currency.

Personality

For some vocations personality is an essential element, just like the quality of work carried out by a person. For example, some tasks can only be given an average rate of productivity/pay, because the rate is determined by the number of customers that enter the premises and need to be served. However, a good personality can increase customers and this needs to be rewarded, whilst a person who is off-hand with a customer is not worth the average rate.

Working hours

The hours of working for many skills are important. With long hours of work, quality and productivity can suffer. In a sustainable economy a working day is based on 8 hours, and this under normal circumstances should allow for consistent quality and productivity.

Where the nature of the work can tire a person quickly, it is suggested that the work is varied so that the desired rates of productivity and quality can be maintained throughout the day.

Table 4

Investment in a skilled occupation during study and training

Year Under	Tradesmen, Clerical & Technician			Professional			Specialist		
Study and training	Pay under training	Effective investment	Value to date	Pay under training	Effective investment	Value to date	Pay under training	Effective investment	Value to date
1	0.3	0.7	0.714	0.3	0.7	0.714	0.3	0.7	0.714
2	0.5	0.5	1.253	0.3	0.7	1.457	0.3	0.7	1.457
3	0.6	0.4	1.711	0.3	0.7	2.229	0.3	0.7	2.229
4	0.7	0.3	2.085	0.3	0.7	3.032	0.3	0.7	3.032
5	0.8	0.2	2.372	0.3	0.7	3.867	0.3	0.7	3.867
6				0.3	0.7	4.736	0.3	0.7	4.736
7				0.5	0.5	5.435	0.3	0.7	5.639
8				0.7	0.3	5.959	0.3	0.7	6.579
9				0.9	0.1	6.299	0.3	0.7	7.556
10				1.0	-	6.551	0.8	0.2	8.062
11							0.8	0.2	8.589
12							0.9	0.1	9.034
13							0.9	0.1	9.498
14							1.0	-	9.878
15							1.0	-	10.273
Totals	2.9	2.1	2.372	4.9	5.1	6.551	8.1	6.9	10.273

Note: 1 Investment is in years assuming 1900 hours per annum

2 Interest on the investment is at the rate of 4% per annum.

3 All figures are in years.

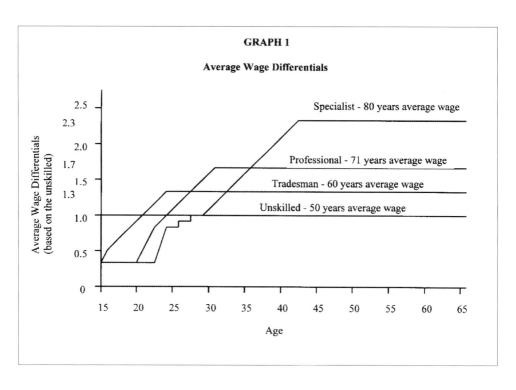

Figure 1

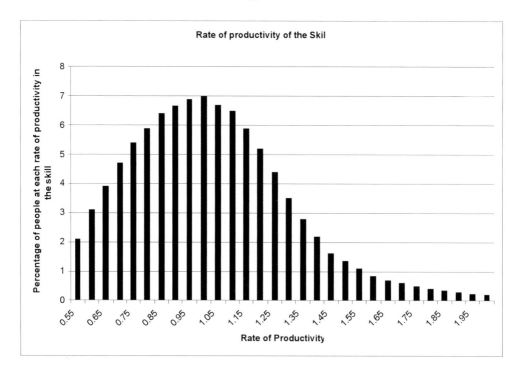

Wage Negotiations

In a sustainable economy wages are negotiated on the basic productivity unit and the master currency, and then where other national currencies are used they are converted into it. To compute the value of the wage for the skilled the productivity is multiplied by the wage differential agreed for that skill. Finally the value of the wage in master currency units (MCU) is multiplied by the appropriate conversion factor to the desired currency. The £ sterling varies in value as shown in Table 5. To calculate the wage the latest value of the MCU would be used. With inflation the buying value of the £ falls as the number of £s to the MCU rises. If the number of £s to the MCU fall deflation would have occurred and a lower figure in £s for the wage would be given. Suppose a person's productivity was agreed to be 0.7 (70%) and he was a tradesman with a wage differential = 1.3 and the value of 1 MCU was £9.77 the hourly wage rate would be:

$$= 0.7 \times 1.3 \times £9.77$$
$$= £8.89 \text{ per hour}$$

It should be noted that when calculating the unskilled workers wage a wage differential is not used as it is = 1 and therefore it would be pointless to use it.

The lowest wage that could be earned would be as an unskilled person with a productivity of 50%. Using the same value of £9.77 per MCU the lowest wage would amount to £4.89 per hour, and the average wage for an unskilled person would amount to £9.77 per hour. Some unskilled persons could be expected to earn up to £19.54 per hour when they achieved a rate of productivity that is twice times the average. A specialist with a 200% productivity/quality rate could expect to receive £44.94 per hour (200% x 2.3 x £9.77).

Wage differentials and productivity must be agreed by the parties concerned and be justifiable to a third party (the public, or government should they query it).

Where a sustainable economic system is fully operational and the Master Currency is the national standard unit of measure for productivity/money the national currency could be fixed at £10.00 per MCU. Table 5 would then not be used. People, businesses and unions would all negotiate wages on 1MCU = £10 per hour. Inflation would not exist.

All wages are renegotiable when either party decides a change has taken place, or the original agreement was faulty. The new wage is not backdated, but takes effect from the time the notice for renegotiation was made.

TABLE 5
The Value of 1 MCU in £s Sterling

Quarter		1 MCU in £ Sterling	Quarter		1 MCU in £ Sterling
1991	4	6.81			
1992	1	6.92	2002	1	9.96
	2	7.01		2	10.12
	3	7.12		3	10.26
	4	7.21		4	10.40
1993	1	7.27	2003	1	10.48
	2	7.32		2	10.56
	3	7.39		3	10.69
	4	7.46		4	10.73
1994	1	7.54	2004	1	10.89
	2	7.62		2	11.01
	3	7.67		3	11.11
	4	7.71		4	11.22
1995	1	7.76	2005	1	11.30
	2	7.80		2	11.38
	3	7.84		3	11.50
	4	7.91		4	11.62
1996	1	7.98	2006	1	11.81
	2	8.05		2	11.92
	3	8.12		3	12.03
	4	8.20			
1997	1	8.30			
	2	8.39			
	3	8.50			
	4	8.60			
1998	1	8.66			
	2	8.66			
	3	8.85			
	4	8.95			
1999	1	9.09			
	2	9.19			
	3	9.30			
	4	9.37			
2000	1	9.42			
	2	9.46			
	3	9.43			
	4	9.45			
2001	1	9.50			
	2	9.55			
	3	9.66			
	4	9.77			

There are many factors that come into wage negotiations and the main ones are now listed.

Productivity negotiation.
Training.
Continued Professional Development (CPD).
Wage differentials.
Trial working period and tests.
Working conditions and climate.
Employer pays for skills required.
Theoretical and practical experience.
Multi-skilled.
Restrictions on working hours.
Risk and insurance.
Piecework.
Overtime and non-social hours.
Tools of trade and clothing.
Payments to professional bodies.
Expenses.
Give and take.
Holidays, illness and pensions.
Mental work not carried out at the work place.
Travelling.
Working one's way up to management duties, in one's skill.
Learning a skill at a very young age as is sometimes necessary in certain vocations.
Intermittent work that requires a full-time presence.
Varied work using different skills.

Each of these is now separately discussed.

Productivity negotiations

Where an industry does not already have agreed rates of productivity they will need to be determined. Productivity rates can be established by an independent body, or directly by the employer and employee/s. There are already recognised methods for determining many types of productivity.

Where an employer has already established the rates of productivity for his business, an employee would agree his rate of productivity with the employer on commencement of joining the business. Prior to accepting employment an employee's skills could be tested, or he could be taken on for a trial period in which his skill could be assessed and agreed by both parties. The employee could also agree to receive some training first.

Fairness by both parties is essential. After all, an employer may have to trust the employee.

Training

The employer usually pays for the employee's training, where a person is classified unskilled (for simple skills). The employee would receive an agreed wage during the training period. Sometimes skilled persons require some training, to allow the employee to become familiar with the firms practices, or the work in hand. This is also at the employer's expense.

On the job, training may only take a few days during say the first month's work and the employer may well suggest a productivity rate of 80% for this period. After that it would be renegotiated from time to time, based on actual results.

Each trade and profession will have its own practices on the amount of training paid for by the business. Sometimes the business products change frequently, and a short period of training may be required each time this happens. Such training and retraining would be normally paid for by the employer.

As economies develop it often changes our working methods, or equipment we use, and it becomes necessary for the unskilled, technicians, clerical persons, tradesmen and professional persons to retrain, or update their occupation. Sometimes, occupations become obsolete, or partly redundant, making learning fresh skills necessary.

Continued Professional Development (CPD)

The employer should not pay for CPD training. If it is paid for by the employer it would mean that the employee should be on a slightly lower wage to take into account the cost of it.

All professional persons need to keep up-to-date with changes in their particular branch of the profession. Sometimes one needs to have more than one branch of one's profession's skills to maintain full employment, and this too would be at the person's own expense, including keeping up-to-date with changes.

Some professions could have a considerable amount of information to keep up-to-date with. In such cases it may mean a shorter working day or working week may become necessary, and consequently a higher wage differential would need to be calculated.

Wage Differentials

Any person who has taken further education for a vocation is entitled to use a wage differential in negotiating the wage, or salary, provided the employment justifies a skilled employee and it is applicable to the employment to be filled.

Present day (2006) wage differentials are market prices for wages and salaries in each trade and profession. For sustainable economies calculated wage differentials should be used based on the master currency. Already in many industries the present wage structure is in the region of sustainability, but disputes frequently take place as inflation progresses and new work arrangements come into force, as businesses develop and become more efficient. The author's sustainable system based on the master currency and fairness is ideal for both businesses and employees to establish a sound wage structure that everybody would be pleased to negotiate, thereby avoiding unnecessary disputes not only disrupting the business, but also its customers. Because wage differentials are all calculated, wages and salaries can be automatically up-dated to cover wage inflation, or deflation as the economy moves forward. A person's productivity and skills would be altered, when changes occurred.

Practical experience in most skilled posts is essential, as shown in Graph 1, where in the earlier years the wage differential has been reduced. A tradesman, therefore, does not have the benefit of a full wage differential until the age of 24, a professional person not until an age of 31, and a specialist person not until an age of 43. However, graph 1 is only a general guide and each trade and profession should establish their own basis for the years of experience required. Employers, who do not have an intimate knowledge of a skill, should use experts to advise them, in order to ensure a fair and properly negotiated salary for the person's experience. In due course all trades and professions will have developed sound guidelines for wage negotiations.

For some very special vocations a substantial amount of further education could be necessary, and it could cover training in several professions, that could all be used simultaneously.

Some people may have learnt their profession entirely at their own expense (not subsidised) and this would raise the value of the wage differential. Employees would want to recover all their investment costs during their working lives, and this could justify some high rates of remuneration.

Trial Working Period and Tests

For skilled vocations, and even for some unskilled occupations, tests are often a convenient way to judge a person's ability. The tests could take several hours and could be unpaid. When testing takes longer periods, the employee's time spent on it should be paid for by the employer.

Even after in-depth interviewing has been completed, for most professions and some trades it is sound practice to take on employees for a trial period (from three to twelve months) before giving long-term employment. After the first three months (where the trial period exceeds three months) the salary could be adjusted for the remainder of the trial period.

Working Conditions and Climate

Working conditions and the climate can affect the rate of human productivity. Working under cold, or hot conditions usually slows the rate of productivity. When using existing statistics the working conditions under which the people worked should also be known. Employees cannot be responsible for reduced rates of productivity caused by poor working conditions. It is essential that the right average rates of productivity be established, in order to be completely fair when negotiating wages.

Employer pays for the skills required

The employer only pays for the skills he requires and not for all the skills the employee may have. However, if the employee's other skills are used, not already taken into consideration in the wage/salary, he should be paid for their use. This could mean an increase in pay, and sometimes a lower rate where the employee agrees to the change that does not use the other skill/s. It is up to the employee to find work using the greater number of his skills, or the best skills that would give the highest wage/salary.

Theoretical and Practical experience

Usually theoretical experience without practical experience is of little use, and the proportions of each of them necessary for a vocation vary depending on the skill/s in use. Each trade, profession, or the type of work determines the appropriate proportions necessary, the rate of productivity and the wage differential used.

Multi-skilled

A vocation may require a number of different trades, or professional activities to be used in the work operation. Assuming only one skill is used at a time the wage negotiated could be on the basis of the average rate of productivity achieved in each trade/profession used for the work. Whatever basis is used, it should be as fair as possible.

Restrictions on Working Hours

If the nature of the work restricts the number of working hours per day and eliminates overtime, because of possible stress, or a national or international law, then the wage differential would need to be increased accordingly. The correction would be based on a 40-hour 5-day working week. For example, supposing the maximum number hours of work permitted was 6 hours, as might apply to a diver working in deep water, the wage differential to apply to correct for this would be 8 divided by 6 =1.33.

Risk and Insurance

In many ways most jobs can carry some form of risk that can cause injury, or shorten one's working life. Normal risks would be covered by the business insurance, one's own insurance, or the State.

There are other types of vocation that are risky, which can cause permanent disabilities, or even early death that are not compensated by normal insurance, or uninsurable. These need compensation in other ways. These types of risk are often covered by an increase in the wage differential to take into account the risk taken and give the person an incentive to take the risk. Such financial adjustment made to the wage/salary should be fairly negotiated and where possible justified on existing statistics.

Piecework

Many vocations are paid for by the actual amount of work carried out and valued on the Master Currency. The price agreed for the work would be negotiated on the basis of the workforce having average skills and rates of productivity.

Overtime and Non-social Hours

Sustainable economic systems cannot justify high overtime rates of pay for overtime. All pay rates and exchanges of labour must be consistent to prevent distortions in the price of goods and services. The employer is expected to ensure that he is not making profit on an overpaid labour force, and as employees are also traders they should also comply with the trading rules and not exceed a profit of 10% on the true value of their skilled labour.

Where people wish to work overtime (more than 40 hours per week) they should not demand overtime, as the object of overtime is to help businesses and other institutions to cope with peaks in their work-load. However, if a person wishes to work longer hours, part-time work should be found in another business or institution. Where industries work three shifts per day it could be unrealistic to expect overtime.

Many people prefer to work night shifts, at weekends, or outside the normal workings hours of between 8.00 in the morning and 6.00 in the evening. In hot climates frequently working hours could be between 7.00 and 12 noon and 6.00 and 10.00 in the evening to make use of the cooler times of the day. People have a choice as to when they wish to work and sometimes businesses work on a flexible time basis. When deciding on a vocation, one can take into consideration that certain trades and professions decide the time of day when employees must be available for work, and it should be noted that some businesses cannot work on a flexible time basis.

In sustainable economies, where governments wish to, overtime can be exempt from income tax, thereby giving people incentive to work longer hours when industry requires extra labour.

In a modern industrial economy many industries are operating throughout the day. This is quite natural, and around the world every business and institution is working somewhere, and some international experts must be available at any time of the day.

Tools of trade and Clothing

Where it is normal in a trade or profession for the employees to provide their own special clothing, tools or equipment, they should be compensated by an increase in their wage or salary to cover the cost of it.

Where special clothing is required for a trade, or to suit a firm's presentation, the cost of the clothing should be paid for by the business. However, normal everyday clothing is the employee's responsibility.

Payments to Professional Bodies and Trade Unions

This forms part of the employee's investment, or shall we say trader's expenses, as we are all traders. Therefore, the employee should not expect his employer to pay them.

Trade Unions too are like a professional body and again it is the employee's choice if he/she belongs to one, and hence they are the ones that pay the cost of their subscriptions.

To keep up-to-date with one's trade or profession one often subscribes to trade journals, these too should be at the employee's expense.

Expenses

Any out of pocket expenses an employee needs to pay to carry out his duties shall be paid for by the employer, but excluding the exceptions mentioned in these sustainable trading rules for wage negotiation.

Expenses payments should not be used as another way of increasing an employee's wage/salary. If a wage/salary is incorrect it should be re-adjusted, as everyone has a right to be properly paid, and in a sustainable economy a person must also pay the tax due on his true earnings.

Give and Take

So far in this book a guide to negotiating has been set out. However, the economy is always on the move and, as it moves forward, peoples' skills and productivity change, and the way our businesses and institutions function. The volume of trade also changes direction. Baskets of different skills used by an employee can also change, and some rapidly in all sorts of directions. To keep pace with all the variations one could forever be renegotiating wages, perhaps even on a daily basis. In a real world, therefore, it is realistic to evaluate wages/salaries on an annual basis and perhaps in certain circumstances every six months, where the type of work would make this fairer. Clearly, there is need for give and take in agreeing our average rate of productivity and quality of work. The important fact to bear in mind is that everyone should be properly paid for their work and skills, so that they are able to support themselves and their families. An error in wages of plus or minus of say 5%, with swings both ways over a lifetime would normally average out in the long term. In present day world economies (2006) many people are being paid less than half of what they should be receiving. In sustainably run economies a small deviation in wage/salary is acceptable and affordable.

In some very special circumstances a greater amount of give and take may be necessary. However, in a sustainable form of economy it is the duty of the parties involved to be as accurate as possible in determining a proper payment for the wage or salary, and they should be able to justify whatever they agree to as being realistic in these circumstances. Employees might agree to lower wages, if they feel that it is in their interest. They may take this action in order that the business, or institution they work for can continue to compete, while it is seeking ways to regain competitiveness, or its sustainability.

Employees should not demand higher wages from their employers than can be justified, as by doing so they are upsetting the balance of the whole economy. Other people would then be forced to give them a gift, as they would be paying more for goods and services they buy than their warrantable value.

Holidays, Illness and Pensions

Illness not caused by work operations is not the employer's responsibility. It is the employee's responsibility to provide for the loss of earnings caused by it. Time taken for holidays and days off work too should all be at the employee's expense. However, employers can deduct the cost for holidays and the cost of a joint insurance scheme to allow for wages lost through illness and paid holidays, and most employees would prefer this basis to be included in their work contract.

Pensions are also an employee's responsibility, but often deductions are made by employers for the state pensions to comply with the law, and for private pensions. Any contributions paid for by the employer at his expense are an extra to the employee's wage/salary and would form part of the amount assessed and agreed in the wage negotiation process.

Mental work not carried out at the work place

In many vocations the brain does not stop working the moment one leaves the work place, but continues working subconsciously and consciously. Often one finds one is sorting out work problems in other places at any time of day and night. One may even be planning the next day's work. Clearly one is working, and it could amount to a substantial number of hours of work during the course of the year. In fact, often at the office one cannot solve the problem, however much one thinks about it. It would be irresponsible when away from the work place to say to oneself 'I am not going to think about it any more, but just forget it', because the thought, if not developed and recorded at that moment, may never again be remembered when back in the work place. Where this happens, and needs to, employees are entitled to be paid for the work. Their wage differentials, therefore, must take such matters into account. There may well be a give and take situation here.

Travelling

Travelling to and from one's normal place of work is at the employee's expense.

From the work place, wherever this is deemed to be, one's time whilst travelling should be paid for, including the cost of transport, whichever means are used. Clearly one should be paid for at least the 40-hour working week, even if one is unable to use one's skill while travelling. It is up to the employer to decide whether the travelling takes place in the normal working hours, or outside them.

When travelling outside the normal working hours, one is clearly working, or losing leisure time, or working time in the family home economy. Sometimes the travelling time can be used for work, study, or leisure. If one is driving and working outside normal working hours, one should at least be paid as a driver at the average rate of productivity. If one is able to work while travelling in the transport being used, one's normal rate should be paid. If it is not possible to work while travelling and the time can be considered your own (you can read etc., or just relax), then the employer need only pay an average unskilled rate in compensation for loss of one's time at home. The matter does need to be negotiated by the parties involved, and there would certainly be some give and take in the agreement.

Working one's way up to management duties

In many trades and professions (gangers, foreman, managers and other types of supervisory staff) employees work their way up into management positions in their vocation. From first starting work one gains practical experience at the various levels of the industry, learning how it functions, what is needed for good results and how it is managed. These persons are known, or observed and guided by the proprietor/s of the business and chosen for their abilities.

The rate of pay for these persons would be above the average productivity rate and would normally rise up to a productivity/quality rate of 200%, depending on the responsibility and nature of the job. They may also receive training paid for by the employer.

Where the employee has also had to take a long management course at his own expense, apart from his normal vocation, this could justify a further increase in the salary.

As with other wage negotiations, both employer and employee must be able to justify the wage agreed, which must be fair.

Learning a skill at a very young age

Some skills and practices can be likened to that of a professional person. For example, if their special skill commences in their childhood, perhaps even at the age of three, and their training is completed when they are say sixteen, they would need to calculate their wage differential from the year they commenced. It is likely they would not be developing their skill fulltime (1900 hours per annum) but less in their younger years. The correct hours of training (self-investment) per annum should be used to work out the wage differential. It should be noted that the hours spent on the person's general education should not be included in the wage differential, as everyone needs this (unskilled and skilled).

Many vocations that may commence at an early age are of an artistic nature and productivity may not apply. However, quality would be important and this is assessed based on the average, just like wage differentials, but judged by experts in the artistic field (not by market forces).

Intermittent work that requires a full-time presence

There are jobs where a person must be present full-time while the business is open, yet they would only be working intermittently. For example: a petrol pump attendant, a baby sitter and a lift operator. Wages for these jobs could be lower where the employees are allowed to use some of the time for their own use, whatever that might be, provided it is in the workplace. The proportion would need to be agreed between the employer and employee for the basis of the wage rate. Students sometimes would be pleased to have such an arrangement, as they could be studying between serving the customers. It is anticipated that the jobs would normally be unskilled. For the jobs mentioned in the example given, the rate of pay would be based on 1 MCU per hour, as productivity does not apply. If the person on average would be working half an hour in each hour for the employer the wage would amount to 0.5 MCU per hour and this would be converted into the national currency. Sometimes a quality of service adjustment could be made to the wage.

Varied Work Using Different Skills

Job satisfaction and productivity can sometimes be improved, by the employee having various tasks to carry out during the day instead of always the same one. It is also useful for the employer to have employees skilled in a number of tasks employed by the business as this gives flexibility when staff become ill or absent unexpectedly. It is useful to the employee to have a range of skills to offer for employment.

Wages would be negotiated in the same way as described for the multi-skilled.

The Wage Negotiation Structure

The methods and the framework for negotiating sustainable and fair wages are now complete. A general approach for all skills has been given. In this book it is not the intention to go into great detail, as this is the task of each trade and profession to establish with the help of experts in their respective fields of competence.

It should be noted that all wages and salaries need adjustment from time to time, or renegotiation due to changes as the economy moves forward. Where difficulties are experienced with wage negotiations expert advice should be sought. Fairness and give-and-take are important elements for success.

CHAPTER 4

MONEY, SAVINGS, PENSIONS AND FINANCIAL INSTITUTIONS

In the first three chapters the manner in which the economy naturally functions has been explained; the form for a sustainable economic system has been described, and so has the basis for negotiating wages. This Chapter is concerned with the financial aspect of a sustainable form of economy, and information everyone should be familiar with concerning money, savings, and pensions.

Money

The purpose of money is to facilitate the exchange process of our hours of work for goods and services. It is also a measure for valuing goods and services. Measures do not alter: they are a fixed unit of quantity that is used for making comparisons (make parts fit, or a mix to be exactly as wanted) and, therefore, can be defined. In a natural world the hours of human productivity are paid for with money. Goods and services can all be calculated in hours of human productive work, and are by the businesses, before being converted to a monetary value. Each hour's work is converted to the nation's monetary unit by multiplying the hours of work by a constant factor to convert its worth into money, the national currency. The monetary units are only a promise to pay and are backed by our collective hours of work in making goods and providing services. We exchange our hours of work for goods and services, or pay someone for their hours of productive work. Money definitely represents our hours of work, which we need to exchange, to buy the goods and services we need. A £, $, Yen, or any other currency could represent one hour's worth of average human production (or the same fixed part of it), in whatever we are employed in at work. One hour's worth of average human productivity is one unit of money in the natural economy; and this is a fixed measure, a natural unit, and a Master Currency (MH unit), that all other units of money can be compared with.

When we are paid for our hours of work, that is the point when the money is created (is born). The employer promises to pay a number of units. When we have spent the money we have earned, the promised payment is fulfilled (and dies). When we save money it can be many years before we spend it. During this period other people, or businesses, can borrow the units to buy goods and services they need, until they have savings to repay the money they have borrowed. When one gives a gift of money, the promise to pay dies when the receiver of the gift spends it.

Money represents goods and services in an as new condition, when the product has just been made, or the service just given. Savings represent goods and services waiting to be bought: they are goods in stock and services ready to be given. Natural money, as the Master Currency, does not lose its value; its purchasing power remains constant. It is most important that money does not lose its value, because long-term savings, as required for a pension, could become worthless. This happens when we have inflation and currencies not fixed to the Master Currency. Natural money is not just printed or issued by governments (or banks); the nation's citizens always create it by the hours of average human productivity in employment. This is sustainable money that has not been distorted. The savings recorded (in our banks and money) balance with the new goods and services each nation has available.

Money, as mentioned, is used as a measure to value goods and services. The goods could be houses, cars, ships, or factories and could be new or second-hand. When we buy one property and sell another each is valued, and we exchange one for another, plus or minus a sum of money to cover any difference in the cost.

Savings

The value of savings in most nations' economies is insufficient to buy all the goods (old and new assets), which could be worth say up to 10 years earnings of the whole population. This does not cause a problem, as we never wish to buy them all at once. We only need to buy what we make each day, and our hours of work each day (week, month or year) balance with what we need to buy. Our savings balance with the money lent and those who borrow it, spend it.

Money as notes and coins and in our bank current accounts are savings belonging to us, and are backed by the goods and services in stock made by us, ready to be bought when we wish. The value of these goods and services will be equalled by business, government and individuals' debts. The savings in current accounts and money should not earn interest. To earn interest money from the current account needs to be transferred to savings accounts. In a natural economy money (as notes and coins and in current accounts) should never fail where the financial system is properly managed. Money in savings accounts can be at risk of loss in badly run loan systems. Loans used as venture capital is the most risky way to invest savings, but can give high rates of interest.

Running current accounts costs money. If a bank does not make charges for the service, it can only cover the cost by lending the money in its clients' current accounts, and by charging interest on the loans it makes to others.

Interest rates must be low on savings to ensure a stable monetary system. They should not exceed 4% A.P.R. (per annum) and should normally be about 2%. Loans should be fully secured and banks should ensure that they are. However, financial institutions dealing in venture capital will need to charge higher rates of interest to balance with the risk being taken.

Pensions

Pensions are paid in advanced economies, like in the developed nations. Pensions can be either provided by the state, or private pension organisations. Sometimes both are required. The state pensions are paid for from taxation, and/or contributions deducted from our wages, and these are likely to be paid throughout our working lives. Private pensions can be paid for in many different ways; often with employers making contributions. The purpose of the pension is to give us sufficient income to support us in our retirement. Many people also accumulate savings to be spent during their retirement.

Pensions are not a human right, and are up to the individual to provide, where governments do not give or organise pensions for us.

In a stable economy, where people do have full employment over their working lives, the most efficient way of providing the pension is for it to be organised by the government and paid by them. If governments do not pay for the pension out of direct taxation, but deduct contributions from wages the most practical time is during the last fifteen years of a person's working life, when families do not have children to bring up and a house mortgage to pay. When pension contributions are paid for over longer periods than 15 years, further years of the administration costs are added.

The proportion of the working population to the retired population can vary. Where there is an imbalance, when there is a high number of pensioners and small working population, governments may be forced to reduce the amount of the pension, or raise the retirement age. The reason for this is not simply the lack of funds (as these would have already been paid in the contributions), but the lack of working population that must do all the work to support the pensioners. It should be noted that it is the working population that does all the work to supply the goods and services for the children and the pensioners. If our average life span is 80 years, 15 years as a child and 15 years as a pensioner, one could say that thirty eightieths of the working population are occupied in supporting children and pensioners. This, say, amounts to 37% of the workforce. If say there are more children and more pensioners amounting to half the population, 50% of the workforce could be needed to support them. This alters the whole balance of our economy and in effect lowers the standard of living. To overcome this problem, governments may allow foreign workers to restore the balance, instead of a later retirement age.

The value of a basic pension for a married couple living in their own home should amount to 37% of the average wage based on the master currency. (In year 2000, therefore, the basic pension should amount to £126.68 per week.) The means of calculating the average wage are given in Chapter 3 'Wage Negotiations'. A couple renting their accommodation would require a larger basic pension equal to 48% of the above-mentioned average wage. (In year 2000, therefore, the desired pension should be £164.34 per week.) Ideally it would be wise to try and achieve a minimum pension equal to 50% of the average wage. This would amount to 15 years x 50% = 7.5 years work per pensioner couple. This is equivalent to 15% of the nation's workforce supporting pensioners' basic requirements, but excludes the cost of health care and all the other free services the pensioners may receive, plus savings they may also spend. These would also create work for the nation's workforce. A single person would need a basic pension equal to 30% of the average wage, amounting to £102.71 per week in year 2000.

Where no pensions are provided, or schemes available to provide pensions, it is the younger working population that has always needed to support the older generations (unable to work) in their families. It should be noted that this still applies in modern economies. The only difference is instead of relations supporting the retired it is the whole nation's workforce collectively supporting them. Consequently, many people can retire before being unfit to work; therefore being able to enjoy their retirement.

Financial Institutions

Banks

For banking, savings and pensions in modern economies financial institutions serve the public and business with this lifetime task. With the MH system banks would provide currents accounts to store our everyday living money, where it would be used to pay our bills, and savings accounts for money we do not wish to spend in the near future. These banks include building societies.

In the MH system current account funds are in the customers ownership and not the banks. The banks only record the transactions and keep the balances. There would, therefore, be a small charge for this service.

Pension Funds

Where pensions are not provided by state schemes they can be provided by various organisations: an organisation's pension fund that actually manages the fund, by placing money into suitable investments, insurance companies specialising in pension schemes, or banks. The funds should not be placed in unsound investments.

Insurance

Finally the other financial institution most of us would be involved with is for insuring our lives and property against major, unexpected losses that could be caused by illness, accidents, fire, theft and natural events like floods and earthquakes.

CHAPTER 5

MODELLING FAMILY ECONOMIES

In this Chapter, using simple stages, tables are built up showing some typical family economies over a complete lifespan. The tables are in MH units, that is, based on our average human productivity (Master Currency). Tables are given for the conversion of the Master Currency into £ sterling over a wide period of years, so that readers using their calculators are able to convert the figures into £s for any particular year they may wish to study.

The basis of the figures shown in the tables is for a modern European standard of living. The figures used are based on the production as it occurred in the year of 1977-78, when a large proportion of goods and services were home production. The reason for this will be explained later when the models are discussed. The figures in the models chosen are for the more basic acceptable standards. Individuals, on the basis described, would be able to make their own models to suit their particular desired standards above the basic levels given.

Overall taxation (income tax, profit taxes, value added tax and various other duties) in the calculations is assumed to be 40%, which is as much as most modern economies can really afford. In 1995 U.K. taxation was close to this figure (different nations overall taxation can vary between 20% to 60%). The value of the goods in the tables given is without tax. Before wages are compared all taxes are first deducted from the wages.

In the following examples five family sizes are considered as follows:
1   A single person.
2   A married couple without children.
3   Married and one child.
4   Married and two children.
5   Married and three children.

The living accommodation in the tables for each of the five families is minimum. Of course there is no reason why a single person or family could not choose larger accommodation, if their budget can afford it.

For a proper appreciation of the family economy the whole life cycle should be considered. This helps to give a clear picture of the necessary expenditure during different periods in our lives. The tables given are on the basis that a wife would spend her time managing the home and domestic affairs, and the tables are also based on the following:
a) A child remains solely at home until the age of 5.
b) A child would receive a general education from the age of 5 to 15.
c) A single person leaves his home at the age of 20 and provides his own accommodation.
d) A person retires at the age of 65.
e) The average age at death is 80.

f) Husband and wife are of the same age and marry at the age of 24.

g) The children are born at two-year intervals commencing 2 years after the marriage.

h) The children receive free education, but not free lunches.

These assumptions would vary from country to country and on individual choices and circumstances but, nevertheless, are realistic examples that can be varied as individuals wish.

The main elements of the domestic budget are food, clothing, domestic maintenance, living accommodation, furnishings and finally our various other requirements, or luxuries.

Food

The amount of food that a person consumes does naturally vary considerably and the figures quoted are those considered adequate for the normal person. It is assumed that all meals are had at home, except school meals bought for the children, and restaurant meals by the husband. Other meals bought outside would not be considered a necessity but a luxury, and therefore excluded from the food budget.

The cost of food eaten at home is based on 3 MH per person per week, including each child whatever age. The amount excludes any savings that could be made by home production from the vegetable garden, and any other home production.

Husband's lunches are based on 2.5 MH per five-day week and children's canteen meals at 1.5 MH per five-day week. The tables assume that the husbands holidays amount to four weeks per annum and the children's are 12 weeks per annum, and outside meals are excluded for these holiday periods.

Table 6 shows the annual cost of meals for each of the five families chosen and Table 7 is their lifetime food budget.

TABLE 6

Annual cost of meals (in MH)

	All meals at home	Midday meals out	Total
Single person	156	120	276
Married without children	312	120	432
Married with one child	468	120 + 60	648
Married with two children	624	120 +120	864
Married with three children	780	120 +180	1080

TABLE 7
Lifetime Meal Budget (in MH)

Age	Single Person	Married	Married + one child	Married + two children	Married+ three children
20-24	1104	1104	1104	1104	1104
24-26	552	864	864	864	864
26-28	552	864	1176	1176	1176
28-30	552	864	1176	1488	1488
30-35	1380	2160	3180	4080	4860
35-40	1380	2160	3240	4320	5400
40-45	1380	2160	3000	3960	5040
45-50	1380	2160	2316	2784	3564
50-55	1380	2160	2160	2160	2160
55-60	1380	2160	2160	2160	2160
60-65	1380	2160	2160	2160	2160
65-70	780	1560	1560	1560	1560
70-75	780	1560	1560	1560	1560
75-80	780	1560	1560	1560	1560
Total	14760	23496	27216	30936	34656

Clothing

An annual allowance of 100 MH per person in the family has been used. This allows for a modest wardrobe only, as it is the needs that are being budgeted for. Table 8 illustrates the lifetime budget.

TABLE 8
Lifetime Clothing Budget (in MH)

Age	Single Person	Married	Married + one child	Married + two children	Married + three children
20-24	400	400	400	400	400
24-26	200	400	400	400	400
26-28	200	400	600	600	600
28-30	200	400	600	800	800
30-35	500	1000	1500	2000	2500
35-40	500	1000	1500	2000	2500
40-45	500	1000	1100	1400	1900
45-50	500	1000	1000	1000	1000
50-55	500	1000	1000	1000	1000
55-60	500	1000	1000	1000	1000
60-65	500	1000	1000	1000	1000
65-70	500	1000	1000	1000	1000
70-75	500	1000	1000	1000	1000
75-80	500	1000	1000	1000	1000
Total	6000	11600	13100	14600	16100

Domestic Maintenance

Finally, the last item of the domestic housekeeping budget, are the various miscellaneous items for cleaning and repairs. A sum of 25 MH per member of the family has been allowed for this item, and this figure has been used to compile the lifetime domestic maintenance budget as show in Table 9.

TABLE 9
Domestic Maintenance Budget (in MH)

Age	Single Person	Married	Married + one child	Married + two children	Married+ three children
20-24	100	100	100	100	100
24-26	50	100	100	100	100
26-28	50	100	150	150	150
28-30	50	100	150	200	200
30-35	125	250	375	500	625
35-40	125	250	375	500	625
40-45	125	250	375	500	625
45-50	125	250	275	350	475
50-55	125	250	250	250	250
55-60	125	250	250	250	250
60-65	125	250	250	250	250
65-70	125	250	250	250	250
70-75	125	250	250	250	250
75-80	125	250	250	250	250
Total	1500	2900	3400	3900	4400

We have now competed the clothing and domestic housekeeping budgets and these are added into one total in Table 10.

TABLE 10

Lifetime budget for meals, cleaning and domestic maintenance (in MH)

Age	Single person	Married	Married+ one child	Married + two children	Married + three children
20-24	1604	1604	1604	1604	1604
24-26	802	1364	1364	1364	1364
26-28	802	1364	1926	1926	1926
28-30	802	1364	1926	2488	2488
30-35	2005	3410	5055	6580	7985
35-40	2005	3410	5115	6820	8525
40-45	2005	3410	4475	5860	7565
45-50	2005	3410	3591	4134	5039
50-55	2005	3410	3410	3410	3410
55-60	2005	3410	3410	3410	3410
60-65	2005	3410	3410	3410	3410
65-70	1405	2810	2810	2810	2810
70-75	1405	2810	2810	2810	2810
75-80	1405	2810	2810	2810	2810
Total	22260	37996	43716	49436	55156

Living accommodation

The areas chosen for each room of the home are based on minimum acceptable standards. Readers would be able to enlarge the accommodation to suit their planned requirements, when preparing their specific lifestyles.

The accommodation shown in Table 11 could be in the form of a flat, bungalow, or house. In the table the first three categories of home do not allow for stairs and the accommodation is assumed to be a flat, as bungalows would be a little more expensive. The remaining accommodation, being shown with stairs assumes it would be in the form of a house.

The cost of building varies depending on the quality of the property, but budget prices can be given on a square metre basis for valuing property. A figure of 85 MH has been calculated for a sound average standard of construction, and this includes the cost of services, as would be provided in a village or town development, and the land costs are based on the rules of the MH System. The costs of the five categories of homes illustrated in Table 11 have been calculated using the figure quoted in this paragraph, and as shown in Table 12.

In some economies, where floating currencies and market forces are the means of running them, the land prices have been well over the natural cost of building the home. There is no need for this to happen in stable economies, based on a sound system as this book describes.

Table 12 shows the cost of buying and renting accommodation. The mortgage is based on the maximum MH loan interest rate of 6% APR, and repayments of capital are over a fifteen-year period. In practice with lower rates of interest envisaged (like 5% APR) some mortgages could be paid off over a shorter period of time. Rents are based on a 6% annual return on the landlord's investment in the property (based on the as new price). A further 2% is charged to cover the cost of maintenance and major refurbishments over the lifespan of the property. The total cost, therefore, of the rent amounts to 8% of the property's value, normally paid in equal monthly instalments over the year. The breakdown of the 6%, the landlord receives on his investment, can be said to comprise of 4% 'net' rent and 2% to cover management expenses and the periods when the property is vacant to let. His 4% 'net rent' can be compared with the proposed maximum interest rate permitted under the rules of the MH System.

A 100% mortgage rate has been shown in Table 12. In practice it would be unsafe for banks to lend the full value of the property in an as new condition, as they have to fully secure the loans for their depositors. Properties are rarely maintained in as an as new condition throughout their lifespan. On new properties, therefore, loans of 90% would normally be considered and probably for older properties up to 80% of the property as new value. Therefore, up to 20% deposit needs to be raised, or saved, to enable a home to be bought, as new houses are not always available in the area one may wish to buy.

TABLE 11
Living Accommodation
(Areas are in square metres)

Room	Single Person	Married	Married + one child	Married + two children	Married + three children
Living room	12	12	12	18	24
Kitchen	8	9	10	10	10
Bathroom	4	4	4	4	4
2nd W.C.	-	2	2	2	2
Single Bedroom	6	-	6	-	6
Double Bedroom	-	10	12	12	12
2nd ditto	-	-	-	12	12
Entrance hall	3	3	4	4	4
Stairs	-	-	-	4	4
1st floor hall	-	-	-	4	4
Total area (square metres)	33	40	50	70	82

TABLE 12
Cost of home (in MH)

Description	Single Person	Married	Married + one child	Married + two children	Married + three children
Floor area square metres	33	40	50	70	82
Cost of home	2805	3400	4250	5950	6970
Annual cost of 100%, 15 year mortgage	286	347	434	607	711
Overheads 4%	112	136	170	238	279
Annual cost of renting	225	272	340	476	558
Overheads 2.5%	70	85	106	149	174

Table 12 includes the cost of overheads to allow for the cost of services of water, electricity, etc. and maintenance. Rented accommodation would normally only require internal decorative maintenance, whilst home ownership requires full maintenance. Home ownership maintenance and services costs would be about 4% of the as new value of the home, whereas rented accommodation would only amount to 2.5%. The expenses are included in the overall costs in Tables 13 and 14.

In compiling the costs of home ownership, Table 14 allows for a mortgage amounting to 90% of its new value.

TABLE 13
Lifetime Cost of Rented Accommodation, including overheads (in MH)

Age	Single Person	Married	Married + one child	Married + two children	Married + three children
20-24	1180	1180	1180	1180	1180
24-26	590	714	892	1250	1464
26-28	590	714	892	1250	1464
28-30	590	714	892	1250	1464
30-35	1475	1785	2230	3125	3660
35-40	1475	1785	2230	3125	3660
40-45	1475	1785	2230	3125	3660
45-50	1475	1785	2230	3125	3660
50-55	1475	1785	2230	3125	3660
55-60	1475	1785	2230	3125	3660
60-65	1475	1785	2230	3125	3660
65-70	1475	1785	2230	3125	3660
70-75	1475	1785	2230	3125	3660
75-80	1475	1785	2230	3125	3660
Total	17700	21172	26156	37180	42172

It should be noted in Table 14 that the house is not bought until the husband and wife are married, therefore, the husband is assumed to be in rented accommodation and the rate for this has been used, including the single person. The home has been purchased during the period of 24 to 39 years of age. After this period overheads only are used. During the time when a person is in the rented accommodation he could be saving for the 10% down payment for the property.

TABLE 14

Lifetime cost of Home Ownership
Including overheads (in MH)

Age	Single Person	Married	Married + one child	Married + two children	Married + three children
20-24	1180	1180	1180	1180	1180
24-26	739	897	1121	1569	1838
26-28	739	897	1121	1569	1838
28-30	739	897	1121	1569	1838
30-35	1847	2242	2803	3922	4594
35-40	1590	1929	2412	3375	3955
40-45	560	680	850	1190	1394
45-50	560	680	850	1190	1394
50-55	560	680	850	1190	1394
55-60	560	680	850	1190	1394
60-65	560	680	850	1190	1394
65-70	560	680	850	1190	1394
70-75	560	680	850	1190	1394
75-80	560	680	850	1190	1394
Total	11314	13482	16558	22704	26395

House Furnishings

House furnishings are listed in Table 15 and 16. Table 15 lists the main items room by room, whilst Table 16 list the overall lifetime cost for each of the five families chosen, and includes a lump sum for replacements during the lifetime. Readers would be able to make their own lists and replacements and convert them into the MH values. The method will be suggested later in the chapter. New furnishings have been assumed in the calculations. The average life assumed for the furnishings is 20 years.

TABLE 15

Cost of home furnishings (in MH)

Room	Description of furnishings	Cost	Totals
Living Room	Three-piece suite	270	
	Table and chairs	40	
	Book shelf unit	25	
	Cupboard unit	35	
	Soft furnishings	60	
	Miscellaneous items	20	450
Kitchen	Table and chairs	25	
	Cooker	60	
	Refrigerator	40	
	Kitchen dresser unit	50	
	Kitchen equipment and soft furnishings	70	245
Bathroom	Medicine cabinet and other equipment	15	
	Scales	6	
	Towels etc.	6	27
Single bedroom	Bed	40	
	Wardrobe	30	
	Other furnishings	30	
	Soft furnishings	50	150
Double Bedroom	Bed	50	
	Wardrobe	50	
	Dressing table	30	
	Other furnishings	20	
	Soft furnishings	65	215

The cost of other requirements (Table 17), the car, washing machine and the colour television could be considered essential and not luxuries. The estimated budget costs assume outright purchase, and that all repairs are carried out by maintenance firms and not do-it-yourself. The sums given include for new items and an allowance for licensing fees, whilst all previous costs excluded these fees. A five-year life is assumed.

The car is assumed to be a normal family saloon and the annual mileage is based on 5,000 miles (8,00 kilometres) per annum.

From Tables 14 and 17 it can be observed that owning and running a motor car can cost as much as a normal family home over a lifetime

TABLE 16

Lifetime cost of Furnishings (in MH)

Room	Single Person	Married	Married + one child	Married + two children	Married + three children
Living room	450	450	450	450	450
Kitchen	245	245	245	245	245
Bathroom & WC	27	27	27	27	27
Single bedroom	150	-	150	-	150
Double Bedroom	-	215	215	215	215
2nd double bedroom	-	-	-	215	215
Total	872	937	1087	1152	1302
Furnishing Replacements	1744	1874	1874	1874	1874
Grand total	2616	2811	2961	3026	3176

TABLE 17

The cost of other requirements (in MH)

Description of cost	Car	Washing machine	Television
Purchase price	1000	60	200
Annual capital cost	200	12	40
Maintenance	60	5	10
Licence and insurance	80	-	15
Running cost	60	2	2
Total cost	400	19	67
50-year cost	20000	950	3350

TABLE 18

Home Ownership

Lifetime Budget Expenditure (in MH)

Age	Single Person	Married	Married + one child	Married + two children	Married + three children
20-24	2784	2784	2784	2784	2784
24-26	1541	2261	2485	2933	3202
26-28	1541	2261	3047	3495	3764
28-30	1541	2261	3047	4057	4326
30-35	3852	5652	7858	10502	12579
35-40	3595	5339	7527	10195	12480
40-45	2565	4090	5325	7050	8959
45-50	2565	4090	4441	5324	6433
50-55	2565	4090	4260	4600	4804
55-60	2565	4090	4260	4600	4804
60-65	2565	4090	4260	4600	4804
65-70	1965	3490	3660	4000	4204
70-75	1965	3490	3660	4000	4204
75-80	1965	3490	3660	4000	4204
Total	33574	51478	60274	72140	81551
Furnishings	872	937	1087	1152	1302
Furnishings Replacements	1744	1874	1874	1874	1874
Grand total	36190	54289	63235	75166	84727

Tables 6 to 20 have shown the cost of some of the main elements of our domestic living costs, the needs and wants. From these tables and Table 5 readers can create their own family models, and vary the tables given to match their requirements exactly. However, the MH value of their chosen items must be established.

Obtaining the correct MH value is not easy in the economy in 1995 as not all products are made in the same currency, nor are people paid correct wages. However, an approximate figure can be established for British goods and services using Table 5. For example a desired kitchen cooker could be £524.00 in a retail shop in June 1993. The VAT was 15% and the MH conversion factor was 1 MH = £7.39. Using your calculator the figure of £524.00 is divided first by 1.15 to give the untaxed value of the cooker and then divided by £7.39 to give the untaxed value of the cooker in MH units. The result would be 61.66 MH. Where goods are made in other nations their MH conversion factor is required; for example, if the product being bought in Britain was made in Spain their price and statistics should be used.

TABLE 19

Rented Accommodation

Lifetime Budget Expenditure (in MH)

Age	Single Person	Married	Married + one child	Married + two children	Married + three children
20-24	2784	2784	2784	2784	2784
24-26	1392	2078	2256	2614	2828
26-28	1392	2078	2818	3176	3390
28-30	1392	2078	2818	3788	3952
30-35	3480	5195	7285	9705	11645
35-40	3480	5195	7345	9945	12185
40-45	3480	5195	6705	8985	11225
45-50	3480	5195	5821	7259	8699
50-55	3480	5195	5640	6535	7070
55-60	3480	5195	5640	6535	7070
60-65	3480	5195	5640	6535	7070
65-70	2880	4595	5040	5935	6470
70-75	2880	4595	5040	5935	6470
75-80	2880	4595	5040	5935	6470
Total	39960	59168	69872	85716	97328
Furnishings	872	937	1087	1152	1302
Furnishing Replacements	1744	1874	1874	1874	1874
Grand total	42576	61979	72833	88742	100504

Using the system, for example, even cars made 30 years ago can be valued in MH, and then compared with the latest equivalent model. Very sound comparisons can then be achieved. It is interesting to note that the figure given for the average, family size colour television in Table 17 was 200 MH (1977-78). This converted into £s (March 1995) with 1MH =£7.90 amounts to £1580.00. However, considerable development has taken place in the design and manufacture of televisions, and the price now would be no more than £400 for an equivalent model, or say 50 MH. Most products and services have not changed very much since the tables given were first prepared. Readers can make their own comparisons, and when they do they will find that reduced costs will vary and some even rise when compared in MH terms.

TABLE 20

The cost of some regular luxuries (in MH)

Description	Unit of time	Amount per item (in MH)	No. of years	Total (in MH)
a) Smoking 20 cigarettes per day per person.	One week	1.05	60	3276
Husband and wife smoking 40 cigarettes each per day	One week	4.20	60	13104
b) Spending 0.25 MH per day on alcoholic drinks.	One week	1.75	60	5460
c) Living at a distance from one's place of work. Say daily cost 0.5 MH per day with 6 weeks deducted for holidays.	One week	2.50	Say 40	4600
d) Private education for one child.	One year	450.00	Say 15	6750
And for two children	One year	900.00	Say 15	13500
e) Average holiday in hotel or tour 50 MH per head per 14 days for family of four.	One per year	200.00	15	3000
For husband and wife	100.00	35	3500	
Total for holidays				6500
f) Domestic help or gardener a day per week.	One week	8.00	1	416
			25	10400

TABLE 21

Average Wage Differentials over a Lifetime

Age	Unskilled	Tradesmen Clerical Technician	Professional	Specialist
15	1.0	0.3	0.3	0.3
16	1.0	0.5	0.3	0.3
17	1.0	0.6	0.3	0.3
18	1.0	0.7	0.3	0.3
19	1.0	0.8	0.3	0.3
20	1.0	0.9	0.3	0.3
21	1.0	1.0	0.5	0.3
22	1.0	1.1	0.7	0.3
23	1.0	1.2	0.9	0.3
24	1.0	1.3	1.0	0.8
25	1.0	1.3	1.1	0.8
26	1.0	1.3	1.2	0.9
27	1.0	1.3	1.3	0.9
28	1.0	1.3	1.4	1.0
29	1.0	1.3	1.5	1.0
30	1.0	1.3	1.6	1.1
31	1.0	1.3	1.7	1.2
32	1.0	1.3	1.7	1.3
33	1.0	1.3	1.7	1.4
34	1.0	1.3	1.7	1.5
35	1.0	1.3	1.7	1.6
36	1.0	1.3	1.7	1.7
37	1.0	1.3	1.7	1.8
38	1.0	1.3	1.7	1.9
39	1.0	1.3	1.7	2.0
40	1.0	1.3	1.7	2.1
41	1.0	1.3	1.7	2.2
42	1.0	1.3	1.7	2.3
42-65	1.0	1.3	1.7	2.3
Total	50.0	60.4	70.8	80.8

Income

Having laid a foundation in tabular form for our needs and wants we now need to have tables on income in MH terms over a lifetime. It will then be possible to shape ones standard of living and decide how money is to be earned.

TABLE 22

Unskilled Category
Income over a lifetime (in MH)

Age	Percentage of earnings based on average productivity								
%	50	70	90	100	110	120	130	140	200
15-20	4750	6650	8550	9500	10450	11400	12350	13300	19000
20-22	1900	2660	3420	3800	4180	4560	4940	5320	7600
22-24	1900	2660	3420	3800	4180	4560	4940	5320	7600
24-26	1900	2660	3420	3800	4180	4560	4940	5320	7600
26-28	1900	2660	3420	3800	4180	4560	4940	5320	7600
28-30	1900	2660	3420	3800	4180	4560	4940	5320	7600
30-35	4750	6650	8550	9500	10450	11400	12350	13300	19000
35-40	4750	6650	8550	9500	10450	11400	12350	13300	19000
40-45	4750	6650	8550	9500	10450	11400	12350	13300	19000
45-50	4750	6650	8550	9500	10450	11400	12350	13300	19000
50-55	4750	6650	8550	9500	10450	11400	12350	13300	19000
55-60	4750	6650	8550	9500	10450	11400	12350	13300	19000
60-65	4750	6650	8550	9500	10450	11400	12350	13300	19000
Sub-Total	47500	66500	85500	95000	104500	114000	123500	133000	190000
65-70	3490	3490	3490	3490	3490	3490	3490	3490	3490
70-75	3490	3490	3490	3490	3490	3490	3490	3490	3490
75-80	3490	3490	3490	3490	3490	3490	3490	3490	3490
Total	57970	76970	95970	105470	114970	124470	133970	143470	200470

Table 21 gives average wage differentials for four main categories for the unskilled and skilled persons. Readers will be able to create their own based on their general, or further education, and create their own personal table.

Tables 22, 23, 24 and 25 give actual earnings and income over a lifetime for the four main categories: one table per category. Each table gives incomes based on the average rate (1 = 100%) for productivity/quality for rates of 50%, 70%, 90%, 100% (average), 110%, 120%, 130%, 140% and 200%. Readers can choose the category that they are in, or build their own more accurate table in line with their skills. These tables are used to discuss how one models family economies in this book. It should be noted that it is not only the family that would wish to make models of their lifetime economy, but also businesses and governments in order to achieve a balanced and sustainable economy for everyone. The tables also include a basic pension that should cover the cost of needs.

TABLE 23

Draughtsmen, Clerical and Technicians
Income over a lifetime (in MH)

Age	Percentage of earnings based on average productivity								
%	50	70	90	100	110	120	130	140	200
15-20	2755	3857	4959	5510	6061	6612	7163	7714	11020
20-22	1805	2527	3249	3610	3971	4332	4693	5054	7220
22-24	2185	3059	3933	4370	4807	5244	5681	6118	8740
24-26	2470	3458	4446	4940	5434	5928	6422	6916	9880
26-28	2470	3458	4446	4940	5434	5928	6422	6916	9880
28-30	2470	3458	4446	4940	5434	5928	6422	6916	9880
30-35	6175	8645	11115	12350	13585	14820	16055	17290	24700
35-40	6175	8645	11115	12350	13585	14820	16055	17290	24700
40-45	6175	8645	11115	12350	13585	14820	16055	17290	24700
45-50	6175	8645	11115	12350	13585	14820	16055	17290	24700
50-55	6175	8645	11115	12350	13585	14820	16055	17290	24700
55-60	6175	8645	11115	12350	13585	14820	16055	17290	24700
60-65	6175	8645	11115	12350	13585	14820	16055	17290	24700
Sub-total	57380	80322	103284	114760	126236	137712	149188	160664	229520
65-70	3490	3490	3490	3490	3490	3490	3490	3490	3490
70-75	3490	3490	3490	3490	3490	3490	3490	3490	3490
75-80	3490	3490	3490	3490	3490	3490	3490	3490	3490
Total	67850	90792	113754	125230	136706	148182	159658	171134	239990

Table 21 is used to develop tables 22 to 25. For table 22 the wage differential remains 1 (= 100%) and the income is only varied by the rate of productivity/quality. The remaining income tables are also varied by the wage differential. The MH income is calculated using the wage differential, the productivity/quality rate and on working 1900 hours per annum. For example, a professional person age 30 has a wage differential of 1.6 and his rate of productivity is 120% (1.2). His annual income, therefore, is 1.6 x 1900 hours = 3648 MH. Income in Table 22 to 25 is based on two and five year intervals so that they may be easily compared with the tables for the lifetime cost of living. Readers may prefer to build their own tables for income on a yearly basis.

TABLE 24

Professional Category
Income over a lifetime (in MH)

Age		Percentage of earnings based on average productivity								
%	50	70	90	100	110	120	130	140	200
15-20	2850	2850	2850	2850	2850	2850	2850	2850	2850
20-22	1520	1520	1520	1520	1520	1520	1520	1520	1520
22-24	1520	2128	2736	3040	3344	3648	3952	4256	6080
24-26	1995	2793	3591	3990	4389	4788	5187	5586	7980
26-28	2375	3325	4275	4750	5225	5700	6175	6650	9500
28-30	2755	3857	4959	5510	6061	6612	7163	7714	11020
30-35	7980	11172	14364	15960	17556	19152	20748	22344	31920
35-40	8075	11305	14535	16150	17765	19380	20995	22610	32300
40-45	8075	11305	14535	16150	17765	19380	20995	22610	32300
45-50	8075	11305	14535	16150	17765	19380	20995	22610	32300
50-55	8075	11305	14535	16150	17765	19380	20995	22610	32300
55-60	8075	11305	14535	16150	17765	19380	20995	22610	32300
60-65	8075	11305	14535	16150	17765	19380	20995	22610	32300
Sub-total	69445	95475	121505	134520	147535	160550	173565	186580	264670
65-70	3490	3490	3490	3490	3490	3490	3490	3490	3490
70-75	3490	3490	3490	3490	3490	3490	3490	3490	3490
75-80	3490	3490	3490	3490	3490	3490	3490	3490	3490
Total	79915	105945	131975	144990	158005	171020	184035	197050	275140

Table 22 shows full employment, however, there could be loss of income when seeking new jobs. In practice most of us would not remain at one productivity/quality rate, and can expect to achieve a mix of rates. These for most of us would be in the range of 70% to 140%.

The comments made for Table 22 also apply to Table 23. However, periods of unemployment could be longer to take into account retraining. The length of time needed for retraining would vary depending on the new skills chosen. Some people would be able to use modified existing skills, which would save time.

The comments made for Tables 22 and 23 also apply to Tables 24 and 25. Periods of retraining, or additional professions, can take a number of years, and may have to be financed without grants.

TABLE 25

Specialist Category
Income over a lifetime (in MH)

Age	Percentage of earnings based on average productivity								
%	50	70	90	100	110	120	130	140	200
15-20	2850	2850	2850	2850	2850	2850	2850	2850	2850
20-22	1140	1140	1140	1140	1140	1140	1140	1140	1140
22-24	1140	1140	1140	1140	1140	1140	1140	1140	1140
24-26	1520	2128	2736	3040	3344	3648	3952	4256	6080
26-28	1710	2394	3078	3420	3762	4104	4446	4788	6840
28-30	1900	2660	3420	3800	4180	4560	4940	5320	7600
30-35	6175	8645	11115	12350	13585	14820	16055	17290	24700
35-40	8550	11970	15390	17100	18810	20520	22230	23940	34200
40-45	10640	14896	19152	21280	23408	25536	27664	29792	42560
45-50	10925	15295	19665	21850	24035	26220	28405	30590	43700
50-55	10925	15295	19665	21850	24035	26220	28405	30590	43700
55-60	10925	15295	19665	21850	24035	26220	28405	30590	43700
60-65	10925	15295	19665	21850	24035	26220	28405	30590	43700
Sub-total	79325	109003	138683	153520	168359	183198	198037	212876	301910
65-70	3490	3490	3490	3490	3490	3490	3490	3490	3490
70-75	3490	3490	3490	3490	3490	3490	3490	3490	3490
75-80	3490	3490	3490	3490	3490	3490	3490	3490	3490
Total	89795	119473	149153	163990	178829	193668	208507	223346	312380

Tables 26 to 29 show the net income, after the deduction of taxation on earnings from employment. The tables assume there are no other forms of taxation. A 40% overall tax rate on the nation's GDP is probably the highest rate governments should ever make. Taxation is discussed further later in the chapter.

TABLE 26

Unskilled Category
Lifetime net income (in MH)
(Earnings taxed at 40%)

Age	Percentage of earnings based on average productivity								
%	50	70	90	100	110	120	130	140	200
15-20	2850	3990	5130	5700	6270	6840	7410	7980	11400
20-22	1140	1596	2052	2280	2508	2736	2964	3192	4560
22-24	1140	1596	2052	2280	2508	2736	2964	3192	4560
24-26	1140	1596	2052	2280	2508	2736	2964	3192	4560
26-28	1140	1596	2052	2280	2508	2736	2964	3192	4560
28-30	1140	1596	2052	2280	2508	2736	2964	3192	4560
30-35	2850	3990	5130	5700	6270	6840	7410	7980	11400
35-40	2850	3990	5130	5700	6270	6840	7410	7980	11400
40-45	2850	3990	5130	5700	6270	6840	7410	7980	11400
45-50	2850	3990	5130	5700	6270	6840	7140	7980	11400
50-55	2850	3990	5130	5700	6270	6840	7140	7980	11400
55-60	2850	3990	5130	5700	6270	6840	7140	7980	11400
60-65	2850	3990	5130	5700	6270	6840	7140	7980	11400
Sub-total	28500	39900	51300	57000	62700	68400	74100	79800	114000
65-70	*3490*	*3490*	*3490*	*3490*	*3490*	*3490*	*3490*	*3490*	*3490*
70-75	*3490*	*3490*	*3490*	*3490*	*3490*	*3490*	*3490*	*3490*	*3490*
75-80	*3490*	*3490*	*3490*	*3490*	*3490*	*3490*	*3490*	*3490*	*3490*
Total	38970	50370	61770	67470	73170	78870	84570	90270	124470

In the tables 26 to 29   the figures given *in italics* are not taxed after the age of 65 because they are retirement pensions. However, any earnings after this date should be taxable. The tables include education grants also shown in italics, and they too are not taxable in a sustainable form of economy.

TABLE 27

Tradesmen, Clerical and Technicians
Lifetime net income (in MH)
(Earnings taxed at 40%)

Age	Percentage earnings based on average productivity								
%	50	70	90	100	110	120	130	140	200
15-20	1653	2314	2975	3306	3637	3967	4298	4628	6612
20-22	1083	1516	1949	2166	2383	2599	2816	3032	3671
22-24	1311	1835	2360	2622	2884	3146	3409	4031	5244
24-26	1482	2075	2668	2964	3260	3557	3853	4150	5928
26-28	1482	2075	2668	2964	3260	3557	3853	4150	5928
28-30	1482	2075	2668	2964	3260	3557	3853	4150	5928
30-35	3705	5187	6669	7410	8151	8892	9633	10374	14820
35-40	3705	5187	6669	7410	8151	8892	9633	10374	14820
40-45	3705	5187	6669	7410	8151	8892	9633	10374	14820
45-50	3705	5187	6669	7410	8151	8892	9633	10374	14820
50-55	3705	5187	6669	7410	8151	8892	9633	10374	14820
55-60	3705	5187	6669	7410	8151	8892	9633	10374	14820
60-65	3705	5187	6669	7410	8151	8892	9633	10374	14820
Sub-total	34428	48199	61971	68856	82627	84725	89513	96399	137712
65-70	*3490*	*3490*	*3490*	*3490*	*3490*	*3490*	*3490*	*3490*	*3490*
70-75	*3490*	*3490*	*3490*	*3490*	*3490*	*3490*	*3490*	*3490*	*3490*
75-80	*3490*	*3490*	*3490*	*3490*	*3490*	*3490*	*3490*	*3490*	*3490*
Total	44898	58669	72441	79326	93097	95195	99983	106869	148182

Pensions

The figures placed in the tables for the pensions have been based on home ownership and the needs based on the tables given as follows:

- Meals at home two persons (Table 6)   312 MH
- Clothing allowance for two persons at 100 MH each   200 MH
- Domestic maintenance for two persons at 25 MH each   50 MH
- Home maintenance for a two-person accommodation (Table 12)   <u>136 MH</u>
  Total   <u>698 MH</u>

Five years pensions amounts to 3490 MH, as in the tables. This pension although based on a husband and wife is also allowed for the single person. Married persons in rented accommodation without savings or any other income would need to move to a single person's accommodation. However, a single person owning his own home having lost a partner does not have to change the accommodation. If the accommodation is rented, the remaining partner would only have sufficient funds to cover a singe person's accommodation.

TABLE 28

Professional Category
Lifetime net income (in MH)
(Earnings taxed at 40%)

Age	Percentage of earnings based on average productivity								
%	50	70	90	100	110	120	130	140	200
15-20	2850	2850	2850	2850	2850	2850	2850	2850	2850
20-22	1520	1520	1520	1520	1520	1520	1520	1520	1520
22-24	912	1277	1642	1824	2006	2189	2371	2554	3648
24-26	1197	1676	2155	2394	2633	2873	3112	3352	4788
26-28	1425	1995	2565	2850	3135	3420	3705	3990	5700
28-30	1653	2314	2975	3306	3637	3967	4298	4628	6612
30-35	4788	6703	8618	9576	10534	11491	12449	13406	19152
35-40	4845	6783	8721	9690	10659	11628	12597	13566	19380
40-45	4845	6783	8721	9690	10659	11628	12597	13566	19380
45-50	4845	6783	8721	9690	10659	11628	12597	13566	19380
50-55	4845	6783	8721	9690	10659	11628	12597	13566	19380
55-60	4845	6783	8721	9690	10659	11628	12597	13566	19380
60-65	4845	6783	8721	9690	10659	11628	12597	13566	19380
Sub-total	43415	59033	74651	78090	90269	98078	105887	113696	160550
65-70	3490	3490	3490	3490	3490	3490	3490	3490	3490
70-75	3490	3490	3490	3490	3490	3490	3490	3490	3490
75-80	3490	3490	3490	3490	3490	3490	3490	3490	3490
Total	53885	69502	85121	88650	100739	108548	116357	124166	171020

The pension provides the safety net most people require, and it is assumed to be provided by the State. Private pensions if badly managed, or for whatever other reason, may not provide the pension intended.

It is interesting to note that the provision of the pension provided by government could amount to 17.5% of the 40% tax collected, or 7.0% of the nation's wage WGDP (Table 31 shows less used).

TABLE 29

Specialist Category
Lifetime net Income (in MH)
(Earnings taxed at 40%)

Age	Percentage of earnings based on average productivity								
%	50	70	90	100	110	120	130	140	200
15-20	2850	2850	2850	2850	2850	2850	2850	2850	2850
20-22	1140	1140	1140	1140	1140	1140	1140	1140	1140
22-24	1140	1140	1140	1140	1140	1140	1140	1140	1140
24-26	912	1277	1642	1824	2006	2189	2371	2554	3648
26-28	1026	1436	1847	2052	2257	2462	2668	2873	4104
28-30	1140	1596	2052	2280	2508	2736	2964	3192	4560
30-35	3705	5187	6669	7410	8151	8692	9633	10374	14820
35-40	5130	7182	9234	10260	11286	12312	13338	14364	20520
40-45	6384	8938	11491	12768	14045	15322	16598	17875	25536
45-50	6555	9177	11799	13110	14421	15732	17043	18354	26220
50-55	6555	9177	11799	13110	14421	15732	17043	18354	26220
55-60	6555	9177	11799	13110	14421	15732	17043	18354	26220
60-65	6555	9177	11799	13110	14421	15732	17043	18354	26220
Sub-total	49647	67454	85261	94164	103067	111771	120874	129778	183198
65-70	3490	3490	3490	3490	3490	3490	3490	3490	3490
70-75	3490	3490	3490	3490	3490	3490	3490	3490	3490
75-80	3490	3490	3490	3490	3490	3490	3490	3490	3490
Total	60117	77924	96731	104634	113537	122241	131344	140248	193668

MH Values

The MH values in Table 5 and 30 as previously mentioned can be used for valuing products old and new. It can also be used for valuing previous services rendered, for example external decorations of a house or repair carried out previously, and being repeated a number of years later. It can also be used to compare past wages against recent awards, where no changes in the work have taken place. The MH is a tool for making comparisons in real values. The tables can also be used for converting the MH units they comprise into £ Sterling and vice versa.

TABLE 30

MH values in £ Sterling

Year	Annual average UK wages in £	Value of 1 MH in £	Rate of inflation % (based on previous year)
1969	1235	0.57	-
1970	1388	0.64	12.38
1971	1556	0.71	12.10
1972	1775	0.81	14.07
1973	2036	0.93	14.70
1974	2419	1.11	18.81
1975	3072	1.41	26.99
1976	3538	1.62	15.17
1977	3895	1.78	10.09
1978	4493	2.06	15.35
1979	5186	2.37	15.42
1980	6141	2.81	18.41
1981	6963	3.19	13.38
1982	7558	3.46	8.54
1983	8207	3.76	8.58
1984	8565	3.92	4.36
1985	9113	4.17	6.40
1986	9835	4.50	7.92
1987	10402	4.76	5.77
1988	11158	5.11	7.27
1989	12561	5.75	12.57
1990	13915	6.37	10.78
1991	14881	6.81	6.94
1992	15742	7.21	5.77
1993	16305	7.46	3.58
1994	16833	7.71	3.24
1995	17280	7.91	2.65
1996	17917	8.20	3.69
1997	18781	8.60	4.82
1998	19559	8.95	4.14
1999	20470	9.37	4.65
2000	20640	9.45	0.83
2001	21344	9.77	3.35
2002	22731	10.40	6.50
2003	23433	10.73	3.09
2004	24519	11.22	4.63

Taxation

Readers may wonder why all taxation in the tables has been lumped together and not in its various forms. In reality, when following through the economic system of exchange it is the public that pays the tax. For example, taxes paid by businesses is money paid to the businesses when goods and services have been sold to families, or people. We all know that government needs a budget and that the citizens supply the funding required. It is much easier when modelling to have one form of tax and to know the real price of goods and services. For government, it is necessary to understand family problems in their cash flow over a lifetime. Comparing the tables for family expenditure against lifetime income, it is soon clear where the problems for families are. From the examples given, an overall tax rate of 40% is really a maximum. Ideally a much lower rate of 30% would improve the standard of living for the majority. A simple tax is far easier for the people to understand and to calculate each year's liability they would have to pay.

Briefly, examining the government tax budget, including the local and regional taxes, it could be as in Table 31. This table shows how the tax could be spent based on 40% of the wage GDP (all forms of money earned). If the tax is cut to 30% of wage GDP (WGDP), and it is not possible to cut the education, health and pension budgets amounting to 22% WGDP, there would be 8% WGDP left for the other requirements. However, all these figures assume only the husband is working in the family unit. In fact it is usually necessary for the wife to work in the outside economy as well, whenever possible, and particularly in the earlier part of the lifespan. This would swell the government budget and alter the figures given in Table 31, making lower taxation possible.

TABLE 31

A Government Expenditure Budget

	% of budget	% WGDP
Education	13.1	5.24
Education grants for students (30% of Unskilled Wage)	12.5	5.00
Health care and prevention of illness and accidents	15.5	6.20
State pensions (36% unskilled average wage) and other welfare payments	14.4	5.76
Defence and national security (police, army and laws)	11.9	4.76
National infrastructure for transport, water and power	17.8	7.12
Government institutions (including regional and local government) to monitor and guide the economy	14.8	5.92
Total	100.0	40.00

Using the tables for family expenditure and income.

The tables can be used as they are, accepting the figures given, and the lifetime models, or used to create new models suiting personal circumstances. It can be noted that renting accommodation over a lifetime is more expensive than owning ones own home, whilst buying a home creates a peak in expenditure over a 15 year period. Having one, two or three children also creates a peak in the earlier part of the lifespan, when one has not reached full earning capacity, or finished education. The lowest paid, after tax deduction, also have problems, as the income is less than expenditure. These problems can be overcome by planning.

People with insufficient income wishing to stay single in the low pay area should have a good look at their situation. The lowest rate of pay after taxation must cover a normal single person's living costs, i.e. a 30% average unskilled wage after the deduction of tax (40% is used in the tables). This would allow the person to share a married person's accommodation. Assuming the person cannot gain a higher wage rate, the alternative is to work longer hours to make good the shortfall in income to reach the minimum living standard for a single person. Tables 26 to 29 show a shortfall in income (under 50% average productivity). It should be noted that the lowest wage shown in the tables are the minimum that an employer should ever pay an employee.

When planning the lifetime family budget for say a family with two children, initially, it would be prudent to work on an average wage for the main breadwinner in the family. It is also reasonable to work on two wages supporting the family, or longer hours by the main income earner. If conditions change, one can re-plan to take into consideration reduced or increased income. The professional and specialist categories have a low income at the start of their lifespan and, if children are desired, a plan having children say five years later in life would help finances considerably. However, in spite of dual salaries say increasing the joint income to 160% (based on an average unskilled wage) there would still be peaks in expenditure where there is a shortfall in income against expenditure. This can be overcome by creating savings made in the years before the peak expenditure arise. When buying a home the mortgage would not cover the whole cost of the investment and savings would also be required, amounting to 10% to 20% of the house purchase price, to buy the home and for furnishings.

The MH system allows savings to be made in MH unit terms, (where the government permit the system to operate) thereby protecting savings from devaluation, caused by inflation that occurs in unstable economic systems. The MH system eliminates inflation. Inflation is erratic, and cannot be accurately forecast, as there are no means by which it can be done, because governments only have partial control. Any interest given cannot be relied upon to make good the loss by inflation. The loss in value of the £ between 1990-94 was (7.70-6.37) x 100%/ 7.70 = 17.27%, and that is based on a low rate of inflation as can be observed in Table 30.

It should be remembered when building the family budget using the tables that luxuries are not included, and must be added.

TABLE 32

A Summary of a Third World Domestic Budget and Wages (in MH)

Description	Single person	Married	Married + one child	Married + two children	Married + three children
Annual living costs					
Food	468	936	1404	1872	2340
Clothing	50	100	150	200	250
Accommodation	192	384	384	384	384
Total	710	1420	1938	2456	2974
Lifetime living costs					
Food	30420	58500	65520	72540	79560
Clothing	3250	6250	7000	7750	8500
Accommodation	11520	23040	23040	23040	23040
Total	45190	87790	95560	103310	111100

Wage (percentage of average)	Annual	Annual less 20% tax	Lifetime	Lifetime wage less 20% tax
70%	1747	1398	87350	69880
100%	2496	1997	124800	99840
140%	3494	2796	174700	139760

Generally over a lifetime people should be able to achieve an overall income between 70% to 140% of the average income. If they find they are not doing so they should try and discover where the problem lies, and try and improve their standards, or try another occupation that gives them a better earning capacity. We are all different, and, therefore, must seek what suits us best to earn our living and meet our personal objectives. However, collectively the skills we possess must be in balance with the products and services we want. This means the work we create (by what we buy) is the work we must be employed in, and for many of us it may not be our choice but, by fulfilling it, we are able to have the hours of work we need to exchange in MH units (money) and to buy the goods and services we desire for our families and ourselves.

The state pension given in the tables would only support the necessities, and at maximum for the married category of home ownership. If one wishes to remain in the family home large enough for say three children, in the tables, a larger pension would be needed, or savings sufficient to supplement the extra cost. The pension and savings would also be required to cover the cost of luxury items. Larger homes than shown in the tables would also require additional income. One's model, therefore, needs building carefully, and the examples given should only really be taken as a basis on which your own can be built.

A sound national economy would allow families to plan according to their capacity to earn, based on the hours they wish to work. If the economy restricts or prevents them from earning, the economy is probably defective. A properly balanced and run economy allows citizens jointly to provide all the goods and services they desire for the hours they are prepared to work to have them, and in balance with the level of technology they have achieved.

Third World Domestic Budgets

Table 32 is based on a lifetime of 80 years, children supported by their parents to the age of 15, a working week of 48 hours, food costing three times more than in the developed nation (because food production is more labour intensive) and a simple two room accommodation for families. However, this does not take into account the standard of living of a small proportion of the wealthier citizens, who sometimes enjoy quite high standards of living.

The basis of Tables 6 to 30 can be rebuilt to apply to a nation at any level of living standards, using local statistics and information. Where countries are working to the MH system a mix of developed nation products can be used in developing the family models.

Standard of Living

The standard of living when working in the MH system is measured by the following:

$$S\% = \frac{\text{Cost of needs for individual or family} \times 100}{\text{Average wage, based on a standard education}}$$

The annual cost of needs and wage are used. The wage would be based on 1900 MH. For example, from Table 19 a lifetime cost of living for needs would be 88642 MH for a family of four. The average annual cost (over a 60 year period) would be 1477.37 MH Therefore, the standard of living:

$$S = \frac{1477.37 \times 100}{1900} = 77.76\%$$

In practice people would have their own personal standards of living, based on their needs, but they would still use the same average annual wage of 1900 MH.

For a third world country using Table 32 for the family of four the lifetime cost of living amounted to 103230 MH, or 1720.5 MH, and the standard of living:

$$S = \frac{1720.5 \times 100}{1900} = 90.55\%$$

However, the model used is at a much lower level, as the home was much smaller and without the same services. If the same model as used for the developed nation was priced using goods made in their country 'S' may have been say 120%. The reason being they lack the skills and equipment of the developed nation.

Conclusion

Families in developed nations should all have an acceptable standard of living, throughout their lifespan, provided they are correctly paid and can work the hours necessary to earn their income.

Government institutions and businesses (government and private) provide the majority of the nation's requirements, and the remainder is imported in exchange for exports. Provided the country's economy is properly managed, all family economies would be self-supporting, including the incapacitated, who would be helped, as necessary. Citizens would expect their government to manage the economy and keep it in a proper balance.

Government would also need to ensure that the citizens are aware of the skills required both in the present and future, as far as they are able. People would then be in a position to judge which skills they should learn for their livelihood.

CHAPTER 6

BUSINESS AND GOVERNMENT SERVICES

As previously mentioned, demands on the national and international economy stem from the outside needs and wants created by the families: the goods and services they do not provide within their family economy. The family budgets for outside purchases, as illustrated in Chapter 5, are the basis for developing the commercial and government service economy. Based on the tables and information given in this book Tables 33, 34 and 35 have been developed. The three tables together form a simple illustration of the whole economy, based on 1000 people as the sum employed.

The figures given in the 'Cost in MH' column represent the expenditure for an average family economy over the whole lifespan (including money from pensions, grants and savings) based on family earnings equivalent to 3040 MH in a balanced economy. This represents earnings from two persons, on an unskilled basis, and is equal to 1.6 person years of 1900 hours. This average represents a complete cross section of all types of family, from single persons to large families over their average lifespan. The weekly expenditure given in the column in the three tables totals 64.77 MH. From this total the education grant and pension money should be deducted as this forms part of the citizens income taken out of their wages, and then immediately returned to them in pensions and student grants; and in effect they spend it, not the government. The average weekly family and single person income, therefore, amounts to 58.46 MH, which over a 52-week year equals 3040 MH. The families earn the 3040 MH income using their skills: all grades of skill, including specialist skills.

The figures in '% of 36.54 MH av. wage' column are based on the working year of 1900 hours as would be earned by an average unskilled person. The 1900 MH is divided by 52 weeks to give 36.54 MH, which represents the average weekly earnings, from a normal 40 hours week to allow holidays during the year. The total of all the items in the three tables, therefore, amount to 160% (of a single average unskilled person's wage) as two persons have provided the income and not one person. However, depending on the person's skills and the hours he is prepared to work, the whole amount could be earned by one member of the family (this can be observed by comparing the subtotals in Table 22, 23, 24 and 25 in Chapter 5).

The 'Producer' column is the first stage in the breakdown of the industrial process providing the goods and services we require, and already illustrates a number of the specialist elements of the economy.

The '1000 Citizens in' column represents a breakdown of the number of persons required in each main element of the economy, in order that the economy maintains a balance. This column is divided into two sections: production of goods and materials, and the sales and services. A thousand persons has been chosen in the model so that it can be easily expanded into a working population of a village, town, region, or country. The citizens in the three tables amount, therefore, to 1000 persons. The 1000 working citizens cover the complete range of skills required.

TABLE 33

Average Weekly Food Expenditure (in MH)

Item	Cost in MH	% of 36.54 MH av. wage	Producer	1000 citizens in	
				Production	Retail and Wholesale + 44%
Bread and cakes	0.82	2.24	Baker	9.8	4.3
Cereals	0.41	1.12	Manufacturer	4.9	2.1
Milk	0.82	2.24	Farmer and Dairy	9.0 3.5	1.5
Meat	0.82	2.25	Farmer and Slaughter House	4.0 7.0	3.1
Butter	0.20	0.55	Dairy produce	2.4	1.4
Cheese	0.41	1.12	Dairy produce	4.9	2.1
Eggs	0.20	0.55	Chicken farm	2.4	1.1
Canned foods	0.58	1.59	Canners	7.0	3.0
Frozen foods	0.41	1.12	Freezer factory	4.9	2.1
Sugar, flour and Other groceries	0.41	1.12	Manufacturer	4.9	2.1
Vegetables	1.64	4.49	Farmer, Small holder, Market gardens	19.6	8.5
Fresh fruit	0.82	2.24	Fruit farmer	9.8	4.2
Other foods	1.43	3.92	Manufacturer	17.2	7.3
Total	8.97	24.55		111.3	42.5

The 'Government Services' in the tables are supported by a total taxation rate of 40% of the GDP (wage earnings). Some of the tax monies are handed back as a basic pension and in education grants to students, in the proportions given in the lifetime income tables given in Chapter 5

It should be noted that the prices in the tables do not include second-hand goods, which all economies use; however, this does not affect the manner in which we build and run our economies.

Balancing the economy

Assuming the correct statistics have been used in Tables 33, 34 and 35, they show a model of the economy that is in balance, the wages are sufficient for the employee's demands, and industry, commerce and government provide all that is wanted. People are in full employment making and providing all our needs and wants. The taxation is affordable. Given the information needed, the model shown could be expanded, including government, in the greatest detail running into millions of elements. This extended model could be in perfect equilibrium and we could all know exactly what we can afford to have.

TABLE 34

Other Average Weekly Expenditure (in MH)

Item	Cost In MH av. wage	% of 36.54 MH	Producer	1000 citizens in:	
				Production	Retail and Wholesale + 50% or Service
Clothing	4.67				
Suits		1.83	Manufacturer	7.6	3.8
Dresses		1.83	Manufacturer	7.6	3.8
Children's clothes		3.65	Manufacturer	15.2	7.6
Other clothing		3.65	Manufacturer	15.2	7.6
Shoes		1.82	Manufacturer	7.6	3.8
Furniture	0.97				
Hard		1.06	Manufacturer	4.4	2.2
Soft		1.06	Manufacturer	4.4	2.2
Carpets		0.54	Manufacturer	2.2	1.1
Home and services					
Insurance	0.58	1.60	Insurance Co.		10.0
Electricity	1.20	3.28	Electric Co.		20.5
Gas	1.20	3.28	Gas Co.		20.5
Water	0.50	1.37	Water Co.		8.6
Building repairs	1.10	3.01	Builder		18.8
Accommodation	2.12	5.80	Landlord		36.3
	1.00	2.74	Building Soc.		17.1
	1.30	3.50	Builders		21.9
	0.60	1.70	Builders mchts.		10.6
Banking	1.17	3.20	Financial Services		20.0
Total	16.41	44.92		64.2	216.4

It has already been explained in Chapter 5 how families can build their individual models, using correct statistics to evaluate each product and service in MH money terms. Knowing the cost of our needs and wants we can then calculate the hours we need to work and the skills we require for our vocation.

TABLE 35

Average Weekly Luxury Family Expenditure
And Government Services (in MH)

Item	Cost in MH	% of 36.54 MH av. wage	Producer	1000 Citizens in:	
				Production	Retail and Wholesale + 50% or Service
Luxuries					
Washing Machine	0.37	1.01	Manufacturer	4.2	2.1
Television	0.42	1.15	Manufacturer	4.8	2.4
Smoking	1.05	2.87	Plantation	5.9	
			Manufacturer	8.0	4.0
Alcoholic Drinks	1.75	4.79	Manufacturer	19.6	9.8
Meals out	2.88	7.88	Restaurant		36.0
			Canteen		13.7
Travelling	1.26	3.45	Public Transport		21.4
Holidays	2.08	5.69	Hotels		29.6
			Travel Agent		1.0
			Transport		5.0
Telephone	0.70	1.92	Telecom Co.		12.0
Car	5.50	15.05	Manufacturer	63.0	31.0
Government Services					
Education	3.05	8.35	Colleges etc.		52.2
Education Grants	2.95	8.07			50.4
Health Care	3.61	9.88	Hospitals etc.		61.8
Pensions	3.36	9.20			57.5
Defence & Police etc.	2.78	7.61			47.6
National Infrastructure	4.17	11.41	Construction		36.3
			Maintenance		35.0
Government Institutions	3.46	9.47			59.2
Total	39.39	107.80		105.5	568.0

Like families, businesses plan and need to know what its customers want from them. They can also offer new products, which they believe are required. Businesses can judge the family demands in various ways:

a) they can either ask us, businesses and government, to let them know what they will be wanting, including the quantities.
b) judge the demand from existing rates of consumption;
c) make their own forecasts for demand, and adjust their supply on a trial and error basis, or
d) judge the demand based on a combination of a), b) and c).

All these methods for obtaining our demands require information. For some products obtaining the information could be more costly than the product itself. At some time we have probably all spent hours, or even days looking for a particular product, that used to exist, does exist, or may exist. Clearly we all need information that is easily and quickly accessible.

Families and businesses are expected to look after their own interests, and it is not their duty to organise the economy that supports them, as that is a Government task.

Families and businesses all use common measures, and a language in their trading activities. Some businesses set up systems to aid this process, but all such systems need to gain acceptance, and remain within national laws. Families and businesses and private institutions are restricted in what they can do to balance the economy, as on their own, they usually lack the necessary powers and resources.

Businesses and families are all traders, but most families only have their skills to trade. They both require a continuous supply of work, or trade to survive and maintain a satisfactory existence. For this they rely on their nation's and the world's economic system for trading. This system is supplied and kept in place by governments, which in democracies are elected.

The family trade activity and businesses are all controlled and guided to keep them on the desired path. When badly managed they go out of balance in different ways, causing distress for them, or even failure. Good management is vital for good results.

Businesses

Businesses have different constructions of ownership. It is important to know something about them, as they supply our livelihood. For example:

a) Some are owned by sole proprietors, and others are owned by partners. They are fully responsible for all the risks in running the business and any financial losses. If they become bankrupt they could lose all their assets and savings.
b) Many businesses, by becoming a Limited Company, avoid the risk of losing their own personal assets; but of course they are likely to lose all the money they have invested in the business itself, if it becomes bankrupt. The private Limited Companies would probably have few shareholders, the minimum being two. They usually ensure they keep full control of the business by owning a large overall proportion of its shares. Maybe a family owns the

Company. Some shares could be owned by employees as an incentive, or by outsider investors, but they would have little control over the policy of the Company.

c) Other businesses become a Public Limited Company and they normally have very many shareholders: individuals and other businesses. At one time they could have been a large private Limited Company, the owners of which decided to become a public company with their shares being sold on the stock exchange. If a Public Limited Company becomes bankrupt its shareholders would lose the money they invested in it, as the shares become worthless. The directors of these companies could own a small percentage of the overall share stock of the Company, or none, as they are really no more than professional managers of big companies. If a single person, or organisation, is able to buy enough shares they can gain control of the company.

The type and size of business would affect its stability. The owners, or managing directors are responsible for its success, and maintaining the business profits; and some of that can be used to expand the business. A small business that lacks capital can have difficulty in sustaining itself when unexpected events occur, like a market for a product suddenly ceasing. Big businesses are likely to have a diverse range of products and, if one fails, it can easily replace it with another, having the resources needed, being wealthier. It can, therefore, maintain its work force. Big companies should have better resources to carry out market research and can plan for replacement products, again ensuring sustainability of its business.

From an examination of the model in Tables 33, 34 and 35, businesses serving certain needs would be more secure than others, provided the supply is in balance with the requirements. If only two businesses are needed there is little point in there being three, which could collapse one of them, due to insufficient turnover. Many items of family budgets require frequent replenishment, like food and fuel. This gives a steady demand and keeps the workforce in employment. It is important that the economy is kept stable to ensure that people and business income remains steady and, in consequence, the demands also remain stable; so businesses should not overproduce, to ensure they would be able to maintain steady employment. Changes in the balance of the economy would then only occur as new and better products are introduced, which only take place gradually, allowing the economy to change shape without creating unemployment.

Small businesses covering a limited range of products sometimes find that their lines cease unexpectedly. To continue in business they need sufficient capital to set up new lines. Only well established and financially sound businesses can manage this. Larger, well run businesses would be more diversified, and cover more lines of business. If one line of business ceases they can replace it with another, already planned, and keep its workforce intact and prevent any loss of jobs. The larger the company the more stable it can be, and they can afford more resources for market research.

Some businesses, like coal mining, have to set up where the resources are situated. Maybe there is sufficient coal to mine over a 30 year period. The company sets up, and new villages, or a small town develops to house and supply the families for all their requirements, and to serve the mining company with the services it requires. Eventually the coal is all extracted and the mines close in the region. The miners have the choice of living and working in another far away mining region, or retraining for work in their present locality, where the mine was the main reason for the community. Its activity created work for the whole region, and, if the miners moved away it could cause the collapse of the rest of the community. Economies, therefore, need to be planned to take these situations into account, so that the community can remain stable. If the original community had been made larger initially, when the mine was established, other industries using the coal could have been set up, diversifying the economy, and visualising that when the mine closed some miners might wish to remain in the community and retrain for other work in the available local industries.

Examining the model business economy further (in the three tables) and bearing in mind villages and small towns, it is clear that the 1,000 strong work force shown in the model lacks all the millions of skills required. Even if the model were increased in size to 10,000 people the same problem remains. However, many trades and businesses would have ample work to supply say 80% of all the everyday needs and wants. The other 20% of their purchases would have to be bought in from other parts of the national economy. To keep the economy in balance, they need other lines of produce that they can exchange with other areas. A rural area may well choose to exchange food products, or other natural resources. A small industrial town would need to exchange a number of manufactured lines. In this manner each area, or region, becomes specialised in a range of products. Its range of products must also be sufficiently diversified so that, when certain lines become obsolete, there are sufficient jobs left to support the village, town or region, while new lines are produced to make good the gap in the number of products needed to support their economy.

Very large cities, or industrial regions of several million people can support big companies with massive production lines. Often these large industries need the support of clusters of smaller specialist firms to support their requirements. Even these much larger and populated regions would not be able to cover the millions of human skills used by modern civilisation to produce all their complicated needs and wants. And even the balance of these big cities needs careful planning to ensure adequate work for everyone. It must be born in mind that it is not the duty of businesses to ensure that the town's workforce always has sufficient work for its citizens. The balance of the economy is a local and regional government task, co-ordinating with other regions and central government when necessary.

Industries need all sorts of specialised products and services to support their activities, plus the relevant human skills. To obtain this information from an uncoordinated information system, when one is in a hurry, can be a nightmare! In a modern industrial world a super information system is vital.

Again, studying the model given in Tables 33, 34 and 35, not all resources are available nationally. For example, smokers need tobacco, and with little imagination when examining other elements of the economy, imported foods and materials are required, various specialised machines and tools, and finally many of us like overseas holidays. To cover the payment for these items others have to be exported, to pay for the imports. In the end the family economies require the support of resources throughout the country and the world.

Businesses need to plan their operations to survive. Many need to buy and sell internationally and to compete with similar industries in other parts of the world. A major element in the cost of goods and services are the hours of human skills employed. In fact everything we use has a human element of work added to it. If this human element of work is valued differently in each country of the world and trading rules are different, the cost of a product made using the same machines and process would be a different cost. In some countries the cost could be much higher than others, therefore, making their products less competitive. Even a more modern process often would not redress the problem. Further, if these monetary values vary from day today, in an irregular fashion and the pattern cannot be forecast, it is an impossible task for a business to establish competitiveness. The MH system uses the same human monetary value nationally and internationally, and trading rules to eliminate such problems. This allows the real competitiveness of a product to be calculated. If a company finds its product is becoming uncompetitive it can plan improvements, or seek other products well in advance to replace the out-dated ones.

Many companies operate internationally and have investments in many countries. They need a trading system that allows them to operate with the minimum of problems across borders. An international commercial language, probably English, should be properly established to aid good communication, transfer knowledge and prevent misunderstandings.

Businesses need personnel with skills to match their requirements, and people need to know which skills are and will be wanted. Key skills for the economy are listed in Chapter 7. Some skills can only be finally shaped in the employment of the business, as only its managers know what is required.

Financial Institutions

Banks and financial institutions are governed by the country's laws and usually can only trade in the legal tender. Though financial laws might not be compatible with the natural economy, the financial bodies still cannot do anything about the situation without government cooperation.

Industry and families require stable monetary conditions so they can save money without loss of purchasing power. They also need to know the maximum rate of interest they would be charged on secured loans. They can then make sound plans and comparisons of costs.

With the MH system clearing banks (handling cheque payments and debit cards) would make an actual charge for this current account service, and would not transfer the costs to the borrowers of funds from the bank. How this develops in the future could be a political decision, provided it does not interfere with the stability of the MH system.

Families and industry need to borrow money to develop their plans. However, the funds needed may not be available, because the financial needs of the economy have not been forecast, or planned. Collectively we produce all the goods and services needed and, therefore, we can create capital in balance with the requirements, provided we are able to work the hours to produce it and have the correct resources available. A body in the economy needs to be occupied with this activity, to establish the balance needed and the level of development achievable.

Government

Like businesses, governments exist to serve families, but also businesses and other institutions. The government forms a vital element of the economic system. Its primary tasks are to manage the balance of the whole national economy, and to ensure that the economic system serving its citizens is compatible with the natural economy, as outlined in Chapter 1.

It has already been explained in this book that, given the right economic structure and technology, economies can be guided to supply our reasonable needs and wants fairly and honestly. However, the economy is complicated and must be thoroughly understood by its managers at all levels. Businesses and other private sector institutions work within the framework set by the government, but their loyalty is to their shareholders and themselves: not to the government, or the general public. This present situation leaves the economy with pieces of the economic system missing, thereby preventing its proper guidance, maintenance and development on a sustainable path, caused by governments who do not know how to manage co-ordination of the elements in their economy, and lack the right system to guide the economy.

Information vital to the smooth running of a modern economy must be coordinated and arranged, so it can be found easily and quickly by those seeking it, to manage and develop their economies. Many incomplete sources of information are unsatisfactory. Collecting and compiling information is a costly process for each village, town and district of a country, and beyond the financial resources of most businesses. Yet if the economies are going to be properly run all information in substantial detail is required. If the business, private institutions and government services are going to provide for present and future needs, it must be known which direction the economy is travelling. Future requirements, goods and materials, need to be prepared for consumption when required. This will not happen if the economy is not guided, and this approach produces the wrong quantities, leaves people unemployed, and the country poorly maintained. There is only one body that can remedy such a situation and that is the government service, to which the public have given the necessary powers for managing the country, i.e. the elected politicians. Government ministers should be aware they are the servants of the families, who pay their salaries.

It is the duty of government ministers, if they are not properly trained in managing and developing economies, to employ experts that are, and who genuinely understand exactly how economies function, are maintained and developed to be sustainable. Clearly they must understand what money (our means of exchange) represents, and how the economy supports families. Every part of the natural economy has a valid purpose and it should be properly understood. Elements of the economy that are out of line with natural events, that have been imposed on a natural economy, will distort it. Those responsible for the economic system and its management must be trained to recognise faults in the system. However, in 2006, how many people in government and outside really do understand how an economy functions? If they do not understand the economy they will not detect the faults in the system they are running, or if they do, would they know how to correct them? The question one might ask oneself: Who really leads the country, the ministers, or the top civil servants?

The industrial process, as it develops, gradually improves the quality of our goods and services and often reduces their cost. This usually results in less human labour being required in the creation of the product. This leads in some industries, where demand for their product is not rising, to shedding employees. If unemployment is to be avoided, these people must be able to step into the next generation of jobs, or retraining courses for the next generation of work. If people are going to remain in full employment, as is necessary to support their families, somebody needs to organise the redistribution of jobs! It is a government responsibility to ensure this is possible.

From the model given, created for this chapter, not all the tax that government receives is used directly for government services. As previously mentioned, some money goes directly back to the people in the form of grants and pensions: Table 35 shows the value of persons receiving grants and pensions equal to 27% of the government budget (amounting to 40% of the wages taxed, and equivalent to 400 persons salary in the example given)

Over the years the industrial process reduces the number of persons required in the existing government services. This produces a financial saving that can be used to create new employment into existing services and new ones, to increase the standard of living for the public. Alternatively the money saved could be used to lower taxation, allowing the public to spend the money in additional goods and services of their choice.

MH System

The MH system introduces the term 'net rent', and this was discussed in Chapter 1 and included in Table 3. The amount of net rent is very important in an economic system. In Table 3 an estimate of 8% of the cost of the average national net rents in wages (resulting from wage differentials based on the MH system) was included in the breakdown of a unit of money. A figure of 10% was given to represent business profits: items 10, 12, 15 and 16 in the table. The total of these net rents given, therefore, in the table amounts to 18%. Other net rents are also paid when borrowing money for the purchase of a home or other essential goods and services. It is very important that the net rents are carefully monitored and controlled to ensure it does not rise above say 25% of a person's money, and that it is affordable. Net rent is like a tax on purchases, allowed solely to give incentive. These net rents in other economic systems are not controlled and lead to inflation. For example, to try and reduce inflation governments raise interest rates, which increase the net rent. All forms of trading should be on a similar sustainable basis. High profits, (net rents) taken by businesses, and speculation, are greediness that distorts the whole economic system when we exchange our money.

The 8% calculated for net rents in wages, results from wage differentials, assume full employment throughout a lifespan and that the special skills were not wasted. In reality perhaps only a 90% use is actually made of them, as at other times unskilled wages are earned, retraining is taking place, or unemployment, preventing the use of special skills. This then would reduce the figure of 8%

The 10% profit that businesses are allowed when using the MH system are to give incentive to the businesses and to investors. It also provides a margin against unexpected events, and allows development. Sometimes products result from a complete chain of a number of businesses activities. Under these circumstances, the 10% maximum profit allowed should be based on the added value that has actually taken place in each business, and not on the profits already charged by previous businesses, whose goods, or services, have already added that permissible profit to their product. Some businesses have substantial capital investment in comparison to turnover and, therefore, a profit of 4% (maximum) is allowed on business capital when pricing the product.

When money is actually spent it can be seen that this is the point where a distribution of wealth also takes place and net rents are given. The net rent given to the employees, in reality is added to the value of the employer's product, and is paid for by the customers. The profits taken by the business is another net rent, which allows the business to retain some of the products, which are sold by the business to its customers to convert into monetary units.

Financial institutions handle money, provide insurance, handle assets and give advice. When handling money, including cheques, credit cards and other forms of money transactions, including loans, they need payment for the service given. The way the charges can be made can result in large sums of net rent being received without proper justification, far more than the 10% profit that the MH system permits. Some of the excess is gained in higher interest rates than needed. The cause is not always created by their own actions, but by governments who confuse the public and banks, by raising and lowering interest rates at erratic intervals and increments up and down. In the MH system financial institutions like other businesses would be obliged to work to the same trading rules. However, on loans, as defined by the MH system, they have a maximum limit of 4% APR imposed on secured loans but, on unsecured loans and venture capital, they are able to charge a higher rate of interest in proportion to the risk taken. Where they use depositors' funds for the unsecured loans they must have their permission, and warn them of the risk that losses could arise.

In the MH system, when money is transferred from country to country, there is no loss in exchanging one currency for another, as they are fixed to the MH unit, and are in effect a single currency.

Insurance companies in the MH system must have no exclusions. However, it is up to them if they cover losses, which could have been allowed for in the normal annual family, or business budget. Their profits too must not exceed the 10% maximum permitted by the MH system. Clearly, they have to allow for the annual fluctuation in claims and, therefore, can set aside surpluses over the profit into reserves against future claims. The government would monitor these reserves and could instruct them to be lowered by reducing insurance premiums. The surplus funds after all really belong to the public.

In the MH system shares would still be bought and sold; but their price would have to take into account their real MH asset value. Currencies would no longer be subject to speculation as in effect there is only one currency value, the MH unit, to which other currencies are established.

Education in understanding the economy is important, as we all rely on it to support our lives. One can say that is the primary purpose of it. The education we receive should cover a clear description of how the economy functions, our rights, duties, and how we can achieve a satisfactory life.

Governments have clear duties to perform in managing an economy, and they can be said to entail all the ones outside those natural to business and family economies. The government must ensure all sectors of the economy, financial and the other elements forming it, are in general equilibrium as it progresses forward. They must ensure the economy has the right structure to support a sustainable living standard, and that its citizens understand what they should be doing to maintain it.

CHAPTER 7

SKILLS AND THE ELEMENTS OF THE ECONOMY

This Chapter is concerned with where we use skills in the economy to earn our living in the industrial economy.

We earn our living in one or more of the following key sectors of our economy, which satisfies the family demands upon it, and those of businesses and government.

The key sectors can be subdivided into branch elements, as has been expanded for the first three sectors of production in tables 37, 38 and 39. Some categories can be divided into thousands of individual businesses and many institutions serving the economy. The elements can be further divided, perhaps many times, and could be said to be similar to a family tree. All these provide work for us, and it is essential that our skills match industry's requirements.

The tables are not complete, but are given only to illustrate the proposed form of a comprehensive information system necessary to building a sustainable form of economy. One which would help people to understand a modern economy. The actual tables listing all the skills used to serve every element of our economy would fill a book containing thousands of pages. The work on this is a massive task that would need a team of the appropriate professional persons to compile, which it is hoped will one day be undertaken.

The tables in this Chapter give an understanding of what a modern economy consists: which industries supply all our services and products and which ones we could be working in. It also forms part of our information system as it classifies all the elements of the economy and indicates where products come from. Each element of the economy can be given a reference number and these can be used to describe our skills and our local form of economy. It can be used to describe the skills used in each business and, therefore, aid in the modelling and development of economies. By there being only one system, the same energy that is used today in compiling many information systems could be used to create one very complete information system. This would aid in finding skills, products old and new, and services more quickly and easily. Each business can be linked directly into this system and they would be able to list the skills they employ as well as the products they provide.

Skills have already been classified under general headings in Chapter 3, which discussed wages and how skills and productivity can be fairly valued. The main classifications used are skilled; tradesmen, clerical and technician; professional and specialist.

The unskilled occupations serve all the production and service elements of the economy. There is a very wide range of tasks that have to be carried out using simple skills that do not require further education. Provided one is trained in the right selection of simple skills (or trained for new ones), there would be no need to seek work in another region away from where one may wish to live. Many skills can be used in more than one type of business, like driving a van, cleaning and assistants to tradesmen, or in offices. Each person needs to discover in which type of skill they are most proficient, in order to achieve their maximum working and earning potential.

Clerical work would be available in all the main elements of the economy, but frequently part of one's practical knowledge would suffice only for the business in which one worked. A certain amount of retraining on changing jobs can be anticipated. In a fairly balanced economy work should always be available in one's region of the country, provided the development process does not reduce the overall numbers of clerical staff needed in the region.

Tradesmen and technicians are specialised in a very wide range of different vocations in businesses, and the industrial development process frequently modifies skills. Skills in a region could come in cycles, and this could result in having to find work in other regions, not within easy travelling distances. However, changing to unskilled types of work, when necessary, could maintain local employment, thereby preventing the need for a person to move to another area. Many persons in this classification could find that their skill is only available in some regions of their country, or only in other parts of the world.

Persons with professional and specialist skills frequently have to seek work nationally and internationally. Depending on their skill, it could serve all the key elements of the economy, only some, or one or a few. With some skills frequent moves may be necessary throughout one's working life: a considerable amount of travelling.

Our skills can be used in the following activities in our work, for example, in production, maintenance, development, or entertainment. Certain activities appeal more to some than others. Everyone needs to make their own decision on the skills they prefer and then seek them.

People's skills must balance with the requirements of businesses, institutions and government. The economy is changing continuously to meet our new collective demands, and this affects the nature of the skills wanted. We, therefore, must all be prepared to retrain in our lives and anticipate having to do work we do not enjoy.

When choosing skills other factors also need consideration, like one's lifestyle, and priorities. The family may be more important than the vocation, or vice versa. Owning a home may be important, or living in rented accommodation may be preferred. If the skill involves international travel, or living abroad, do we wish to learn and speak foreign languages? We also need to consider where we wish to live when we retire. In fact we need to consider the objectives of our whole lifespan.

It is essential to have sound information to make decisions on skills during our lives. This is an important service necessary in our economy. Our initial education in this matter should also help us plan our lives in the economy. It is important to both industry and individuals to know where skills can be located and where they are, or will be required.

TABLE 36

The Key Sectors of the Economy

Production	1 Natural materials	a)	Agriculture
		b)	Forestry
		c)	Fishing
		d)	Petroleum and natural gas
		e)	Water
		f)	Mining and quarrying
	2 Manufactured materials	a)	Wood
		b)	Metal
		c)	Chemical - solid liquid and gas
		d)	Plastic
		e)	Glass
		f)	Cloth
		g)	Leather
	3 Manufactured products	a)	Food
		b)	Domestic
		c)	Transport
		d)	Industrial
		e)	Packaging
		f)	Office
		g)	Pleasure and luxury
	4 Construction	a)	Building contractors
		b)	Civil Engineering contractors
		c)	Plant installation contractors
Services	5 Distribution	a)	Merchants – Wholesale and retail
		b)	Delivery and postal
	6 Transport	a)	Road
		b)	Rail
		c)	Canal
		d)	Shipping
		e)	Air

Services	7 Accommodation	a)	Domestic
		b)	Land
		c)	Office
		d)	Industrial
	8 Energy	a)	Water
		b)	Wind
		c)	Sea
		d)	Electricity
		e)	Coal
		f)	Oil and gas
		g)	Wood
		h)	Solar
	9 Water	a)	Domestic
		b)	Irrigation
		c)	Industrial
	10 Maintenance	a)	Domestic
		b)	Cleaning
		c)	Machinery
		d)	Repairs
		e)	Checking
	11 Recycling resources	a)	Water
		b)	Materials
		c)	Liquids
		d)	Clean air and gases
	12 Communication	a)	Literal - books
		a)	Verbal – Radio and television
		b)	Electronic – telephone, computer Software, etc
	13 Information	a)	Skills and jobs
		b)	Family
		c)	Commercial
		d)	Industrial
		e)	Travel
		f)	Geographical and statistical
		g)	Historical
		h)	Species

Service	14 Professional	a)	Domestic
		b)	Medical
		c)	Agriculture
		d)	Engineering, architecture and scientists
		e)	Management
		f)	Education
		g)	Research
		h)	Development
		i)	Business and financial advisors
		j)	Religions
		k)	Charities
		l)	Professional institutions
	15 Financial	a)	Clearing banks
		b)	Loan banks (secured funds)
		c)	Commercial banks (venture capital)
		d)	Insurance
		e)	Stock markets
		f)	Pensions
	16 Government	a)	Local
		b)	Regional
		c)	Central
		d)	International
	17 Defence	a)	Law
		b)	Police
		c)	Military
	18 Education	a)	General
		b)	Further education – vocational
		c)	Pleasure activities
	19 Health	a)	Medical service – accident and illness
		b)	Preventative service
	20 Entertainment	a)	Active – sports and games
		b)	Cinema, theatre, concerts and television and computer
		c)	Holidays

TABLE 37
1 Natural Materials

a)	Agriculture	1	Grain
		2	Vegetables
		3	Fruit
		4	Cattle
		5	Sheep
		6	Poultry
		7	Other animals
		8	Plants
		9	Tea
		10	Coffee
		11	Cocoa
		12	Sugarcane and sugar beet
		13	Tobacco
b)	Forestry	1	Forests and woodlands
		2	Tree nurseries
		3	Rubber
c)	Fishing	1	Sea
		2	Freshwater
		3	Fish ponds
		4	Fish breeding
d)	Petroleum	1	Petroleum
		2	Natural gas
		3	Natural bitumen
e)	Water	1	River
		2	Borehole
		3	Catchment reservoir
		4	Desalination
		5	Mineral waters
		6	Hot springs
		7	Sea chemicals
f)	Mining and quarrying	1	Metal ore
		2	Diamonds and precious stones
		3	Chemicals
		4	Slates
		5	Facing stone – marble, granite
		6	Building stone
		7	Stone aggregate and sand
		8	Lime
		9	Coal
		10	Clays
		11	Silica sand
		12	Rock salt

TABLE 38

2 Manufactured materials

a)	Wood	1	Sawn and prepared timber sections
		2	Paper using wood pulp
		3	Cardboards and corrugated materials
		4	Hardboards
		5	Plywood
		6	Veneers
		7	Chipboards
b)	Metals	1	Steels of various types and sections, flat sheets and wire
		2	Cast iron
		3	Copper of various types and sections, flat sheets and wire
		4	Aluminium ditto
		5	Silver
		6	Gold
		7	Lead
		8	Tin
		9	Other metals
c)	Chemicals	1	Solid
		2	Liquid
		3	Powder
		4	Salts
		5	Gas
d)	Plastics	1	PVC in various sections and sheets and for injection moulding
		2	Polythene ditto
		3	Resins
		4	Cord
e)	Glass	1	Wool
		2	Sheet
		3	Tube
		4	Fibres
f)	Cloth	1	Wool
		2	Cotton
		3	Manmade fibre
		4	Various fabrics
g)	Leather	1	Natural
		2	Dyed
h)	Glues	1	Natural
		2	Resin
		3	Other materials

TABLE 39
3 Manufactured Products

a)	Food	1	Cooking ingredients
		2	Bakery products
		3	Prepared foods in packages
		4	Canned foods
		5	Frozen foods
		6	Drinks – non-alcoholic
		7	Wines, beers and spirits
b)	Domestic	1	Clothing
		2	Furnishings
		3	Domestic home appliances
		4	China, pottery and glassware
		5	Leather and plastic goods
		6	Televisions, radios, clocks, watches, etc.
		7	Garden tools and equipment
		8	Prams and equipment for babies and children
c)	Transport	1	Bicycles
		2	Motorbikes
		3	Cars
		4	Buses and coaches
		5	Lorries
		6	Trains and trams
		7	Tractors
		8	Boats and ships
		9	Aircraft
		10	Other forms of transport
d)	Industrial	1	Tools – all types, including purpose made
		2	Machines for manufacture
		3	Special machines purpose made
		4	Agricultural machines
		5	Machines for construction
		6	Component manufactures of standard items
		7	Component manufacturers for purpose made items
		8	Electric motors
		9	Pumps and turbines
		10	Computers
		11	Instruments for measuring
		12	Other forms of instruments as used by professions
		13	Industrial equipment
		14	Rubber and plastic products
		15	Lenses

d)	Industrial	16	Building and construction products
		17	Retail, wholesale, warehouse machines and equipment
		18	Telecommunication equipment
		19	Industrial photographic equipment and materials
		20	Scientific equipment
		21	Testing equipment
e)	Packaging	1	Wood
		2	Paper and cardboard etc.
		3	Metal
		4	Plastic
		5	String and cord etc.
f)	Office	1	Stationery
		2	Furnishings
		3	Equipment
		4	Computer software
		5	Systems
g)	Pleasure	1	Games
		2	Toys
		3	Sports equipment
		4	Videos, records, tapes, etc.
		5	Hobby products

CHAPTER 8

KEY SECTORS OF THE ECONOMY

As has been previously explained, the economy has developed from the needs of families, who buy products and services that they cannot provide for themselves, or do not wish to. Table 36 in Chapter 7 lists 20 key sectors of the economy, and some of the sub-divisions. Every element of the economy is created for a definite purpose, or duty, that must be efficiently and properly performed to produce the best results. Although most of the key headings may be self-explanatory, they do require further explanation, or discussion as follows.

1 Natural Materials

Food products and other materials in the environment need careful protection, and some minerals and resources, even water in some countries, may need to be used sparingly.

Modern farming, material extraction and manufacturing processes, and the type of economies we live in, create pollution, which must not reach such an extent that living organisms are damaged, or completely destroyed. The natural organic foods and materials must not be over-extracted to ensure that natural replacement can be sustained.

The use of many metals, minerals, gasses, and chemicals can have a drastic affect on the environment and all its living creatures. For our happy and safe survival the economy must be developed to preserve all the natural resources, by completely understanding the effects of our industrial economy.

Few nations in the world have all the natural resources needed for modern economies and, therefore, they will need to share perhaps many of their resources with other countries. For example, many rivers serve a number of countries, so these must be managed and shared to enable all the countries to remain sustainable: if there is a shortage they are jointly responsible for solving the problem.

Natural resources include special species and human skills and knowledge that every nation may require. In a sustainable world economy these special resources must be shared.

2 Manufactured Materials

They are created from the natural resources. Generally they are not the finished products, but only the materials to help make the final products.

3 Manufactured Products

They are important elements of the human economy and a large workforce is employed in their production. The goods we create in this sector have a substantial bearing on our standard of living, and how sustainable our economies can be.

4 Construction

Industry and families rely on this sector to construct all the accommodation for living, working, storage and the national infrastructure, including transport by various means to take place effectively. The construction forms much of the long term fixed assets, which are a large part of a nation's wealth.

5 Distribution

This section of the economy deals with selling the products, including services, created to support families, industry and government services. It has a considerable amount of information on the quantity of goods and services used and consumed.

6 Transport

This element of the economy is concerned with carrying goods and people travelling, by various means. Each type of transport could have characteristics making it the most efficient, or suitable for the specific purpose required.

7 Accommodation

The building and other construction, where required, forms the family homes and accommodation for businesses, like offices, shops, warehouses, factories and leisure activities, and government buildings. Temporary accommodation would be included in this section.

8 Energy

All the human activities at home and at work require different forms of energy, other than animal and human. The vast amount of energy derived from the various forms available in modern economies has allowed our industries to be maintained and developed. Without that energy they could not have been developed to present day levels. Some sources of energy are not plentiful, but finite, and should not be wasted. Other forms of energy to replace them will be required when the supplies are exhausted. Further, certain fuels create pollution and accordingly should be used sparingly, and methods should be sought to extract and dispose of their waste safely, without affecting the natural balance of our environment, including the atmosphere.

9 Water

This is the world's most vital resource. Without it we do not survive. No one should be denied sufficient water for safe survival, particularly when for centuries it has been a natural right. However, natural events beyond our control can do so; but entitlement to water from another area must remain a human right.

Water specifically required to sustain the earth's necessary bio-resources must not be abstracted at the expense of the natural environment. Development should only take place where the water required is adequate. This may need planning and sharing of water resources.

Water resources, including the seas, must not be polluted by industrial and domestic developments, but should be protected to ensure a safe environment.

Fresh water in many parts of the world is scarce and frequently has to be increased by use of desalinated water, or imported one way or another. Very careful planning of our economies is essential to avoid insufficient water for future development.

10 Maintenance

Maintenance is a very important element of our economy, not only to preserve our assets, but to also ensure our safety and that the assets function correctly. Lack of maintenance can be inefficient not only in monetary terms, but by allowing natural resources to be wasted. Human lives can be ruined by accidents, caused by lack of maintenance.

Well-maintained property adds to the quality of life for most people.

11 Re-cycling resources

Throughout the world a considerable amount of domestic and industrial waste is dumped or scattered over its surface, and the atmosphere is polluted by the combustion of fuels and industrial processes. Much of the waste, some of it toxic, has been disposed into dumping areas over decades of industrialisation, before it was understood that it harmed the environment. It can be attributed to our collective lack of knowledge, bad organisation, and unwillingness to rectify the problem; and to people not caring where their litter and rubbish is thrown away. We now know that waste must be properly disposed and pollution should be minimised. We also know much waste can be recycled, often saving precious resources.

The recycling process should allow for all waste to be properly collected so that useful resources can be saved, and waste that cannot be re-used can be disposed of safely and pollution prevented. Dumping waste anywhere in our towns and countryside can cause disease, is costly to collect and very unpleasant for those living in such an environment. Our towns and countryside free of litter will help to protect the environment and make it safe for everyone, and the wildlife. We are all responsible for ensuring that our nation educates us to dispose of waste in a manner that suits the authorities disposal and recycling process, and ensuring we bring up our children to understand to dispose of waste properly and safely.

12 Communication

Communication enables people to converse and understand the world we live in. A single commercial language is very necessary to prevent misunderstandings, to transfer knowledge, technology and other information, and to prevent accidents.

Modern technology has produced many electronic aids and devices to communicate easily and quickly, and this is now a massive industry.

13 Information

The modern world is complicated, because of the millions of skills, products and services available and needed to maintain our high standard of living. It is essential that information can not only be located, but also found easily and quickly. The information system is a very vital sector of the economy and needs to be re-organised based on the key sectors of the economy as listed in this and the previous Chapter.

14 Professional

The services given by professional people must be to a high standard, sound and affordable. Advice should be available for all the elements of the economy, as necessary, to create safe, enjoyable and sustainable economies. Without these key people economies could be unstable in various ways.

15 Financial

This sector provides:
A mechanism to effect monetary exchanges to pay for goods and services,
A system for financing development and for raising capital for families and businesses,
Systems for spreading risk,
Bodies to check that the financial system is sustainable, and
Advisers for financial planning.
These five elements are the main purpose for the sector. Many governments seem to believe the financial sector is the centre of the economy, but they are no more important than the other sectors. They all have to be properly managed and used to create sustainable economies. Governments are responsible for establishing a sustainable financial sector structure.

16 Government

National economic activities should be co-ordinated at local, regional, and central levels of government.

Just as families and businesses have to maintain the equilibrium of their economies, government bodies at each level of the economy have also to ensure the nation's economy is in balance, evenly throughout the country. Businesses and families are not responsible for this.

Governments have many duties to perform on all the elements of the economy. The planning at each level would need to take into consideration skills, availability of work, businesses compatible with the local districts and regions, and that the overall developments are affordable.

17 Defence

This is concerned with creating security and fairness, essential for stable and safe economies to live and work in.

18 Education

This is a very vital section of the economy. Firstly, its task is to educate the young generation about our economy and their responsibilities in it, giving reasons for its form, including the moral aspect essential for the stability of the economies. They need to be properly taught in the basic subjects, to serve their family and working life. The basic education should equip them to make the decisions on how to develop their lives to attain their reasonable desires.

Secondly education is required to form the foundation for the various work skills needed by the economy, including further education, refresher courses, and retraining courses, later in life to suit the changing conditions in the economy.

Thirdly, education is concerned with pleasure activities. This enhances the quality of life for many people, who wish to carry out many activities, including the arts.

Finally, preventative education as an insurance against unwanted events occurring. Many accidents could be avoided, or minimised, if people were given a broader knowledge of the element in each sector of the economy they are likely to use. They could be normal domestic elements, or highly specialised elements in the course of their work. Many items, for which insurance is claimed, could perhaps have been avoided, if one's education had covered the matters causing accidents, or other events. Many of the every day events could be covered in one's general education.

19 Health

It can be seen in Table 36 that health has been subdivided into two main parts: a) accidents and illness, b) prevention. The latter is the most important element that should not be dismissed so lightly as it often is. All prevention is a form of insurance, but instead of paying for the compensation after the event, one pays before it. Compensation never gives the same quality of life. Loss of life, being crippled for life, or suffering in some other way cannot be replaced by treatment that could have been avoided, or money.

20 Entertainment

We all need relaxation of some form, and it does form a very important element of our lives. It is natural to have hobbies, including sport and games and entertainment, which are a natural part of life, and consequently a key part of all economies.

General Comments

Examining Tables 37, 38 and 39, Chapter 7, which are further subdivisions of the key sectors, every element has a specific purpose and there are millions that can be listed. The use of each must be understood and their relationship with the other elements.

It is so often assumed that persons owning a business have one sole objective, to make massive profits and no other motive. In fact, if people made careful observations they would discover only a few really have this as their main objective for running a business. We all need to be paid for our activities in the general economy supporting all our lives. People who choose to run a business do so for many reasons, apart from it being a means to support their families. All businesses, like families, need to earn money and require profit to maintain the stability of their service. As explained, even those taking further education take risks, as the demand for their skills can vary; and, as the economy changes shape, they need to update their knowledge, usually carried out in their own time, often at their expense.

Many people are dedicated to the service they provide to other people, and can become frustrated when working for an employer who prevents them using what they believe to be their best talents. Eventually, many of these persons decide to have a business of their own. Providing one has full financial control of one's business, it allows individuals to develop their ideas, or concepts, completely. They would be well aware of the risks they would be taking, but would not be satisfied until they would have proved, or tried to, that their product is viable and wanted. Many businesses do not produce high incomes, but only serve to support a normal standard of living for their families. If these persons were in business solely to make money, they would not be concerned with the public's satisfaction, nor the quality of what they provide.

Government should be elected solely for the purpose of co-ordinating all the activities in the economy, and to ensure that the system that operates serves its proper purpose. That is to supply the reasonable needs and wants of families that cannot, or prefer not to, supply them using their own labour. Economies need to be kept sustainable and this is another vital government duty. Whatever is needed for the nation's stability and cannot be supplied by the private sector (families, businesses and non-governmental institutions) must be provided by the government bodies.

Another duty of governments is to monitor the economies to ensure they are performing correctly and efficiently, and if not take the necessary action to ensure soundly performing economies. They must also care and ensure the environment is kept sustainable.

CHAPTER 9

LIFECYCLE PLANNING

In Chapter 5 basic tables have been given so that families can build up their own lifecycle plans. Generally speaking, families need to create an average income over their lifespan equal to 1.6 times the average earnings over a fifty-year working life. In this Chapter such a plan is going to be studied on the basis that both husband and wife work and that the husband's earnings are in total average and the wife's earning are as close to 60% as possible, when not looking after their two young children at home. One can say this size of family keeps the population and the workforce sustainable.

All figures used come from those in the tables in Chapter 5 for the cost of the necessity items, some of luxury items listed and for income, including the state pension. In the first five years only the man's income is included and it is based on a productivity of 70% i.e. 70% x 1900 MH per annum. He is assumed to be living at home, but paying for the housekeeping needed and an accommodation rent equivalent to one quarter of a standard family home for four people as shown in the tables. The amount is as shown in Table 40.

TABLE 40

A single persons expenses between the age 15 –20

Expense Item	Amount in MH
Basic	
Food	276
Clothing	100
Domestic	25
Rent (25%)	119
Total	520
Luxuries	
Drinks	91
Holiday	50
Total	141

The married couple's luxury items are as follows:

Washing Machine	19 MH
Television	67 MH
Alcoholic drinks	91 MH
Holidays	100 MH
Total	277 MH

TABLE 41

Family expenditure and income over a lifetime
Married + 2 children – Home Owners

Age	Expenditure MH			Earnings MH		
	Basic	Luxuries	Total	Husband	Wife	Total
15 - 20	2600	705	3305	6650	-	6650
20 - 24	2984	1108	4092	7600	4560	12160
24 - 26	3033	554	3587	3800	-	3800
26 - 28	3595	654	4249	3800	-	3800
28 - 30	4157	754	4911	3800	-	3800
30 - 35	10752	1885	12637	9500	5700	15200
35 - 40	10445	1885	12330	10925	5700	16625
40 - 45	7300	1835	9135	10925	5700	16625
45 - 50	5574	1385	6959	9500	5700	15200
50 - 55	4850	1385	6235	9500	5700	15200
55 - 60	4850	1385	6235	9500	5700	15200
60 - 65	4850	1385	6235	9500	5700	15200
Earnings Total						139460
65 - 70	4250	1385	5635	*3490*	-	3490
70 - 75	4250	1385	5635	*3490*	-	3490
75 - 80	4250	1385	5635	*3490*	-	3490
Total	77740	19075	96815	105470	44460	149930

Note: The figures in italics are the state pension.

The figures in Table 41 are based on the luxury items as shown on the previous page and on Tables 12, 17, 18, 22 and 40. The husband's income between 35 and 45 has been increased by 15% and therefore over his life span his income has an average rate of 1 MH per hour. The wife's income has been based on approximately a 60% working life at 1 MH per hour. 50 MH per annum has been allowed for furnishings from age 20. The above basis is a realistic goal for any family as it should be achievable.

Table 41 does not take into account government taxation. The author considers a flat tax on all income is the most efficient and practical tax. This tax would be applied to all earned income. No other taxes would be paid on any other form of income: pensions would be free of taxation, any interest earned on savings accounts, presents; and no death duties. Two rates of taxation are used in Table 42 30% and 40%. A lifetime cash flow is given for both rates of taxation.

TABLE 42

Family MH cash low after flat taxation
Married + 2 children – home owners

Age	Expenditure	Income	After 30% Flat tax	Cash flow	After 40% Flat tax	Cash flow
15 – 20	3305	6650	4655	1350	3990	685
20 – 24	4092	2160	8512	5770	7296	3889
24 – 26	3587	3800	2660	4843	2280	2582
26 – 28	4249	3800	2660	3254	2280	613
28 – 30	4911	3800	2660	1003	2280	- 2018
30 – 35	12637	15200	10640	- 994	9120	- 5535
35 – 40	12330	16625	11638	- 1686	9975	- 7890
40 – 45	9135	16625	11638	817	9975	- 7050
45 – 50	6959	15200	10640	4498	9120	- 4889
50 – 55	6235	15200	10640	8903	9120	- 2004
55 – 60	6235	15200	10640	13308	9120	881
60 – 65	6235	15200	10640	17713	9120	3760
65 – 70	5635	3490	-	15568	-	1621
70 – 75	5635	3490	-	13423	-	- 524
75 – 80	5635	3490	-	11278	-	- 2669

The expenditure and income figures in Table 42 come from the totals shown in Table 41. Income tax is paid on all earnings and the amount shown in the tax columns is the amount remaining after tax has been deducted. The cash flow columns show the earned income remaining after paying the amount shown in the expenditure column. As one goes down the table the savings are added to the past savings. However where the cash flow becomes negative there is not enough income or past savings to cover the family expenditure. This is caused by the cost of buying a home and bringing up two children. With only a state basic pension it can be seen that the savings reduce during retirement and, with a 40% tax rate there is not enough savings left, and subsidies are necessary. However, with the 30% tax rate there is approximately a saving of six years average wage for one person. The expenditure tables exclude running a car. From Table 16 the cost of a lifetime's furnishings for a family of four amounts to 3026 MH, the approximate amount used in the Table 41; and from Table 17, 50 years motoring amounts to 20000 MH. These last item amounts to more than the savings left under the 30% tax rate. However, the tables provided in this book are all based on new goods with perhaps shorter life spans than would normally take place.

Much can be learned from these tables and the others produced in this book. The tables produced in this book are based on the actual hours of work used to provide goods and services. These MH rates were based on manufacturing and production methods in 1978. Since those days productivity has probably increased by about 60% on many manufactured items, but many services are still very labour intensive so overall maybe the family budget costs have only reduced by about 20%. However, items like motorcars could have reduced by 40%. Many people are happy to buy second-hand goods, like furniture and cars and considerable savings can be made by this practice. It should be noted that The Economist (weekly paper) cost £0.80 = 0.25 MH in 1981, £1.40 = 0.27 MH in 1988 and £3.10 = 0.26 MH in 2005, so its price has stayed more or less the same and has not been reduced in price resulting from modern technology.

Using the latest MH value in Table 5, 1MH = £11.5 Sterling and the cost of clothing allowed at 100 MH per annum per person this now in Sterling values amounts to £1150. Today most of the clothing we can afford to buy is made in countries like China where wages paid could be as low as one fiftieth of U.K. wages. Shops selling here still have to pay UK wage and expense rates but, even with these, clothes are costing little compared with prices in 1978, when most of our clothes were manufacture in our country. The budget allowed for food in 1978 for the family of four was 964 MH per annum and this converted into Sterling now amounts to £11,086 per annum, or £213 per week. Some people may find this figure somewhat excessive, but under the MH System local farmers would be paid properly for their products without any need for subsidies. Much of our food is now imported from countries with much lower wage costs than the U.K. However, the cost of wages where the goods are grown or made are MH values in those counties or even lower: they, therefore, are paying prices like those used in the tables in this book. Eventually, the developing nations will reach the same levels of industrialisation as the developed nations, and the value of the currencies would rise making their products as expensive as ours. Our lifetime budgets must take this into account and not rely on more overseas goods and services than necessary.

The present world economies try to operate on a free market system, based on currencies kept at various levels created by market forces, not real natural values. Provided a product can be sold it can be sold at any price people are prepared to pay for it. The value of a product does not have to be based on the real time taken to provide it! Very large profits do not break international trading rules. In 1978 when Table 12 for the cost of housing was made most prices in the UK, generally speaking, would have been within the estimated building costs given. Now, 28 years later, one can pay two or three times more and most properties are worth well above their true cost: MH costs based on real human effort and work. If we had proper trading rules the distortions just discussed would not happen. Price and wage distortions cause considerable problems for people, and given the right political policies it would not happen.

One might ask, why were the negative cash flow rates left in the Table 42? The reason was to highlight this difficult point in our life cycle. People can make their own plans on how they wish to move this negative cash flow problem. It could be removed by having children later in life, by working longer hours, by the wife being younger than the husband and having the benefit of his savings, or by cash funds from senior members of the family. There are many solutions possible. However, it is most important not to pay inflated prices for the home, the major purchase in everyone's life. It is interesting to note that from the age of 50 – 65 is a good time to save for the second pension, where living expenses have lowered, when the children are able to support themselves. It should be noted that do-it-yourself activities could make savings on maintenance costs. The wife being in fulltime, instead of part time, employment would also add to funds for retirement. In this latter 15 year period both should be able to manage an average rate of productivity.

From Table 42 it is clear that taxation should not be at the 40% rate but somewhere in the 30% range. It is up to government to lower the rate of taxation by running their services with less unnecessary administration. It is also most important people are paid fairly for their productivity. The low minimum basic wage paid (£5.30 in April 2006) is insufficient. Wages must be enough to pay normal living costs. There are also too many people being overpaid with amounts that cannot be justified.

Governments could make considerable savings by creating fuller employment by cutting the international rate of the £ Sterling; by a better education leading to healthier living, preventative measures, reducing crime, and better management of our nation. An improved financial system and currencies pegged to the MH would maintain the purchasing power of money and people's savings: it would also enable sound financial planning.

With reference to the standard of living index in Chapter 5, and based on a 30% flat tax rate, an average index can be established on a family lifetime. Basic expenditure over a lifetime is 77740 MH (Table 41). Total earnings from the same table amount to 139460 MH for both husband and wife, and a 30% tax on the earnings amounts to 41838 MH. This added to the basic expenditure amounts to 119578 MH.

$$S = \frac{\text{Cost of basics} \times 100}{\text{Total income}}$$

$$= \frac{119578 \times 100}{139460} = 85.74\%$$

The balance of the funds left are, say for luxury items, amounting to 14.26% or 19882 MH roughly 10 years earnings for the family.

CHAPTER 10

POLITICAL POLICIES

How does one decide on a political policy and how can they affect our lives? Many of our early observations concern what we can obtain from life and what we would like to do with it. When grown up we all realise we will need to work to support our standard of living. We obviously want our fair share of available resources and not to be excluded from what we see others enjoying. Most of us like to just get on with our own family lives, wanting the economic system to be fairly organised to serve our various requirements, without involvement. Voting for a political party can be a nuisance, yet if we do not we could end up with a party that could make life very difficult for us. We find that we must be involved! If we feel we are being unjustly treated by the economy, and it cannot be explained, we are going to question why, and resent being in that situation. This in later years can lead to retaliation in some way against the successful: crime and conflict in various forms as is now happening throughout the world Decisions on political issues are based on making sound comparisons of the events taking place around us, the purpose of this Chapter.

To make sound decisions it is necessary to understand sufficiently our natural economy, particularly how the family is supported, our participation in the economy, and our rights. The first six chapters of the book have given a picture of the standard of living we can achieve in the economy and how one can shape one's own economy. For the economy to function properly the type of education we receive is most important, as it should guide us on a route that leads to maintaining a sustainable economy. There are three main parts to the economy: the families, who set the demands for it; the business services that provide the needs and wants; and the government, who are responsible for its general shape, co-ordination and sustainability, to achieve the levels families can realistically have. We are concerned with government duties and policies, so these must now be discussed.

Clearly it is very important that we have an economic system that can be guided in the right direction and sound policies to support us. This then should be examined. We can now ask the following questions:

1   Does the system allow full employment?
2   Does the system allow everyone to support themselves without state help, when in good health; and how are the disabled helped?
3   Does the system protect our savings for future requirements and pensions without loss in its purchasing power, and would the pension funds be secure and reliable?
4   Is the education system compatible with all levels of development of the economy?
5   What rights does the economic system and government polices allow?
6   Does the policy include for a sound health system and guidance on the prevention of ill health and accidents?

7   How does the policy protect the nation?

8   How democratic are the policies, how open will government be, and would referendums be held on major issues?

9   Have the party politicians the right skills to govern a country, and would they ensure that the top civil servants have been properly trained in understanding exactly how an economy should function? Will the politicians be able to judge the top civil servants skills?

10 What are the policies on laws and codes of practice to guide the economy and give security?

11 What would the policies be on improving the information system?

12 What is the policy on protecting the environment and natural resources?

13 What are the foreign policies?

14 Are the government policies affordable?

These questions need examination and now will be commented on in the same sequence.

1 Employment

Provided an economic system is properly chosen and managed, employment in any country can be assured during the course of our lifetimes; but may not always be in the type of work we would prefer. The MH system is managed to achieve the right to work before and after normal retiring age, when able. It also allows people to choose their achievable standard of living, for the hours they are prepared to work This observation should be compared with the actual employment situation and availability of work, and political policies offered.

2 Wages

With reference to the MH System and the tables given in Chapter 5 for developed countries, even the lowest wages would support a single person to a very acceptable standard of living. In developing countries there is no reason why the basic needs should not be available in politically stable economies, using their most productive skills possible, and the application of the Master Currency System would help generally to achieve stability, globally. Existing national wage standards need to be compared against what is known to be possible, and then a decision made on the proposed policies offered.

3 Savings and Pensions

As explained in this book, given the right economic system, the purchasing power of savings can be protected. Secure pensions can also be given if a sustainable economic system is used. Pension funds would be placed in sound savings deposit accounts, where money would not be at any risk of loss, by being fully secured by assets of borrowers. Government pensions are mainly funded from taxation. The existing national financial structures should be compared with MH System structure explained to determine whether the existing or proposed policies are satisfactory.

4 Education

As previously mentioned one of the primary reason for education is to teach us the skills to support our economic activities. The education needs to explain the reasons for the various elements of the economy: how we use it and how it should be cared for. Again the existing education system and proposed policies must be checked to determine they are compatible with requirements.

5 Rights

Apart from the usual human rights, one right often missed is the right of work. Without work one cannot support oneself. One also needs to be paid properly for one's productivity and skills being used, as underpaid wages would leave insufficient income to buy needs and wants. There is little point in subsidising people's income through the tax system when they could earn it. Subsidies cost money to distribute and the human energy used can be better employed. People are also entitled to their share of the earth's resources needed for their survival, particularly water.

Proper education rights are also essential, so people can understand when a give and take process is applicable, including a sound basic education. Because we are sharing the world with millions of other people and nature's environment we cannot do just as we please. To do so would take away the rights of others. Our education should teach us where constraints are, and that these must be respected.

6 Health

Prevention of accidents and ill health is very important, as this can not only save suffering and money, but increases the quality of life. For those needing medical attention, the sooner the better, and for this an efficient service is needed. Some medical care is very expensive, but necessary. However, the service should be affordable, and where a private enterprise system is used, state health subsidies should be available for all the major expenditure a family may have to pay for. It is in everyone's interest that the nation has good health and treatment should be provided by the state, rather than be paid for by medical insurance creating an unnecessary labour force to manage it. How the medical service is provided would depend on the policy, but should not overlook the matters mentioned.

7 Defence

The form of military defence and the extent of it would depend on the economies in the rest of the world. Where unstable political economies exist, political unrest, border and resource disputes exist, etc. national and international defence forces are unfortunately necessary. Policies should not spare resources on these, but ensure the national economy can be protected, but nonetheless efficiently.

Governments should be working towards a world economic system and policy that would eventually remove the need for present day military expenditure. Such forces should eventually transit to being equipped to working on major internal catastrophes caused by natural environmental forces.

8 Democracy and Open Government

Voting is a start, but often the election process has finished when a government is in power, and little can be done to stop their inappropriate actions, with many of these not meeting the approval of the general majority.

Election policies do not always cover all the important matters that government needs to handle, and minorities are often ignored. If the general public and politicians had a better understanding of their economies, government policies would be more sustainable. Government needs to be open and honest, and involve and keep the public well informed on changes they propose to make, or of unexpected problems with international bodies.

Countries running on a sound economic system, like the MH System, would be very stable. It allows for open government and more public participation. However, for progress and to maintain a sustainable economy, unpopular decisions sometimes need to be made though more acceptable with transparency.

9 Government Skills

The authors experience with ministers and senior government civil servants is that frequently they lack the skills needed. Often they are elected into posts for which they have no training, or experience. It is not surprising, therefore, that good sound solutions pass by them without being detected! Many specialist advisors can be accused of tunnel vision, or wanting to impose their own ideas, or solutions, without wanting to consider, or discuss others.

It is very important for the public to have widely experienced and well trained Ministers, who know how to engage with top civil servants and specialists to obtain the sustainable solutions they should be seeking. It is prior to an election that political parties should be seeking the right solutions, but often at this period they too are suffering from tunnel vision! It is only the voters that can remedy this problem, if they find the party and politicians are unsound. They must influence their politicians to change, or create sounder political policies. As explained in this book sustainable economies are quite feasible, but the will of everyone is needed to engineer the economy into the form desired. It should be clearly understood that the present free market economies do not adjust themselves, but must be guided to become sustainable and efficient.

10 Laws

Laws alone will not guide an economy on the right path. Laws, rules and codes of practice, also need sound explanation for their use. Education would assist considerably in the smooth running of the economy and aid in its security. It should be noted that if there are too many regulations and laws, no one will have the time to learn them. Good information supplied in the right parts of the economy can be more effective to ensure sound practice.

11 Information

Modern economies live on information, which needs to be very accessible. So many incomplete sources, with insufficient detail, waste valuable time and increase costs. Policies should ensure information, as needed for the economy, is given adequate financial resources. Information needs to be placed into one complete as possible system, based on the key sectors of the economy.

12 The Environment

The economy forms part of the environment, and it is the only force that can protect it. The environment, in which we live, provides the natural resources for the economy and it is up to us to ensure the resources are sustainable and the world is kept pleasant to live in. Present world economies are only starting to care for the environment, and many of our activities are not in harmony with it and are unsustainable. This results in pollution, resources being used faster than they regenerate, and habitats destroyed or made unsafe to live in.

By understanding how the natural economy functions and arranging our economic system to suit the country, it can be cared for properly, as a soundly run economy releases the necessary resources and allows the economy to be properly balanced.

Stable economies allow home production in developed countries to become productive, like forests. When timber production becomes economic it is possible to afford to look after the forests and woodland properly. When farm profits are higher, it releases funds to care for the countryside. When local resources are used, this lowers transport costs and fuel which then reduces pollution of the atmosphere.

Stable economies require a sound economic system. A standard method measurement is also required to compare costs, which are stable, and do not become distorted. The MH System uses its Master Currency, the MH unit, for this purpose. This allows comparisons of costs to be made internationally and work out affordable solutions. The system when adopted, being stable, also allows increased human production to take place creating the capital required to pay for the work needed to guide our economies onto a sustainable path.

13 Foreign Policy

Countries in a modern world can no longer live in isolation from others. What happens in one country often affects others. Therefore, nations must work with others to solve common problems, and national problems too.

When trading and discussing problems, it is highly desirable to be able to do so in a single language, so that everybody has a sound understanding. It is also important to have an understanding of each other's cultures and religions. This would help to prevent misunderstandings, which sometimes lead to terrible conflicts.

The care of the environment is not only a national problem, but an international one, as are also problems of scarce natural resources. It is essential that all nations work towards trusting other nations. Confidence can only arise by a sound understanding of our natural economy and each other's problems, and by generally supporting each other in solving the problems. This process should protect everyone's rights throughout the world.

To aid this foreign relations process, it is most important that the developed countries ensure their economies are very sound, and that they are not wasting any resources, and that includes eliminating any unemployment. Strong nations would then be in a better position to help the weaker nations to solve their problems, essential for the sustainability of developed countries.

The MH system and the three volumes of this book are designed to inform how a natural economy should function; as a basis to rebuild our economies to be sustainable, and help people to understand how to solve the world's present day problems, peacefully.

14 Affordable Policies

Although a substantial amount of information is required and needs to be studied, individuals can use a common sense form of analysis by comparing key elements of the economy. For the example, suppose the national state of the economy is that 10% of the work force is unemployed; 30% of the families are under-paid; pensions only cover 70% of the needs; the housing stock, through lack of maintenance, requires substantial repairs averaging 9% of their as new value instead of 2%; the transport system has a backlog of maintenance equivalent to 11% of its as new value, whereas on an annual basis it should be no more than 4%; health care and education are little below the standard they should be, but are otherwise satisfactory and has acceptable resources; crime is on the increase; and there is little finance available for the massive research necessary to determine why the economy has become so distorted. Let us now study two proposed policies:

The first is to cut all taxes from 40% to 37% of the GDP, the saving being made on all luxury items provided by the state. This would stimulate the market. Savings in research, defence and education of 1.3% of the GDP would be made. More aid is going to be given to developing nations equal to 0.5% of the GDP; a further 0.5% of the budget is going to support sport, the arts, and other leisure activities; 0.3% of GDP will go to hospitals' expensive operations to save lives even if success cannot be guaranteed; and a further 1.5% of the GDP will be spread over the remaining government and local government services. Growth in the economy will create tax revenue equivalent to 1.5% of the GDP and balance the budget.

Such a policy does little to re-stabilise the economy, in fact it is likely to increase its instability. However, to many voters it is an attractive policy, as it will increase their standard of living. But for others, who have insufficient income for the necessities, the policy is a bleak one. Some will become unemployed and others will become employed, but overall it would not create much increase in employment.

The second policy for the same economic condition previously given could be as follows: The party policy will keep taxation at its present level and will increase the revenue by gradually restoring the balance of the economy. For this purpose it would use the MH System as a tool to remodel the economy into a sustainable one that will allow all citizens to support themselves by being paid a proper wage. Adequate resources will be given to a new government research team to produce the master plan to reform the economy and remove the distortions, and lead it onto a sustainable path. This is estimated to cost 0.1% of the GDP. One of the distortions in the economy is the overvalued currency. In the first stage of the policy the currency would be reduced in value by being fixed to other currencies making purchases far more attractive, increasing exports, but slowing the expensive imports. The increasing exports would increase employment. In the second stage, extra taxes resulting from increased employment would be used to increase pensions, which would again stimulate employment. In the third stage the results of the economic research would be used to restore the balance in the national wage structure. As the nation gradually moves to full employment and imports balance exports, the increased tax revenue resulting from full employment and proper wages would be used to restore the condition of the national housing stock, and the national infrastructure. It is anticipated that the level of crime would fall as poverty is eliminated. The lower cost of export goods would aid the developing countries more than subsidies.

The two policy samples given show how different the policies can be. The MH System can be used, and common sense goes a long way to analysing policies. However, the better one's understanding of the natural economy and the way it functions, the easier it will be to compare the merits of political policies.

Observations

It is very useful to prepare lists of questions before analysing political policies. It is also useful to have a sound basis on which to compare the policies and to know what is possible.

Using the MH System as a tool political parties could construct better policies and could update models as described in this book. As development takes place, new methods reduce costs of production and services, and introduce new products. When the family lifetime tables in Chapter 5 were modelled (1979) computers were very expensive, but now are no more costly than a television.

Using sound technology politicians can study all sectors of the economy, to discover weaknesses, and see how they can improve them. However, they need both time and money for this, yet frequently have neither. The parties with the best resources should be able to produce the best policies, but they must also understand what they are doing in order to direct sound policy making.

MASTER CURRENCY SUSTAINABLE ECONOMIC SYSTEM

VOLUME 2

PRIVATE SECTOR

CHAPTER 1

BASIC KEY MODELS
FOR BUSINESSES AND INSTITUTIONS

The MH system uses key models so that the economic system can be understood and comparisons can be made. The models are needed to show the main composition of businesses and institutions and where skills, machinery and equipment are used in the economy. The information can then be used to analyse, maintain, plan and develop economies to be in the form desired.

The first set of tables, for maximum business profit, are needed to understand the amount of profit that can be taken by traders and businesses and yet still maintain a fair and honest trading system that is acceptable by everyone. Tables 101 to 110 show businesses and institutions divided into 10 categories, which cover the complete range that presently serve the world economy. There are three main components to every business and institution: they are employees, bought in products and services, and initial capital. The first four columns of the tables apply to both businesses and institutions, including sole traders and all government bodies. The second four columns apply to business permissible maximum profits, which are necessary to ensure economies remain in a sustainable form, so that people have sufficient income to support themselves and their families.

In the MH system everything is measured in the master currency, which is explained in Volume 1, and it is both a monetary unit and a basic productivity unit. The tables shown can be used in MH master currency units, in man-years or any existing currency. It should be noted that for any category the sum of column 2 (the workforce) and column 3 (bought-in materials and services) always add up to 100 units. With reference to the Business Category, column 1, the first numbers, before the category letter, represents the quantity of materials and services (column 3) and after the letter for the category the number/s represent the 'Fixed and liquid assets' employed in the business. This column can also represent the initial share capital or investment. One could say that the business category represents the type and financial structure. As '100' has been used to represent columns 2 and 3 the figures also represent a percentage, which is ideal for converting any existing business figures into the format, to compare it with the business category tables, thereby determining its standard MH system classification.

Not one of the 10 tables actually list every category shape, or code. For example, Category A for 'Fixed and liquid assets' could have every number from 1 to 1000 in its column. One of the numbers not listed being 898 and this business category would be 0A 898. The Category B code starts with 10 and Category A code starts with 0. However, Category A also includes the proportion of materials and services from 1 to 9, and Category B from 10 to 19 and the other categories also include a range of 10 variations. For example we could have a business, or institution 37D 88. In this manner a very accurate shape of a business can be determined.

Table 101
Business Maximum Profit Category A

Business Category	Employees and directors (X)	Materials and services	Fixed & liquid assets (Y)	Total profit 10% + 4% (X) (Y)	Turnover	Profit as % of (or unit of money)	% Share-holder's returns 5% X + 4% Y
0A 1	100	0	1	10.04	110.04	9.12	504.00
0A 2	100	0	2	10.08	110.08	9.16	254.00
0A 3	100	0	3	10.12	110.12	9.19	170.67
0A 4	100	0	4	10.16	110.16	9.22	129.00
0A 5	100	0	5	10.20	110.20	9.26	104.00
0A 10	100	0	10	10.40	110.40	9.42	54.00
0A 20	100	0	20	10.80	110.80	9.75	29.00
0A 30	100	0	30	11.20	111.20	10.07	20.67
0A 40	100	0	40	11.60	111.60	10.39	15.50
0A 50	100	0	50	12.00	112.00	10.71	14.00
0A 100	100	0	100	14.00	114.00	12.28	9.00
0A 200	100	0	200	18.00	118.00	15.25	6.50
0A 300	100	0	300	22.00	122.00	18.03	5.66
0A 400	100	0	400	26.00	126.00	20.63	5.25
0A 500	100	0	500	30.00	130.00	23.08	5.00
0A 1000	100	0	1000	50.00	150.00	33.33	4.50

Table 102
Business Maximum Profit Category B

Business Category	Employees and directors (X)	Materials and services	Fixed & liquid assets (Y)	Total profit 10% + 4% (X) (Y)	Turnover	Profit as % of (or unit of money)	% Share-holder's returns 5% X + 4% Y
10B1	90	10	1	9.04	109.04	8.29	454.00
10B2	90	10	2	9.08	109.08	8.32	229.00
10B3	90	10	3	9.12	109.12	8.36	154.00
10B4	90	10	4	9.16	109.16	8.39	116.50
10B5	90	10	5	9.20	109.20	8.42	94.00
10B10	90	10	10	9.40	109.40	8.59	49.00
10B20	90	10	20	9.80	109.80	8.92	26.50
10B30	90	10	30	10.20	110.20	9.26	19.00
10B40	90	10	40	10.60	110.60	9.58	15.25
10B50	90	10	50	11.00	111.00	9.91	13.00
10B100	90	10	100	13.00	113.00	11.50	8.50
10B200	90	10	200	17.00	117.00	14.53	6.25
10B300	90	10	300	21.00	121.00	17.36	5.50
10B400	90	10	400	25.00	125.00	20.00	5.13
10B500	90	10	500	29.00	129.00	22.48	4.90
10B 1000	90	10	1000	49.00	149.00	32.89	4.45

Table 103
Business Maximum Profit Category C

Business Category	Employees and directors (X)	Materials and services	Fixed & liquid assets (Y)	Total profit 10% + 4% (X) (Y)	Turnover	Profit as % of (or unit of money)	% Share-holder's returns 5%X + 4% Y
20C 1	80	20	1	8.04	108.04	7.44	404.00
20C 2	80	20	2	8.08	108.08	7.48	204.00
20C 3	80	20	3	8.12	108.12	7.51	137.33
20C 4	80	20	4	8.16	108.16	7.54	104.00
20C 5	80	20	5	8.20	108.20	7.58	84.00
20C 10	80	20	10	8.40	108.40	7.75	44.00
20C 20	80	20	20	8.80	108.80	8.09	24.00
20C 30	80	20	30	9.20	109.20	8.42	17.33
20C 40	80	20	40	9.60	109.60	8.76	14.00
20C 50	80	20	50	10.00	110.00	9.09	12.00
20C 100	80	20	100	12.00	112.00	10.71	8.00
20C 200	80	20	200	16.00	116.00	13.79	6.00
20C 300	80	20	300	20.00	120.00	16.67	5.33
20C 400	80	20	400	24.00	124.00	19.35	5.00
20C 500	80	20	500	28.00	128.00	21.88	4.80
20C 1000	80	20	1000	48.00	148.00	32.43	4.40

Table 104
Business Maximum Profit Category D

Business Category	Employees and directors (X)	Materials and services	Fixed & liquid assets (Y)	Total profit 10% + 4% (X) (Y)	Turnover	Profit as % of (or unit of money)	% Share-holder's returns 5%X + 4% Y
30D 1	70	30	1	7.04	107.04	6.58	354.00
30D 2	70	30	2	7.08	107.08	6.61	179.00
30D 3	70	30	3	7.12	107.12	6.65	120.67
30D 4	70	30	4	7.16	107.16	6.68	91.50
30D 5	70	30	5	7.20	107.20	6.72	74.00
30D 10	70	30	10	7.40	107.40	6.89	39.00
30D 20	70	30	20	7.80	107.80	7.24	21.50
30D 30	70	30	30	8.20	108.20	7.58	15.67
30D 40	70	30	40	8.60	108.60	7.92	12.75
30D 50	70	30	50	9.00	109.00	8.26	11.00
30D 100	70	30	100	11.00	111.00	9.91	7.50
30D 200	70	30	200	15.00	115.00	13.04	5.75
30D 300	70	30	300	19.00	119.00	15.97	5.17
30D 400	70	30	400	23.00	123.00	18.70	4.88
30D 500	70	30	500	27.00	127.00	21.26	4.70
30D 1000	70	30	1000	47.00	147.00	31.97	4.35

Table 105
Business Maximum Profit Category E

Business Category	Employees and directors (X)	Materials and services	Fixed & liquid assets (Y)	Total profit 10% + 4% (X) (Y)	Turnover	Profit as % of (or unit of money)	% Share-holder's returns 5%X + 4% Y
40E 1	60	40	1	6.04	106.04	5.70	304.00
40E 2	60	40	2	6.08	106.08	5.73	154.00
40E 3	60	40	3	6.12	106.12	5.77	104.00
40E 4	60	40	4	6.16	106.16	5.80	79.00
40E 5	60	40	5	6.20	106.20	5.84	64.00
40E 10	60	40	10	6.40	106.40	6.02	34.00
40E 20	60	40	20	6.80	106.80	6.37	19.00
40E 30	60	40	30	7.20	107.20	6.72	14.00
40E 40	60	40	40	7.60	107.60	7.06	11.50
40E 50	60	40	50	8.00	108.00	7.41	10.00
40E 100	60	40	100	10.00	110.00	9.09	7.00
40E 200	60	40	200	14.00	114.00	12.28	5.50
40E 300	60	40	300	18.00	118.00	15.25	5.00
40E 400	60	40	400	22.00	122.00	18.03	4.75
40E 500	60	40	500	26.00	126.00	20.63	4.60
40E 1000	60	40	1000	46.00	146.00	31.51	4.30

Table 106
Business Maximum Profit Category F

Business Category	Employees and directors (X)	Materials and services	Fixed & liquid assets (Y)	Total profit 10% + 4% (X) (Y)	Turnover	Profit as % of (or unit of money)	% Share-holder's returns 5%X + 4% Y
50F 1	50	50	1	5.04	105.04	4.80	254.00
50F 2	50	50	2	5.08	105.08	4.83	129.00
50F 3	50	50	3	5.12	105.12	4.87	87.33
50F 4	50	50	4	5.16	105.16	4.91	66.50
50F 5	50	50	5	5.20	105.20	4.94	54.00
50F 10	50	50	10	5.40	105.40	5.12	29.00
50F 20	50	50	20	5.80	105.80	5.48	16.50
50F 30	50	50	30	6.20	106.20	5.84	12.33
50F 40	50	50	40	6.60	106.60	6.19	10.25
50F 50	50	50	50	7.00	107.00	6.54	9.00
50F 100	50	50	100	9.00	109.00	8.26	6.50
50F 200	50	50	200	13.00	113.00	11.50	5.25
50F 300	50	50	300	17.00	117.00	14.53	4.83
50F 400	50	50	400	21.00	121.00	17.36	4.63
50F 500	50	50	500	25.00	125.00	20.00	4.50
50F 1000	50	50	1000	45.00	145.00	31.03	4.25

Table 107
Business Maximum Profit Category G

Business Category	Employees and directors (X)	Materials and services	Fixed & liquid assets (Y)	Total profit 10% + 4% (X) (Y)	Turnover	Profit as % of (or unit of money)	% Shareholder's returns 5%X + 4% Y
60G 1	40	60	1	4.04	104.04	3.88	204.00
60G 2	40	60	2	4.08	104.08	3.92	104.00
60G 3	40	60	3	4.12	104.12	3.96	70.67
60G 4	40	60	4	4.16	104.16	3.99	54.00
60G 5	40	60	5	4.20	104.20	4.03	44.00
60G 10	40	60	10	4.40	104.40	4.21	24.00
60G 20	40	60	20	4.80	104.80	4.58	14.00
60G 30	40	60	30	5.20	105.20	4.94	10.67
60G 40	40	60	40	5.60	105.60	5.30	9.00
60G 50	40	60	50	6.00	106.00	5.66	8.00
60G 100	40	60	100	8.00	108.00	7.41	6.00
60G 200	40	60	200	12.00	112.00	10.71	5.00
60G 300	40	60	300	16.00	116.00	13.79	4.67
60G 400	40	60	400	20.00	120.00	16.67	4.50
60G 500	40	60	500	24.00	124.00	19.35	4.40
60G 1000	40	60	1000	44.00	144.00	30.56	4.20

Table 108
Business Maximum Profit Category H

Business Category	Employees and directors (X)	Materials and services	Fixed & liquid assets (Y)	Total profit 10% + 4% (X) (Y)	Turnover	Profit as % of (or unit of money)	% Shareholder's returns 5%X + 4% Y
70H 1	30	70	1	3.04	103.04	2.95	154.00
70H 2	30	70	2	3.08	103.08	2.99	79.00
70H 3	30	70	3	3.12	103.12	3.03	54.00
70H 4	30	70	4	3.16	103.16	3.06	41.50
70H 5	30	70	5	3.20	103.20	3.10	34.00
70H 10	30	70	10	3.40	103.40	3.29	19.00
70H 20	30	70	20	3.80	103.80	3.66	11.50
70H 30	30	70	30	4.20	104.20	4.03	9.00
70H 40	30	70	40	4.60	104.60	4.40	7.75
70H 50	30	70	50	5.00	105.00	4.76	7.00
70H 100	30	70	100	7.00	107.00	6.54	5.50
70H 200	30	70	200	11.00	111.00	9.91	4.75
70H 300	30	70	300	15.00	115.00	13.04	4.50
70H 400	30	70	400	19.00	119.00	15.97	4.38
70H 500	30	70	500	23.00	123.00	18.70	4.30
70H 1000	30	70	1000	43.00	143.00	30.07	4.15

Table 109
Business Maximum Profit Category I

Business Category	Employees and directors (X)	Materials and services	Fixed & liquid assets (Y)	Total profit 10% + 4% (X) (Y)	Turnover	Profit as % of (or unit of money)	% Share-holder's returns 5%X + 4% Y
80I 1	20	80	1	2.04	102.04	2.00	104.00
80I 2	20	80	2	2.08	102.08	2.04	54.00
80I 3	20	80	3	2.12	102.12	2.08	37.33
80I 4	20	80	4	2.16	102.16	2.11	29.00
80I 5	20	80	5	2.20	102.20	2.15	24.00
80I 10	20	80	10	2.40	102.40	2.34	14.00
80I 20	20	80	20	2.80	102.80	2.72	9.00
80I 30	20	80	30	3.20	103.20	3.10	7.33
80I 40	20	80	40	3.60	103.60	3.47	6.50
80I 50	20	80	50	4.00	104.00	3.85	6.00
80I 100	20	80	100	6.00	106.00	5.66	5.00
80I 200	20	80	200	10.00	110.00	9.09	4.50
80I 300	20	80	300	14.00	114.00	12.28	4.33
80I 400	20	80	400	18.00	118.00	15.25	4.25
80I 500	20	80	500	22.00	122.00	18.03	4.20
80I 1000	20	80	1000	42.00	142.00	29.58	4.10

Table 110
Business Maximum Profits Category J

Business Category	Employees and directors (X)	Materials and services	Fixed & liquid assets (Y)	Total profit 10% + 4% (X) (Y)	Turnover	Profit as % of (or unit of money)	% Share-holder's returns 5%X + 4% Y
90J 1	10	90	1	1.04	101.04	1.03	54.00
90J 2	10	90	2	1.08	101.08	1.07	29.00
90J 3	10	90	3	1.12	101.12	1.11	20.67
90J 4	10	90	4	1.16	101.16	1.15	16.50
90J 5	10	90	5	1.20	101.20	1.19	14.00
90J 10	10	90	10	1.40	101.40	1.38	9.00
90J 20	10	90	20	1.80	101.80	1.77	6.50
90J 30	10	90	30	2.20	102.20	2.15	5.67
90J 40	10	90	40	2.60	102.60	2.53	5.25
90J 50	10	90	50	3.00	103.00	2.91	5.00
90J 100	10	90	100	5.00	105.00	4.76	4.50
90J 200	10	90	200	9.00	109.00	8.26	4.25
90J 300	10	90	300	13.00	113.00	11.50	4.17
90J 400	10	90	400	17.00	117.00	14.53	4.13
90J 500	10	90	500	21.00	121.00	17.36	4.10
90J 1000	10	90	1000	41.00	141.00	29.08	4.05

The object of limiting profits is to ensure that economies remain sustainable and efficient: with the minimum of unemployment and subsidies to support families. Generally speaking many business profits do not exceed the figures shown in the maximum profit tables. The limitation on annual profits does not prevent shares, or businesses becoming more valuable, as this is quite normal where businesses are properly managed and developed. When economies are sustainable interest rates would be low, probably in the region of 2% to 3%, and this would allow businesses to expand to meet demand, which with time would increase the labour forces and the fixed and liquid assets.

The tables for developing sustainable family economies as in Volume 1 and these business maximum profit tables can be used by governments to establish currencies at values that maintain the efficient balance of their economies. Currencies must not be overvalued, and this would ensure full type employment and allow businesses to compete fairly.

Table 111

Business Divisions

1	Management
2	General office
3	Research
4	Designing
5	Estimating
6	Planning
7	Maintenance
8	Buying
9	Training
10	Raw materials
11	Manufacture of material products
12	Manufacture of each product
13	Product assembly
14	Product information, including operating instructions and maintenance
15	Packaging
16	Storage
17	Transport
18	Distribution
19	Sales promotion
20	Sales
21	Wholesale
22	Retail

Table 112

Skills Employed

The Business				
Business Division	Unskilled	Clerical Tradesman Technician	Professional	Specialist
1 Management 2 General Office 3 Research 4 Designing 5 Estimating 6 Planning 7 Maintenance 8 Buying 9 Training				
10 Raw materials 11 Manufacture of material products 12 Manufacture of each product 13 Product assembly 14 Product information 15 Packaging 16 Storage				
17 Transport 18 Distribution 19 Sales promotion 20 Sales 21 Wholesale 22 Retail				

Tables 111 to 118 are all based on natural events and sequences that take place in the business, institution and government sectors of the economy.

With reference Table 111 the business divisions are shown in three sections. The first section mainly applies to the business office, whilst the second applies mainly to the production of the physical products that are made, and the third section concerns distribution of products. Some businesses could actually carry out all the operations listed, but other businesses would only carry out some of the operations. The activities of institutions including government bodies would all be involved with the office operations listed in the first section, and they could also be involved with storage in section 2 and transport and distribution in section 3.

All studies made in the MH system, where applicable are based in MH units, the master currency, which is the only monetary building block that is sustainable and suitable for undistorted comparisons. For development sound information is required and tables 112 to 116 record statistical information that businesses, institutions, government bodies and specialists need to monitor, maintain and develop the economic activities they are involved with.

Table 118 shows other natural elements of the economy, which constitute the elements of cost in providing a product. By improvements to the various elements a product can be made more competitive. The net rent component is a matter that governments need to monitor and perhaps adjust to ensure the economy is sustainable. The table can be used for all business products or for each individual product

Table 113
Summary of Machines and Equipment
and Asset Value

| The Business | | | | |
Business Division		Machines and Equipment	New MH Value	Discounted MH Value
1	Management			
2	General Office			
3	Research			
4	Designing			
5	Estimating			
6	Planning			
7	Maintenance			
8	Buying			
9	Training			
10	Raw materials			
11	Manufacture of material products			
12	Manufacture of each product			
13	Product assembly			
14	Product information			
15	Packaging			
16	Storage			
17	Transport			
18	Distribution			
19	Sales promotion			
20	Sales			
21	Wholesale			
22	Retail			

Many businesses, institutions and government bodies would probably prefer to use the currency in force, leaving others to convert the monetary values into MH units. This is quite acceptable. However anyone involved with the development process involving productivity and efficiency would need to work in the MH productivity unit, as this master currency unit is the same for all countries.

Table 114

Product - Skills Employed

The Product		Unskilled	Clerical Tradesman Technician	Professional	Specialist
Business Division					
1 Management 2 General Office 3 Research 4 Designing 5 Estimating 6 Planning 7 Maintenance 8 Buying 9 Training					
10 Raw materials 11 Manufacture of material products 12 Manufacture of each product 13 Product assembly 14 Product information 15 Packaging 16 Storage					
17 Transport 18 Distribution 19 Sales promotion 20 Sales 21 Wholesale 22 Retail					

These standard tables can be used for many purposes. Each business, or organisation, can use the tables to record the statistical shape of their own establishment. They can compare their activity with similar organisations to help establish their competitiveness. The tables can be used to check that the overall salaries paid actually approach the average, or are right for the productivity achieved. When using the individual product tables, comparisons can be made using different production lines using different machines, or equipment.

The tables 111-118 are all summary tables and can be used, and arranged as applicable for just for one business division, like management, or the manufacture of a single product. The bigger the organisation the greater the number of divisions, and subdivisions, would be used.

Tables 112 and 114 could define the skills based on the subdivisions of the 'Key sections of the Economy' (as proposed in Tables 36-39 Volume 1). For example it could be 2 a) 5 x) 21 in connection with a wood product, based on the international framework proposed for the economic information system. Coding the economic system on this system has not yet commenced. It will be a massive task that will be needed to be organised by information institutions.

Tables 113 and 115 gives new MH values and Discounted MH values. It should be noted that, when discounting, the value should take into account that new replacement products could be much less a few years later than the original product cost, therefore requiring perhaps a much larger discount to ensure one is working on a sustainable accounting basis.

Table 115

**Product - Machines and Equipment used
and Asset Value**

The Product			
The Business Business Division	Machines and Equipment	New MH Value	Discounted MH Value
1 Management 2 General Office 3 Research 4 Designing 5 Estimating 6 Planning 7 Maintenance 8 Buying 9 Training			
10 Raw materials 11 Manufacture of material products 12 Manufacture of each product 13 Product assembly 14 Product information 15 Packaging 16 Storage			
17 Transport 18 Distribution 19 Sales promotion 20 Sales 21 Wholesale 22 Retail			

Table 116
Business/Institution Fixed Assets

Asset	Description	MH Value
Land		
Buildings		
Infra structure		
Other major Assets		

Table 117

Company Annual Financial Report

Description	Amount MH
1 Fixed assets	
2 Current assets	
3 Creditor amounts falling due after one year	
4 Net assets	
5 Turnover	
6 Operating turnover	
7 Labour costs	
8 Outside purchases	
9 Profits	
10 Other income	
11 Total profit	
12 Taxation and minority interests	
13 Retained profit	
14 Dividends	
15 Value of ordinary shares	
16 Shareholders funds	
17 Par value of shares	

The object of the tables is not only to be used by businesses and other organisations, but by anyone wishing to understand how the economy functions and is interested in the statistical shape of each element of the economy. It is hoped that many organisations will supply statistical information to help students learn how sustainable businesses are managed and developed. Development specialists, or consultants, would require the information so that they can analyse and develop businesses and the economy. The information needs to be exchanged between developed nations and developing countries.

Table 118
Some of the elements of spent money.

Elements of the economy	Percentage of monetary unit spending power.
1 Actual goods or service the customer buys	
2 Cost of selling	
3 Storage while awaiting sale	
4 Packaging	
5 Transporting goods	
6 Wastages	
7 Rent for premises	
8 Interest on loans	
9 Royalties	
10 Cost of development (net rent)	
11 Writing off outdated stocks	
12 Net rents in wage differentials	
13 Maintenance of business assets (buildings and machines)	
14 General expenses in running the business	
15 Retained profit to be used later in business (net rent)	5 (max.)
16 Profit for proprietors (net rent)	5 (max.)
Total percentage of all elements	100

Note: Elements numbers 15 and 16 for net rents may be adjusted by governments.

Table 119 shows the Master Model for an economy based on the key sectors of the information system as illustrated in Table 36 Chapter 7, Volume 1. The Model is used for a large village, a local district, a region, a country and the world economy. The upper part of the master model shows the workforce employed in each business and organisation in the economy and the trade among them: business purchases and sellers. The bottom part of the model shows the buyers (domestic and commercial / industrial turnover), which balances with the upper model transactions.

The figures placed in Table 119 are based on a hypothetical model economy as illustrated in Chapter 2, Table 120 and this latter model was based on Tables 33, 34 and 35 in Chapter 5 Volume 1. The models were created in a simple form and therefore not all sectors of the economy were included. However, this helps to make it easier for persons studying the model to see how an economy functions.

Businesses and institutions are also economies, so they too would need to record all their purchases in the same format as Table 119. This information is then available for the government statistics. However, if they do not actually buy natural materials, manufactured materials, or manufactured products direct, but they come from a service supplier, it is a service supplier purchase.

Every economy is likely to be different, but with respect to services serving the general public these could be similar, in say the regions of a country. The statistics for these models would be gathered and maintained by the local districts and regions in each country. They would obtain the information from the business and government bodies in their sectors. This information would be obtained from the completed Tables 112, 114, 117 and 119 by all the organisations supporting the local economy.

Table 119

Master Model for an Economy

Category	Suppliers (Sellers)	1	2	3	4	5	6	7	8	9	10	11	12	13	14	15	16	17	18	19	20	Total
		Business Purchases																				
	Workforce	52.11	34.66	292.54	91.33	102.51	14.12	46.55	60.73	7.98	77.17		18.51		21.69	65.33	45.24	16.17	26.03	27.33		1000.00
1	Natural Materials			27.43																27.43		
2	Manufactured Materials			30.29	8.58	3.06			3.31											45.24		
3	Manufactured Products	3.93	12.53	66.63	23.60	30.29	77.40	11.79	17.32	2.60	6.25		6.20		20.17	5.54	5.32	15.47	11.23	14.51		330.78
4	Construction	0.64	1.74	25.04	5.05	2.28	32.93	33.23	13.14	2.62	2.50		3.96		0.71	1.12	0.89	4.76	3.92	5.59		140.12
5	Distribution	0.80	0.15	5.06	22.90	0.61	0.13	0.55	3.65	0.24	0.06		0.55		0.12	1.15	0.74	0.19	2.18	2.38		41.46
6	Transport																					
7	Accommodation																					
8	Energy	0.09	3.25	31.36	2.10	6.22	0.55	2.63	1.41	0.72	2.90		1.20		2.14	2.86	2.96	0.48	3.27	4.76		68.90
9	Water	0.09	0.19	1.69	1.49	0.24	0.11	1.01	0.11		0.38		0.04		1.48	0.22	0.22	0.02	0.55	1.19		9.03
10	Maintenance	1.23	1.64	13.69	11.81	3.97	31.38	1.28	7.65	1.41			3.08		1.93	0.52	9.52	0.33	0.83	90.27		
11	Recycling																					
12	Communication	0.58	0.64	6.70	1.60	4.64	0.16	1.45	0.84	0.24	0.75				1.20	1.23	0.59	1.19	0.55	0.71		23.07
13	Information																					
14	Professional																					
15	Financial	1.53	2.26	23.72	6.84	8.53	4.20	5.37	4.38	2.24	2.43		2.37		3.39	3.69	4.14	0.95	5.40	5.99		87.43
16	Government																					
17	Defence																					
18	Education																					
19	Health																					
20	Entertainment																					
	Insurance funds spent															43.12						43.12
Buyers	Domestic turnover	31.80		204.50	40.70	85.20	157.05	101.55	41.00	8.60			12.00		49.70	47.10	59.20	47.60	52.20	61.80		
	Commercial / Industrial Turnover	8.89	22.40	231.61	83.97	59.84	146.86	57.31	51.81	10.07	15.27		17.40		29.21	17.74	15.38	32.58	27.43	35.96		
	Insurance Claims	1.38	1.33	11.98	4.24	3.63	3.78	2.44	2.64	0.42	2.17		0.84		1.20	1.75	1.42	1.15	1.26	1.49		
	TOTAL	42.07	23.73	448.09	128.91	148.67	307.69	161.30	95.45	19.09	17.44		30.24		80.11	66.59	76.00	81.33	80.89	99.25		1906.85

CHAPTER 2

THE PURPOSE OF THE MH MODELLING

Volume 1 of the MH economic system generally gives all the information that the general public needs to follow and understand, so that people and their families know what they need to do to achieve a sustainable living standard during their lifetime. Many models are provided to help plan one's lifetime family economy.

Volume 2 is concerned with what businesses and the non-governmental section of the economy needs to understand about the MH system, and how it is used to develop sustainable economies. This Chapter is concerned with how economies are kept in balance using the MH system, and the purpose of the models.

So far in Chapter 1 of this book the key models have been given for the business/institutional structures. All models are in the master currency: years of productive work based on 1900 hours per annum. However, what has not yet been explained is why the author proposes a maximum 4% interest rate and, a maximum profit of 10% based on the labour employed in the business, including directors. At this stage all figures in the models are realistic and are based on acceptable assumptions. The models show how the economy functions, and the explanations indicate how we actually build, maintain and develop our goods and services.

What must next be explained is how we get interest rates and profits affordable and sustainable. People must also know how to convert existing currencies into MH units.

Table 121 has been prepared to give an appreciation of the value of a nation's fixed and liquid assets. These are needed to help calculate affordable profits: interest rates and business profits. The MH system calls these profits 'net rents', which is a profit where no work has been done for their payment, not even the work of collection. They could be classified as a gift! Tables 122 and 123 are used to calculate the value of net rents as given in wage differentials, where this system is the political policy, and quite acceptable in a sustainable economic system provided it is affordable.

Table 121 determines the real assets supporting the business economy: the needs and wants in real use, but not those which for much of the time are idle, (like collections of goods that may rarely be used, but may be of interest from time to time, as antiques, ancient monuments and collectors' items and disused buildings). The assets in Table 121 are based on the turnovers obtained from Table 120. For example, building contractors (number 26) is the sum of 49.83 + 50.22 = 100.05 (own employees plus commercial/industrial turnover, under buyers at the bottom part of the table). The first five items of 'turnover' in the table are taken from Table 120. Then 6 years has been judged, per 1000 persons, to represent land development for agriculture, and 10 years for other business assets produced by their own labour force. The last two assets are 80 years to represent savings held by financial institutions and 1875 years held by non-state, or private pension funds. The total assets amount to 6750 years.

Table 120
A Hypothetical model Economy

Number		Suppliers (Sellers)	1 (5) Food Retail & Wholesale	2 (3) Processed foods	3 (3) Baker	4 (3) Dairy
		Own employees	40.80	3.36	8.32	11.69
5	(1)	Slaughter –house				
9	(1)	Fruit farmer				
10	(1)	Farmer		0.81		7.98
1-11	(3&5)	Food retail and Wholesale			1.00	
18-21	(3)	Furnishings				
22	(15)	Insurance	1.76	0.08	0.16	0.19
23	(8)	Electricity	1.76	0.03	0.64	0.98
25	(9)	Water	0.07	0.01	0.03	0.06
24	(8)	Gas		0.03	0.48	
26	(4)	Builder	0.77	0.08	0.16	0.22
29	(5)	Builders merchant				
30	(15)	Financial institution	1.00	0.11	0.22	0.45
34	(1)	Tobacco plantation				
39	(12)	Telephone	2.23	0.17	0.16	0.19
45	(3)	Tools & equipment	2.63	0.14	0.08	0.06
46	(3)	Machines	0.26	0.17	0.02	0.94
47	(3)	Vehicles & tractors	0.44	0.33	0.16	0.19
48	(10)	Garage and fuel	0.42	0.33	0.16	0.19
49	(2)	Timber				
50	(2)	Metal manufacturer				
51	(3)	Building material manufacturer				
52	(5)	Stationary and Packaging	0.21	0.17	0.05	0.38
53	(4)	Civil engineering contractors				
54	(2)	Domestic material manufacturer				
55	(3)	Electrical component				
22	(15)	Insurance claim funds spent				
Buyers		Domestic turnover	42.50	4.90	9.80	19.80
		Commercial/industrial Turnover	11.55	2.46	3.32	11.83
		Insurance claims	1.12	0.14	0.27	0.55
		Total	55.17	7.50	13.39	32.18

Table 120
A Hypothetical model Economy

Number	5 (3) Slaughter house	6 (1) Chicken	7 (3) Canners farm	8 (3) Frozen foods	9 (3) Fruit farmer
	5.21	2.20	4.65	3.96	12.87
5			0.25	0.34	
9			0.25	0.11	
10	6.30		0.75	0.42	
1-11					
18-21					
22	0.09	0.06	0.08	0.09	0.15
23	0.06	0.01	0.49	0.09	0.01
25	0.06	0.01	0.03	0.02	0.01
24	0.28		0.30		
26	0.09	0.02	0.15	0.09	0.07
29					
30					
34	0.25	0.05	0.16	0.12	0.26
39	0.19	0.11	0.15	0.19	0.15
45	0.06	0.01	0.08	0.02	0.01
46	0.02	0.01	0.15	0.19	0.07
47	0.19	0.13	0.30	0.37	0.16
48	0.19	0.13	0.30	0.37	0.16
49					
50			0.15		
51					
52					
53	0.08	0.11	0.08	0.14	0.37
54					
55					
22					
	11.00	2.40	7.00	4.90	9.80
	7.86	0.65	3.67	2.56	1.42
	0.31	0.07	0.20	0.15	0.31
Total	19.17	3.12	10.87	7.61	11.53

Table 120
A Hypothetical model Economy

Number	10 (1) Farmer	11 (3) Manufactured foods	12 (5) Clothing, retail and wholesale	13 (3) Suits	14 (3) Dresses
	31.54	15.77	22.54	3.52	3.52
5		0.10			
9		1.33			
10		2.66			
1-11					
18-21					
22	0.18	0.55	0.38	0.13	0.13
23	0.07	0.78	1.02	0.51	0.51
25	0.07	0.08	0.03	0.01	0.01
24		0.47	0.64	0.25	0.25
26	0.55	0.37	0.41	0.11	0.11
29					
30					
	0.83	0.51	0.53	0.15	0.15
34					
39	0.32	0.32	0.25	0.13	0.13
45	0.37	0.08	0.13	0.13	0.13
46	0.35	1.57	0.64	0.76	0.76
47	2.82	0.32	0.25	0.25	0.25
48	0.94	0.32	0.25	0.25	0.25
49					
50		0.09			
51					
52					
	0.32	0.94	0.17	0.06	0.06
53					
				1.52	1.52
54					
55					
22					
	19.60	22.10	26.60	7.60	7.60
	6.82	10.49	4.70	4.26	4.26
	1.00	0.62	0.64	0.18	0.18
Total	27.42	33.21	31.94	12.04	12.04

Table 120
A Hypothetical model Economy

Number	15 (3) Children's clothes	16 (3) Other clothing	17 (3) Shoes	18 (5) Furnishings retail and wholesale	19 (3) Hard furnishings
	7.69	7.69	3.45	6.13	3.09
5					
9					
10					
1-11					
18-21					
22	0.18	0.18	0.13	0.90	0.20
23	0.94	0.94	0.51	0.45	0.60
25	0.02	0.02	0.01	0.02	0.02
24	0.47	0.47	0.25	0.34	0.29
26	0.23	0.23	0.11	0.18	0.14
29					
30					
	0.30	0.30	0.15	0.22	0.17
34					
39	0.12	0.12	0.13	0.22	0.20
45	0.23	0.23	0.13	0.22	0.20
46	1.40	1.40	0.76		0.99
47	0.47	0.47	0.25	1.34	0.40
48	0.47	0.47	0.25	1.34	0.40
49					1.98
50					
51					
52					
	0.12	0.12	0.06	0.11	0.10
53					
	2.93	2.93	1.59		
54					
					0.40
55					
22					
	15.20	15.20	7.60	5.50	4.40
	7.88	7.88	4.33	5.34	6.09
	0.37	0.37	0.18	0.27	0.22
Total	23.45	23.45	12.11	11.11	10.71

Table 120
A Hypothetical model Economy

Number	20 (3) Soft furnishings	21 (3) Carpets	22 (15) Insurance	23 (8) Electricity	24 (8) Gas
	3.27	1.30	10.40	36.67	24.06
5					
9					
10					
1-11					
18-21					
22	0.20	0.12	0.91	0.66	1.50
23	0.60	0.45	0.83		0.75
25	0.02	0.03	0.09	0.06	0.05
24	0.30	0.22	0.83	0.66	
26	0.14	0.07	0.86	0.86	0.65
29				2.65	
30					
34	0.17	0.08	1.21	1.30	0.92
39	0.20	0.22		0.34	0.50
45	0.20	0.12	0.45	0.66	0.50
46	1.19	0.45	0.73	3.31	2.00
47	0.40	0.22	0.83	2.65	5.00
48	0.40	0.22	0.83	2.65	5.00
49					
50				3.31	
51					
52					
53	0.10	0.07	0.55	0.50	0.50
54				6.63	5.00
55	1.99	1.01		3.20	
22			43.12		
	4.40	2.20	10.00	20.50	20.50
	5.91	3.28	8.12	29.44	22.37
	0.22	0.11		1.55	1.09
Total	10.53	5.59	18.12	51.49	43.96

Table 120
A Hypothetical model Economy

Number	25 (9) Water	26 (4) Builder	27 (15) Building Society	28 (7) Landlord	29 (5) Builders merchant
	7.98	49.83	14.99	31.00	8.68
5					
9					
10					
1-11					
18-21					
22	1.89	1.95	0.29	0.75	1.81
23	0.48	0.97	0.14	0.40	0.36
25		0.63	0.03	0.07	0.04
24	0.24	0.25	0.14	0.40	
26	0.26		0.06	0.18	0.08
29					
		19.21			
30					
	0.35	1.94	0.34	0.72	0.67
34					
39	0.24	1.22	0.29	0.80	0.73
45	0.24	0.97	0.57	0.95	0.73
46	0.95	2.91			
47	1.41	2.43	0.26	0.75	1.09
48	1.41	2.43	0.26	0.75	1.09
49		6.08			
50					1.81
51					
					16.61
52					
	0.24	1.46	0.14	0.40	0.73
53					
	2.36	4.86			
54					
55		2.91			
22					
	8.60	40.70	17.10	36.30	10.60
	10.07	50.22	2.52	6.17	25.75
	0.42	2.49	0.41	0.87	0.72
Total	19.09	93.41	20.03	43.34	37.07

Table 120
A Hypothetical model Economy

Number	30 (15) Financial institution	31 (3) Washing machine manufacturer	32 (3) Television manufacturer	33 (3) Tobacco company	34 (1) Tobacco plantation
	39.94	3.73	4.83	4.87	5.90
5					
9					
10					
1-11					
18-21					
22	0.94	0.48	0.48	0.50	
23	0.46	0.24	0.24	0.20	
25	0.10	0.01	0.01	0.02	
24	0.46	0.12	0.15	0.30	
26	0.20	0.06	0.08	0.17	
29					
30					
		0.08	0.09	0.27	
34				5.90	
39	0.94	0.12	0.12	0.10	
45	1.85	0.12	0.12	0.10	
46		0.48	0.36	1.00	
47	0.85	0.12	0.12	0.20	
48	0.84	0.12	0.12	0.20	
49					
50		0.60	0.48		
51					
52					
	0.46	0.12	0.12	0.40	
53					
54					
55					
22					
	20.00	6.30	7.20	17.90	
	7.10	2.67	2.49	9.36	
	1.34	0.10	0.12	0.33	
Total	28.44	9.07	9.81	27.59	

Table 120
A Hypothetical model Economy

Number	35 (3) Brewery	36 (14) Restaurant and canteen	37 (7) Hotels and cars	38 (6) Transport	39 (12) Telephone
	24.03	21.69	13.47	12.02	18.51
5					
9	0.92				
10					
1-11					
		17.77	5.90		
18-21		1.20	2.36		
22	0.69	2.40	2.36	0.83	1.71
23	0.46	0.72	0.71	0.21	0.69
25	0.20	1.48	0.94	0.10	0.04
24	0.35	1.42	0.94	0.16	0.51
26	0.29	0.71	0.45	0.08	0.55
29					
30					
	0.39	0.99	0.59	2.42	0.66
34					
39	0.12	1.20	0.59	0.10	
45	0.23	1.20	1.18	0.10	1.03
46	0.92				0.38
47	0.46		0.35	77.00	3.08
48	0.46		0.35	31.20	3.08
49					
50					
51					
52					
	0.35	0.12	0.12	0.10	0.55
53					
					3.41
54					
55					1.71
22					
	29.40	49.70	29.60	121.40	12.00
	5.84	29.21	16.84	112.30	17.40
	0.47	1.20	0.71	2.92	0.84
Total	35.71	80.11	47.15	236.62	30.24

Table 120
A Hypothetical model Economy

Number	40 (16) Government institution	41 (18) Education	42 (19) Health care	43 (17) Defence law and police	44 (6&7) National infra-structure
	45.24	26.03	27.33	16.17	4.16
5					
9					
10					
1-11					
			1.78		
18-21	3.32	5.45	3.57	1.19	
22	2.96	4.36	4.76		0.48
23	1.48	1.09	2.38	0.36	0.24
25	0.22	0.55	1.19	0.02	0.01
24	1.48	2.18	2.38	0.12	0.12
26	0.89	3.92	5.59	1.19	29.75
29					
30					
	1.18	1.04	1.23	0.95	1.42
34					
39	0.59	0.55	0.71	1.19	0.12
45	1.48	4.36	4.76	2.38	0.24
46		1.09	3.57	1.19	
47	0.52	0.33	0.83	10.71	0.36
48	0.52	0.33	0.83	9.52	0.36
49					
50					
51					
52					
	0.74	2.18	2.38	0.19	0.06
53					
				3.57	35.70
54					
55					
22					
	59.20	52.20	61.80	47.60	71.30
	15.38	27.43	35.96	32.58	68.86
	1.42	1.26	1.49	1.15	1.72
Total	76.00	80.89	99.25	81.33	141.88

Table 120
A Hypothetical model Economy

Number	45 (3) Tools	46 (3) Machines	47 (3) Vehicles	48 (10) Garage and fuel	49 (2) Timber
	30.76	52.01	72.09	77.17	7.25
5					
9					
10					
1-11					
18-21					
22	1.00	4.00	3.75	0.63	0.13
23	1.25	5.00	5.00	2.75	0.25
25	0.09	0.38	0.38	0.38	
24	0.38	1.25	1.25	0.15	
26	0.38	0.75	1.88	1.25	0.06
29					
30					
	0.84	1.65	2.74	1.80	0.18
34					
39	0.75	1.50	0.88	0.75	0.13
45		2.50	6.25	1.25	0.13
46	3.75		25.00	2.50	0.63
47	0.88	1.75		2.50	0.38
48	0.88	1.75	4.38		0.38
49					
50	2.50	7.50	12.50		
51					
52					
	0.19	0.38	0.75	0.06	0.01
53					
	1.25	2.50	3.75	1.25	
54					
55					
22					
	14.14	30.91	68.51	15.27	2.28
	1.05	1.95	3.30	2.17	0.22
Total	15.19	32.86	71.81	17.44	2.50

Table 120
A Hypothetical model Economy

Number	50 (2) Metal manufacturer	51 (3) Building material manufacturer	52 (5) Stationery and packaging	53 (4) Civil engineering contractor	54 (2) Domestic material manufacturer
	19.87	7.76	9.66	41.50	7.54
5					
9					
10					
1-11					
18-21					
22	0.40	0.36	0.25	1.50	0.63
23	1.25	0.73	0.63	0.63	0.50
25	0.06	0.04	0.06	0.86	0.13
24	1.25	1.81	0.25	0.25	
26	0.05	0.36	0.19	0.19	0.25
29				1.25	
30					
34	0.65	0.32	0.35	1.45	0.27
39	0.38	0.36	0.38	0.38	0.13
45	1.25	0.36	0.38	1.25	0.13
46	5.00	0.73	3.75	3.75	3.75
47	0.88	1.09	0.63	9.38	0.38
48	0.88	1.09	0.63	9.38	0.38
49			1.25		
50		1.09		2.50	
51					
52	0.01	0.18		0.25	0.13
53	1.38	0.73	0.38		
54					
55					
22					
	13.44	9.25	9.13	33.02	6.68
	0.78	0.40	0.44	1.75	0.33
Total	14.22	9.65	9.57	34.77	7.01

Table 120

A Hypothetical model Economy

Number	55 (3) Electrical Manufacturer wholesale	56 (5) Luxury goods retail and	Totals
	5.59	14.70	1000.00
5			0.69
9			2.61
10			18.92
1-11			
			26.45
18-21			17.09
22	0.13	0.30	51.73
23	0.50	0.71	44.06
25	0.13	0.02	9.03
24			24.84
26	0.05	0.27	56.86
29			
			23.11
30			
	0.15	0.36	35.70
34			5.90
39	0.13	0.83	23.07
45	0.04	0.83	43.85
46	1.00	0.12	80.97
47	0.13	0.24	137.30
48	0.12	0.24	90.27
49			9.31
50			32.53
51			
			16.61
52			
	0.04	0.12	18.35
53			
			83.26
54			
			3.40
55			7.82
22			43.12
	2.42	4.04	
	0.19	0.44	
Total	2.61	4.48	1906.85

145

From this, home ownership assets must be deducted, and this is approximately equal to 90% of 625 homes of 3 to 4 person size, average value 60 sq m x 85 MH = 5185 MH = 2.684 years each and total value amounting to 1509 years. After deducting government assets for national infrastructure, approximately 30%, the value of the private sector business assets amounts to 3668.7 years, created by 1000 working population.

Table 121

National estimated fixed and liquid assets
(based on 1000 strong workforce)

Description	Turnover	Investment life in years	Years of permanent investment	Amount invested in category	Permanent investment created
Building	100.05	100	50.5	25.00	1265.5
Contractors		50	25.5	17.00	433.5
		40	20.5	18.00	369.0
		20	10.5	20.00	210.0
		Maintenance	None	20.05	
Civil	74.52	50	25.5	22.00	561.0
Engineering		40	20.5	20.00	410.0
Contractors		30	15.5	20.00	310.0
		Maintenance	None	12.52	
Machinery	82.92	15	8.0	58.00	464.0
		Maintenance	None	24.92	
Tools	44.90	5	3.0	40.00	120.0
		Maintenance	None	4.90	
Vehicles	140.60	5	3.0	98.00	294.0
		Maintenance	None	42.60	
Land	6.00	100	50.5	6.00	303.0
Other					
Business assets	10.00	10	5.5	10.00	55.0
Financial					
Institutions				80.0	
Private pension					
Funds & savings		40	40.0	46.875	1875.0
Sub total					6750.0
Deduct home ownership					1509.0
Business and government assets					5241.0
Deduct government assets (30%)					1572.3
Business assets					3668.7

The next operation is to determine the affordable profits, using the 4% maximum for interest and 10% for profit on labour force employed.

Table 122
Net rent in wages based on 1975 statistics

Skill	Number of persons	Average maximum net rent per annum + average wage	MH man years net rent	Percentage
Unskilled	742500		742500	
Technicians	143075	1.237	176984	
Sub degree	32050	1.303	41761	
Degree	56592	1.655	93660	
Post Graduates	15783	2.027	31992	
Total	990000		1086897	9.8

Table 123
Net rent in wages based on 1988 statistics

Skill	Number of persons	Average maximum net rent per annum + average wage	MH man years net rent	Percentage
Unskilled	575000		575000	
Technicians	296021	1.237	366177	
Sub degree	96300	1.303	125479	
Degree	94055	1.655	155661	
Post Graduates	26133	2.027	52972	
Total	1087509		1275289	17.3

Calculating net rent in wages is not a simple task to do accurately, because it would require a vast number of statistics over a period of fifty years. Therefore, the approach in this book is simply to establish an appreciation of the amount. Statistics for it are taken from the U.K. Department of Education and Science Statistical Bulletin ISSN 0142-5013 9/90 July 1990 and ISSN 0142-5013 11/90 August 1990.

The figures for the five grades of skills are derived from the student numbers in the bulletins. Tables 122 and 123 show the calculations for the net rents created by wage differentials for the five grades. Column 2 in each table shows the number of students taking further education, and the number of unskilled not taking further education. Each Table also shows the total number of persons taking education for that year's generation. Column 3 shows the average annual wage the person could receive, plus the average net rent that could be added, when based on the MH system, assuming full employment. This has been derived from Chapter 3, Volume 1. For the unskilled grade no net rent is added, in accordance with the MH system. Column 4 shows the total wages paid in the country for each grade, and column 5 shows the percentage of net rent created in the economy due to the system of wage differentials.

From the two tables it can be observed how the education pattern has changed and how much more net rent is added to wages, when year 1988 is compared with year 1975. Each year has a different structure, and to obtain a complete pattern, the whole fifty-year working cycle is required, showing the structure of the whole workforce. The percentage of the net rents would then be averaged. However, in this book the figure used is the average based on Tables 122 and 123, which is 13.55%. It should be noted that net rents are always included when calculating the average wages in the skilled rates.

Table 124
Total net rents

Item	Percentage
10% net rent on the annual workforce	10.00
4% net rent on business assets 3.6687 years per person (Table 121)	14.67
Wage differentials, approx. 90% of 13.55% (based on Tables 122 and 123)	12.20
Total	36.87
Proportion of net rent per unit of money (MH basis)	
Wages - 10% divide by (100 + 36.87) x 100	7.31
Business assets -14.67% divide by 136.87 x 100	10.72
Wage differentials-12.20% divide by 136.87 x 100	8.91
Total	26.94

Table 124 shows how the unearned net rents are calculated and then added to labour costs. This could be considered as the Gross National Product and amounts to 100% labour plus 36.87% pure unearned profit. Therefore, the proportion of the net rent per MH unit is 36.87% divided by 136.87% = 26.94%. This means that, for every unit of money a person earns, a gift of approximately a quarter is passed on to others when he spends the money, to cover risk and as an incentive to businesses and persons investing in special skills. Approximately 8.90% of the unit of money goes to persons with specials skills and 18% to investors in businesses, financial institutions, including pension funds, and savers. Generally speaking interest rates are expected to be between 2% and 3% and one can say an affordable amount for net rent is 25%, i.e. a quarter of the real purchasing power of the money, and this is sustainable as illustrated by all the tables in Volumes 1 and 2 so far included.

The tables in Volume 1, Chapter 5 are based on goods and services where the above interest rates and profits have been taken into account, and with an overall government taxation amounting to 40% of the national wages earned. The proposed MH master currency and trading rules all follow natural sequences and the manner in which economies are managed and developed. The system allows for the sustainable development of economies, and each step forward in developing them can be carefully thought through. However, at present all other currencies are floating and continually changing in value. To use the MH system, a method of conversion into MH units is required. With reference to Tables 122 and 123, the average figure for the net rent used to calculate the value of the wage differentials amounts to 13.55%, and this information is used to value the MH unit. To give the MH value, the average annual national wage income is divided by 1.1355, (i.e. 1 + 0.136) and the average hours worked per person (taken to be 1900 hours). However, this was based on statistics up to 1988 and more people are taking further education, so the author at present is using 1.15 for the conversion factor and the figures given in his books are on this basis.

Every currency needs to have an estimated conversion factor, where it is not pegged to the MH master currency, so that real comparisons can be made on the cost of products throughout the world. In the EU, each nation too should value the Euro, from which an average rate could be calculated for the EU currency area. This will help to determine the economic differences in the EU nations.

Table 120 has also been provided to explain turnover and GDP. The trading transactions have approximately doubled the labour force figure of 1000 to 2000. The profit in Table 124 amounted to 36.87% of the labour employed: i.e. labour of 100 persons creates a G.D.P. of 136.87. In present economies national G.D.P can vary from say 100 to 400 based on a labour force of 100, and sometimes even much higher. Even if GDP is the same as calculated for a sustainable economy it does not confirm the economy is not distorted, as low wages, high profits and interest rates and high unemployment can produce the same GDP. Suppose the 10% business profit was also made on the 1000 turnover due to trading as in Table 120 and interest rates and wage differentials were double, the GDP would rise from 136.87 to 173.74, increasing the net rent to 73.74 and taking 42.4% of the purchasing power of money from each unit of money. Generally in present economies about half the purchasing power of money is being taken out in net rents. Therefore, compared to a sustainable form of economy where the purchasing power of a monetary unit falls to 75% to pay for the net rents, in present economies it falls to 50%. Anyone, therefore, on a 50% average wage, when it should be an average wage, has the purchasing power for his money reduced to 50% x 50% = 25%, instead of 75% proposed by adopting a sustainable form of economy. This is a very serious distortion in the present form of market economy.

It should be noted that in Table 120 each business, or a government service, has been given a number between 1 and 55 and after it another figure, in brackets, which denotes the key sector of the economy that it is in. This will help those wishing to follow through the transfer of the figures in Table 120 to Table 119, the Master Model for the Economy.

No doubt many economists will wish to say the figures and assumptions are wrong. However the purpose of the tabular models is to show the structure, statistics and methodology needed to create sustainable economies. The tables given indicate the key elements of the economy and how they interact. Without this understanding of the economy, the better and fairer economy we all wish to have cannot be created. The right education for everyone in the economy is most important, as without it stability can never be achieved. The MH system has been designed to maintain and develop economies, at whatever level they may now be, into sustainable forms in the whole world. The right education and a sustainable form of economy can achieve very low levels of conflict and high levels of fairness and honesty. Businesses and professional persons will need to understand how trade should be conducted and how economies should be developed to maintain a sustainable state.

The next steps are for actual business and national statistics to be used in the proposed key models, and the use of the MH system as a tool to study the shapes of the various economies; determine the flaws in the economies, and then steer them onto a sustainable path. Governments would then also be able to decide whether the author's proposed ceilings for maximum interest and profit rates should be adjusted. His other proposals should also be checked, and improved and developed as may be necessary.

CHAPTER 3

BANKS

When discussing the sectors of the economy in Chapter 8, Volume 1 the financial services were divided into five categories: The first (a) was a mechanism to effect exchanges of goods and services and this means our current accounts; and the second (b) a system for financing developments and capital for purchasing assets, our loan accounts. (a) is normally carried out by our high street banks, and (b) is also carried out by these banks, and by special banks dealing with venture capital projects. In the MH system current accounts banks only operate the monetary exchange process (banks type 1), savings banks provide secured loans (banks type 2) and venture capital for projects (banks type 3).

The author proposes that these three types of bank account only are suitable for a sustainable system:

Type 1 banks	- current account,
Type 2 banks	- saving deposit accounts earning interest rates between 0% to 4% AER, where loans are fully secured, and
Type 3 banks	- venture capital accounts, where higher rates of interest are offered to compensate for higher degrees of risk, and where loans are not fully secured.

Type 1 Banks

Current account banks form the source of our finance, particularly in a sustainable economy. The reason for this is that money is no more than a promissory note to exchange units of productive human labour, and the current account banks are needed to witness the exchanges. These notes form the nation's money supply, the only money that is used to exchange all the goods and services we have collectively created to match our needs and wants (each day, week, month or year).

From the research and modelling carried out by the author, it is clear that banks dealing with current accounts should be separate from those accepting deposits for loans to customers. Money represents promises that allow the exchange of human labour for the products gathered, created and distributed by human labour. The first part of the exchange takes place when wages are paid for work done and the second part of the exchange occurs when the wage earner buys products (goods and services) with the wages earned, in balance with the promissory note, thereby completing the exchange. Money representing a promissory note, whilst in a bank current account, belongs to the account holder and not the bank. The bank provides a service that witnesses the transactions and keeps account of the units in the current account. This is an important process that is essential to the stability of the monetary system. This money must not be devalued in any way. Banks that use current account money to loan to others can lose it. Naturally, the bank can charge for the current account service on the same basis that any other form of business needs to. It can also aid in the recovery of failed promissory notes (cheques) as part of its banking service. However, any loss in the current account caused by failing cheques is at the current account holder's expense. Each citizen, business, or institution should be permitted one current account only (at the bank of his or her choice).

One of the main tasks of current account banks is to ensure that their clients are keeping their accounts in general balance. All this is necessary to ensure economies remain sustainable. Obviously where accounts are unsatisfactory the problem must be solved. Where they cannot, it may become the duty of a government department to rectify; for example, where a citizen's private account is overdrawn beyond his capacity to repay, because he, or she has become incapacitated.

Where customers are defaulting the bank must step in by first informing the customer to rectify the fault, or supply further information justifying that the debt can be repaid. Where there is a problem to be solved the defaulter must take professional advice, and it can either be given by the bank, or an advisor the customer may prefer to use. The action taken must be very prompt and positive to ensure payments of promises made. The extra service of course would have to be paid for. The monetary exchange system must never be allowed to fail. Clearing banks would be allowed to take security against customer's debts, as is normal for most loans; however, it is not the intention that debts on current accounts should be a permanent low cost form of finance for businesses.

From the figures in the current accounts, banks would be aware of the customer's potential and from this information they would be able to judge the strength of the account, and this would comply with the MH system rules. Normally accounts would be in surplus, but no penalties should be taken for being overdrawn; effective action should be taken to determine the cause. Overall, customer's accounts must be in surplus to ensure equilibrium and soundness of the current account monetary exchange system.

It is important that the records of these current account transactions are never lost. Copies should always be available and safely stored in one or more safe locations situated miles from each other, in addition to the bank's main branch, or sole office. With the right precautions the current account should be foolproof, and therefore, customers would never loose their money, if the current account bank failed, or one of its records were destroyed, by accident or some natural destructive event.

Banks type 2

These banks (and building societies) would only lend money against adequate security, valued in the Master Currency.

These institutions would be dependant on money people would wish to save for short, medium, or long term. Pension funds would be ideal to support long-term loans. Very short-term savings are likely to stay in current accounts, as they would not wish to have a hold-up in withdrawing savings, when perhaps an unexpected withdrawal load from the bank could delay a payment from it.

With the author's form of sustainable monetary system, where money is pegged to the master currency, there is no inflation and no need for central banks to vary the interest rates as the money supply is self-regulating. When money is in short supply, depositors interest rates will rise to a maximum of 4% AER (excluding bank charges for services); and, when the money supply is adequate, interest rates will fall to approximately 2% AER, and may be to 0% AER when there is a shortage of borrowers. If there is little demand for loans and interest rates fall to 0% APR, banks may make a service charge for holding the savings account open. However, under such conditions savers may well move savings back into their current accounts, where it is not at any risk from loss. The borrower's maximum interest rate for the secured loans would not exceed 6% APR. This allows the bank 2% gross profit, however, this is based on manual operation. With modern high-tech equipment the gross profit figure should be much lower.

Savings deposit accounts can offer either fixed or variable interest on their loans. This form of savings account would always be fully secured and in practice never fail. However, should existing depositors decide to withdraw funds quicker than the inflow of new deposits and repayments, they can be refused repayment or repayments could be in stages, until the bank has rectified its cash flow problem, which it must do under the trading rules. All banks must also hold a residue of liquidity as determined by the central bank. Under these circumstances it is unlikely that withdrawals would ever be withheld for very long. These banks would also be permitted of course to offer varying types of periodic notice of withdrawal, like say one year, six months, three months, and one month notice, and immediate withdrawals. Only under very exceptional circumstances would these banks ever become bankrupt.

Careful management of secured loan banks should result in these banks rarely making any losses, due to default by borrowers, or unfavourable markets, lowering the value of assets. It should be noted in bankruptcy, or liquidation, governments normally have the first call on the funds and then the holders of security on the loans. Banks should ensure they have not over-lent on the security they hold and should, therefore, check on the value of the security at regular intervals.

Many banks have savings accounts that are used also as current accounts, which allows the holders of these to have free banking. With this type of account the bank owns their funds and bank type 2 rules apply. These funds therefore are at some risk, but should not normally fail, as these banks are not allowed to participate in type 3 banking. However, the customers' deposits could be insured against any loss, the cost of the insurance being paid for by the bank.

Banks Type 3

These banks specialise in commercial products, development projects and other business risk ventures. They should have properly trained personnel who understand the projects they are assessing, and wish to support. They are taking risks, as they cannot always judge that the projects will be successful. They can expect a number of failures that would have to be financed by successful projects. Investors in these banks would be willing to risk their capital for a greater percentage of profit. They could be backing patents and copyrights, which could gain substantial royalties. They may wish share participation in companies. They would need to abide to the MH system rules and have an appropriate financial structure that covers for the unsuccessful ventures.

As venture capital banks are taking risks they will need to be very well managed to selected sound ventures, to ensure that their rates of interest do cover the inevitable failures that occur in the real world. Central Banks may need to set the maximum rates of interest payable to depositors, to ensure the stability of the economy. Any profits in excess of the figures given by the trading rules shall be set aside against future losses. Again Central Banks could vary the rates of interest and fees charged by the venture capital banks for their services. Depositors in these banks would receive a minimum interest rate of 4% AER. Higher rates of return would depend on the risks taken. Risk can be compared with ordinary shares, and these banks may well raise money this way.

General notes

Any of the three types of banks mentioned may also sell low risk services, like other companies' insurance.

Banking failures in the sustainable system just outlined will not affect the money supply, or the stability of the monetary system. Money remains a stable value, as it is a productivity unit, and so is always backed by goods and services ready for use. Funds lost by failing banks are spent money, when not in their current accounts and, therefore, does not form part of the money supply. Any failed current account bank, would either need to be sold to another bank, or the clients asked to select their new bank, so that their current account holding can be transferred from the failed bank to the new bank. This is possible, because the money remains in the ownership of the depositor, and the bank is only recording the monetary exchange transactions.

Banks type 2 and 3 will have their liquid funds (money not lent) in a current account of their choice. In the MH system the only money available for spending is in the current accounts. Banks type 2 and 3, therefore, can only loan funds they have available in the current accounts and can only repay withdrawals by depositors when the funds are in the current account. For this reason they would normally always have a sufficient cash reserve in their current account to pay the majority of withdrawals by the depositors on demand where deposited on that basis. It would be rare for a sound banking system to withhold payments for lack of liquidity. All money in the MH system current accounts has been created by average hours of human labour in creating products and services. The money in current accounts is in balance with goods and services ready for purchase. The money in current accounts and all secured loans are backed by a greater amount of assets, generally speaking.

It has already been mentioned that the current account records should be stored in several safe locations to ensure records are never lost. These records also apply to other banks and financial institutions handling customers' funds and loans. Customers should also keep records of their financial accounts. Electronic banking systems must also be foolproof, as none of the transactions would be recorded on paper. Therefore, the system must establish permanently safe records that cannot be destroyed, until they are no longer required.

Central Banks

Central Banks need to supervise these three types of banks, including building societies. Building societies, like banks, must keep current accounts separate from loan accounts. However, banks can have holding companies that own the three types of banking business.

Central Banks, in a sustainable system, will need to continue to oversee all financial institutions. They could also need to hold deposits (in their current account) to ensure the liquidity of loan banks, particularly for fully secured loans in savings banks of low risk. They will also need to check the money held in banks' current accounts to ensure they are in balance with the notes and coins in circulation, as these are promissory notes forming part of the overall money supply. However, apart from holding government money collected from taxation, there is no need to hold reserves to back the notes and coins in circulation (or the currency), as these are already backed by goods and services ready for immediate purchase. Gold held by central banks should slowly be sold off.

Within a country, financial balances among the local districts and regions must also be maintained to ensure stability, as the economy moves forward with time. This can be checked using the current accounts, and banks should make this information available to the government authorities. Ideally, to aid the checking process, the banking services within each region should follow the boundaries of the region, and not cross into neighbouring regions. Under certain conditions governments may need to subsidise unstable regions, which need funds to reshape their economies, or following a natural catastrophe.

Central Banks are responsible for overseeing the activities of all banks and financial institutions, to ensure sustainability. They do not need to be 'lenders of last resort', but may well need to co-ordinate the use of the nation's money supply, which is recorded in the nations' current accounts, including the government's current account. In a well-managed economy this would not require too much effort, as the system is more or less self-regulating. However, balances can be upset by major catastrophes.

International Banking

Each nation's currency is supported by the goods and services backing its money supply. When a bank lends money to another nation it can either be lent in the bank's local currency, when the borrower spends the money in the lending bank's country, or supplied in the borrower's currency (exchanged using the master currency) when the borrower buys goods in his country. However, with the latter option the loan bank would need to exchange the foreign currency for local currency to balance his accounts. This is necessary to keep each nation's financial balance in proper equilibrium.

It is important to note that when money is received in another nation's currency it does not alter its own nation's money supply, as the foreign currency is backed by the foreign nation's products. When banks convert foreign currency into local currency, goods and services in its own nation, in effect, should be set aside for export to balance the value of the foreign exchange converted. If this does not happen there will be more money than goods and services produced, and the monetary exchange system would be out of balance. Exports and imports among nations and their currencies exchanged must always be in equilibrium, as the economy moves forward with time. The author considers that export/import agencies (or banks) should be responsible for maintaining these balances, which form a vital part of the international economy.

Balances are essential for sustainable economies and require sound human effort on a continuous basis. Free markets and market forces on their own do not, and never will, create sustainable economies. Every element of all economies has to be guided into balance (family units, businesses, institutions, local districts, regions, countries and trading areas, like the EU). Trading rules are essential, and sound planning and development must be within the capacity of the citizens to create. Economies should not move forward faster than the people can collectively manage and comprehend. Nowadays, as never before, humanity has the technology for the requisite data collection, direction and retrieval, to do the job.

If the economies of the world are to become sustainable, their economies must converge and follow a natural path, using the Master Currency and a sound trading system that almost all citizens can be taught to understand at some level, feel comfortable with, and follow.

Islamic Banks

As no interest is normally charged by Islamic banks, type 1 banks are ideal for exchange, via the current accounts. The type 2 banks would not charge any interest, but would create current accounts that are free of any bank charges, which would be paid for from the fees charged on loans to cover all the banks expenses and permissible MH system profits. The depositors' funds would also need to be insured to protect against any loss. Bank type 3 is still required for venture capital. Its fee on venture capital loans would reflect the risk taken and the cost of their services, and the depositors would collectively receive a fee for their risk taken amounting to 50% of the Bank profit, as permitted by the MH system trading rules. The depositors would be like shareholders.

CHAPTER 4

OTHER FINANCIAL INSTITUTIONS

When discussing the sectors of the economy in Chapter 8, Volume 1 the financial services were divided into five categories. The first (a) was a mechanism to effect exchanges of goods and services and the second (b) a system for financing developments and capital for purchasing assets: these have already been discussed in Chapter 3 – Banking. The other three categories are: (c) a system for spreading risk, (d) a system for checking that the dealings remain sustainable and (e) advisors for financial planning. These are being dealt with in this Chapter.

Category (c)

Category (c) includes insurance, stock markets and commodity trading, and these are essential natural elements of our economy.

One can divide these three financial areas into two sections:
- insurance and commodity exchange,
- stock markets.

Insurance and commodity trading are used as tools in the economy to reduce risk, and they substantially aid family and business economies. Stock markets allow savings to be rolled over to maintain the purchasing power of money into the latest goods and services available many years later, as would be required for pensions, and by business when using their savings to modernise, or expand their businesses. Current accounts and savings also permit this to happen. However, for reasons explained, savings accounts do not always allow funds to be withdrawn when required; but shares in the stock markets can be bought and sold at any time, with, unfortunately, the disadvantage that their price varies depending on the health of the companies the shares represent. An advantage in a sustainable form of economy is that, when shares are held in sound companies, the dividends should produce a better rate of return than from bank interest earned in savings accounts.

Taking the present free-for-all form of capitalism, the manner in which insurance, commodities and stock market businesses operate can be said to favour the financial business sector rather than the customer's interests, so we will next examine the purpose of these institutions in a sustainable economy.

Insurance

Insurance covers loss or damage caused by various events. Some losses for families without insurance could create considerable difficulties, especially if they lost their home, worth a number of years earnings. The uninsured losses are often beyond the earning capacity of the person/s involved. With the insurer's clients contributing an affordable annual fee to an insurance fund, with premiums balancing with their clients' claims, security for the insured is achieved. This is the true purpose of insurance. One of the present-day problems for customers is the exclusion of certain risks from their insurance. The system can be complicated as many items need insurance and insurance companies vary their conditions from year to year. It is the author's opinion that sustainable economies need all items to be insured. However, it is appreciated that companies may wish to have a simple classification system to cover each type of insurance, like buildings, land, vehicles, machinery, furniture and electronics. Small claims, those that could be easily paid from a family or business contingency budget, should be excluded. The contingency budget could be assumed to be 1% of family earnings or business turnover. This would assist in making the insurance system more efficient as small claims can be costly to administer. Therefore, in a sustainable economic system each insurance category would not have any exclusion, except for small claims. Insurance companies, where they underestimate, or overestimate, the expected value of claims due to changing conditions and demands, would readjust their premium rates to maintain their premium/claims balances probably on an annual basis. Money may be borrowed by insurance companies to smooth out the cost of annual variations in the premiums. An insurance system based on the foregoing is likely to be more efficient and acceptable to insurance companies' clients. Insurance companies, like banks and businesses, should also comply with the trading rules determined to satisfy sustainable economies as already indicated in Volume 1 Chapter 2.

Life assurance is another product devised to assist families to cover, for example, the unexpected death of the main wage earner. The with-profit option of a life assurance is another useful way to save, or pay off a home mortgage when an economy is sustainable. With-profit life insurance policies can also be used on maturity to provide a pension.

The actual structure supporting the insurance industry can be achieved in various ways, but in exceptional circumstances may also have to be supported by individual governments and sometimes collectively. For example, a natural catastrophe could destroy the insurers assets backing its financial structure, and hence the need for government-aid to restore the economy.

Commodity Exchange

Commodities and many other natural resources are subject to cycles from low to high demand, high and low production, and low to high costs. Advanced purchases for crops have the effect of smoothing out income for the producers and also prices for the purchasers of the final product. However, the commodities system for sustainable economies should not be used to squeeze producer prices at short notice, but take into consideration the whole economy, and allow time for needed structural changes to take place at a realistic and sensible pace, bearing in mind all relevant factors. The reason for this observation is that the economy exists to serve people and their requirements, including a right of employment.

Stock Markets

Production fluctuates, to meet demand. Budgets of individuals, families, businesses, organisations and government bodies also fluctuate, creating debt and savings. Overall debt and savings will balance, and assets would be greater than debts in a sustainable form of economy. The stock market plays an important role in diverting resources where they are required. Families and businesses require capital for peak expenditure, and for contingencies, improvements, business expansion and pensions. This creates the need for savings. Money in loan accounts, bonds and shares assist both debtors and savers, provided markets and money are stable and finance is available, and all participants of the economy are trading using the same rules.

Stocks and shares, or any other similar products, should not be created to off- load a bank's bad debt that will probably never be paid. Likely bad debts should be written-off as they are unreliable investments that clients may believe to be sound. This can then lead to people suddenly finding their assets to be worthless. Honest, transparent dealings are an essential part of a sustainable economy.

The use of shares not only allows capital to be raised to commence, or expand a business, but it also allows investors to share in a number of companies to minimise the risk of loss due to failures, and to even out the fluctuation of income from dividends.

Bonds like those issued by central or local governments, companies, banks and other institutions are used to raise capital. Whatever the form of the bond it must conform to the MH trading rules to ensure economies remain in a sustainable form.

Limited liability companies should not be set up purely to gain a financial advantage at the expense of others, by creating products and businesses expected to fail. Bankers and financial institutions including pension funds should ensure they have a thorough knowledge of the businesses they are supporting, to safeguard and minimise the risk of losing their clients' money. If an investor lacks the right personnel to assess the risks, the risks should not be taken.

Financial institutions dealing in venture capital should ensure their personnel are qualified to assess the projects they wish to invest in, as failing projects not only unnecessarily waste resources, but also impede maintenance and improvement of the standard of living.

Category (d) – Monitoring the economy

With the MH system economies are monitored regularly to ensure they remain sustainable. All businesses, therefore, would need to be checked to ensure they are complying with the trading rules. This task would be carried out by local and regional government bodies and the Central Bank. They would use the statistics that would be submitted annually, by businesses and institutions and records supplied by the banking system.

Category (e) Financial advisors

The MH system is a natural structure, which follows the manner we development and maintain our economies. It works on sound measures including its master currency. Its trading rules and method of modelling and monitoring the economy allows the economies to move forward steadily at a pace that people can follow. It is designed to gradually converge economies and correct the flaws in them. The structure used for the information system would be so arranged that people would be able to understand how the economy functions, by studying its structure. The economic information structure is based on production and services, which generates the employment that gives all the products that supports the population's standard of living, and stable salaries to finance their purchases.

This stable form of economic foundation allows long term planning and allows individuals, families, businesses, institutions and government to build feasible living standards within human capacity. It allows sound financial planning. Collectively, it allows everyone in the economy to understand what their duties and role are in the economy. This is because everything about the economy can be explained.

The task for financial advisors in running the MH form of economy will be to guide individuals and industry and government on the transition to a sustainable form of economy, and then in the economy as it moves forward.

Although a sustainable form of economy would be much easier for everyone to understand, there will always be those that will require help as modern economies are complicated, and not everyone can grasp all that is required in managing their economic lives. Advisors would need to help with property purchases, pensions and investments and many small businesses.

Partnerships and large family businesses would continue to need advice on their business structure and expansion, and limited companies would also need to learn how to structure and expand their organisations.

CHAPTER 5

INTERNATIONAL TRADE

Referring to the Hypothetical Model Economy Table 120, Chapter 2, supplier 34, the tobacco plantation, it made no purchases from the sellers in the economy, but did show 5.90 persons annual production working in the industry. The reason for this is that the supply came from an overseas economy. The imported tobacco will have to be paid for by exports of some of the goods shown in the table. Had the table been based on a more complete economy many other imports would have been shown. Imported goods and services could all be ones that the nation cannot provide itself. Holidays taken in another country are also like imports. It is these items that give rise to international trade.

It has already been mentioned that all economies have to keep their trade in balance: the cost of goods and services they import must be balanced with what they export, like businesses have to keep their costs in balance with income from sales. The trade balances start with the local districts and regions in every country. Each country, therefore, must also balance the cost of imports with the export sales. This is not an easy process, particularly in present day economies. The value of national currencies are nearly always changing and when compared with the MH Master Currency they all have a very different purchasing power, as shown in Tables 125 and 126.

Tables 125 and 126 have been prepared to show how different a selection of 40 nation's economies are, based on 1982 statistics, which are still similar at the time of publication of this book. The first 15 countries shown are developed nations and the remaining 25 countries are emerging economies (developing nations). Table 125 compares the U.K. against the other nations, and its currency value has the highest purchasing power of the ones listed, except for Switzerland. Table 126 compares India against the same other nations in Table 125, and its currency was the weakest at that time. It can be observed that in 1982 the value of labour at the extremes varied by a ratio of more than 1:60, see UK buying power column Table 125. These ratios among countries are continuously varying in the present form of market economy, the reason being that the currencies are all 'floating' measures, valued by market forces or pegged to another currency. Each day these rates vary up and down, making it difficult to calculate the value of exports and imports.

The last column in Table 126 shows the ratio of wages to G.D.P. As mentioned previously 1.00 represents the cost of wages and the amount exceeding 1.00 is all net rent. For example, when the ratio is 1:2, 50% of the unit of money is extracted as net rent (money not earned by anyone), and when 1:3, or 1:4 the net rent amounts to 67% and 75% respectively. Consequently the wage earner's purchasing power is reduced to 50%, 33%, and 25% respectively. This means that a considerable amount of wealth has been transferred to individuals and businesses. Some governments try to redress this situation by taxing those who have had the unearned profit, and also tax the high wage earners to pay subsidies to the poor. There are various reasons for the GDPs being high. Sometimes it results from royalties on oil and natural resources, paid direct to governments. When comparing competitiveness both wages and GDP should be studied because they are different in each country.

TABLE 125
UK Purchasing Power

Country & Currency	1 MH in nation's currency	£ at current exchange rate	Value of 1£ based on MH unit	UK buying power in other nation's (UK is 1.00)	Percentage of UK cost
Australia A $	4.28	1.721	1.24	1.39	72
Austria Sch	60.41	29.86	17.46	1.71	58
Belgium B Fr	164.58	79.98	47.57	1.68	59
Britain £	3.46	1.00	1.00	1.00	100
Canada C $	5.80	2.16	1.68	1.29	78
Denmark Dkr	36.63	14.59	10.59	1.38	72
France Fr	26.39	11.50	7.63	1.50	67
Germany DM	10.38	4.25	3.00	1.42	70
Italy L	3410.52	2368.00	958.70	2.47	40
Japan Yen	873.23	436.00	252.38	1.73	58
Netherlands Gld	10.51	4.67	3.04	1.54	65
Spain Pa	211.44	192.30	61.11	3.15	32
Sweden Skr	29.76	11.00	8.60	1.28	78
Switzerland S Fr	13.09	3.55	3.78	0.94	106
United States $	5.35	1.75	1.55	1.13	89
China Yen	0.19	3.306	0.055	60.11	1.7
Hong Kong HK $	12.81	10.63	3.70	2.87	35
India IR	0.94	16.55	0.27	61.30	1.63
Indonesia Rp	157.89	1158.00	45.63	25.38	3.9
Malaysia Ma $	1.72	4.088	0.497	8.23	12
Philippines PP	2.72	14.95	0.786	19.02	5.3
Singapore S $	5.49	3.746	1.586	2.36	42
South Korea Skw	511.21	1280.00	147.75	8.66	12
Taiwan NT $	41.92	68.18	12.12	5.63	18
Thailand Bt	7.25	40.26	2.10	19.17	5.2
Argentina Arg $	2.97	4.538	0.858	5.29	19
Brazil Cr	173.91	314.2	50.26	6.25	16
Chile Ch $	39.58	89.12	11.44	7.79	13
Colombia Col $	32.95	112.2	9.52	11.79	8.5
Mexico Mex $	52.63	96.25	15.21	6.33	16
Venezuela Bs	8.38	7.527	2.42	3.11	32
Greece Dr	110.50	116.90	31.94	3.66	27
Israel Sk	54.00	42.48	15.61	2.72	37
Portugal Esc	73.23	139.10	21.16	6.57	15
South Africa R	0.929	1.897	0.268	7.08	14
Turkey TL	82.38	284.5	23.81	11.95	9
Czech Republic Kcs	17.39	10.64	5.03	2.12	47
Hungary Ft	31.94	64.12	9.23	6.95	14
Poland Zl	68.65	148.00	19.84	7.46	13
Russia Rub	1.14	1.27	0.33	3.85	26

TABLE 126
Indian Purchasing Power

Country & Currency		1 MH in nation's currency	IR at current exchange rate	Value of IR based on MH unit	Indian buying power in other nation's (India is 100%)	Ratio of wages to GDP
Australia	A $	4.28	0.104	4.55	2.28	2.43
Austria	Sch	60.41	1.80	64.27	2.80	2.64
Belgium	B Fr	164.58	4.83	175.09	2.76	2.54
Britain	£	3.46	0.06	3.68	1.63	1.23
Canada	C $	5.80	0.131	6.17	2.12	2.47
Denmark	Dkr	36.63	0.882	38.97	2.26	2.19
France	Fr	26.39	0.695	28.07	2.48	2.65
Germany	DM	10.38	0.257	11.04	2.33	2.57
Italy	L	3410.52	143.08	3628.21	3.94	2.74
Japan	Yen	873.23	26.34	928.97	2.84	2.42
Netherlands	Gld	10.51	28.20	11.18	2.52	2.90
Spain	Pa	211.44	11.62	224.94	5.17	3.26
Sweden	Skr	29.76	0.665	31.66	2.10	2.19
Switzerland	S Fr	13.09	0.21	13.93	1.51	2.27
United States	$	5.35	0.106	5.69	1.86	2.33
China	Yen	0.19	0.200	0.202	99.00	2.79
Hong Kong	HK $	12.81	0.642	13.63	4.71	2.24
India	IR	0.94	1.00	1.00	100.00	3.98
Indonesia	Rp	157.89	69.97	167.97	41.66	2.93
Malaysia	Ma $	1.72	0.247	1.83	13.50	3.29
Philippines	PP	2.72	0.903	2.89	31.25	3.30
Singapore	S $	5.49	0.226	5.84	3.87	2.34
South Korea	Skw	511.21	77.34	543.84	14.22	3.03
Taiwan	NT $	41.92	4.12	44.60	9.24	2.45
Thailand	Bt	7.25	2.43	7.71	31.52	2.39
Argentina	Arg $	2.97	0.274	3.16	8.67	3.41
Brazil	Cr	173.91	18.98	185.01	1.026	3.51
Chile	Ch $	39.58	5.38	42.11	12.78	3.91
Colombia	Col $	32.95	6.78	35.05	19.34	3.94
Mexico	Mex $	52.63	5.82	55.99	10.39	4.10
Venezuela	Bs	8.38	0.45	8.91	5.05	3.57
Greece	Dr	110.50	7.06	117.55	6.00	2.84
Israel	Sk	54.00	2.57	57.45	4.47	3.52
Portugal	Esc	73.23	8.40	77.90	10.78	2.10
South Africa	R	0.929	0.115	0.988	11.64	4.39
Turkey	TL	82.38	17.19	87.64	19.61	2.50
Czech Republic	Kcs	17.39	0.643	18.50	3.48	2.05
Hungary	Ft	31.94	3.87	33.98	11.39	2.42
Poland	Zl	68.65	8.94	73.03	12.24	2.04
Russia	Rub	1.14	0.077	1.21	6.36	2.07

When trading in the sustainable MH system each country would be using the same trading rules and in consequence wages in each nation would be similar and the GDP would be in the region of 1:1.3, as net profits would amount to about 25% of Master Currency's purchasing power. However, present economies are not trading using the MH system, but it can still be used as an economic tool to analyse economies.

When studying a nation's economy to determine possible markets the ratio between wages and GDP has an important bearing on demand. For example taking 1:4 ratio against 1:1.3 ratio (MH type GDP): it transfers to the wealthier 0.75% - 25% = 50% more money earned by the employees, leaving them with only 25% of the wealth they created to spend to support their family economies This means that there would be three times more trade with the wealthy and businesses, than with the employees. Even two developed nations with the same potential could have vastly different markets, as the employees in one country could have much more wealth than the other. Rich people and businesses will spend their money on different products, many of which the poorer cannot afford. The actual wages paid to people can also change trading patterns. The MH system works on the basis that no one should be paid less than half the average unskilled rate. Many countries have large populations on much lower pay rates and this also distorts the pattern of trade. Market surveys must be carefully carried out in present day economies. One EU country can be very different from another. The same analysis applies to similar developing countries. One should not jump to conclusions on market potential being similar.

The international exchange of goods and services is vast in modern economies as few countries have all the resources to be self-sufficient. The exchange allows the imports and export of vital raw materials, very special skills serving the whole world, and many special products in small to large quantities that could be made in just a few countries or anywhere in the world. Many goods can be imported in vast quantities until perhaps they are made in their own country.

Generally speaking all countries of the world are using similar measures for all the products we produce, except money: the medium we use to measure the value of our labour and products. Tables 125 and 126 illustrated how distorted this has made trading in our economies. In consequence developed nation's currencies have much greater purchasing power for goods and services from developing countries and, for developing countries, purchase of goods and services can be very expensive. Fifty years ago the developed nations economies and skills were considerably more advanced comparatively speaking, than they are now, but gradually over this period developing countries have been catching up with the developed nations skills, infrastructure and production technology. This has led to the situation where with free markets, and a distorted monetary system it has become more economic for industries formerly in the developed nations to transfer to suitable developing nations, where labour costs are very low when compared against developed countries currency labour charges. Even with the cost of additional transport perhaps half way round the world substantial gains are made. Businesses in competition, when other competitors are operating in those countries, have no option than to follow, or not survive.

The free market concept is fine from the point of view of lowering the price of goods and services in the developed nations. Further, it is allowing technology and vital resources to reach developing countries that will help to raise their standard of living. The more educated we collectively become in the world the more and quicker will be the discoveries and developments. However, the rate at which these changes are taking place affects the stability of developed nations, particularly the problem of unemployment and supporting those with insufficient work, or income due to lower wages from the pressure of overseas competition. Businesses in the developed nations, if they wish to survive in them, must compete. Lowering wages is one element that helps, but with the 1:60 ratio it does not solve the problem. However, with 1:2, or 1:3, and the most modern equipment and advanced techniques, it probably can. In spite of industry's best endeavours since say the early sixties, unemployment has been steadily rising in the developed nations. Unfortunately more jobs are being lost than sustainable jobs can be created. The balance can be restored by using the MH system, but that can probably only be implemented by governments, or massive support by business and citizens to force the change, where governments refuse to correct the unsustainable situation.

The present free market trading and monetary system is out of control. It is impossible to forecast whether, in relation to each other, the purchasing power of the currencies will draw closer; and if it does how long this will take. Markets can become very distorted and can even be manipulated to create certain results. Countries with large strong economies, or large multinationals can do this. Businesses in developed countries affected by international competition may well decide there is only one solution, to set up in the nation with the best wage and infrastructure advantage. However, will national wage advantages seesaw, and what sort of cycles can be expected? All this uncertainty does not create stability and efficient economies, as much wasted effort could result by setting up the business in the wrong countries.

One important major change in the world economy is the still developing European Union (EU) with the Euro single currency. However, to date it has not solved their collective economic problem. The decision for the single currency was sound, but no guidance was given to the citizens and businesses on its convergence with the values of the purchasing power of their very different currencies, and it has not solved the unemployment problems, caused by the present international trading system. It is interesting to note that wages and prices are slowly becoming more similar, but the economy is not sustainable.

A modern complicated world economy needs a single international trading language essential for sound and safe communication. English is being widely used in business and India has continued to use it since independence. People in all nations are searching for products and information. Poor translations often lead to wrong information and misunderstanding.

The MH system divides trade into two main categories, necessities and luxuries (desirable products not necessary for survival, but used to improve the quality of life). It should be noted these would not be the same in every nation: it would depend on many factors, such as national culture, climate, the degree of development of the country and its location in the world. International businesses setting up in other counties should not therefore assume consumption of their product would be the same in every country.

All businesses have different characteristics and when setting up in another nation these must be carefully examined, bearing in mind, which markets are going to be served. The important elements for the cost of production can be high and if the intention is also to supply local demands the final product must be affordable. A best solution may well be a combination of local and imported products that will give the optimum result. Although the Tables given in this book indicate wage levels, up-to-date information of actual wages paid should be used in calculations. The MH system can be used to also determine whether wages are distorted. Provisions for distortions may need to be taken into account in estimates.

Further tables like Tables 125 and 126 can be made to compare against the national currency in which the business exists or could exist. On having figures for one table they can be used for any country listed to study another country based on its currency, i.e. Table 126 was based on Table 125. In relation to labour one can establish which currencies are overvalued or undervalued, based on the chosen country of reference. For example in Table 125 the Swiss franc was overvalued against the £ and all other currencies were undervalued against the £.

From Table 125 (and similar) initial calculations can be made to decide whether there is an advantage of one's business moving to another country. For example, businesses are normally run on local produce, materials and the labour force, and other requirements are bought from other nations. It is necessary to determine whether there is an advantage to be gained by moving, for the business being considered. Calculations for the best country to produce in would take into consideration where the markets are for the product and quantities, and how much deliveries would cost. The calculations would take into account as much as possible being carried out by local labour, materials and products in the chosen country. The remaining labour, materials and products could be supplied from any other countries having what is needed.

Import/Export Agencies

It really is necessary for nations to keep their external national accounts in balance, for reasons already explained. If they are not, a country's economy could become unbalanced, causing all sorts of problems.

There are many items that have to be kept in balance, when importing and exporting, apart from the monetary balance. Spares have to be imported for the foreign goods in a country. Some businesses manufacture goods, or provide services, that need a world market, as the home market would be too small to operate a viable business. Some commodities, goods and services must be imported, as they cannot be obtained in the nation. Therefore, international trade is necessary for most countries.

The MH system uses import/export agencies to fulfil and balance the international exchange. Businesses would contact these organisations to help them in whatever manner is required to ensure that they can buy what is needed, and to ensure the supply of the foreign exchange needed for the purchase. The agencies could aid in finding sales to obtain foreign currency, in the desired amounts to meet imports. To effect balances agencies could exchange foreign currency in their possession for the currencies they really need. The agencies could be businesses specialising in exchanging goods and services, or they could be large multinational companies and banks. The agencies might not serve one country only, but could be a group of agencies working together and operating in any number of countries. However, each agency would have to keep its external account in balance. They must not allow sales, either way, to go ahead without the funds for the purchases.

For small businesses that cannot afford to send salesmen to foreign countries, the agencies can assist by finding sales for them, as they would have their own contacts, or agencies, in other foreign countries. The agencies could also be linked to international transport companies.

The agencies should be able to keep the national external accounts in balance, with governments overseeing the operation, but otherwise with little involvement in the exchange process.

Current account banks would be involved with the agencies, as they would witness their clients' monetary transactions. These banks would also need to supply cash for those requiring it for foreign holidays and business trips, where not arranged by a travel agency.

Governments and individuals could require foreign currency loans. These loans would be arranged by the banks and in accordance with the MH system banking/trading regulations. However, long-term international loans over many years would create an imbalance, but this is acceptable where necessary, just as it is nationally.

The agency service will have to be paid for in a manner mutually agreed. Profits of the agencies would comply with the MH system trading rules.

CHAPTER 6

PRODUCTION AND SERVICES

Basically businesses and government bodies provide two main sections to support the family requirements and industry. The first is **production** that creates all the physical assets, and the second are **services** that support our activities that, in effect, are consumed at the minute, hour, or other period of time it is being given. The assets of production can have a long life, like housing, whereas other assets could have a shorter lifespan, like cars and many electrical products, or a short use, like packaging and food products. Excluding products like materials, equipment and business organisation, or institution assets, services are all supplied by human labour using skills that are all used while the service is being given. The production and service sectors provide all the activities needed by the economy, including information and the purpose of the economy and how it should function and be supported.

The information system can be based on Table 36, Chapter 7 Volume 1, which commences to subdivide the industries in the economy, including the government sector. The following tables, 37, 38 and 39, continue the process of listing all the elements of the economy. Modern economies need millions of production and service units, which specialise in all the elements needed to support the world economies. In the early days of industrialisation the number of elements was small in comparison with the present-day; and it was easier to locate the products and services required. Present modern economies have expanded to such an extent that no one has the mental capacity to know, or absorb all the information concerning the complete economy, consisting of millions of products. We can only collectively absorb this knowledge. Consequently, to permit the economy to function efficiently, a complete structure for the economy is needed so that people can understand their economy and find whatever they require, that exists. This form of information system has to be developed, and it is an essential key element, required to build sustainable economies in harmony with the environment. Clearly, the information system needs to be broken down in a very logical pattern and table 36 commences this process.

At one time a business, or organisation, could have been completely self-supporting, and did not have to buy in outside help, except labour with the required skills. In a modern world, for most products/services, one must buy in goods and services provided by other organisations, and one needs to know where they are located. Frequently, under present conditions it can be an impossible task, as the information system is incomplete, leaving the question of whether, or not, a product does, or does not exist: much time can be wasted. It is not unknown for products to be imported, only to find later they existed locally.

In a modern world the information network in each country should be linked to every nation to allow businesses, including government bodies and other institutions, to interact on a sound structure, and preferably in one international trading language. This is essential to minimise inefficiencies, errors and misunderstanding. This proposed information system is a vital component of the production/service industry serving the world economy.

In a sustainable form of economy each organisation (business, institution, or government body) has its own objectives and duties to perform, with its chosen supply task, or delegated task. They, however, must also comply with the trading rules and the natural processes that allow economies to be sustainable. Collectively, as closely as possible, the economy needs to supply the actual goods and services the economy requires.

Whatever business, or other organisation forming part of the economy, it must be understood that in a natural world they exist to serve the needs of people. People have rights, and the object of the MH system is to respect these rights and also their environment. The manner in which the economy functions can make the world a marvellous place to live in. However, if the world economy is abused, life on earth can be turned into hell. The people working in the economy all have a duty to make sure their actions are fair, honest and sustainable. They must make sure that everyone they know understands what we must collectively do for success. The world resources must be shared as required among the economies while people serve the families and their environment. People and organisations will have to keep within the natural constraints. Any form of profit, must be sustainable, and this is why the MH system is modest with financial rewards. Production and services need to take into account the observation made in this paragraph.

All families have objectives or agenda for what they want, which can change at any time and perhaps many times. Like families, businesses and other organisations also have objectives that can change with time, as they reshape to meet the demands of the economy. Each business will decide on special functions that form its type/s of trade. Each is like an individual with quite different characteristics, like size, internal structure and service provided. They all interact with the rest of the economy differently to support the activities the world economies require. Some of the demands on the economy are wanted immediately, whilst others would be at a later date. Some products could be made to order, and it could be an asset, or a service.

Many activities in economies have to be planned and this would depend on the development decisions made. Many sectors of the economy have to plan to supply the future needs for when they could be required. To achieve this sound information on future development trends is essential. Development, or the rate of it, would depend on affordability, funding, materials, services and skills all being available. Unstable economies, making unforeseen changes, upset all the planning and quantities estimated. Sound long-term plans lead to efficiency and a satisfactory standard of living.

Other activities provided by the economy are based either on the trends of flow of normal demand, and anticipated fluctuations, or from market research. Some demands can only be established by a trial and error process, or intelligent deduction. This applies to some new products and services. Forecasts all need stable economic conditions to determine for industry the short, medium and long-term requirements to ensure that the economies develop smoothly, hence avoiding bottlenecks in the supplies. Many businesses do need to know the actual direction the economies are planned to develop. It is appreciated that unexpected disasters and other events will happen, but these would only slow the general direction envisaged.

The foundation and framework of the economic system must take all the foregoing matters into account. Economies should be able to re-adjust, without massive distortions, like 10% unemployment and industries and homeowners going bankrupt from unnatural high rates. The MH system is in a form arranged to accomplish this.

Regions

It is not unusual for various regions throughout the world to specialise in certain agricultural, mining or manufactured products that result from the region's natural resources and location. As some natural resources are used up their industries close, but the economic activity has not always died, as other industries have taken over that are not so dependent on the local natural resources. One of the problems in depressed economies is the previous investment in homes, villages and town infrastructures. The people living in these areas frequently want stay in an environment they like and where their families and good friends live. Moving for many families also has other factors to consider, like the children's education and perhaps having to care for their parents, or a disabled person. Some people are quite happy to move, but this is usually a minority.

Many industries and services do not have to be local and could be in any region, and this applies much more in modern economies than in past ones. This is partly helped by telecommunications and electronic systems, which have advanced and become quite low in cost. Many industries do no longer have to locate in local clusters that support them. Many developing nations now also have good road links and other excellent transport facilities, which in the past were not available nation-wide. Finally, there is the advantage in having a workforce that is happy in their environment, rather than employees moved in from other areas, whom may have all types of problems caused by the move, distracting their attentions to family problems, and reducing their work performance.

Bearing in mind the observations made, businesses might do well to consider expansion to declining regions that could have a suitable skilled workforce for their activities; employed and unemployed. Many forms of business do not need highly skilled personnel, but a large workforce that can be trained, or retrained, in a relatively short period of time.

Business Location

When it is anticipated that a business is going to grow, location needs to be taken into account, particularly if enlargement would need to be on the same site, or same district. It could be important for local, or regional authorities to understand this. Hopefully, this would be part of the planning authorities function.

There needs to be close co-ordination between business and government on the location for some special businesses. They must be located taking all factors into consideration, including the public and the environment. Many businesses are essential to the stability of the nation and must have a sound location, somewhere, that fulfils all conditions.

The nation' assets can be located anywhere. Changes in the economy can render buildings and constructions no longer being needed for the original purpose. Government bodies should co-ordinate with the owners in seeking a new use for the assets and not just force them to be wasted, by non co-operation.

Skills

Governments and businesses should understand people, and the fact that the skills of most communities would cover a large proportion of the skills naturally needed in a region. There will be people also wanting unskilled work, manual work, mental work, a combination of manual and mental work and professional work, all with various degrees of responsibility. Older generations will often need different work from younger generations.

Businesses, institutions and government bodies exist to serve families. That fact does not only apply to supplying goods and services, but also to provide work, that is their natural right. All these matters need to be taken into account to ensure sustainable economies.

A shortage of the right skills is not solved by unemployment. There will always be a shortage of some skills, particularly where new technology has been developed and a rapid demand, exceeding expectations. Skilled shortages can only be solved, or minimised, by good planning, and by training people well in advance, ready for when they are wanted. Good planning needs the right information on which to make forecasts. Education authorities and businesses need to work closely together.

Many skills can only be learnt at the place of work. Sometimes, only businesses can transfer technology, and this could be worldwide. Businesses could be requested to set up organisations in other parts of the world to train staff, which could be in the use of their special plant. This is a necessary part of the services given by businesses to the public.

Business Stability

People running businesses in any form of economy will always be taking a risk that the demand for their product could cease, and if the business cannot change to products that are in demand their business could fail. Many smaller businesses could be at greater risk than large ones that are often cover a larger range of products, have better purchasing power and are wealthier. It should be noted that, as economies change, markets alter the demand for some lines quite quickly. Competition can also reduce turnover and force other businesses to close. Businesses will always have to understand how to survive and build sustainable businesses. They will need to know when to cease certain lines of business and when to start others. Failed and failing lines of business are part of the industrial process and development of our economies. The MH system helps businesses by creating more stable economies and a superior information system.

There are many businesses that customers will always support, provided the service is given fairly and remains of sound quality. Individuals that are not liked against those who are can change a business from being successful to having to close. Goodwill can be very important for many businesses, and this would not be changed by the MH system.

All businesses need to be well understood, and developed at a rate that is affordable and backed by sufficient reserves. Where they are situated is important. Markets should always be carefully assessed and the trends of the economy should be followed and understood. Short, medium and long-term local, regional and national plans should be carefully studied. When using the MH system economies are more stable, allowing businesses to make proper financial plans for development and expansion to meet sound market forecasts, although it will not remove the need for contingencies to cover unexpected events.

One of the arts of sustaining a business is to have it large enough, and with sufficient financial backing to change to new types of business as markets change. This is not easy for a small business that has just started; but if it is successful, the owner/s should bear in mind that markets could change one day, and, therefore, provide for such an event by creating back-up capital and expanding into other lines of business. Each business is different, but their owners should be aware of the nature of competition that could affect them. Sometimes some areas for a business would give them a more sustainable location, than others: maybe rural, or town location. Even businesses that have a monopoly may only last until their lines are no longer popular, or in demand, for whatever reason.

Some successful businesses may wish to join others to form a larger business, and spread risks. They could be in a similar line of business, or quite different. The MH system does not stop take-overs, or monopolies, but only regulates the maximum profits. More stable trading conditions and economies, and the manner in which they are managed by governments, should allow businesses to improve their forecasts, and be able to make sounder business development plans. Secured loans would remain at low rates of interest, making financial planning easier.

Research and Development

There are still many problems in our world and research continues to be necessary in an endeavour to solve them. Many ideas can only be gradually developed, and they usually have to be tested to ensure the solution sought has been achieved.

Many businesses should be carrying out R & D, yet do not; and this sometimes is caused by too much competition, that reduces the profits needed to finance research. Some professional firms cannot admit they do not have all the answers and, therefore, cannot let it be seen that they are carrying out research. This attitude needs to change.

Many industries do carry out a substantial amount of research, particularly manufacturers. Each specialised industry should determine the amount of research needed, and decide how it should materialise. Individuals often wish to carry out research, but often do not have the means. A sound economic system needs to help these persons whenever possible.

The rate of research like all other elements of the economy needs to be affordable. A regular budget could be a solution ensuring sufficient research is done.

Market Surveys and Advertising

Although these are useful tools to determine markets and to increase sales respectively they can create a nuisance to the receiver. The right balance needs to be struck.

Market surveys require people to give information verbally or by completing forms, sometimes covering many pages, which can take up peoples' time. Time for some costs money and for others their leisure time.

Advertising can reach such proportions that tons of paper is printed and distributed to people having neither time to read nor wishing to read it. Sorting out important documents, or faxes, from the junk mail and disposing of the waste (much of which may not be recycled) again wastes natural resources and a considerable amount of total human effort. Frequently advertising material can also end up littering the streets.

For certain services market information is requested that is not always applicable to the service. Although sometimes one can indicate that the information is not to be passed on to other organisations, except a group's organisation, people miss the small print, and box, to confirm the information is confidential some businesses sell on their lists, which again helps to swell the junk mail sent.

However, a certain amount of advertising is necessary and also market surveys, but in an efficient economy they should be properly targeted to those that really need it, or want it. The MH system is used to examine better and more efficient ways to achieve the objectives. It uses a properly organised information service that classifies every business and other element of the economy, including people. In modern economies a substantial part of it is connected to the internet. This already links most businesses and many homes. The MH business classification system lets the advertiser know the nature of products or services each business needs, and software could be used to prevent advertisements, and it could also be used to request specific information. Families could have software to reject adverts, or invite certain ones. By visiting a business website, one can already scan over their products. Other advertisements would all be viewed on the television and not sent by mail, and this form of advertising causes less inconvenience to the general public.

In less developed economies many businesses deal with selected suppliers, who already know their clients requirements, or know they will contact them for the latest information. With a background knowledge selective advertising would be more effective than mass advertising sent anywhere.

Market surveys may best be carried out in conjunction with the information that needs to be compiled, or updated, in the single MH information system. Information could be paid for via the telecommunication system, say when the user enters direct into a business website.

Accounts Rendered

The MH system operates on the basis that all bills are paid promptly, i.e. invoices (or equivalent) are to be paid no later than the end of the following month. Banks should not refuse the clearance of cheques or other forms of payment. If the business, or person, cannot meet the payments the banks should sort the problem out as previously mentioned in the chapter describing the banking service. This form of banking procedure allows a secure and smooth cash flow for businesses, as payments cannot be delayed. Where businesses are short of liquidity they should raise the funding necessary.

The National Economy

It will be understood that the MH system is designed to serve families, and that it also creates a fair economic system for both families and businesses. They support and help each other in a co-ordinating process, and they do not work in isolation. The economy is simplified by using a clear set of trading rules and a super information system. Where possible, the MH system is made self-regulating.

Economies need to be guided in the desired direction to ensure they remain sustainable. People must have sufficient work to be self-supporting, and be properly paid for their productivity. The environment must be cared for and kept in balance. The national economies are a collection of local economies all keeping their areas sustainable and in harmony with the regional, national and international economy.

Businesses serving the economy must provide needed elements in the economy and that is its real function. Persons managing businesses are given incentives to run the business in the form of net rents taken in accordance with the trading rules. However, the funds that support and allow the business to function successfully and to develop are provided by the public for that purpose when they buy from the business. The funds therefore, must be used honestly in the business to create the best possible deal for the customers. It should not be forgotten that without customers the business would not exist. In reality businesses owners are in partnership with their customers. Wealthy, successful business owners have partly gained their wealth by collecting net rent, (which does not include the wealth created by their own labour). This wealth, although in their ownership, morally should be used to support the business, and not other purposes.

Business owners should also be aware that while the employees' earnings accumulate, their wages are backing the business. They are in effect a form of un-rewarded shareholders. They only benefit from their wages deposited in their current account when they spend money, or have placed it in an interest bearing deposit account.

Finally, economies are such that no one is independent from other people, but tied into a complex network in which all the elements are dependant on each other.

CHAPTER 7

ESTIMATING AND VALUATIONS

Estimates and valuations can be carried out in many ways, and using the MH system does not necessarily alter many methods already in use; but it can simplify some methods used in business.

When using the MH system one main difference is that values are not placed on any natural resources, before a human labour input. The value of the natural resources derives solely from added human productivity in extracting, transporting, selling, etc. For example, coal in the ground has no monetary value with the MH system, before it is actually extracted using average hours of human work based on the MH productivity/monetary unit. The machines and other capital investment used are all created by human productive effort and this also forms part of the cost of extraction.

Existing business costing practices

Businesses have many ways in which they arrive at costs for their product or service. Many industries work on a percentage basis, the percentage addition varying considerably depending on the industry or service.

Many retail and wholesale businesses add a percentage of their buying cost of the goods to cover both expenses and profit. Sometimes the same percentage would be used throughout their whole range of sales, and at other times various percentage rates would be used to suit each form of product. Certain retail trade organisations would have their own recommended retail rates for products sold by their members. Frequently location and turnover does not affect the percentage rate used. At other times competition determines price, or sales prices can be used to clear stock, or attract more business.

Other industries, like in manufacturing and certain services, would calculate the cost of the product before fixing a price, and then add a percentage to cover the cost of overheads and profit. Alternatively, a fixed price based on an estimate plus a contingency figure and another percentage to cover overheads and profit.

Other pricing methods used, as in the steel industry involved with fabricating steel materials into finished products, could base costs on the weight of the material used and classified into size of sections and types of work. A monetary figure would be used to cover the material and labour cost, to which might be added delivery and then as before a percentage for overheads and profit. Many businesses use their own individual percentages rates in manufacturing industries.

Many smaller businesses, where the service supplied may be labour only, would give lump sum prices; and these are often not based on any calculation, but just judged, based on experience. Materials are often at cost without additions, thereby the overheads and profit being all made on the labour element only. Other tasks may be on an hourly basis for labour at a stated rate per hour, plus materials and a percentage for overheads and profit.

Large businesses and prices for massive projects are usually based on a detailed bill of quantities with every item of work and supply of materials valued. Percentages could be added to allow for wasted materials. Every type of machine used would take all kinds of factors into account, including depreciation, repairs and fuel. Average productivity rates would be used for labour and, perhaps, percentage additions to take into consideration quality and working conditions. There is a vast range of methods used in pricing and for planning the work.

Many professional activities work on a fee basis set and determined by their professional body, or trade organisation. If high quality is to be maintained too much competition can lower standards. Therefore, it is important to have the right balance.

Using the MH system does not change the pricing methods mentioned, but whatever system is used by businesses they must abide by the trading rules that limit profits to a maximum of 4% APR on capital used and 10% APR on the labour costs. If the percentages they use for profits are too high they must reduce them. For example a large super market with a substantial turnover would be able to work on lower profit margins than a small village store with a small turnover, being in an area of low population and isolated.

The rest of this Chapter discusses types of businesses, methods of estimating and valuations, and the basis on which they can be built. The key types of economic sector are next described, giving a picture of how economies are naturally formed, commencing with natural materials, as Item 1, Table 36, Volume 1, the first item in the production section.

Natural materials

Table 37, Volume 1 lists some of the main natural resources we use. Agriculture and forestry are both very dependant on land. Originally the land was unlikely to have been in a state that it could be used without first carrying out improvements to it. Clearly some land was more suitable than others for agriculture. For example flat river plains are more fertile than mountain slopes. For some form of agriculture flattish land and good soil is essential, whereas for other types, hills and mountain slopes can be adapted without too much loss in productivity. Various types of farming, therefore, would have taken place in the most suitable regions for them. For example, on the river plains grain and vegetables on areas easy to plough, and on the steeper slopes of hills and mountainous areas, say sheep farming, fruit farms and forestry. In warm climates and mountainous regions hillsides would be terraced and grape vines planted, etc.

So the most suitable, or best, land would have been chosen first to serve the particular need. Then land that had to be cleared of unwanted growth, stones and rocks or needed drainage. Roads and tracks would have been built for access, and boundary walls, fences and hedges erected to protect crops and keep animals from wondering, or being lost. All this work has added value to the land and allowed it to be farmed efficiently. The valued added to the land by our hours of human activity is then the basis for calculating what it is worth. Values would not be similar in every region, as in some locations more work would have been necessary than in others.

Once land has been fashioned to the particular need for the type of farming chosen the land must be maintained in good condition, including all roads, tracks and ancillary items built. Land can go out of condition very quickly when not looked after.

Newly planted forests and natural ones all need attention if the best results are desired. If quality timber is required the forests must have regular maintenance.

Some land, like for tobacco plantations, become poisoned by the crop and then will need to be restored to its original condition.

Irrigated land must also be carefully managed to avoid salts rising and polluting the land. Land for irrigation would be more expensive to provide than other agricultural land, due to the additional cost of providing the irrigation supply network and laying land to falls where flood irrigation is operated.

Fishing from natural water resources is the least expensive, the only human input being the management of the water to ensure sustainable regeneration. The main capital cost would be for the fishing boats and tackle. However, fish ponds would have a much greater labour input, that would probably include building the ponds, keeping them well stocked and also feeding the fish.

For the petroleum industry the first task is finding where the natural oil, gas and bitumen are located. This is an expensive exploratory process. For some sources extraction is very expensive, where wells are very deep or under the sea. Capital investment is considerable before the first drop can be extracted and processed. Pipelines and tankers for distribution are necessary. If oil spills should occur the cost of protecting the environment is added and finally when the installations are no longer needed the land needs to be reinstated.

Water supply is a vital industry to our economies. Water extraction, treatment and supply can be from low to very high cost, depending on its natural availability, the quantity needed and the location of the source. Land may also be required for its abstraction, reservoirs, treatment plants, pipelines and canals.

Apart from the drinking water consumed, the waste water that has been used for other purposes must be treated to ensure land, rivers, lakes and the sea are not contaminated. This often involves constructing sewerage systems and treatment plants. The cost of sewage disposal is usually greater than the cost of water supply.

The mining and quarrying industries are the ones we use to create most of our structures and manufactured products, apart from forestry products and bi-products of agriculture. Land use is not so high, but is required whilst the mining and quarrying activities take place. Ideally after these operations the land can be reinstated in some way to care for the environment.

Compensation for loss of land use while the operation takes place may also have to be paid.

None of the natural resources discussed should receive a royalty. As explained not a single resource can be extracted without human labour. If a royalty is paid on one of them: why not all of them? Often, when royalties are paid, the money is paid to a minority of the population. Clearly, if a nation has a resource, it can use it to supply employment for its citizens, instead of employing people from other countries. By this process they are gaining from the product. As has already been stressed natural resources are to be shared throughout the world, particularly the scarce ones; and the latter resources should be used sparingly and responsibly.

Manufactured Materials

Some of these are listed in Table 38 Volume 1. These industries use the natural materials, farmed or extracted, to produce their products. Relatively speaking their land useage is small. However, they require the support of the economy, its workforce and infrastructure to support their activity. These industries can be located close to the source of materials they need, or in an industrial region where they may form part of a cluster of industries.

Some of the activities of these industries create toxic waste, which must all be disposed of safely to avoid damaging the environment. This will add to the cost of their product.

Manufactured Products

Typical industries are listed in Table 39 Volume 1. Some of these industries would be involved in heavy engineering and are often sited close to material suppliers. For many light industries it is not so necessary to be located in industrial regions, or in clusters, but good communications and sound transport systems are usually essential. Generally the same remarks as made for manufactured materials would apply to manufactured products.

Construction

Most of the foregoing industries are dependant on the construction industry, to build the factories (every one being tailored to suit its own requirements) and the nation's infrastructure, on which they all rely.

The construction industry relies on the first three production sectors of the economy for its supplies of tools, machines and materials, and the service sector.

Services

Services supply the other needs of the production sector and the requirements of the general public, and the key elements have already been listed in Table 36 Volume 1.

Before services can be priced they must know the value of each of the products they buy from the production sector of the economy.

Pricing

Although businesses are all different they all need to work to basic costing structures. Some businesses would use every part of the structure, whereas others only certain key parts.

Table 118 lists the sixteen main elements for the price of a product, excluding taxes. The product could be as little as a pin, or as large as an oil super tanker. It could be for a service like the supply and installation of a cooker, or just a haircut. The percentages shown against each element, however, varies dependant on the nature of the product, and for some products not all elements would be used to calculate the price. Some of the items listed from 1 to 16 needing further explanation are made next.

Item 1, for the actual price of the goods or service needs to be calculated. This price could be separate from the other items listed, Items 2 to 14, or included in them.

The cost of selling the product Item 2 would vary depending on the value of the product, or the method of calculating the sale price adopted by the business. For example, the actual cost of manufacturing a single pin is very small in comparison with say a tailored wedding dress. To sell the pin could cost several times the actual cost of the pin, but to sell the wedding dress say only 1% of the cost of making the dress, yet the business practice would probably be to say the cost of selling all products is 2% of the actual cost of the product value. It should be noted that the 2% would be sufficient to cover the costs of the sales staff.

The storage of products while awaiting sales, Item 3 would apply to products that are not purpose made. Some products, like frozen foods and grain could be kept for say a whole season. Other products could be made in batches, and each batch may be made in one month and then could take up to six months to sell; or if books, or spare parts they might be stored for several years. Some products are bulky and not very costly, whilst others could be expensive and only take a little space. The cost of storage, therefore, depends once again on the nature of the product.

Many businesses would have to pack their product, Item 4. Some businesses may treat this as a separate item, whilst others would treat the cost as part of their overheads.

Transporting goods Item 5 would certainly apply to many businesses and once again the cost would depend on the type of goods and how far they must travel to reach their final destination.

Wastage of materials Item 6 would occur in all businesses. Some businesses can expect a greater proportion of waste than others due to the nature of their tasks. It should be noted that there would also be loss of hours of labour caused by errors, causing further wastage.

The cost of development Item 10 would apply to fewer businesses, as many businesses do not need to carry out research and development. The production industries are the ones that would carry out the majority of development projects. Certain services would also specialise in research and development for clients in industry and for government. Governments too would probably carry out some of its own research to develop its polices.

Many industries would need to write off out-dated stacks, as provided in Item 11. This can be caused in many ways: such as the products being superceded by new ones, by manufacturing a greater quantity than needed, by overbuying due to overestimating the demand for products, and goods passing their safe date.

The net rents, Item 12, forming part of the wage bill would not normally be treated separately, but would be included in the actual wage paid, or estimated, when calculating the cost of running the business, or a price of a product.

All businesses would be carrying out maintenance as provided by Item 13, even if it is only to office equipment and cleaning. Many businesses also have buildings and equipment to maintain.

All businesses have overheads to pay for as provided under Item 14. Some businesses would treat this item separately and could use a percentage addition to cover for this expense. Other businesses like retail shops would add a percentage addition to cover for all expenses in running their business.

In Chapter 1 the business maximum profit tables 101 to 110 showed that profits were made on the hours of labour employed and on the capital investment in the business, and this is common to every business. Item 15 is for retained profits in the business and would probably be limited to 5% of the added value and item 16 represents the maximum profit for the business owner/s, or shareholders, as calculated using the basis described for tables 101 to 110 in Chapter 1. The added value is calculated on the hours of work carried out by the business' own labour force. Profits must not exceed the limits set as they would then be unsustainable and would upset the balance of the economy.

Price of individual products

Very many products and services are based on the actual cost plus a single percentage addition to cover profit and all expenses to sell them. Factories would first calculate the price of the item made in the production line. A simple product could be made by a small workforce and one, or a few machines. This could be a product normally sold to other businesses for sale to the public, or as a part in another product. The product, however, could be one of many used in a business production line. A price of each of the products used would need to be calculated and then further priced in each of the further production processes, until the final article is complete.

The price of a complete product, having been calculated net of overheads and profit, would then be finalised to include the overhead costs, items 2 to 14 that apply, and items 15 and 16 for the permitted profit, as shown in Table 118. When working to the MH system rules the percentage additions would need to comply with the maximum profit basis shown in Tables

101 to 110. Past business records of turnover and profit would be used to calculate actual percentages to be used.

Wholesale and retail service businesses would buy their supplies from manufacturers, and other producers of products. They would add a percentage addition to each item that would cover the cost of their expenses plus profit. The profit element again would be based on the capital invested in the business plus their wage bill, and take into account their turnover to ensure the profits do not exceed the permissible rate for their business maximum profit category.

Many other services work on lump sum fees, a rate per hour, or both. Additional costs for materials, supply of products and/or expenses could also be charged. Their fees would also need to take into account their turnover and the MH system maximum annual profit rules. For example, a country hairdresser may not always be fully booked, but one in a town could be, which would increase the turnover and lower their overhead charges, and this could lower the cost of their service in comparison with the country hairdresser. The types of hair style could also vary, affecting their rates of turnover, etc. Other services making charges could be electrical appliance repairers, dentists, solicitors, architects, garages, jobbing builders, or shoe repairers, banks and financial services. Professional fees can often be based on the final cost of a customer's asset, like a new building, an infrastructure project, or a production line, and the fees could be paid in stages. Whatever the type of business they must all comply with the maximum profit conditions, when economies are developed on the MH system basis.

Pricing a wooden folding chair

To illustrate how estimating is applied when using the MH system, a small business making folding wooden chairs is used as an example. It bases its calculations on a country with 25 million homes, and on 1% of the families buying the chairs, which have a life of 25 years. Assuming 4 chairs per family, annually they need to make 40,000 chairs. To commence the proprietor decides to make 10,000 chairs per annum, say 200 per week equal to 40 per day. The land for the factory will allow for expansion. Each folding chair consists of the parts shown in the following Table127.

Each week 200 chairs are made and the working week is 40 hours per person. Each chair takes 40 minutes to make, say 0.67 hours and 200 chairs take 134 hours equal to 3.35 man-weeks. Say with other work, including receiving materials and maintenance etc. 4 man-weeks are required. Time per chair then amounts to 4 x 40 divided by 200 chairs equals 0.8 hours per chair. For the work two tradesmen are needed paid 1.24 MH per hour and 1 assistant at 1 MH per hour and 1 spray painter at 1 MH per hour. Therefore, the cost of the labour force in the workshop amounts to 4.48 MH per hour and the labour cost in making each chair amounts to 4.48 MH x 40 hours divide by 200 chairs amounts to 0.896 MH per chair.

TABLE 127

Wooden folding chair

Parts or operation	Time to make
8 seat slats	8 mins.
1 curved seatback	2 mins.
4 round bars (dowels)	4 mins.
2 seat sides mortised for slats	6 mins.
4 legs including sides for seat back and holes for dowels	6 mins.
Assembly of chair	10 mins.
Spray painting.	4 mins.
Total time	40 mins.

Overheads and profit	Value in MH
Building 4800 MH divide by 30 years	160.00
Machinery 5210 MH divide by 15 years	347.33
Building maintenance 4800 MH x 2%	96.00
Machinery maintenance 5210 MH x 5%	260.50
Office staff (1.5 + 1.3) MH x1900 hours	5320.00
Office expenses	1400.00
Insurance	242.20
Deliveries	625.00
Profit on capital 13010 x 4%	520.04
Profit on labour (4.48 +2.8) MH x 1900 hours x 10%	1383.20
Total cost	9354.27

The business buys the timber in bulk and requires 0.1593 cubic foot per chair plus 10% to allow for waste = 0.0159 cubic feet. It pays 0.69 MH per cubic foot for the timber. Therefore, the timber cost per chair amounts to (0.1593 + 0.0159) x 0.69 MH = 0.12 MH per chair. Each chair has 4 small triangular brass plates and they are connected by 6 special brass nuts and bolts. There are also two brass pins that run in slots in the legs and bolts in a sleeve to act as a hinge, allowing the legs of the chair to fold. These items are purchased at 0.09 MH per chair. The spray paint costs 0.025 MH per chair. Heating and power costs amount to 0.023 MH per chair. The total cost of these outside purchases amount to 0.258 MH and add to this the cost labour at 0.896 MH the manufacturing cost amounts to 1.154 MH per chair.

Overheads on the business would include the cost of the factory accommodation, the machinery used, and the office staff. The size of the factory building is 6 metres by 20 metres = 120 square metres. The construction cost is 40 MH per square metre and this includes the cost of the land. Therefore the cost of the accommodation amounts to 4800 MH and the building has a 30-year lifespan. The machinery costs 5210 MH and it has a 15-year lifespan. Building maintenance costs amount to 2% of the capital cost and for the machinery it is 5% of the capital cost. The business has a manager at a cost of 1.5 MH per hour, and a secretary/book-keeper at 1.3 MH per hour. The office expenses amount to 400 MH per annum, for the telephone, power and stationery. Deliveries cost 625 MH and insurance costs 242.20 MH per year. The liquid capital employed is 3000 MH. Fixed assets amount to 4800 MH for the building and 5210 MH for the machinery making a total of 10010 MH. Therefore total capital employed amounts to 13010 MH. Profit on capital allowed by MH system is 4% per annum and 10% per annum on the business' own labour-force. The total cost of the overheads and profit is as shown in Table 127 MH amounting to 9354.27 MH. The cost for overheads and profit per chair amounts to 9354.27 MH divide by the annual production 10000 chairs = 0.935 MH. The total cost for the workshop manufacturing, overheads and profit is 1.154 MH + 0.935 MH = 2.089 MH. per chair.

The business turnover amounts to 2.089 MH x 10000 chairs = 20890 MH. The estimated gross profit is 520.04 + 1383.20 = 1903.24 MH giving a 9.11% profit, based on the turnover. The overheads, including profit, amount to 44.8%, based on turnover.

A retailer could be working on 30% to cover his expenses and profit. The retail price of the chair would then amount to 2.089 MH x 130% = 2.716 MH (or MCU). With reference to Table 5 Volume 1, 1 MCU in December 1991 was worth £6.81 and in December 2001 it was worth £9.77: the chair value in £ Sterling was therefore worth £18.49 and £26.54 respectively.

With reference to the supply of timber for the chair manufacture the material could have been supplied from woodland in the region. The wood could have come from 100 years old trees, and each one would have given a yield of about 60 cubic feet. Each tree would have given a turnover of 60 x 0.69 MH = 41.4 MH. Each chair uses 0.12 cu. foot and 10000 chairs uses 1200 cu feet, or 20 trees per annum. Say there would be 100 mature trees per acre, of which 20% were suitable for chair manufacture. With a 100-year tree cycle a 100 acres of woodland would be required to initially supply the factory, and 400 acres (160 hectares) when it expanded to 40000 chairs per annum. The felling, transport and sawmill costs of the trees would absorb about half the sale value of the timber, leaving gross profit of about 20.70 MH per acre. Woodland maintenance costs would amount to 16.7 MH for maintenance and 4 MH for profit on the investment. The value of the woodland would be approximately 100 MH per acre (250 MH per hectare).

Pricing a range of products

Many projects, or schemes, are made to order. The contract for the work can be based on a specification and valued using bills of quantities, where each item has to be priced, including profit. The projects could contain thousands of items, including, research, temporary and permanent work. Some work might have to be on a cost plus basis. Such projects could be as follows:

• Houses and flats
• Factories, shops and offices

- Power stations, pipelines and treatment plants
- Roads, railways, canals and airfields
- Schools, hospitals, swimming pools, hotels and concert halls
- Ships, aircraft, turbines, cranes, tanks and computer systems
- Designs for the above projects and the management of them.

There are of course many thousands of products wanted to create the desired projects, whatever they may be. Each item is priced in the manner required, for example:

- Labour only
- Materials only
- Machines and equipment only
- Labour and materials and equipment used
- The above including expenses
- The latter including profit
- Designs only
- Management only
- A group of operations as a lump sum with, or without profit
- Temporary work only
- Research work only.

These would be calculated and built up in the manner used in the example for the folding chair. The information to achieve it could be based on a businesses own records and experience for similar work, or built up from tables of information, or supplied by other businesses. Experience estimators would be used for each type of specialist work, to ensure accurate pricing. Average productivity rates are needed to build up rates for both manual methods and using machines and equipment. Many productivity rates would need to be determined by businesses themselves, where they have their own special machines and methods of operation. The cost of subcontracts and materials can be judged by obtaining quotations from other specialist businesses.

Many types of contract are only for information; they do not provide the finished product, but only its form, for example, research, designs and management plans. These consultancy services often have to be priced before the work is undertaken. Experienced businesses would be able to plan all the stages of the work to be undertaken and fix a time to each element and price it, including the expenses for bought-in services.

Trial runs to determine price

Prices are based on productivity and it needs to be determined for untried methods, new machines and equipment, and working in new locations. Accurate data can be achieved by trial runs to obtain sound information. Future pricing can then be based on the studies and test results of the trials.

It should be noted that the MH system not only creates greater stability, but it can also reduce profit margins normally applied by some businesses with high profit margins. Accurate estimating is important to avoid underestimates.

Cost plus

Where accurate pricing is not possible, due to lack of information, or unforeseen events, a cost plus basis should apply to contracts for work. Sometimes insufficient time is allowed to obtain information, or it is too costly to carry out for a tender.

Prices would be agreed on the time worked by each trade, including their accepted wage productivity rate, as previously determined, plus materials, fuel, plant and equipment used. Overheads and profit would be added as previously explained. Where site overheads apply these would also be added.

Gains and losses

There would always be some gains and losses on items tendered. Overall the gains and losses should average out. Great care should be taken on pricing large valued items as a loss may not be balanced by smaller gains. Further a large gain may breach the MH trading rules. Under such circumstances a repayment may be due to the customer.

The average profit made on all the business turnover, or contracts, should be within the maximum profit limits set by the MH system trading rules.

There would always be variations causing under and over estimates in pricing, so a certain amount of 'give and take' is unavoidable and should not be abused by either party.

Contingencies

When applying the MH system trading rules contingency allowances are still used to cover unforeseen events, but they must not be used to boost profits.

Average costs

Many services given would vary in value for a similar, or the same result. For example, a surgeon in a hospital would carry out a routine operation, perhaps 10 or more times a day, and they may average 55 minutes each, but one could be as short as 40 minutes and another as long as 70 minutes. It is quite acceptable to base the price of the operation on their average cost, including materials and assistance.

Many professions could also apply an all-in hourly rate that not only covers their professional time, but the team supporting them, including overheads and profit.

Some services are based on appointments and an average time for a particular service. This too does not breach the MH trading rules. However the maximum profit limit over the year should not be exceeded.

Budget prices

Many customers may require budget prices on which they base their costs, or make provisional comparisons. Guidance should also be given concerning their degree of inaccuracy, for example plus or minus 10%. The business from past experience should know how accurate the budgets are, against projects completed. They can also mention the factors that increase, or decrease the budgets prices, like the type of materials used and natural conditions.

Budget prices can be given based on similar projects they have previously completed. The MH system can be used to update currencies that have devalued by using tables, like Table 30, Volume 1. However, if all the prices are first calculated in MH units, the prices would not normally require correction.

Buildings can be classified in types and be measured in square metres. In Volume 1, 85 MH has been used to value average domestic construction like houses and flats. Lump sum standard rates can be derived for many structures.

Certain types of metal fabrication can also be classified and paid for by a ton rate. Industries have developed various ways of pricing that are standard practice and these need not be altered by the use of the MH system. However, the profit criteria must be complied with.

Some budget estimates could be given on the large bulk items quite accurately and then a percentage added to cover all the small miscellaneous, or ancillary items, which might add 20% to the total estimate.

Natural resources

The harvesting or collection of natural resources vary depending on their location, and for crops, whether the year has been average, good, or bad. The resources can be either sold at the actual cost of growing and harvesting, or the cost of extraction as applicable. The important matter is to keep within the MH system profit limits. Average prices, over a number of years are acceptable, but all traders would need to work to the same system for the commodity. Market forces can also still be used to determine the price. Which ever system is used it must keep within the maximum profit criteria of the MH system to ensure stable and sustainable conditions.

One could say that it is common sense and human nature to buy the resources that are the best value, which in turn means those easiest to collect, or abstract. How global prices even out would vary and depend on international trade relationships.

The location of resources varies the price of them among and within nations. The present monetary system employed also affects their price as previously explained, probably to a much greater extent than just the resource location.

Climate

The national weather climate affects the animal and vegetable natural growth rate and the rate of human productivity. These factors all influence the final price of goods and services.

Quantity discounts

Using the MH system these can still apply. They can apply by making savings on storage and distribution, and in other ways, such as a large order that can increase the business efficiency.

Discounts for prompt payment

The MH system is designed for payments to be made within the normal trading period, either promptly or by the end of the month following the invoice date for accounts holders. If businesses, or individuals are in financial trouble, whatever the cause, bills are still honoured. The banking system picks up the troubled account at an early date and ensures the correct action is applied to solve the problem. Therefore trade discounts for prompt payment are not needed.

Safety at work

Clearly this is very important, as the whole object of the economy is to serve people and not the contrary. The level of safety has to be sensibly chosen, in that it must be affordable by the nation as a whole. The government, including sensible public opinion would set the standards that should be applied.

The responsibility does not rest only at government level and business managers, but also the employees, who must act responsibly. Safety is a collective responsibility and needs to be taught to the young generation from an early age in their education and in the family. The extra expense of preventative accident education would be more than offset by the savings in damage caused by accidents and this includes accident medical care. This would then ensure that the competitiveness with nations paying no attention to safety are not gaining an advantage. The policy would be long termed, but no more than many other investments made by businesses.

Pricing would need to take into account all safety issues including education and updating on knowledge concerning safety. Safety at work is part of the quality of life.

Wage rates

These rates have been covered in Volume 1, Chapter 3 Wage Negotiations, and therefore, no further information is given here.

General comments

The purpose of this Chapter has been to explain how natural valuations should be made and how the MH system modifies trading and pricing practices.

Many businesses are very experienced already and would not want a lengthy explanation on how to value products for sale, but would want to know how trading practice is modified by the MH system. Business and people not so familiar with estimating can find many books giving information they require, or can seek advice from specialists in business pricing and development.

The MH system techniques can be used for valuing existing assets in MH units (Master currency). Many assets can be revalued using the most modern creative methods to replace a product. Older assets, therefore, could be overvalued because modern methods are more efficient (the asset is made with less hours of human effort). Therefore, when using the MH conversion factor to revalue a product made on an old production line to correct for inflation, it would be more expensive than that made on a modern production line using a smaller labour force.

The owner of a project or business in the MH system is responsible for insuring his completed assets, and not the contractor.

CHAPTER 8

COMPETITIVENESS

Buyers are the cause of competition, because they seek good value for money, good quality and reliable products. However, some businesses do not have competitors, because they are the only maker or supplier of their product. Not all buyers have time to compare products and buy trusting the product is sound and fairly priced. Some customers are loyal to a business (goodwill), and support their activities without taking monetary value into account. This Chapter concentrates on those businesses that are or could be in competition.

Competition could arise solely at local level, or at regional, national and international level. Local competition is most likely in the service sector, whilst at all other levels in the production sector.

Under present circumstances most of the domestic products would be sold in shops and by mail, or email orders, and little bought direct from the manufacturer and other producers. Business purchases would be mainly from the producers and only smaller purchases from the retail sector.

The nature of competition

Although prices of products are very important to most buyers they are not the sole qualities sought. Goods of the same price would also be compared for various qualities. The design, or nature of the product is very important and must appeal to the buyer's tastes or requirements. It is also important that the product is adequate for the duty it is wanted. Products offered with guarantees also influence buyers. This latter requirement could make price and even quality sometimes irrelevant.

Businesses need to choose products that are wanted and also conform with the qualities buyers could be seeking. Producer's lines must allow for competition from similar products to ensure sufficient quantities for economic production. Generally, the more costly the product the greater care buyers take to ensure they have made the right choice. It should be noted that sales potential and quality for large purchases are often subject to quality control. Some products are reported on by buyer's organisations like 'Which' magazines.

Many low cost items sell if they appeal to the buyer at the time, and that is the only consideration given by the buyer. Not much is lost if the product is later found to be useless.

Selling products in a competitive market can be classified into two sections:
Those that are easily affordable and are wanted and bought against other competitors'
Quality products designed to meet the buyer's approval.
The MH system does not solve the problems in choosing products: it can only assist in making prices more competitive, and as a tool to estimate the cost of various solutions to find the

lowest cost of production and marketing. The other qualities that may be required would best be solved using the present market survey methods.

Business structures

In Chapter 7 the folding chair business was used to illustrate production of a simple product. Market experience could indicate that the price should be reduced. On examining the business structure two possible solutions were identified, one to increase productivity in the workshop and the other to reduce office expenditure.

Solution 1 is to increase the workshop productivity. It would also be necessary to increase the annual rate of production. This would allow a different process that would double the rate of production to 20000 chairs per annum, but it would be at a greater capital cost. It would also require two extra staff in the workshop, each at a rate of 1MH per hour. The office staff, being already of greater capacity than needed now that the business is established, can cope with twice the turnover. The additional capital of 4500 MH needed for the new and modified machinery would be borrowed at a rate of 6% APR. Solution 2 is to reduce the office staff to just the fulltime manager and a part-time book-keeper at 12 hours per week on the same rate of pay.

Solution 1

TABLE 128

The workshop wage bill	
2 tradesmen at 1.24 MH per hour 3 assistants at 1.00 MH per hour 1 spray painter at 1.00 per hour	2.48 MH 3.00 MH 1.00 MH
Total labour cost	6.48 MH
Overheads and profit	
Building 4800 MH divide by 30 years Machinery 9790 MH divide by 15 years Building maintenance 4800 MH x 2% Machinery maintenance 9790 x 5% Office staff (1.5 + 1.3) x 1900 hours Insurance Deliveries Interest payments 4580 MH x 6% Profit on capital 17590 MH x 4% Profit on labour (6.48 + 2.8) MH x 1900 x 10%	160.00 MH 652.67 MH 96.00 MH 489.50 MH 5320.00 MH 358.47 MH 1250.00 MH 274.80 MH 703.60 MH 1763.20 MH
Total cost	11468.24 MH

The labour cost per chair would amount to 6.48 MH x 1900 hours per annum divide by 20,000 chairs = 0.616 MH. The material power costs would remain at 0.258 MH and the total workshop cost would amount to 0.874 MH.

The revised figures for capital investment on machinery would be 5210 MH + 4580 MH = 9790 MH and the total capital employed would be 17590 MH. The over- heads would be as in Table 128 amounting to 11468.24 MH and divide this by 20000 chairs = 0.573 MH per chair. The total cost per chair for workshop and overheads is 0.874 MH + 0.573 MH = 1.447 MH. The business turnover amounts to 1.447 MH x 20000 chairs = 28940 MH. The gross profit amounts to 703.60 MH + 1763.20 MH 2466.80 MH: an 8.52% profit based on the turnover. The overheads including profit amount to 39.63% based on the turnover.

Solution 2

The reduction in cost for this solution would result from having a part-time book-keeper. Wage savings (40 – 12) x 1.3 MH x 52 weeks = 1892.80 MH, therefore profit would be reduced by 1892.80 MH x 10% = 189.28 MH and total savings would be 2082.08 MH a reduction of 0.208 MH per chair. The new price for the chair would be 2.089 MH – 0-.208 MH = 1.881 MH. The new turnover now amounts to 1.881 MH x 10000 = 18810 MH and the profit is reduced to 1903.24 MH – 189.28 MH = 1713.96 MH, a 9.11% profit based on the turnover.

Clearly solution 1 is the best. The increase in profit amounts to 2466.80 MH – 1903.24 MH = 563.56 MH. If the loan is paid off at the rate 458 MH over a 10 year period, the increase profit would clear the loan. If the turnover does not increase as anticipated the existing profits can cover the interest payments and the repayment of the capital, 274.80 MH and 458.00 MH respectively, a total of 732.80 MH.

International competition

At the present time the MH system is being used as a tool to study the world economies and its trading system. Tables 125 and 126 Chapter 5 illustrate the value of currencies in 1982 among developed and developing nations. By using the MH unit (MCU), one is able to compare the purchasing power of other currencies and the weakest in the Tables was approximately worth one sixtieth of the strongest. We now examine this in relation to business competitiveness. As an example the manufacture of a folding chair will again be used, but manufactured in a developing nation.

Making the folding chair in a developing country is assumed to be far more labour intensive. It is based on machinery being purchased from a developed country, but otherwise labour and materials are indigenous. It is decided to buy the chair from an Indian manufacturer.

The imported machinery to make the chair is bought in Italy at a cost of 1500 MH. Shipping adds 20% to the cost of the machinery = 300 MH making a total cost of 1800 MH. From Table 126 Indian buying power from Italy amounts to 3.94%. The MH capital value to allow for this is 1800 MH divide by 3.94% = 45685.28 MH (India) because they are unable to trade in MCU (MH units) Working capital used amounts to 60000 MH. The cost of the factory amounts to 9200 MH. Total capital employed would, therefore, amount to 45685.28 MH + 60,000 MH + 9200 MH =114885.28 MH.

TABLE 129
Wooden folding chair made in India

Parts or operation	Time to make
8 seat slats	32 min.
1 curved seat back	14 min
4 round bars (dowels)	6 min
2 seat sides mortised for slats	36 min
4 legs including sides for seat back and holes for dowels	20 min
Assembly of chair	15 min
Spray painting	6 min
Total time per chair	129 min (2.15 hr.)
Overheads and profit	Value in MH
Buildings 9200 MH divide by 30 years	306.67
Machinery 45685.28 MH divide by 15 years	3045.68
Tools (local) 250 MH divide by 15 years	16.67
Building maintenance 9200 MH x 2%	184.00
Machinery and tool maintenance 45685.28 MH x 5%	2284.26
Office staff (1.5 + 1.3 + 2 x 1.1) MH x 1900 hours	9500.00
Office expenses	400.00
Insurance	1262.70
Deliveries	1250.00
Profit on capital 114885.28 MH x 4%	4595.41
Profit on labour (14.16 + 5) MH x 1900 hours x 10%	3640.40
Total cost	26485.79

The estimated time to make one folding chair is 2.15 hours. 9 tradesmen would be employed on making the wooden parts of the chair at a rate of 1.24 MH per hour. 2 assistants would be employed assembling the chair and one spray painter each paid 1 MH per hour. The total cost for labour would be:

-	Tradesmen 9 x 1.24 MH =	11.16 MH
-	Assistants 2 x 1.00 MH =	2.00 MH
-	Spray painter	1.00 MH
Total		14.16 MH

Cost per folding chair for labour based on 200 chairs per week would be 14.16 MH x 40 hours per week divide by 200 = 2.832 MH per chair. The brass parts and power would cost 0.516 MH, double the cost than in the developed nation. Total workshop cost per chair amounts to 2.832 MH + 0.516 MH = 3.348 MH. Cost of overheads per chair 26485.79 MH divide by 10,000 MH = 2.649 MH. The total workshop cost for manufacturing one chair would be 3.348 MH + 2.649 MH = 5.997 MH.

Shipping costs to Europe amounts to 0.83 MH per cubic foot and the volume per chair amounts to 0.9 cubic feet. The shipping cost amounts to 0.83 MH x 0.9 = 0.747 MH per chair. Delivery cost in the country of import is 625 MH per 10000 chairs, therefore cost per chair amounts to 0.063 MH per chair. The cost of importing and selling the chair in the UK is shown in Table 130. Therefore, the wholesale price of the chair amounts to 0.908 MH + 0.685 MH = 1.593 MH per chair.

TABLE 130
Imported folding chair

Import cost of chair to UK	MH
The chair at 5.997 MH, divide by 61.30 (India UK buying power Table 125)	0.098
Shipping	0.747
Delivery in UK	0.063
Total	0.908
Wholesaler's costs	MH
Warehouse and office 2400 MH divide by 30 years	80.00
Building maintenance 2400 x 2%	48.00
Office staff 2.5 MH x 1900	4750.00
Office expenses	400.00
Insurance	242.20
Deliveries	625.00
Profit on capital 5800 MH x 4%	232.00
Profit on labour 4750 MH x 10%	475.00
Total	6852.20
Cost per chair 6852.20 MH divide by 10000	0.685

The revised UK cost for a folding chair is 1.447 MH against 1.593 MH for a chair imported from India. It is interesting to note how important transport costs are. The chair when assembled is quite bulky. The volume of timber used per chair amounted to 0.16 cubic foot per chair, 18%

of the volume of the assembled chair; i.e. one fifth of the volume of the assembled chair, a considerable saving. Let's now consider importing the parts only for the folding chair from India and only assembling and painting the chair in the UK.

The Indian manufacturing costs per chair as a result of the proposed change would be reduced by 21 minutes per chair as assembly and painting are now excluded. Only the tradesmen would now be employed at 11.16 MH per hour. Based on a 40-hour week the cost amounts to 2.232 MH per chair. Let it be assumed that the cost of the brass fittings and power requirements remain the same at 0.516 MH and the overheads remain at 2.652 MH. Therefore, total Indian factory costs are 5.400 MH and this divided by the UK buying factor, 61.30 (Table 125) = 0.088 MH per chair. Shipping cost is reduced by one fifth, i.e. 0.747 MH x 20% = 0.149 MH, delivery costs remain at 0.063 MH, giving an imported cost for the chair parts amounting to 0.30 MH per chair.

The UK factory importing the folding chair parts has only to assemble and paint the chairs, taking a time of 21 minutes per chair. Say 2 employees in the workshop are required at 1 MH per hour. Annual cost for this labour is 2 x 1.00 MH x 1900 hrs. = 3800.00 MH. With an annual production 10000 chairs the cost per chair amounts to 0.38 MH.

TABLE 131
With parts imported for folding chair

Office overheads	MH
Warehouse and office 2400 MH divide by 30 years	80.00
Machinery 1100 MH divide by 15 Years	73.33
Building maintenance 2400 x 2%	48.00
Machinery maintenance 1100 MH x 5%	55.00
Office staff 1.5 MH x 1900 hours	2850.00
Office expenses and workshop power	500.00
Insurance	242.20
Deliveries	625.00
Profit on capital 6400 MH x 4%	256.00
Profit on labour 2850 MH x 10%	285.00
Total cost per annum	5014.33
Cost per chair 5394.53 MH divide by 10000	0.501

Total cost per chair, imported parts 0.30 MH, workshop assembly 0.38 MH and overheads 0.501 MH amounts to 1.181 MH. This is a much better price with the parts manufactured in India and assembly and painting in the UK factory: this last method is the one that could be adopted.

The above estimating process illustrates the process needed to make a business more competitive under present economic conditions. Had the Indian business been able to buy the machinery in its own country it would have saved a considerable some of money due to the buying power factor caused by the world currency distortions Tables 125 and 126. If the world had already implemented the MH system the UK business would not have considered importing from India, instead it would have been exporting to it at affordable rates, or investing in the developing nations making products for their consumption, thereby improving their standard of living..

It is hoped that the simple examples chosen have highlighted the problems that the producer sector of the economy is facing in the present form of free market trading. The present system only helps the trading part of the service sector to become more competitive and often very profitable at the expense of the rest of the economy: it is unfair to the skilled and unskilled labour force and the production sector of the economy (Volume1 Table 36). The present system is overvaluing many products which it sells, and undervaluing the products of the production sector and peoples' wages and pensions. The instability this creates fuels unfairness and poverty in both developed and developing nations.

The MH system as a tool

The examples given in this book are based on correct and sustainable wages for their productiveness, which includes for the investment in their skills. In the present economic system people are paid market prices. Therefore, the figures calculated must also be adjusted for market wage rates. Different countries wages rates can be compared against the MH unit wage negotiation structure as in Volume 1 Chapter 3. These could be more or less than the MH true value based on real productivity and skills investment. Each skilled used must be checked. However, in present economies labour market rates fluctuate, necessitating a safety margin to be added to the estimates. The safety margin would also need to take into consideration fluctuating currency rates. The present international economic system creates risks due to its instability. One cannot forecast how markets will react. The MH system removes varying labour rates and currency risks and allows economies to become stable.

Where markets rates for wages are above the MH value, and a product requires them to be more competitive, a business can try and negotiate wages on the MH basis. The negotiations would need to include reasons for the need to adopt a fair wage system.

It can be observed that the MH system allows businesses to engineer their competitiveness.

CHAPTER 9

TAXATION

So far all the modelling and pricing excludes the different forms of taxation, or if used is a simple flat tax, an income tax on a person's earnings. The MH economic system is based on the natural principle that the sole purpose of the economy is to serve people. The tax is collected to pay for services given by government bodies that are responsible for managing and guiding the economy, and in most countries also providing health, education, invalidity benefits and pensions: these latter type services could be supplied by the business private sector and could be paid for that way instead of from taxation.

In present economies there are many forms of taxation, some being paid by businesses and institutions, and the rest by the population. The following are some of these taxes:

Income tax
Purchase tax or value added tax,
Customs duties and excise duties
Business or corporate taxation
Capital gains
Wealth taxes
Local authority taxes
Licences of various forms
Taxation on income from interest payments and dividends
Death duties
National health and pension taxes

One could say a whole army of people are employed by government bodies and the private sector calculating and agreeing the sums to be paid. The taxation systems can be very complicated, needing many experts to help businesses and people on how to save on taxation by altering their business methods, structures or timing of sales, etc. Each nation's taxation system is different and some small countries are tax havens.

Pensions are built up from savings: however, on retirement the pensions received are often taxable although tax was already paid on the person's earnings. When this happens the earnings are taxed twice. This means a person needs a much larger pension to cover the unknown tax rate that could be required from his pension!

In a natural modern world economy the real purpose of taxation is to pay for the services of government bodies that manage our economies from the local district level to the international level. The taxes would also pay for services which are not available from the private sector, or best provided by the government sector. The taxation rate would differ among nations, as the structure and degree of development of each country is different.

It has already been explained that all exchanges for goods and services take place in businesses and institutions. It is here that the money we have earned is distributed to those that have provided the goods and services, and where it is most economic to pay taxes. Anyone supplying labour to others for employment works in a business, (that includes the self-employed), or an institution of some form, and this includes government bodies. The tax could be an income tax, a value added tax, or a license fee. What is important is that the tax is collected for the least human effort and in a way that the majority believe to be honest and fair. The taxation system must also take into account how people support their families and businesses function in competition internationally.

It is important for government to have a regular flow of income. Money is created from people in employment, who need employment to earn their living. Generally speaking in any well-run economy there is always more work to be done than the labour force can achieve. This is because, as a nation, we have a planned future direction for the improvement of our economy to serve our desired needs and wants. The business economy has to take more risk than the individual employee; and government economies and employees are a more stable source for tax revenue than the business and the private sector economy. The government has records of the working population and can base its tax revenue calculations on normal working hours of 1900 hours per person. With a soundly run economy unemployment would be very low.

The business and private institution sector can be involved not only with the national economy, but the international economy, resulting in unstable income patterns, created by competition, new and better products, and resource problems. Any taxation taken from businesses is passed on to buyers, therefore returning it back to the national labour force. In other words, it is not sensible to tax institutions and businesses, but only to use them to collect taxes payable on the labour force. This would then help all businesses internationally to assess their competitiveness more accurately.

From the explanation of the economy given in Volume 1, the general public would understand why they are being taxed on their earnings, and how they need to conduct their lives in a sustainable form of national and world economy. They would understand how to budget for their family and lifestyle, and that when their financial needs are greatest they may need to work longer hours to support their children and house purchase. Government could help by not charging any tax on hours of work exceeding 1900 per annum. Government could help the savings problem for pensioners by excluding pensions income from taxation, but any earnings from work activities could still be taxable.

From the above form of analysis, the MH system would recommend that the majority of tax would be collected by the local district authority on a flat tax basis, a single percentage rate on income earned on 1900 hours of work per annum. The local districts would fund the regions and central government budgets. The minimum of other local taxes would be charged, for specific services to the business/ institution sector, but not based on their profits, only for the service given.

CHAPTER 10

ANALYSING AND UNDERSTANDING ECONOMIES

The previous chapters of this book have been concerned with the key elements of the economy and how they should be structured and developed to be sustainable. In this Chapter some existing businesses are going to be analysed and discussed; and then various matters concerning the economy.

Using Tables 101 – 110 and Table 132 the maximum permitted profits for the four businesses are now studied. The figures in this paragraph represent millions. Let us assume 'A' has labour costs amounting to £55 and 'B' £210, as they were not given in the company statements. The MH System maximum permitted business profit for business 'A' is 10% x £55 + 4% x £835 = £38.9, and based on the turnover the maximum profit should not exceed 26.6%, but its profit was 49.8%. The MH System maximum profit for business 'B' is 10% x £210 + 4% x £900.4 = £57.0, and based on the turnover the maximum profit should not exceed 3.4%, but its profit was 9.3%. The MH System maximum business profit for business 'C' is 10% x £246 + 4% x £2790 = £136.2, and based on the turnover the maximum profit should not exceed 2.3 %, but its profit was 9.8%. The MH System maximum business profit for business 'D' is 10% x £93 + 4% x £2757 = £119.6, and based on the turnover the maximum profit should not exceed 7.17%, but its profit was 12.6%. The following list shows by how much the businesses exceeded the MH system recommended sustainable profits:

> Business 'A' 187%
> Business 'B' 274%
> Business 'C' 426%
> Business 'D' 176%

The total profits of the four businesses amounts to £1021.2 million and the permissible profit based on the MH system amounts to £351.7 million. Therefore, the profit taken amounts to 2.89 times more than permitted when using the MH system. As mentioned previously, most of the profit has been retained, and no doubt each business would have its reasons.

All profits need to be affordable, just like taxes must be. If they are not, the peoples' standard of living is going to fall. With reference to the businesses 'A' to 'D' the dividends paid on the shares owned by citizens, or their pension funds, are not being paid more than they should under the MH system rules, and they are not benefiting from the high profits, which are being used by the businesses. Can the businesses really justify the excessive profits that are being taken, to allow them solely to grow more quickly, and for no other reason? Clearly, like families, businesses also should have financial constraints. The MH system allows businesses to borrow money, based on security, at low rates of interest, never exceeding 6% APR.

How efficient are economies? Are they wasting human effort when 10% of the working population is unemployed, and all have to be supported by subsidies? Suppose taxation is raised to cover half an average wage for the unemployed on the 90% of the workforce remaining in employment and this equals 5% of the tax budget based on full employment. This would increase the taxation on the employed by 5.55% just to support the unemployed. Are business investments being properly utilised and not written off too early? Are all take-overs making production more efficient, or is it purely empire building? To answer these questions stable economies are required and a sound set of calculations. This can only be achieved using the MH system. The 5.55% Tax mentioned has the same effect on the purchasing power of money as net rent, and can be added to the other net rents already mentioned.

TABLE 132
Based on actual company financial reports
(Figures in £ millions)

Description	Company			
	A	B	C	D
1 Fixed assets	670.7	943.7	354.0	3368.0
2 Current assets	202.2	206.9	493.0	431.0
3 Creditor amounts				
falling due after one year	37.9	250.2	-	1040.0
4 Net assets	835.0	900.4	847.0	2757.0
5 Turnover	146.0	1680.4	5914.0	1668.0
6 Operating turnover	-	-	955.0	-
7 Labour costs	-	-	246.0	93.0
8 Outside purchases	-	-	262.0	1302.0
9 Profit	55.3	-	-	-
10 Other income	17.4	-	-	-
11 Total profit	72.7	155.5	582.0	21
1.0				
% based on turnover	(49.8%)	(9.3%)	(9.8%)	(12.6%)
% on shareholders' funds	(8.7%)	(17.2%)	(20.9%)	(7.7%)
12 Taxation and minority				
interests	3.3	46.6	205.0	57.0
13 Retained profits	60.0	31.0	252.0	98.0
% based on turnover	(41.1%)	(1.8%)	(4.3%)	(5.9%)
% on shareholders' funds	(7.2%)	(3.4%)	(9.0%)	(3.6%)
14 Dividends	9.4	77.9	83.0	56.0
% based on turnover	(6.4%)	(4.6%)	(1.4%)	(3.3%)
% on shareholders' funds	(1.1%)	(8.7%)	(3.0%)	(2.0%)
% on value of shares	(6.5%)	(38.9%)	(63.4%)	-
15 Value of ordinary shares	144.1	200.0	131.0	-
16 Shareholders' funds	835.0	900.4	2790.0	2757.0
17 Par value of shares	100.0p	50.0p	10.0p	50.0p

As has already bean related, when money is spent this is the point when our human effort is distributed to various parties for the goods, or services received, and Table 3 Volume 1 shows a typical distribution. If businesses are efficient with all resources, including the human element, the best value would be available for the buyer. At the same point, the business (or the self employed person) can collect taxes. Governments can either take all taxes needed from the employee's wages (and self employed), some of it, or all from the profits of the business. It does not really matter. But, to be truthful, in reality it is the employees and self-employed (all the working population) that really pay the tax. Further, as tax really in the end comes from the buyers and the economy is theirs, as they have collectively created it, they are the ones that should pay the tax, not the businesses. However, it does makes sense for the businesses to be the tax collectors, on behalf of the government.

Most people are well aware that they really pay all the tax and most appreciate that it is for the services rendered by government, usually without profit. There is no need for governments to make a profit, as tax is collected to cover all their requirements to provide the service and pensions. Provided government personnel are properly trained there is no reason why they should not be just as skilful as persons in the private sector. On this basis some services can be provided at less cost than in the private sector. However, if a business is too large it is not possible for its top manager to devote the attention needed, to ensure efficiency. Government policy should take this into account.

Many factors affect the efficiency of a business. Basically, for equal quality, it is the production of the product for the minimum human effort, i.e. with the MH System the minimum number of MH units. To achieve this there is frequently a vast range of human aids from the simplest tools and machines to some of the largest and most complicated tools and machines, computers and software. Using the aids and taking into account the human hours of productivity to provide them, they together with the human productive effort, can lower the cost of the product, compared with previous methods of production. The manner in which products are produced, whatever they may be, is an art, and requires very skilful persons. The personnel with the best resources would be able to produce the most economic products.

The scale of production for any given product can also affect the price of it. Often the larger the quantity needed, the lower the production cost can be made. This results from being able to use more productive methods due to the larger scale operation required. However, oversized production lines can increase costs if the line cannot be run near to maximum capacity. Forecasting turnover is most important, and the more stable the economy the easier it is to do so. Over-production can mean additional storage. Using the same production line 24 hours a day can make the best use of the capital cost and lower the product price.

Stable money internationally would make it easier to plan the life of production lines. If labour costs sea-saw among nations, the lines may be economic one year in one country and the next in another, or they may never be economic again and have to close down before full use of them has been made. The MH System's monetary unit has the same value internationally. All that is required when using it is for businesses to ensure the same equipment and human skills and wage structures are used in each country.

Some businesses have more stable markets than others. For example given a population, they would all require necessities: food, clothing and shelter throughout their lives. These markets are fairly stable and only gradually change shape as new and more products are introduced. Luxuries, our other human wants, are very numerous and demand can change more quickly, or even cease over night. If a catastrophe should occur funds first maintain the necessities before the luxuries, therefore luxuries are less stable. Businesses in a monopoly situation do not have the same problem as those in competition and, if a necessity, can be very stable provided there is a continual flow of work to keep the business working full time.

Clearly for business to survive they should be aware of market fluctuations for their products. They must also understand the life expectancy of their products and how quickly they can sometimes cease, caused by the introduction of new products. The fewer the products the business has, the greater the risk of the workload fluctuating or ceasing. The more the products lines a business has, the smoother the overall workload. A business specialising in a sector needs to try and cover the whole range in that sector to give a smooth workload. Obviously one needs to choose lines of business that are well understood by the business.

Teamwork helps in most businesses. A quickly changing workforce is unlikely to achieve this. Most businesses have in-house information and methods of working that have to be learnt and properly understood. All sorts of facts and information belong only to the particular business and are of no use to others. Often a labour force, or parts of it, cannot be easily replaced and accordingly can be considered as part of the business. They are vital partners, but their skills are their own.

Many businesses are associated with local areas, towns and regions, and the people's skills serve those industries. Some industries do not have steady workloads, and if the workforce were retained in periods of slack work this would add to the cost of the product. It is practical for the workforce to have other skills they can use in other industries, or other work needed to be carried out at some time in the locality. Clearly industries and regional authorities need to work closely with each other to create sustainable work conditions in their region's economy. Sound information readily available is needed for this purpose.

It is often stressed that competition creates lower prices and better products. However, when considering the millions of products and skills, in fact, for many industries there is no competition: as there is insufficient time to compare all the products. Probably most products are bought in good faith: that they are sound and good value. Many products are special and produced in small quantities, because the national or world demands are small. Many product prices are being continually varied, and it is not only inflation causing this.

There are few products that are bought frequently allowing people to remember whether the price has changed. Given a stable MH System it is possible to create an information service giving prices of items that can be compared. However, local conditions can also influence prices, where sale turnovers of products are low: for example, because of the small size of a community, or the distance from the sources of production. Guidance can of course be given on extra costs for these situations.

New methods do not only produce cheaper production, but can also create products that improve the quality of life. Many such products are bought not because they are cheap, but are wanted. The form of the MH System takes into account the price of what we buy, which frequently is not governed by competitive forces. That is why it sets limits on net rents distributed at the time of sale of the product. The first control is a macro one; and involves checking through tax return information to ensure that the profits taken do not exceed the limits set. However, depending on results of further studies, governments may well except average profit over the years, but not exceeding the limits set, because business turnovers can vary from one year to another in an unpredictable way. As deemed necessary, other micro economic checks would also be made. It can probably be said that most of us accept in life constraints are a natural event. For example, businesses need to control their operations and in doing so set constraints as necessary within which employees must comply: like not to waste materials, only to buy materials at the required rate and to only carry out extensions that are necessary. Governments need to ensure the right balance of products, particularly the ones we need, and that the people are willing to work for them. After all the very purpose of the economy is primarily to serve families.

For best results the management levels must be carefully chosen as each manager must be fully in control and qualified to supervise the operation he is responsible for. Senior managers must be fully aware of the capabilities of their managers and be able to guide them whenever required. At the lower levels foremen, section leaders, or department heads, should be intimate with the abilities of their staff, or workforce, and able to guide them whenever required.

From the foregoing calculations and information in Table 121 (National estimated fixed and liquid assets) and in this Chapter, it is clear a considerable amount of capital is in used in industries and national infrastructure. Much of it is in the private sector. Most of the assets are in a fixed form and, in the example given, amount to approximately five times the workforce annual earnings. The capital employed does of course vary from nation to nation and is different among businesses, and what it can produce would also be different. But in general terms the higher the industrial technology and development, the more it would produce for its citizens, provided the economy is in equilibrium. The assets giving the best results must be the ones really needed by the economy, i.e. those in daily use. The fixed assets and the liquid assets (goods and services), must all be maintained by the nation's workforce. The more the assets the more there is to be maintained. Clearly there is a limit to how much the workforce can maintain, and on their willingness to work the hours required to do so.

Further, private housing assets equivalent to one and a half year's earnings has also been identified. To these must be added the domestic fixed assets, we use, including motorcars and our other treasures, or objects like antiques and hobby items. These could well amount to another year's earnings. These too must be maintained. Some family assets are maintained by outside services, but much of what we own is looked after in the family economy. Some maintenance is a hobby activity. The goods are cared for to varying degrees of repair. The lack of repair would affect the MH value.

A nation also has other assets that are not in demand and therefore not in use. They are either perfectly sound, or in various states of deterioration. Many are not maintained, allowing their value to deteriorate until someone wants them. Then, if required they can be valued in MH terms, either based on original methods of production, or using modern methods.

The money to buy assets is restricted by how frequently we exchange the fixed assets and the money supply, our annual earnings. Much of the annual earnings are spent on consumable items and maintenance. The savings are used to buy new or second hand assets, and this applies to both family and the business sector, including government services. The money supply only increases if people work longer hours. Developed nations are likely to allow families to decide their own working hours in the general economy, provided they are supporting their family. Developing nations may well require people to work longer hours than in developed nations.

How safe is our money? Business and private fixed assets and products for sale back money in circulation, current accounts, and saving accounts. In a very sound economy, where we are providing all the goods and services we really need, and understand our economy at all levels, family, business and government, our money is very safe, i.e. a sustainable economy. However, there will always be natural and manmade catastrophes that could upset the stability of the economy. Dependant on the severity of the catastrophe, it could collapse the economy, or put fringe industries at risk, as a result of resources being redirected. Some businesses could find that sales could slow or cease, until the damage to the economy has been repaired. Money backing industries affected by the crisis could be lost. However, funds received from insurance cover would aid in minimising the loss.

In stable economies, based on sound information and moving in a planned step by step direction, it would be clear which industries are in decline and need regeneration to meet fresh demands. Well-run businesses would stop production of failing lines at an optimum point and reshape to other lines that are in demand. Its shareholders, or owners, would use their money to back their calculated risks and the profits permitted by the economic system. Banks would have to check that the businesses are soundly based ensuring repayment of loans. Commercial, or venture capital banks would use money that is intended to be at risk, in order to give a better return than on safer investments. With the MH system such banks would only deal in that form of business, and would carefully choose the ones expected to be successful.

Although the MH System sets levels for net rents, it does not mean that governments cannot lower them if they determine that they must be lowered, based on statistical evidence, investigation, and sound analysis. Governments must balance the effect of all net rents taken with the needs of the economy, and ensure they are truly affordable.

Governments would need to decide whether business profits, share income and other income should be taxed. Clearly net rents should be kept as low as possible, and one way of ensuring they are is not to tax them. Businesses, including shareholders, are the ones that maintain the value of the assets and are taking risks. Where royalties are the property of a business they are treated as a business. Investment income frequently comes from the retained profits reinvested in the business and this can increase the business size and turnover, which in turn could increase the value of the shares and the dividends.

One of the real purposes of shares is to spread risk and produce a higher return on one's investment. It also allows larger business ventures to commence, where the proprietor lacks the capital required. Ordinary shareholders place their investment at 100% risk, so should choose the investment carefully. Preference shares are the first to receive a dividend where profits are low. Or in an event of bankruptcy, or liquidation, they should have prior call on funds in advance of ordinary shareholders; but their share investments are also at risk to the value of 100%.

With the MH system insurance is used to protect against any major risks, of fire and theft, or other major events causing loss. The calculated business risks should not be covered by insurance companies, but by the other risk measures discussed, and by those persons who are prepared to back those risks. The clear purpose of insurance is to protect against major misfortunes, and accordingly there should be no exclusions. The assets of insurance companies would need to be relatively flexible as they cannot forecast in which sector peak claims would come from, although generally claims can be expected to cover a normal pattern of events.

Pensions can be provided in various ways: from taxation, pension funds, or by a combination of these two forms. At one time one could say that pensions were provided by the family or community, where younger generation working members would support the elderly, who were no longer able to work and support themselves, but who contributed to the assets that backed the local economy. In modern economies this is not so easy, as frequently specialised skills prevent families living closely. The service therefore needs to be bought in, and the payments covered by the parent's savings. Where the size of the population remains stable one can say that the government pension tax element taken from the working families are immediately transferred to the retired parents. This is a very efficient method for the basic pension, and eliminates the cost of managing pension funds and solves the problems of those that cannot save, but who must spend at the same rate as they earn! Where there are large population bulges, governments can create investments to cover these events, i.e. they always tax at the right rate from every taxpayer and save the surpluses they do not pay out (due to smaller numbers of pensioners) until they are required. Bulges in population come before the people retire, so governments can budget in advance the amount that would be wanted. The problem now in the U.K., due largely to six million abortions these last 25 years, is the converse of the bulge: too few young workers to support an increasing geriatric population. This new situation is true of the west generally. The MH system is supportive of stable family life, which itself would help to redress this problem.

The funds people may require above the basic pension can be provided for in the manner they choose: their own savings, or pension funds. However, these pension funds must be very safely invested and rolled over in various sound investments until they are required. Pension funds used to finance house mortgages is one sound solution, particularly in stable economies, as the risk is very well spread in an essential part of the economy.

The existing economic system, driven by market forces, supply and demand, and the payment of large net rents causes major instabilities. In the UK property prices have sawed to levels considerably higher than their net worth, their construction cost. They have sometimes sold for more than double their real value. Businesses and speculators have done well, but many ordinary citizens have suffered damage that should never have happened. The MH System allows all prices to be valued in MH units and its rules do not allow excessive profits. By having lists of products priced in MH units, stable examples are available for comparison, and people can always obtain a professional valuation on the MH basis. For certain precious arts of work, which are not basic needs and everyday wants, the MH system does not prevent anyone from purchasing and paying higher net rents than can be justified, but the original proper production cost of the item should be available, so the buyer knowingly pays the net rent offered to gain the product. Governments would need to keep a watchful eye on such transactions, so that net rents taken never get out of hand, and upset the balance of the economy. Another example where excess net rent may be paid is for land that is needed for expansion adjoining existing development. Yet clearly exceptions must be limited.

Summarising the points made

The management of net rents in an economy is vital to ensure its proper balance, and fairness in distributing the goods and services we have collectively made. Suppose the 10% net rents on labour employed in the businesses, and 4% on capital employed, were doubled. The original 36.87% net rent (Table 124) added to each unit of money would double to 0.7374 units. Therefore, actual net rent that would be taken out of the purchasing power of each unit of money would be 42.4% (i.e. a GDP of 173% based on wages) reducing the purchasing power of money to 57.6%. Businesses and the richer population with shares and savings, and the skilled, are the ones receiving the net rents that would help them recoup some of the loss of some of the reduced purchasing power of the money; but the other say 50% of the population without any investments, or very little, and with unskilled occupations would not receive any net rent. Yet they are just as important to the success of the overall economy as the skilled and the investors. Such a system is not a fair distribution of wealth created and could cause unnecessary hardship for the unskilled. The economy would not be looking after their interests. Using the MH System and the proposed maximum net rents limits on the profits, increases the purchasing power in the foregoing example, as it would go from 57.6% to 73%, giving 15% more purchasing power. The economic system belongs to all of us and must therefore serve everyone and not just some, as is happening to date in most economies. With wage to GDP varying 1:1.3 in the UK overall this appears to be satisfactory, without a detailed analysis being made. It should be noted that people on the UK minimum wage are losing about 26% of their money's purchasing power.

Sound economies should not have high rates of unemployment and underemployed, nor wages not reflecting people's real productivity.

This Chapter highlights the fact that when money is spent is the point when an individual's labour is distributed: as Table 3, Volume 1. The distribution takes place within the business. Taxes can be collected, and net rents paid on the purchase of labour, goods and services.

The labour sold should balance with the products bought. At this same point governments can allow certain key services, forming say a part of the national infrastructure, to take additional profit to be used only to develop their service: it could be like a tax. It could be suggested by businesses themselves, or by government, but would need to be approved by government, who would ensure it was affordable, bearing in mind other local or national priorities and conditions. This would be more economic than borrowing money, or increasing its share capital.

Banking regulations require banks taking public deposits to have 8% liquidity based on the deposits held, to cover variation in the rates of deposits and withdrawals. This covers the turnover of all the customers' deposits in both current accounts and savings accounts. In the MH System the money in current accounts remains in the ownership of the depositors, so the banks do not need the 8% liquidity for them, but only for the money in the savings accounts, on which interest is normally paid. The banks, therefore, do not have to tie up assets for the risks in handling the current accounts. They do, however, have to check that the promises to pay are honoured. The MH System ties up less capital and allows it to be used more efficiently, thus is more efficient.

National economies do have to be managed to keep them in equilibrium, and should not be just left to market forces, businesses and families to run. It has been shown how these economies become out of balance without a proper measure for money and a corresponding standard for trading rules.

Adequate and sound information is necessary in modern world economies, which in 2006 are becoming out of touch with the millions of skills and products available.

The main points mentioned explain why modern economies are performing so unfairly, and are also contributing to many of the world's other problems.

CHAPTER 11

THE BENEFITS OF STABLE ECONOMIES

Sustainable economies can give the following benefits:

1 A complete explanation of the purpose of the economy,
2 Stable government structures to manage the economies,
3 Sound information system,
4 A trading system that is stable, fair and honest,
5 A very stable financial system that eliminates inflation,
6 An economy people business and government can understand,
7 A sound education system and,
8 Sound business products for the private sector.

We will now enlarge on the above headings in the order just given.

A complete explanation of the purpose of the economy.

In Volume 1 the nature of the key elements of the natural economy were given with simple models showing the shape of an economy that supplies the family needs. The key purpose of the economy is to provide goods and services that families cannot, or wish not to provide. The business private sector and government sector provide these requirements. These sectors have specific duties, which include the way we naturally develop sustainable economies using our skills in making and planning our economies within our capacity. This process takes into account our human capabilities and weaknesses and how dependant we are on each other throughout the world, studying the natural economy and past mistakes, and correcting them. Conflicts and wars need not happen. There are restraints on what we do. We should protect each other's rights and live in harmony with the environment: our home and provider of natural resources. We need to be fair and honest and support cultures and ethics that are just; improve our quality of life, and not create harmful conflicts that can cause hell instead of paradise. The majority of the world population want peace and harmony. The minority that cause conflict must be taught to understand it is not wanted, and this can only be cured by sound explanation, sometimes a long education process, correcting perhaps unbalanced previous experience that could have caused the problem. There is no other way to create the trust needed.

The knowledge in the world is available to make it a better place to live in, and what is required is the sustainable management system and the will to create it.

Stable government structures to manage the economies.

MH System develops its government strategy from how local districts, regions and countries economies naturally work, interact and develop. Local districts and regions are self-supporting as they can be, within the capacity of the resources they have. They then need to buy in the resources they lack, by selling the resources they have in surplus. They are the ones most likely to have the greatest amount of knowledge concerning their region. Governments are required to co-ordinate the balances of the regional economies and provide a sound common trading system, which in turn works with the other nations of the world to manage a sustainable and achievable world economy in harmony with the rest of the natural environment. Such governments do need to understand how the world's workforce and industry need to function and interact to develop the right management structure and international trading rules. The MH System is based on this form of specification.

With this form of government structure, the private sector of the economy would be able to maintain and plan its operations more easily. Governments would oversee the stable direction in which the economies were moving and be able to plan its operations on sounder information.

Sound information system.

The proposed world information system would use one international language and be integrated and made as complete as possible. As already indicated in Volumes 1 and 2, it would have a structure based on the key components of the economy. The benefits of this would be that it would form a basis on which everyone could learn the content of our complicated economy and find information more easily. The information layout also forms the basis of the economic model of each local district and region, making it easier to compare economies. Every business would be in the system.

The system would be used to locate products, skills and potential business throughout the world, and access information on the economies.

A trading system that is fair and honest.

The MH rules of the trading system have been designed to take into account that people must be properly supported by the economy in balance with their hours of productive labour, and the business sector: an environment that allows fair competition and profits that are sustainable, and lets all sectors of the economy function properly.

All businesses would be entitled to make profits, but none would be allowed to overcharge as this upsets the balance of the economy. However, if too many businesses were in competition some would fail. It would be up to businesses to ensure they were investing in the right products and lines of business, which would be easier in the stable form of economy to assess.

Planning business in stable economic conditions would be easier as prices would be stable and markets for goods and services steadier over the whole range of the economy.

A very stable financial system that eliminates inflation.

The financial system is based on a Master Currency: a defined productivity unit based on the hour. Such a unit eliminates all the problems created by inflation and allows prices of goods and services throughout the world to be compared accurately. Ideally the national currencies should be pegged to the Master Currency into a convenient number of units like 6 or 10, and it would be better if all nations made the same choice.

For stability of the monetary system interest rates must be low, to prevent distorting the monetary exchange system, as has been explained in other Chapters. Net rents, completely unearned income, are restricted to sustainable levels. This allows very stable long term monetary planning, important to both families and businesses. The very low interest rates make borrowing easier. Islamic countries do not have to charge interest, which is quite acceptable and sound.

Tables 101 to 110 indicate the permissible sustainable profits for the business and the shareholders, or proprietors. Businesses can expand by raising capital by issuing more shares, or borrowing from banks and other financial institutions.

Inflation would not exist, so saving would not be eroded. Both businesses and families need savings. Savings for pensions would be very long-term. Table 121 indicates the amount that could be available and other savings, which would be shorter termed, as some of the family models in Volume 1 indicate. Businesses and other institutions too would have savings for shorter periods, until required. With Master Currency economies the pattern of savings and borrowings would also become more stable, all helping to make planning easier.

With a single world currency there would be no losses due to fluctuating currencies. However, countries would need to keep imports and exports generally in balance. As the MH System comes into operation the currencies would converge step by step so that the world economy could adjust at a suitable pace without creating economic shocks, thus giving the economy time to reshape efficiently.

As economies return to natural skill balances for each country, full type employment would return. With this happening, and so more income, more business would result. Countries would become increasingly sustainable, with a fairer, more informed political direction.

An economy people and business can understand.

People and businesses would know the direction in which the economy was going, given a well set up structure, and paths of good communication. The economic system can be well explained so people would know how it operates to support our standard of living. Everyone would know what the taxes are for and where they were spent. They would know that work is needed to support their family and the economy. Children would soon learn money does not grow on trees, and education was an essential serious matter! In short, all parts of the MH Economic System can be explained and justified.

With easier trading conditions and communication it would be easier for many businesses to set up in other countries. Some countries could want to export more than it needs to import. Where its businesses have products with considerable international demand they could set up factories in countries that lack exports. The integrated information system would help to obtain all the details required.

A sustainable economic system would allow people and businesses to make long term plans, and this would help to generate business and work, increasing everyone's standard of living.

A sound education system

The education system is the engine that will drive the sustainable economy forward. It would explain to people how we would need to respect each other and support each other's human rights. This is because we are all dependant on millions of other people's work to support our lives. Therefore, we need to be fair and honest and not destructive, which only destroys our assets and causes unnecessary ill feeling. Children from an early age do understand the difference between right and wrong given good guidance and not left to do as they please. Parents must have time to spend with their children, so that they can patiently explain the world to them and how they must behave. This is why in the MH models in Volume 1 only one parent is working: see Chapter 9 Volume 1.

Children have much to learn for both their domestic lives and working occupations. Good health too is very important, including avoiding accidents. People need to know much about the everyday activities we all need. This would help to avoid damaging and spoiling all the aids and facilities we use everyday. Because past education has lacked many important daily activity knowledge £ millions of damage occurs, that given the right form of education could have been avoided. It is in both business and government interest that children's education from the earliest age is not neglected, and will help to make parents tasks much easier. Economies need to get all balances right.

The structure of the information system will help people to learn what the economy consists of. There is a vast range of exciting and interesting occupations available, even within one's own local habitat. It is good for children to learn how all the items we use have developed. Often children prefer real jobs to toys. Practical toys are often more interesting. It is amazing how skilful young children can be.

The general education we all need must prepare us for both our domestic and working lives, and for special skills. It must ensure we understand the nature of the world we are living in, and our duties and responsibilities. Crimes and conflicts must be avoided, as they destroy our lives. Fairness, honesty, sound morals and ethics, and manners make life worth living.

Sound business products for the private sector.

The MH System of sustainable development would make major changes to the world economies. Its Master Plan would not only create an enormous amount of work, but it would also create a much better world to live in. Setting up the sustainable infrastructure and reshaping the world economies is many years work. As this work takes place the economies would become more efficient and taxation would fall to the lowest levels possible. Unnecessary imports would reduce and each country would live on more home production. Necessary imports would increase, like medicines third world countries need badly, and they would become affordable, because they would be paying Master Currency prices, which could be 40 to 50 times cheaper in the very poor countries.

Careful planning and design would create many new products that are wanted, to save not only fuel and scarce materials, but human effort too. There is no point in producing more products than are needed. Often they do not improve the quality of life, or make us any happier. Too many goods and assets all need maintenance, and this work would reduce time for leisure activities. All the balances need to be got right, so the rate of change would need to be at a pace we can collectively manage.

For the financial services there would be a massive increase in business, as everyone would need a bank account and savings accounts. Each current account would have one plastic card to replace notes and coins: these cards would be used for normal cash purchases. Sustainable economies ensure unemployment is minimal and this too would increase business transactions. There will also be a considerable amount of savings that would need careful management to ensure the minimum of losses.

The farming industry would become sustainable, although it may well have to reshape to take account of natural events like global warming. Reforestation would be necessary to ensure a sustainable environment and the material resources. They would have to ensure the natural supplies needed to support the world economies.

The manufacturing industry would need to restart many of the industries closed down in the developed nations through the flawed international currency valuations and the present day form of free market force management. They would also need to be active in the developing nations, setting up suitable industries to move their economies forward onto a sustainable path, using appropriate technology.

The construction sector, responsible for making possible the present day standard of living, builds and sets into operation the worlds physical asset infrastructure and all the buildings we use for habitation, and production. The infrastructure involves transport systems, water, electricity and gas supplies, communications systems, and docks, harbours and airports, being the major ones we are all aware of. Perhaps, space stations should also receive a mention! There is an enormous task to be tackled in the developing world, just for the basic requirement of water and to allow food to be produced.

The service industry in a modern world is now probably the largest sector of the economy. It covers both the government and private sectors. It is these sectors that are involved with supplying all the human tasks supporting families, including leisure activities. It also supplies much of the maintenance activities, planning and design and specialists that deal with all the problems in the development process. This sector would also be responsible for properly managing the recycling or safe disposal of all waste.

Conclusion

There is no doubt that a sustainable form of economy has enormous benefits for the private sector in the form proposed, the Master Currency Sustainable Economic System. However, to make the changes possible it is vital for the private sector to drive the process forward and ensure that governments and civil servants have all the information and tools required to move the process forward, the reason for the drafting of this three volume book.

CHAPTER 12

MARKETING, TURNOVER AND GOODWILL

Generally speaking the MH system doe not interfere with the majority of the existing practices of marketing, turnover and goodwill. Its major affect is to make conditions more stable and efficient. The Chapter will mainly deal with general matters and not detailed for every type of business.

Marketing

The MH information system splits the economy into local districts, regions, national and international sectors. The activities of many local businesses are local or regional and they would mainly be involved with trade in these sectors. Information on their customers would be located in the system. They would use the system to find their potential buyers, which they may target at just a few at a time, depending on the nature of their business. Others may target them with information of their product at regular intervals.

Many businesses mainly serve national or international clients, and they would use the national and international sectors of the MH information system to select potential customers.

There are two main business sectors, production and services. Many businesses would have their own websites. Once the MH information has been set up, all businesses would be recorded, and other institutions. Through this information system people would be able to find the type of business with the service, or product, they are interested in. The businesses with websites would be able to use them to advertise their products, whatever they may be in production or services. And this would probably be the cheapest form of advertising.

Again making use of the information on businesses, institutions and people that are on the inter-net, one could select potential customers and send emails to them of products they could be interested in. This again is a not too expensive way to advertise.

Trading organisations are another useful way to sell products. For example, a wholesaler could act as an advertiser, by bringing to the notice of their customers new products they would be stocking. These trading organisations could be operating nationally and internationally. They could also balance imports and exports, so that countries can keep these balances more easily.

Much advertising takes place in newspapers, magazines, and on television; but even the cheapest way can be costly, and there is often no real proof that the advert was the reason for the sale. Frequent and continuous adverts can brainwash people into remembering their organisations and products, and this can be useful and effective.

Advertising with posters on billboards is another way that businesses can make people aware of their products. These can be out in the open on purpose-made billboards, or on walls of buildings, in subways and in buildings. They could also be shown on electronic screens, like at post offices. Advertisements can also be placed in trains and buses and on other transport vehicles, from cars, vans, lorries to buses. Finally, they can be in any buildings, where permitted and the public visit, or pass through.

Products once displayed in shops and other business premises are being advertised, and this is a positive way to sell without the cost of advertising.

Probably the most expensive way to sell products is by the use of sales persons. This could be by telephone, or visits to potential customers, and by giving small gifts with the business name marked on the gift in some way. Finally, business product literature, advertising the business product and services can be supplied to potential customers.

The type of marketing used would depend on the nature of the business, and the finance available. Each business needs to work out their own solutions, and whether they are worth the investment. With the MH system and the proposal that business would not be taxed, the cost of advertising could not be offset as a tax relief on profits!

Turnover

With the MH system one cannot make large profits (net rent) without justification as has been explained in previous chapters, because it would throw wealth distribution out of a sustainable balance, among the working population and business/institution sector. The bigger the capital investment and the size of the business workforce, the greater the turnover can be. Possible profits made on the investment capital is 4% AER, and on the labour force it would be up to 10% of the wage bill.

The stock turned over in the business would depend on the nature of the business. For example a retail shop would turn over a lot of stock, but a solicitor would not as his service is labour intensive. The shop would make much of its profit on the capital employed in the business and not so much on the labour employed. Tables 101 to 110 indicate the turnovers made on people, bought in products and capital employed over a complete range of financial business structures.

From the business category tables mentioned in the previous paragraph the turnover is built from the employees working in the business, and the materials and services bought in from other businesses. The employees add value to the bought in items. The capital, the fixed and liquid assets, is needed to support the business activity. Although the tables show the possible turnover for each different business structure, the turnover cannot be achieved without the business supplying what the market wants. The business must make or provide what people need and want to buy. The business needs a steady flow of customers, old and new. As old products become out of date or unwanted, they need to be replaced with new ones to keep the business sustainable. Where the demands for the products increase the business can grow to a larger size, provided the capital for expansion can be raised. Where businesses cannot maintain products that the market wants it will begin to fail until the right product lines replace the failing ones. If new lines cannot be found as old lines die out eventually, the business would be forced to close, as there would be no turnover and profit to support its activities.

Usually the more lines and the greater the diversity of them the more stable the business is likely to be. Small businesses with just one, or a few lines, are more vulnerable than the larger businesses. However, one could just have one product that just keeps on selling, decade after decade. The life of any product is really impossible to forecast. There are manner factors to take into account that could quickly and unexpectedly remove the demand for a product. This is why business activities are always at risk. However, some product turnovers can indicate when the market for them is falling, and businesses must learn where some products demands run in cycles, before ceasing supplies.

For many businesses the rate of turnover of each item or product is important, as if it is not used or sold, it must then be stored, and storage costs money. Unused services, or goods not sold are profit lost. Turnovers need careful management, and sometimes research and planning.

The turnover of basic items we all need for families and business are more likely to have a continuous demand, in comparison with the luxury, or unessential products. Businesses should understand this and be prepared for unexpected slow turnovers that can be caused by various events taking place in economies, natural and man made.

Turnovers can be improved by presentation and quality of goods and service. For new products sound marketing is necessary. Sometimes marketing can cost many more times the value of a product. Producers, or manufactures need to take this into account when deciding on new lines, as the advertising cost could make the product uncompetitive.

Goodwill

Goodwill is the value that can be placed on an established business. When new businesses are set up one does not always know whether they will be successful. Even if one is certain that it will be, its viable turnover would have to be established and for most businesses this can take time. Perhaps before the business can function the premises and equipment have to be established taking weeks or months. Then sufficient customers have to be found and this again takes time to establish. Generally speaking one can say in the first year one is lucky to break even (wages paid but no profit), and it can take three years for a business to become established.

If one wants to make a profit from the start of owning a business, it is best to buy an established business. The business one would pay for can be divided into: the premises, or the leases of them, the fixtures and fittings and the goodwill. The goodwill with MH system would amount to one year's profit, up to the value given in the profit column in Tables 101 to 110 for the right category of the business being bought. For example Table 108, category 70H 20 which gives 3.8 man-years of 1900 MH and at 1 MH = £11.50 would amount to

£83,030. Such a business employs 30 people and has invested capital amounting to 20 man-years of 1900 MH. This business could be a large shop. Suppose one was buying a business of the same category, but it only employed 3 persons, the value of the maximum goodwill then = 3/30 x £83,030 = £8,303. To this goodwill figure the proprietor's wage would be added, as he would be considered to be working in the business. This would be about one year's average wage, based on the skill required.

To save goodwill costs many small businesses can be started on a part time basis, where the proprietor gradually builds up customers to a point where he can then have fulltime employment. Some businesses can be built up by working from one's home. By this process, if the business is unsuccessful, there is a minimal loss of capital.

The goodwill of some businesses depends not just on the quality of the work or product, but also on the personality of the owners and sometimes the employees. Upset the customers and a business can soon loose its goodwill, its amount of business. Poor standards too can loose goodwill.

Location for some businesses is also very important and the presentation of the product also. This would apply to many shops and to leisure activities.

CHAPTER 13

BUSINESS GROWTH

In Chapter 1 ten key models (Tables 101 to 110) are given for business maximum profit categories A to J. With the MH system many persons may worry that permissible profits on which the tables are built would not allow enough profit for businesses to grow. In this Chapter business growth based on the MH rules is discussed. For this purpose ten further tables are made showing the maximum investment based on the maximum annual profit from the business being invested every year.

The ten tables show continuous growth over a 20-year period for the five categories used. Five of the tables represent companies, which invest 5% of the profit based on employee's wages. The other five tables are based on one, or more owners who are partners, but not in a limited company and this allows the person/s to reinvest all their maximum profit permitted allowed by the MH rules, as there are no shareholders to be paid dividends. The company tables are called 'Business maximum growth category' and the other tables are called 'Owner maximum growth category'. The tables are in pairs so that they may be compared for the same category of business. Only five examples have been given as to give them all would amount to a very large number. However, one can make one's own table for the category of business wanted.

It can be observed from the tables that companies have ample profit to grow steadily using their permitted annual profits. The sole owner, partnership, or family type business can grow very rapidly on its maximum permitted profits. If further investment funds are required funds can be borrowed from banks, or raised by issuing further shares, or bonds.

With the MH system businesses can construct their own models to determine the most advantageous way to expand a business.

It should be noted that many businesses could be started on little capital. Renting accommodation and equipment can reduce start-up capital. Other people's services can also be used. However, other types of business do require substantial start-up capital.

Not all businesses grow. Some businesses have a limited market for their product, or a limited number of customers. There may be no need to use the profits made in the business, in the business. The money, therefore, could just be saved by the business for possible future requirements. The savings would earn interest and it would add to the capital value of the business. Alternatively instead of the business retaining the 5% profit earned on employee's wages, this could be paid out to the shareholders, or drawn by the other types of business owners.

Where businesses save their profits, this money could eventually be used to start or buy another business.

Table 133

Business maximum growth Category 10B 100

Year	Employees and directors (X)	Materials and services	Fixed & liquid assets (Y)	Total profit 10% + 4% (X) (Y)	Turnover	% Profit on turn- over	Share- holders % return Par value	5% (X)
1	90.00	10.00	100.00	13.00	113.00	11.50	8.50	4.50
2	94.05	10.45	104.50	13.59	118.09	11.50	8.89	4.70
3	98.28	10.92	109.20	14.20	123.40	11.50	9.29	4.91
4	102.70	11.41	114.11	14.83	128.94	11.50	9.69	5.14
5	107.33	11.92	119.25	15.50	134.75	11.50	10.13	5.37
6	112.16	12.46	124.62	16.20	140.82	11.50	10.59	5.61
7	117.21	13.02	130.23	16.93	147.16	11.50	11.07	5.86
8	122.48	13.61	136.09	17.69	153.78	11.50	11.57	6.12
9	127.99	14.22	142.21	18.49	160.70	11.50	12.09	6.40
10	133.75	14.86	148.61	19.32	167.93	11.50	12.63	6.69
11	139.77	15.53	155.30	20.19	175.49	11.50	13.20	6.99
12	146.06	16.23	162.29	21.10	183.39	11.50	13.80	7.30
13	152.63	16.96	169.59	22.05	191.64	11.50	14.42	7.63
14	159.50	17.72	177.22	23.04	200.26	11.50	15.06	7.98
15	166.68	18.52	185.20	24.08	209.28	11.50	15.75	8.33
16	174.18	19.35	193.53	25.16	218.69	11.50	16.45	8.71
17	182.02	20.22	202.24	26.29	228.53	11.50	17.19	9.10
18	190.21	21.13	211.34	27.47	238.81	11.50	17.96	9.51
19	198.77	22.08	220.85	28.71	249.56	11.50	18.77	9.94
20	207.72	23.07	230.79	30.00	260.79	11.50	19.61	10.39

Table 134

Owner maximum growth Category 10B 100

Year	Employees and directors (X)	Materials and services	Fixed & liquid assets (Y)	Total profit 10% + 4% (X) (Y)	Turnover	% Profit on turn-over	Owner % return (start-up capital)	5% (X)
1	90.00	10.00	100.00	13.00	113.00	11.50	13.00	
2	101.70	11.30	113.00	14.69	127.69	11.50	14.69	
3	114.92	12.77	127.69	16.60	144.29	11.50	16.60	
4	129.86	14.43	144.29	18.76	163.05	11.50	18.76	
5	146.74	16.31	163.05	21.20	184.25	11.50	21.20	
6	165.82	18.43	184.25	23.95	208.20	11.50	23.95	
7	187.38	20.82	208.20	27.07	235.27	11.50	27.07	
8	211.74	23.53	235.27	30.58	265.85	11.50	30.58	
9	239.26	26.59	265.85	34.56	300.41	11.50	34.56	
10	270.36	30.05	300.41	39.05	339.46	11.50	39.05	
11	305.51	33.95	339.46	44.13	383.59	11.50	44.13	
12	345.23	38.36	383.59	49.87	433.46	11.50	49.87	
13	390.11	43.35	433.46	56.35	489.81	11.50	56.35	
14	440.83	48.98	489.81	63.68	553.49	11.50	63.68	
15	498.14	55.35	553.49	71.95	625.44	11.50	71.95	
16	562.90	62.54	625.44	81.31	706.75	11.50	81.31	
17	636.08	70.67	706.75	91.88	798.63	11.50	91.88	
18	718.77	79.86	798.63	103.82	902.45	11.50	103.82	
19	812.21	90.24	902.45	117.32	1019.77	11.50	117.32	
20	917.80	101.97	1019.77	132.57	1152.34	11.50	132.57	

Table 135

Business maximum growth Category 30D 20

Year	Employees and directors (X)	Materials and services	Fixed & liquid assets (Y)	Total profit 10% + 4% (X) (Y)	Turnover	% on turn-over	Profit Share-holders % return Par value	5% (X)
1	70.00	30.00	20.00	7.80	107.80	7.24	21.50	3.50
2	72.45	31.05	23.50	8.19	111.69	7.33	22.85	3.62
3	74.98	32.14	27.12	8.58	115.70	7.42	24.15	3.75
4	77.61	33.27	30.87	9.00	119.88	7.51	25.60	3.88
5	80.33	34.43	34.75	9.42	124.15	7.59	27.00	4.02
6	83.14	35.61	38.77	9.86	128.61	7.67	28.50	4.16
7	86.05	36.86	42.93	10.32	133.23	7.75	30.10	4.30
8	89.06	38.15	47.23	10.80	138.01	7.83	31.75	4.45
9	92.18	39.49	51.68	11.29	142.96	7.90	33.40	4.61
10	95.41	40.87	56.29	11.79	148.07	7.96	35.10	4.77
11	98.75	42.30	61.06	12.32	153.37	8.03	36.90	4.94
12	102.21	43.78	66.00	12.85	158.84	8.09	38.70	5.11
13	105.79	45.31	71.11	13.42	164.52	8.16	40.65	5.29
14	109.49	46.90	76.40	14.01	170.40	8.22	42.70	5.47
15	113.32	48.54	81.87	14.61	176.47	8.28	44.70	5.67
16	117.29	50.24	87.54	15.23	182.67	8.33	46.85	5.86
17	121.39	52.00	93.40	15.87	189.26	8.39	49.00	6.07
18	125.64	53.82	99.47	16.54	196.00	8.44	51.30	6.28
19	130.04	55.70	105.75	17.27	203.01	8.51	53.85	6.50
20	134.59	57.65	112.25	17.94	210.18	8.54	56.05	6.73

Table 136

Owner maximum growth Category 30D 20

Year	Employees and directors (X)	Materials and services	Fixed & liquid assets (Y)	Total profit 10% + 4% (X) (Y)	Turnover	% Profit on turn-over	Owner % return (start-up capital)	5% (X)
1	70.00	30.00	20.00	7.80	107.80	7.24	39.00	
2	75.46	32.34	27.80	8.66	116.46	7.44	43.30	
3	81.52	34.94	36.46	9.61	126.07	7.62	48.05	
4	88.25	37.82	46.07	10.67	136.74	7.80	53.35	
5	95.72	41.02	56.74	11.84	148.58	7.97	59.20	
6	104.01	44.57	68.58	13.14	161.72	8.13	65.70	
7	113.21	48.51	81.72	14.59	176.31	8.28	72.95	
8	123.42	52.89	96.31	16.19	192.50	8.41	80.95	
9	134.75	57.75	112.50	17.98	210.48	8.54	89.90	
10	147.34	63.14	130.48	19.95	230.43	8.66	99.75	
11	161.31	69.12	150.43	22.15	252.58	8.77	110.75	
12	176.82	75.76	172.58	24.59	277.17	8.87	122.95	
13	194.03	83.14	197.17	27.29	304.46	8.96	136.45	
14	213.13	91.33	224.46	30.29	334.75	9.05	151.45	
15	234.33	100.42	254.75	33.62	368.37	9.13	168.10	
16	257.86	110.51	288.37	37.32	405.69	9.20	186.60	
17	283.98	121.71	325.69	41.43	447.12	9.27	207.15	
18	312.98	134.14	367.12	45.98	493.10	9.32	229.90	
19	345.17	147.93	413.10	51.04	544.14	9.38	255.20	
20	380.90	163.24	464.14	56.66	600.80	9.43	283.30	

Table 137

Business maximum growth Category 50F 200

Year	Employees and directors (X)	Materials and services	Fixed & liquid assets (Y)	Total profit 10% + 4% (X Y)	Turnover	% Profit on turn-over	Share-holders % return Par value	5% (X)
1	50.00	50.00	200.00	13.00	113.00	11.50	5.25	2.50
2	51.25	51.25	202.50	13.23	115.73	11.43	5.34	2.56
3	52.53	52.53	205.06	13.45	118.51	11.49	5.41	2.63
4	53.85	53.84	207.69	13.69	121.38	11.28	5.50	2.69
5	55.19	55.19	210.38	13.93	124.31	11.21	5.59	2.76
6	56.57	56.57	213.14	14.19	127.33	11.14	5.68	2.83
7	57.99	57.98	215.97	14.44	130.41	11.01	5.77	2.90
8	59.44	59.44	218.87	14.69	133.57	11.00	5.86	2.97
9	60.92	60.93	221.84	14.96	136.81	10.93	5.96	3.05
10	62.45	62.44	224.89	15.25	140.14	10.88	6.07	3.12
11	64.01	64.01	228.01	15.52	143.54	10.81	6.16	3.20
12	65.61	65.61	231.21	15.81	147.03	10.75	6.27	3.28
13	67.25	67.25	234.49	16.11	150.61	10.70	6.34	3.36
14	68.93	68.93	237.85	16.40	154.26	10.63	6.48	3.45
15	70.65	70.66	241.30	16.72	158.03	10.58	6.60	3.53
16	72.42	72.41	244.83	17.03	161.86	10.52	6.71	3.62
17	74.23	74.23	248.45	17.36	165.82	10.47	6.83	3.71
18	76.09	76.08	252.16	17.70	169.87	10.42	6.95	3.80
19	77.99	77.99	255.96	18.04	174.02	10.37	7.07	3.90
20	79.94	79.94	259.86	18.38	178.26	10.31	7.19	4.00

Table 138
Owner maximum growth Category 19B 100

Year	Employees and directors (X)	Materials and services (Y)	Fixed & liquid assets	Total profit 10% + 4% (X) (Y)	Turnover	% Profit on turn-over	Owner % return (start-up capital	5% X)
1	50.00	50.00	200.00	13.00	113.00	11.50	6.50	
2	56.50	56.50	213.00	14.17	127.17	11.14	7.09	
3	63.59	63.58	227.17	15.45	142.62	10.83	7.73	
4	71.31	71.31	242.62	16.84	159.46	10.56	8.42	
5	79.73	79.73	259.46	18.35	177.81	10.32	9.18	
6	88.91	88.90	277.81	20.00	197.81	10.11	10.00	
7	98.91	98,90	297.81	21.80	219.61	9.93	10.90	
8	109.81	109.80	319.61	23.77	243.38	9.77	11.89	
9	121.69	121.69	343.38	25.90	269.28	9.62	12.95	
10	134.64	134.64	369.28	28.24	297.52	9.49	14.12	
11	148.76	148.76	397.52	30.78	328.30	9.38	15.39	
12	164.15	164.15	428.30	33.55	361.85	9.27	16.78	
13	180.93	180.92	461.85	36.57	398.42	9.18	18.29	
14	199.21	199.21	498.42	39.86	438.28	9.09	19.93	
15	219.14	219.14	538.26	43.45	481.73	9.02	21.73	
16	240.87	240.86	581.71	47.36	529.09	8.95	23.68	
17	264.55	264.54	629.07	51.62	580.71	8.89	25.81	
18	290.36	290.35	680.69	56.26	636.97	8.83	28.13	
19	318.49	318.48	736.95	61.33	698.30	8.78	30.67	
20	349.15	349.15	398.28	66.85	765.15	8.74	33.43	

Table 139

Business maximum growth Category 70H 10

Year	Employees and directors	Materials and services (X)	Fixed & liquid assets (Y)	Total profit 10% + 4% (X) (Y)	Turnover	% Profit on turn-over	Share-holders % return Par value	5% (X)
1	30.00	70.00	10.00	3.40	103.40	3.29	19.00	1.50
2	30.45	71.05	11.50	3.51	105.01	3.34	19.90	1.52
3	30.91	72.11	13.02	3.61	106.63	3.38	20.60	1.55
4	31.38	73.19	14.57	3.72	108.29	3.44	21.50	1.57
5	31.85	74.29	16.14	3.83	109.97	3.48	22.40	1.59
6	32.33	75.40	17.73	3.94	111.67	3.53	23.20	1.62
7	32.82	76.53	19.35	4.06	113.41	3.58	24.20	1.64
8	33.31	77.68	20.99	4.17	115.16	3.62	25.00	1.67
9	33.81	78.85	22.66	4.29	116.95	3.67	26.00	1.69
10	34.32	80.03	24.35	4.41	118.76	3.71	26.90	1.72
11	34.84	81.23	26.07	4.53	120.60	3.76	27.90	1.74
12	35.36	82.45	27.81	4.65	122.46	3.80	28.80	1.77
13	35.89	83.69	29.58	4.77	124.35	3.84	29.80	1.79
14	36.43	84.94	31.37	4.90	126.37	3.88	30.80	1.82
15	36.98	86.21	33.19	5.03	128.22	3.92	31.80	1.85
16	37.54	87.50	35.04	5.16	130.20	3.96	32.80	1.88
17	38.10	88.82	36.92	5.29	132.21	4.00	33.80	1.91
18	38.67	90.16	38.83	5.42	134.25	4.04	34.90	1.93
19	39.25	91.51	40.76	5.56	136.32	4.08	36.00	1.96
20	39.84	92.88	42.72	5.69	138.41	4.11	37.00	1.99

Table 140

Owner maximum growth Category 70H 10

Year	Employees and directors	Materials and services (X)	Fixed & liquid assets (Y)	Total profit 10% + 4% (X) (Y)	Turnover	% Profit on turn-over	Owner % return (start-up capital)	5% (X)
1	30.00	70.00	10.00	3.40	103.40	3.29	34.00	
2	31.02	72.38	13.40	3.64	107.04	3.40	36.40	
3	32.11	74.93	17.04	3.89	110.93	3.51	38.90	
4	33.28	77.65	20.93	4.17	115.10	3.62	41.70	
5	34.53	80.57	25.10	4.46	119.56	3.73	44.60	
6	35.87	83.69	29.56	4.77	124.33	3.84	47.70	
7	37.30	87.03	34.33	5.10	129.43	3.94	51.00	
8	38.83	90.60	39.43	5.46	134.89	4.05	54.60	
9	40.47	94.42	44.89	5.84	140.73	4.15	58.40	
10	42.22	98.51	50.73	6.25	146.98	4.25	62.50	
11	44.10	102.89	56.98	6.69	153.68	4.35	66.90	
12	46.11	107.57	63.67	7.16	160.84	4.45	71.60	
13	48.26	112.58	70.83	7.66	168.50	4.44	76.60	
14	50.56	117.94	78.49	8.20	176.70	4.64	82.00	
15	53.02	123.68	86.69	8.77	185.47	4.73	87.70	
16	55.65	129.82	95.46	9.38	194.85	4.81	93.80	
17	58.46	136.39	104.84	10.04	204.89	4.90	100.40	
18	61.47	143.42	114.88	10.74	215.63	4.98	107.40	
19	64.69	150.94	125.62	11.49	227.12	5.06	114.90	
20	68.14	158.98	137.11	12.30	239.42	5.14	123.00	

Table 141

Business maximum growth Category 90J 30

Year	Employees and directors (X)	Materials and services	Fixed & liquid assets (Y)	Total profit 10% + 4% (X) (Y)	Turnover	% Profit on turn-over	Share-holders % return Par value	5% (X)
1	10.00	90.00	30.00	2.20	102.20	2.15	5.67	0.50
2	10.05	90.45	30.50	2.23	102.73	2.17	5.77	0.50
3	10.10	90.90	31.00	2.25	103.25	2.18	5.80	0.51
4	10.15	91.36	31.51	2.28	103.79	2.20	5.90	0.51
5	10.20	91.82	32.02	2.30	104.32	2.20	5.97	0.51
6	10.25	92.28	32.53	2.33	104.86	2.22	6.07	0.51
7	10.30	92.74	33.04	2.35	105.39	2.23	6.10	0.52
8	10.35	93.21	33.56	2.38	105.94	2.25	6.20	0.52
9	10.40	93.68	34.08	2.40	106.48	2.25	6.27	0.52
10	10.45	94.15	34.60	2.43	107.03	2.27	6.37	0.52
11	10.50	94.62	35.12	2.45	107.57	2.28	6.40	0.53
12	10.55	95.10	35.65	2.48	108.13	2.29	6.50	0.53
13	10.60	95.58	36.18	2.51	108.69	2.31	6.60	0.53
14	10.65	96.06	36.71	2.53	109.24	2.32	6.67	0.53
15	10.70	96.54	37.24	2.56	109.80	2.33	6.73	0.54
16	10.75	97.03	37.78	2.59	110.37	2.35	6.83	0.54
17	10.80	97.52	38.32	2.61	110.93	2.35	6.90	0.54
18	10.85	98.01	38.86	2.64	111.50	2.37	7.00	0.54
19	10.90	98.50	39.40	2.67	112.07	2.38	7.07	0.55
20	10.96	98.99	39.95	2.69	112.64	2.39	7.13	0.55

Table 142

Owner maximum growth Category 90J 30

Year	Employees and directors (X)	Materials and services	Fixed & liquid assets (Y)	Total profit 10% + 4% (X) (Y)	Turnover	% Profit on turn-over	Owner % return (start-up capital)	5% (X)
1	10.00	90.00	30.00	2.20	102.20	2.15	7.33	
2	10.22	91.98	32.20	2.31	104.51	2.21	7.70	
3	10.45	94.06	34.51	2.43	106.94	2.27	8.10	
4	10.69	96.25	36.94	2.55	109.49	2.33	8.50	
5	10.95	98.54	39.49	2.67	112.16	2.38	8.90	
6	11.22	100.94	42.16	2.81	114.97	2.44	9.37	
7	11.50	103.47	44.97	2.95	117.92	2.50	9.83	
8	11.80	106.12	47.92	3.10	121.02	2.56	10.33	
9	12.11	108.91	51.02	3.25	124.27	2.62	10.83	
10	12.44	111.83	54.27	3.41	127.68	2.67	11.36	
11	12.78	114.90	57.68	3.59	131.27	2.73	11.97	
12	13.14	118.13	61.27	3.76	135.03	2.78	12.53	
13	13.52	121.51	65.03	3.95	138.98	2.84	13.16	
14	13.91	125.07	68.98	4.15	143.13	2.90	13.83	
15	14.33	128.80	73.13	4.36	147.49	2.96	14.53	
16	14.76	132.73	77.49	4.58	152.07	3.01	15.27	
17	15.22	136.85	82.07	4.80	156.87	3.06	16.00	
18	15.70	141.17	86.87	5.05	161.92	3.12	16.83	
19	16.21	145.71	91.92	5.30	167.22	3.17	17.67	
20	16.74	150.48	97.22	5.56	172.78	3.22	18.53	

Depending on the category of business, particularly those employing a high percentage of labour, their growth can be considerable, as can be seen from Tables 134 and 136.

Table 143

Growth of £0.57 invested in 1969

Year	Average Bank rate (%)	Depositor's actual interest rate (Bank rate – 2% & 30% Income tax).	Rate of inflation (%)	Loss or gain for year (rate of inflation - actual interest rate).	Value of £0.57 invested. Compound interest. (interest after Taxation).
1969	7.84	4.088	-	-	£0.570
1970	7.28	3.696	12.38	- 8.684	£0.598
1971	5.92	2.744	12.10	- 9.356	£0.640
1972	5.90	2.730	14.07	- 11.340	£0.687
1973	9.79	5.453	14.70	- 9.247	£0.706
1974	11.90	6.930	18.81	- 11.880	£0.744
1975	10.81	6.167	26.99	- 20.823	£0.796
1976	11.74	6.818	15.17	- 8.352	£0.845
1977	8.15	4.305	10.09	- 5.785	£0.902
1978	9.13	4.991	15.35	- 10.359	£0.941
1979	13.75	8.225	15.42	- 7.195	£0.988
1980	16.30	10.010	18.41	- 8.400	£1.070
1981	13.60	8.120	13.38	- 5.260	£1.177
1982	12.04	7.028	8.54	- 1.512	£1.272
1983	10.01	5.607	8.58	- 2.973	£1.362
1984	9.65	5.355	4.36	+ 0.995	£1.438
1985	12.18	7.126	6.40	+ 0.726	£1.515
1986	10.88	6.216	7.90	- 1.684	£1.623
1987	9.74	5.418	5.79	- 0.372	£1.724
1988	10.04	5.628	7.29	- 1.642	£1.817

Table 143 is given to show the past loss to the depositor of funds in a bank or similar investment. The actual percentage loss of the investment each year is shown in column 5, and in column 6 the value of the deposit made in 1969 and adjusted for the annual interest is given after tax deductions.

Table 144 compares the same sum of money invested in 1969 converted into MH units and in each year reconverted back into £. Had the MH monetary system been in use at that time and the money deposited in MH units instead of £ Sterling the investor would have been 4.755 times better off at the 4% rate of interest used. Clearly the tables show that the MH monetary system not only protects the person's capital, but can also give real interest.

Table 144
Growth of 1 MH and compared with Table 143

Year	1 MH invested at 4% Per annum less 30% income tax	Value of MH investment converted to £ Sterling using Table 30 Volume 1	Value of £0.57 invested as shown in Table 143
1969	1.000	0.570	0.570
1970	1.028	0.657	0.598
1971	1.057	0.750	0.640
1972	1.086	0.879	0.687
1973	1.117	1.039	0.706
1974	1.148	1.274	0.744
1975	1.180	1.664	0.796
1976	1.213	1.965	0.845
1977	1.247	2.220	0.902
1978	1.282	2.641	0.941
1979	1.318	3.124	0.988
1980	1.355	3.807	1.070
1981	1.393	4.444	1.177
1982	1.432	4.955	1.272
1983	1.472	5.535	1.362
1984	1.513	5.931	1.438
1985	1.556	6.489	1.515
1986	1.599	7.200	1.623
1987	1.644	7.825	1.724
1988	1.690	8.640	1.817

It should be noted that the income tax deducted in Table144 is based on an annual rate of 30%, however, this varied most years and the rates also depended on the taxpayer's actual income or the business taxation rate at that time. The table, therefore, must be taken as a realistic indication of how much people's savings were devalued by wage inflation. Since 1990 the wage average rate of inflation in the UK has been below 4% per annum.

Table 145 is given to show the growth of 1MH saved each year over a period of 20 years in a stable economy. In such an economy 2% per annum would be a realistic rate of interest. Such an interest rate would not be subject to any form of taxation, making it worth much more than in present-day economies and the savings would not be devalued by inflation. This considerably helps financial planning.

Table 145 can be used to plan saving rates. For example, suppose one saved 1000 MH per annum for a period of 12 years it should produce with interest 13.4062 MH by the end of that year. Alternatively, one might want to save 12000 MH and this could be achieved after 11 years at 1000 MH per annum.

Table 145
Growth of 1MH saved per annum with interest at the rate of 2%

Year	Annual saving	Interest added per annum	Total savings
1	1	-	1.0000
2	1	0.0200	2.0200
3	1	0.0404	3.0604
4	1	0.0612	4.1216
5	1	0.0824	5.2040
6	1	0.1041	6.3081
7	1	0.1262	7.4343
8	1	0.1487	8.5829
9	1	0.1717	9.7545
10	1	0.1951	10.9496
11	1	0.2190	12.1685
12	1	0.2434	13.4119
13	1	0.2682	14.6801
14	1	0.2936	15.9737
15	1	0.3195	17.2932
16	1	0.3459	18.6391
17	1	0.3728	20.0119
18	1	0.4002	21.4121
19	1	0.4282	22.8403
20	1	0.4568	24.2971

Businesses needing to expand more rapidly could borrow from banks or other financial institutions. In a stable economy the borrowing rate could be expected to be at a rate of 4% APR. On the employee element of the business the trading rules allow up to a 10% profit. The business may wish to employ more people and need to have a minimum sum to cover a months employment so they can finance the extra monthly wage cost. Say they borrow for each new wage earner 190 MH, which is 10% of the person's annual wage. This is more than a months wage, but equal to the 10% permissible profit allowed by the MH trading rules. The bank interest for the loan on this amount would be 4% of the 190 MH, which amounts to 7.60 MH per annum. For a limited company half the profit of 190 MH equal to 85 MH would be set aside for shareholders, leaving 85 MH – 7.60 MH = 77.40 MH to pay off the loan, which at that rate would be quite rapid. Once the MH system has been fully implemented no tax should be payable on business profits. However, the examples given are based on maximum profits and businesses should understand that profits could be lower than the examples given in this book and are likely to vary from year to year.

It is hoped that the examples given in this Chapter will be sufficient for managers and planners to develop their own models to suit their business requirements. Each business would need to obtain their own statistics relevant to their business. They would then be able to create various models to develop the most suitable financial structure to advance their business and maximise their profits.

MASTER CURRENCY SUSTAINABLE ECONOMIC SYSTEM

VOLUME 3

GOVERNMENT POLICY SECTOR

CHAPTER 1

PEOPLE

Government and politicians are involved with managing a country for its citizens. How much do politicians and civil servants know about the people they serve? Do they really understand what people really want? If they do not, it is going to be very difficult to know how to run a sustainable economy and care for the environment. In this Chapter the author is going to note some of his lifetime observations.

It is probably best to make a start from childhood. When we come into this world our brains have recorded little information about it. As we grow up our brains record various forms of information so we can function, live and survive. The sort of information we record is: how we need to behave, about surviving, having or not having to work, and hobbies and pleasure activities These are influenced by the environment we inhabit. Children record what they observe and what they are taught. This information would be recorded to make comparisons. They would gradually become aware of right and wrong and the constraints in life. However, if a child's education is not guided, and the constraints in a sustainable culture are not explained, what ever they may do, good or bad, could become a right to do. The longer a child or person continues to do whatever they wish, the more it becomes a right to do, and the harder it becomes to accept it might be wrong.

Concerning our characters we are all different. We could be some of the following: weak to strong willed, caring, selfish, good to bad tempered, helpful to un-co-operative, greedy to sharing, follower to leader, and bully. We all have different proportions of these characteristics. Education can modify some of them. Economically some people require a substantial number of possessions to satisfy their lifestyle, whereas others want little. Finally, we all have a conscience and this too has a strong influence on what we do, and how we could behave.

Our human capacities vary like: good to bad memories, analytical minds, linguists, good at memorising names, poor to good at organising and managing, weak to strong physically, poor to good manual skills. We all have our natural skills. We all have tasks we prefer, or are happy to do. Yet, in our working lives are likely to have to carry out tasks we do not enjoy to earn our living, or survive.

Without good guidance and education it would take anyone a very long time to understand the world they are living in, and this reduced knowledge would lower the standard and security of living, and the number and quality of material goods we could possess.

The amount of time we spend on learning our skills and remembering information determines how much overall knowledge we have. To make judgements we make comparisons. If we could have a complete knowledge we would be likely to make correct judgements. The older and more experienced we are, the more knowledge we are likely to have, plus we can use other peoples' knowledge, or recorded information we can study. Young children have very little knowledge and experience and little to compare and hence would make mistakes, unless guided. For example: 'Do not touch because it is very hot. If you do you will burn your fingers'. Alternatively, a child might take sweets from a store without paying for them, because he does not know that it is wrong. Guiding and teaching from a very early age helps to prevent unnecessary accidents and doing wrong.

By working together in groups people can pool their knowledge and support each other's family economy. By using special skills and human aids, each of us can produce more in less time, allowing the standard of living to rise and more time for leisure. The bigger the group, the greater the knowledge and skills and the more diverse the economy can be. Complicated economies rely on many millions of skills throughout the world, and this process creates the modern world trading system.

When people do not work together it leads to breakdown of families and economies. People also become violent and destructive and kill smash and blow up our creations. Some people become terrorists. The cause of violence is serious, and the world does not seem to understand why it is happening. Governments must solve the cause of the crime problems.

Conflict and disagreement problems are frequently caused by dishonesty, unfairness, stress, broken agreements, greed for resources, abuse of human rights, misunderstandings and neglect in sorting out problems by discussion and sound reasoning. The present day unsustainable economic system where people are not properly paid is also a major cause of family problems. Human rights are also being ignored. Communication and sound, honest explanation is essential to solving all problems, and where language is a problem excellent interpreters are vital. Controlling by fear, or force, is never a permanent solution. Conflicts and the killing of opposition is also negative, as frequently they can escalate into major wars lasting years and causing massive destruction of people's lives. The right form of education would eliminate most forms of misunderstanding and conflict.

The Master Currency Sustainable Economic System (MH System) takes into account the character of the human race, its weaknesses and strengths; and honesty and integrity are vital components that can ensure its success, plus human determination.

CHAPTER 2

MH ECONOMIC SYSTEM

As mentioned in the Introduction 'The MH System' is the abbreviate name for the economic system and its productivity unit is a stable Master Currency, based on time and a defined average human productivity unit: this allows accurate comparisons to be made as inflation has been eliminated. The MH system follows natural events and takes into account all the factors mentioned in Chapter 1 concerning us. Unlike any other economic system every matter is taken into account, the whole environment. It is not a political policy, but an economic tool, the skeleton of the natural economy for guiding the world economy onto a sustainable path. The models used are all based on fact, or what really should happen, when we collectively make the right observations. It allows us to make comparisons with the past, and it allows us to create various solutions for the future, that allows feasible developments, that are sustainable. It provides the basis for keeping our world economy in harmony with the environment.

Volume 1, The Family Sector, and Volume 2, Private Business Sector, give the basis of the MH System and its key form of models and how they are applied to those sectors. This information is used in this volume to explain how the MH System is used for governments and politicians. Readers should therefore be familiar with the content of the first two volumes. This Volume discusses the form and operation of the government economic structures and how they should be managed and developed.

The main levels of government are as on page 17 of Volume 1 'The World Environment' heading, being Local Districts, Regions, National and International, the European Union being another level that can also be used. The MH system does not alter this structure, being quite natural and practical.

Local Districts

Local district authorities have the primary contact with their population. Their area, wherever it may be, is largely their responsibility as it forms their citizen's home surroundings and is more important to them than the rest of the country. For most families, the local district could have their most important assets, such as their home and livelihood on which they rely to support their individual economies. It is the place where most likely they spend the greater part of their time, and this could apply to the majority of the population.

Local district economies may consist of hamlets, villages and small towns, or may be only a part of a very large town. In the majority of circumstances they would probably be where individuals both live and work. Even in an advanced world economy, such places may well be where citizens spend most of their time, because they do not wish to live and work anywhere else.

Collectively, in the local districts, the inhabitants would have a considerable knowledge of themselves, their problems, the local businesses and infrastructure, including the natural resources. These local districts, with correctly trained personnel and a reasonably trained public, should be the most capable of managing their economy and developing it, given the reasonable freedom to determine their own path, in co-operation with regional and. government authorities all co-ordinating to maintain their economy in balance.

If modern economies are to be run effectively, all relevant information of the general economy is needed. In the local district, community members best gather this information, as they are usually the most familiar with it and they also have the easiest access to it. Some specialist help may also be required. The essential information is as follows:

1. natural resources
2. citizens' skills and work experience
3. composition of the existing economy
4. nature of imports and exports, from or to the rest of the nation and world respectively
5. state of the existing economy
6. plans to maintain and develop the economy

This information should be freely accessible to all e.g. those that play key roles in shaping the economy, local district authority, business and specialists and individuals needing to know the skills that are required to serve their present and developing local economy. Individuals should update their c.v. at least annually, and businesses need to update their information as appropriate, perhaps daily, weekly, monthly or annually.

The author visualises that most local districts would need to serve a population of about 100,000 people, but this is flexible to suit circumstances, each to be decided at local level. However, it is necessary that they are not larger than can be efficiently managed and comprehended by staff, who must have a good knowledge of the economy they are responsible for.

The local district authority is the nerve centre of its economy, responsible for co-ordinating its activities and providing the services not given by the non-governmental organisations and businesses. It is the best place to gather the local district statistics and information, which needs to be complete. Its planning department would, of course, work closely with its economic development department. A clear picture of the skills required is important and it would work closely with the education authorities, which would assist in training the required skills for the local districts and its region.

Each business and institution in the local district knows the skills it uses, the number of staff and the hours they work. From this information the skills of its total workforce can be classified. Further, all businesses and institutions can be listed into a complete information classification.

Each business and institution can give sales' turnovers and the goods and services it bought within its local district, in the region, the country and those imported from abroad. Each business can list the products they exported to the region, the country and to other countries.

This information is important for businesses and for establishing the shape of the economy at each level of the world economy.

Local district authorities, using the foregoing information, can build tabular models of their economy based on man-years (1900 hours per year). The models would include all businesses and institutions in the local district economy in their respective 'information' classification, horizontally and vertically (see Volume 2, Tables 119 and 120). All businesses and institutions would head the vertical columns and those that trade would describe the sales to each vertical column. Such a model gives a clear picture of the shape of the local economy and what the individual balance and business turnover is. This model is the one which is used by the authority to understand how to sustain and develop its economy, as it changes and moves on.

The planning and economic development department of each local district would be responsible for these models and for making them available to all other parties, including the departments at regional and central government levels. The models would be up-dated at yearly intervals and used in the development process of the local district. Certain developments would also be co-ordinated at regional and national levels. Businesses and institutions would be expected to give advance information concerning reducing or increasing, their labour force, including the nature of the skills being reduced or wanted. This information is required to plan future employment skills, and to help new businesses that would be needed to sustain the local district economy, and to ensure full employment.

Via this information system, the planning and economic development department of the local district authority would be able to make available the changes anticipated in the economy. This would assist businesses to find the workforce and locations for proposed new developments in order to expand their businesses. The local authority would work closely with businesses and other institutions to develop their economy soundly. The local district staff would be very familiar with their economy, its resources, strengths and weaknesses and, therefore, in the best position to steer the economy onto the best path possible. These departments are critical in the creation of sustainable economies, as they are the only ones who have the complete knowledge of their own economy and the latest changes taking place or in the pipeline. They would also be aware of the plans of adjoining local districts and their region.

The planning and economic development department of the local districts would be responsible to ensure all relevant information is collected and available, even if they do not themselves organise the collection, because the service is carried out by the private sector. They themselves would have access to the data. The information would include all the different products made and services supplied, and the skills experience of the workforce, including skills available, but at the time not used in employment.

Ideally local districts should collect all taxes, including those required to service the region and central government, as this is the most efficient way to collect and monitor the balance of the local district economy. Banks dealing in current accounts would serve as closely as possible the local district area, in order to assist in checking the financial balances of the district. Information on the businesses and institutions could be collected via the taxation department.

In a sustainable economy it is a human right for people to have work. Local districts are best placed to help their citizens to find work, or assist them to retrain for new jobs that should be available in a balanced well-run economy. As previously mentioned, they have all the forward information concerning development in their locality, the adjoining local districts and their region.

Local districts would assist in co-ordinating all businesses and institutions in their area, and also make them aware of the types of business needed to keep the local economy in balance. This information is useful for businesses seeking new locations for their trade. All activities of the local district need to be carefully monitored, co-ordinated and planned to meet new conditions as the economy moves forward. If this work is not properly carried out using well trained personnel, it is likely the economy would not be sustainable, jobs would not be available and the standard of living would fall, for all the citizens, as we all rely on each other's efforts in modern economies.

Regions

Regions are likely to serve at least a population of a few million and, of course, would serve many local districts. Some regions may serve populations of ten million or more, as may be necessary to serve a very large city. Regions might serve a water catchment area of a river or several rivers, or a large island, for example.

The main task of the regional level of government is to co-ordinate all the local district authorities and their activities, to ensure that their economies can be collectively maintained in general equilibrium within their region, and country. They would also co-ordinate their regional activities with central government.

The overall activities of the regional economy would be in better balance than the local districts, as this economy would contain a more complete overall economy due to the increased variation in skills, products and services, necessary for their standard of living. Regions, therefore, would be more self-supporting than local districts, which would need to exchange a higher proportion of their production than at regional level. It is likely that businesses and institutions within the region could supply 80% of all goods and services their population requires, whereas a local district may be able to supply only 60% of local requirements. The remaining 20% of goods and services the region desires would need to be brought in from the other regions of the nation and other countries in the world market, being paid for by the sale of their export products. These products could be surplus production over and above their own needs and special products intended for export. For economies to remain sustainable the value of imports and exports should be kept in general equilibrium. A region should have all the important key elements of an economy that are essential to sustain it.

As just mentioned, regions are far more complete and balanced than most local districts. For example, taking a family economy of two persons (and any children supported by them), they can produce 40% (say 40 hours work) of their own needs and wants within the family unit and, therefore, need to buy in 60% (say 60 hours work) from the general economy (which is paid for from their wages earned by working in the local economy); the local district general economy produces 60% of the needs and wants of that economy and the remaining 40% has to be imported, whilst the region provides 80% of its required products and imports only 20%. Naturally all local districts and regions are different and the percentages in this illustration would vary.

Like local districts each region would produce its own models of the economy, which would be based on the information supplied by the local district authorities. Regions would, in the main, be responsible for planning and co-ordinating major developments that could involve some or all their local districts. They would also assist central government with national maintenance and development projects.

Regions would also be responsible for local codes of practice and regulations that only need to apply to their area.

They would be funded by the local districts, which would also have to fund central government via the regional authority.

Regions would be responsible for monitoring their economy, and this leads to giving guidance to local districts and maybe assisting with experts and training, where universities or colleges do not cover this subject. Financial institutions would also work closely with regional authorities, particularly as they witness the region's cash flow and are aware of the demands for finance, including the knowledge of the level of savings. It is also important to know the value of the assets owned by citizens, businesses and all institutions, as these all have to be maintained. The amount and the nature of the maintenance can alter the type of economy needed. Insurance companies would collectively be insuring quite a large proportion of the assets, and they would also need to classify these.

Central Governments

In a sustainable economy central governments have extra main tasks. Firstly it is their job to select a sustainable monetary and economic system suitable for developing their economy. Such a system must function within a world economy. Governments, however, would need to comprehend why such a system is necessary and how important it is for many people to have an understanding of their economy, including what citizens need to know and do to support their economy.

A key role of central government is to co-ordinate the activities of its regions, and also to ensure that its economy is in a sustainable balance with the rest of the world. This is to ensure that the development path they are taking would be stable and not overload the world's resources and ecosystems etc. The local district and regional authorities should not undertake this task, as they do not have the resources, and because it is a central government task. Governments should have the appropriate personnel needed to understand how economies must be steered. These specialists would also be available to give expert advice to regions and local districts when required, and monitor the resources and the environment to ensure a sustainable world. Private sector consultants can also be involved in this process.

Any region of the world can suffer unexpected shocks caused by natural events that could require assistance from outside their region. Governments must aid these regions as necessary, which could involve arranging assistance from other regional authorities, or international help.

Wars cannot really be justified in a sustainable world. The author believes they are primarily caused by the wrong international economic structure and poorly educated national administrators. A sound training in how our economies function should considerably reduce such conflicts. Governments must find the will to try to ensure that their economies are built on a sustainable basis, including fair trading rules.

Central governments would work closely with central banks in order that the banks can adopt a sustainable form of fixed currency, as proposed by the author. Provided central banks operate soundly, they cannot be held responsible for failures in the economy, caused by governments not understanding how economies should function and how they should guide it.

Regions would carry out all the short, medium and long term planning of the economy and co-ordinate their plans with other regions. However, central government would be responsible for monitoring the plans and ensure these were sound and feasible.

Governments should understand that having much legislation is undesirable, particularly when much of it is liable to become out of date because of the pace of new technology and modern developments. Codes of practice make a sounder basis on which to build and guide our economies. Professional persons and tradesmen should be responsible for elements of the economy for which they have specialised knowledge, and generally follow the codes that apply. Codes can be suspended, where they are not applicable or found to be unsound; laws cannot. The economy needs to be organised so that individuals specialising in certain areas of the economy can easily absorb all information they need to know. When alterations are made to codes of practice, the government or private sector bodies should ensure that the appropriate specialists are notified. Lists of specialists should be available from the information system.

Central government would be responsible for organising or overseeing a sound national information system, vital for modern world economies. The information sought would be so arranged that it could be easily and quickly found. A single complete and comprehensive system is needed. The skeleton of the structure is commenced in Volume 1 Tables 36 to 39. Local districts would collect and supply the bulk of the information.

The local districts would collect the tax revenue supporting the regions and government.

Central government would, of course, be responsible for providing all services not provided by the private sector, local districts or regions.

Education

Present-day education does not properly prepare many people for their economic lives, and people are not sure what they need to do to achieve a successful working life. Many practices, and advice often given, are very different from those required to create sustainable economies. When rebuilding an economy to function on a sustainable basis, it is not only the children's education that requires reformulation, but many matters also need to be brought to the attention of both the working and retired population.

The present global economies are at different levels of development because economies have advanced at a different pace, mainly due to the amount of investment and the nature of the technology used. Some countries have made little progress. However, the author's solution for building sustainable economies applies to all nations, whatever the level an economy has reached. Education applied to each nation would be given at the appropriate level.

It is important that people should realise that past education and lack of trust can be expected to slow the progress in eliminating crime, civil war and wars. The ability to become fair and honest are essential elements for the creation of sustainable economies. The education process will need to justify why honesty and fairness are vital and that, in sustainable economies, people's trust must not be broken. Crime and wars are costly, create fear and everyone looses. Dictators should not profit from their situation.

In a natural world people's ability is intended to vary, as also are their objectives during their lifespan. Not everyone wishes to lead and take responsibilities, nor is this necessary. Some people in their vocation may be considered to be in an elite situation, but such a position should not entitle privileges. When an economy collectively provides all the goods and services we need, every human task is equally important, and someone is needed to carry it out. All skills are required, the simple skills being just as important as the complicated ones. It takes many kinds of people to build a complete economy, which should also enhance our quality of living. In reality no one can be considered superior in a sustainable form of economy.

We all need to earn our living to support our families and ourselves. However, we do not all live just to make money or amass fortunes. Most of us are simply content to be just properly paid for our work in the general economy. Many people are dedicated to their trade, or profession, and take a pride in what they do and achieve. For some citizens their hobbies are the more important to them. We are not all greedy and most of us are content to have our fair share of what the world has to offer us, and in time of need would be willing to help others. We do not all wish to compete but solely wish to enjoy what we are doing. Governments and economists need to understand the various desires and objectives of the population.

When purchasing goods, many of us do not want to be comparing prices to determine whether or not we are being overcharged, or that the service has been correctly given. In a busy world there is often little time to allow for this process to take place. People wish to trust traders and expect the workforce to be conscientious.

Freedom is not without any constraints. In any economy none of us can have complete freedom, as our world has to be shared and other people's rights need to be protected. Give and take and morals are important and assist in building our quality of life. Discipline from a young age is important, to prevent the wrong message, that, because something has always been allowed it is correct and a human right.

How previous generations behaved, perhaps before our grandparent's time, (the crimes that they may have committed in civil war and disputes of various kinds), should not be paid for by the present generations, by ethnic cleansing, vendettas, or similar acts. This is a difficult problem to solve, but much explanation and education on how a sustainable form of economy works will help to eliminate these situations. However, it is appreciated that this is a very slow process, although essential in the development of building sound economies.

Governments and their education authorities have many problems ahead of them to lead people in the right direction. Clearly, how our children are educated from a young age is important. In modern economies much needs to be learned by the adult population to ensure they would be confident with the sustainable form of economy. It is hoped that booklets like 'Everyone's Simple Guide' would help this learning process. Many other short books should also help in explaining in greater detail how the economy will work, and give everyone greater security. Videos too could aid to explain how the economy would be reshaped and why changes are necessary.

CHAPTER 3

FAMILY ECONOMIES

A considerable amount of key information has been given in Volume 1, so that people can build lifetime economic models for both expenditure and income. The tables have also taken into consideration taxation on a flat tax basis, as this is considered to be the most efficient and acceptable method. Much can be learnt from making realistic models of family expenditure over the complete lifespan. In Volume 1 Chapter 9 one example for a typical average family of four is given, for expenditure and income (Tables 41 and 42). This example is now going to be used to discuss the cash flow problems.

In Table 42 two flat income tax rates have been used, 30% and 40%. For the 30% tax rate between the age of 30 to 40 years the cash flow was negative; the family was just in debt, by approximately 30% of the husband's annual earnings. With bank interest added to this it would have been much more. At the end of the 80 year lifespan they had 7.74 years savings based on his earnings income of 1900 MH per annum. However, this money could soon have been spent on furnishings, presents and travelling, like motoring expenses, not included for in the Table 41. With a 40% tax rate there is little left in savings at the end of the 80 year lifespan. What is left would say have covered for the presents only. To prevent the debts resulting from a 30% flat tax rate the family would have had perhaps to buy second-hand goods. With the 40% flat tax rate the family would have been continually in debt from the age of 28 to 50 and that does not take into account the amount of bank interest on that debt, which at its peak reached 4.59 years earnings based on the husband's wage of 1900 MH per annum. The 40% tax rate would have created real hardship.

With the 40 flat tax rate the family could not be self-supporting. They would have needed subsidies. It is not unreasonable to assume 50% of working families would have required the subsidy. Under present economic conditions where the present tax collected in various forms amounts to 40%, 5% would need to be returned to subsidise family incomes. The administration to collect all the different forms of taxation could also amount to 1 or 2%, and then all the unemployed we have to pay for also need to be subsidised, shall we say the remaining 3%. Then of course many families are paid a minimum wage, and this is less than half an average wage based on an unskilled rate, i.e. less than 0.5 MH instead of 1 MH. Clearly with a sustainable form of economy carefully thought through, a 30% flat income tax could be very feasible.

From the cash flow example in Table 42, money is very much a problem for families with children. Renting a home saves some money when the children are being brought up, but long term it makes sense to buy the home as over the whole lifespan this is the cheaper solution. Having the children at a later date allows more savings that can be spent while one partner stays at home to look after the young children. This means it may be preferable to start having children around the age of say 28, assuming a 30% flat income tax. This sort of family cycle pattern would appear sustainable. This applies particularly to men, because the prime childbearing time for women is naturally between 17 and 29.Of course individuals will make such a decision for themselves.

Where children are born when the married couple are much younger, there is no doubt they would need to earn as much as possible and would need to work in occupations that need little training and where productivity is at least average. They would need to make as much saving as possible on accommodation: renting would save money and increase cash flow. Buying a home would have to be a later option, when the children are able to support themselves.

Many economies are now suffering from inflated property prices raising rents and house prices, making living accommodation unaffordable. There is no logic to this situation, which has been caused by an unsound monetary and trading system. It is creating hardship for a large sector of the population, particularly the young workforce. Yet governments have done nothing to prevent grossly overvalued properties, distorting the balance of the economy.

The minimum wage set at a level insufficient to support people must be abolished. People should be properly paid for their skills, quality of work and productivity. Only sound money and trading rules as the MH System can allow this to happen. This would allow natural redistribution of wealth to take place and economies to be in the right balance: people to be in fuller employment and able to be self-supporting.

Another major distortion taking place is the value of our savings. Two Tables are given in Volume 1, Table 5 gives the quarterly value of the MH in £ Sterling and Table 30 gives the annual value plus the rate of inflation over the previous year. In 1969 1 MH was worth £0.57 and in 2004 was worth £11.22. In 35 years the £ sterling has lost nearly 95% of its original value. Taxed or untaxed interest given by banks does not normally compensate for the loss caused by wage inflation. Savings shown in the cash flow Table 42 would be eroded by inflation: the greater the wage inflation the bigger the loss in the savings shown. If people are to use their savings to support their future family budget they cannot afford a loss in value of their savings.

The savings in the example given in Table 42 were partly used to supplement the state pension given. The savings shown in the table could be said to partly represent the second pension that most retired persons need to avoid lowering their standard of living. Savings left in the current accounts in the proposed MH System are safe and do not devalue. However, they represent goods and services ready for use. If the funds remain in that form of account for years, or perhaps even several decades as required for pensions, the goods and service produced could not be sold as they back the money waiting to be exchanged (this does not apply to present-day current accounts as this money banks are permitted to lend, and do). The money with the MH System does need to be transferred into savings accounts, where others can borrow the money and spend it, on goods and services produced by the work force, thus allowing the promissory notes to be honoured with the wage earners, and completing the cycle of earning the money and exchanging it for goods and services. The borrower of money allows others to keep their savings for decades, until they need to use it. With sound bank management banks lend the money in the savings accounts fully secured, so assets can always be sold if a borrower defaults, and the bank can repay the loans in savings accounts when required by the depositor, or in accordance with the savings bank account terms and conditions.

If families did not have to repay capital when bringing up the children, but only pay interest this would vastly improve their cash flow. Further, it would be cheaper to only pay interest, instead of renting the same size of accommodation. This can be checked using the information and tables given in Volume 1. One could also say that the interest one pays when paying ones mortgage is paid back later when earning interest on one's own pension savings. By using the MH System, planning and modelling one can solve many problems to make life easier.

It makes sense for people to own their own homes. However, for various reasons some families may have to make frequent moves, often to follow their careers. This leads to the need for having a reasonable choice of properties to let. With frequent moves it is often cheaper to rent than the cost of buying and selling.

From Table 12 Volume 1 it can be established a family home is equivalent to 2 to 3.6 years work based on a person's average income of 1900 MH per annum. Some homes would be less expensive and others more. Lets say the average value of a home is 2 years, allowing for depreciation, as the homes are not all new. With a 1000 strong work force in the economy there would be about 650 families, and their properties would be equivalent to 1300 years work. From Table 121 Volume 2 the value of government assets supporting the community were valued at 1572 years work. Add to the domestic and government assets say the shopping centre: we could say these assets are worth say 3000 years work or 4.6 years per family. This is a vast investment. To this must be added the other private sector services. Should a large industrial complex close down or other large employers, it is probably cheaper to bring work in, than people moving out to where there might be work but no homes. Many people do not want to move away from an area where they were brought up, have friends and relations and are happy.

CHAPTER 4

THE PRIVATE SECTOR ECONOMY

The private sector covers all forms of business, and includes institutions, clubs, charities and religious bodies. It can also include a government service not provided by the private sector, but acting like a business. A sole trader, or self-employed person is also treated as a business. Banks and other financial institutions are all considered to be businesses. The business models in Volume 2 and the MH trading rules all apply to the foregoing bodies. The models also apply to government bodies.

Generally speaking the private sector is the force providing the majority of the goods and services supporting people's lives and standard of living, and providing the goods and services needed by the private sector and government bodies. Governments are responsible for establishing the trading rules and guiding the balance of the economies.

Families look after the balance of their economies, and businesses and institutions look after their interests and stability. They are not responsible for the local national, or international economies: that is their government's duty. Governments need to understand their citizens' realistic demands, and how the private sector needs to function and be managed to keep the world on a sustainable path. Governments need information on how all the elements of the economy should interact and be kept in sustainable equilibrium as the world moves forward, including how they should be managing the task.

The MH System is designed to serve the purpose of the private and government sector tasks. It sets up all the key models needed for: people, to understand the world they are living in, the private sector to maintain and develop their activities, and the government sector duties. The MH System tools allows family, private sector, countries and the environment to be gradually set on to a sustainable course.

In Volume 1 the minimum explanation and rules are given, so that families have sufficient information to understand what they need to support their lives and families. Volume 2 adds to the information in Volume 1, and sets out the skeleton models of the key parts of the economic structure and starts to explain how the economy interacts, is maintained, managed and developed. In this Chapter this process will be further expanded.

Volume 2 Tables 101 to 110 define the financial structure of a business or any other organisation in the private or government sector. The layout of these models can be extended if found necessary, but probably cover the statistical shape of most organisations. They are necessary for a number of different reasons. They give the shape of an organisation and the permissible profits that each grade can produce to be within the trading rule requirements and for maintaining sustainable economies. All values are in MH units or years of 1900 MH units. Labour employed in the business plus bought in material services are based on a hundred. Varying the percentage of labour against the bought in products creates the category of the business. The fixed and liquid assets of 1MH to 1000MH, backing the business varies the category. The rest of the figures in the tables are based on maximum profits of 10% on labour employed and 4% on the capital employed in accordance with the MH rules. The form of the rest of the tables is self-explanatory and gives key information on the financial model of each category of business. Any business however big or small can be classified using the tables as also explained in Volume 2 Chapter 1. Businesses, when establishing the hours or years of work by employees and working directors, would use wage differentials where applicable, but not their productivity rate. The total wage paid may well be above or below the average figure in the tables. This would be caused by the quality and productivity of the employees employed.

The Business Maximum Profit Category tables have been produced to ensure the economic system can be held on a sustainable path. That is that the net rents paid do not distort the economy to such an extent that wage earners income and purchasing power is eroded. Yet on the other hand there is enough incentive for people to take sound risks in learning skills needed, running and investing in businesses, and creating new innovations to improve and solve world problems. The larger the organisation the nearer should the wage paid to employees match its business category. The government would monitor these statistics.

With every type of business and organisation having a financial category based on original investment, useful information data is recorded. Using the information each one could determine the initial capital funding required for a chosen business. This is very useful information for development planning. Developers may be consultants, individuals, businesses, private or governments. The information is needed to develop sustainable economies. Similar business would want to compare their situation with others to determine their competitiveness. Local districts and regions may have had a number of business closures, no potential inward investors but collectively have funds available to set up new suitable activities using the present workforce. The business category data would be a starting point for selecting feasible projects.

Developing economies need ideas, albeit, some are very rich and others very poor. The business category information would be very useful for them to determine perhaps what can be started on low capital cost, or how to use up massive capital reserves.

Although the business category tables give useful information for both the government and private sectors, a considerable amount of more general information is required, the reason for the further key tables given in Volume 2 Chapter 2, Tables 111 to 118. The tables set up give the natural form of structure for all organisations, even if only some of the economic elements apply to their organisation. Naturally, although a business would have all details of their organisation listed in the tables for their own use, they would not have to make any sensitive information available for others or government without justification. Much of the information for government statistics is of general nature, like people and skills employed, fixed asset values, financial reports and the elements of the economy they use. For other organisations and businesses they would be interested in information that would be beneficial to others and that indicates they should interact where it would be jointly helpful. The information gathered would be used to set up a detailed and as complete as possible information system, and local district economic models of the economy. This would benefit everyone. The local district model economies would also form the basis for the regional and national models of the economy. Tables 33 to 35 Volume1 and Tables 119 and 120 Volume 2 show a very simple local district model. The economic models in Volume 2 are based on the model in Volume1. The information system would be set up in the type of format shown and commenced in Chapter 7 Volume 1. The information system and the layout of the economic system are interrelated, or based on the same format.

Table 119, Master Model for an Economy, would be used to construct the local district economy model, and would be produced from a similar format supplied by each business, private sector organisation, and the local district authority, and any other government organisations within the local district. This information would then be used to create the regional model and finally the national model of the economy. These models would then be up-dated annually. These models can then be compared with each other to determine the various patterns of trade and determine the similarities of each economy. Comparing similar areas can help to identify flaws in an economy, or enable improvements to be made. The developed nations models can also be used to help developing nations.

The master economy model can also be used to study GDP as the buying and selling process creates turnover. Even with the simple model the buying and selling process has increased the labour force turnover from 1000 to 1906.85. The more businesses trading with each other, the greater would be this figure. For this reason businesses in the MH system are not permitted to make a profit on any bought in goods or services, as the suppliers have already made a profit on it them-selves. Adding net rent (unearned profit) increases the turnover and G.D.P. The more the unearned profit the more expensive the products sold to families, and the less their money will buy. This then leads to wage inflation. This process makes economies and money unstable and distorts all the value of products. Prices are changing when they should not be. Prices should only change when more or less labour is used to create the product or service.

Goods and services produced with local resources can expect to be a similar price. However, the greater the area in which the product is supplied the more is the transport cost. For a true but extreme example, a bag of cement sold in the UK has a value of 0.34 MH; however, the cost in Somalia was about four times more in 1978 i.e. 1.36 MH purely resulting from the cost of transportation. With a fairly large country, should businesses sell their product including transport, or with transport as an extra? When examining petrol filling station prices in the UK, there appears to be a large variation and no logic to the pricing, other than perhaps to make as much profit as possible! With the MH system, provided a business does not exceed the permissible profit, a uniform price can be charged for a product that includes delivery anywhere: they have a choice.

The private sector businesses need to make profits on their activities, to cover development, unexpected losses, contingencies and the cost of capital employed in the business, like dividends on shares. Generally speaking well-run businesses and organisations are efficient.

When the managers are also the owners they have an incentive to be efficient and proud of the business, taking care to run it properly. Where larger businesses have professional managers they should be conscientious and again make sure the business was well managed and developed. However, what is also most important is that the managers and the employees understand the business they are in and have pride in their work. The larger the business unit, the more likely that those who are in charge could be out of touch with the organisation. The natural balance is needed, and that is probably at the point that managers can still keep in frequent contact. Such a business might just produce one special product as anticipated in Tables 114 and 115. At this point businesses should not be made larger, but instead new ones created with the businesses then owned by a parent company or organisation that is not involved with the detail, but only there to support it.

The MH system is based on three natural main sectors, family, private sector and government sector. Each sector has its own responsibilities and should not transfer them to the other sectors. Businesses are responsible for paying their employees properly and promptly, but individuals are responsible for themselves and their families. If families need help, that is a government task; the reason for their existence, to serve people. Businesses, however, are responsible for health and safety on their premises or work sites. However, they should only have to cover risks involved with projects in their ownership, which might be their only business without other assets. Depending on their wealth, businesses would insure with a company outside their organisation, or would decide to cover their own risks. Companies should not be expected to provide a pension, care service for employees, or redundancy payments. What is needed on becoming redundant is work, and the necessary support from government services until work is located. However, the task of tax collection does occur in the business resulting from the trading exchange process. Without having to take on responsibilities for staff welfare, businesses and other organisations would be free to spend their energies on their own product.

Sustainable development involves taking into account the environment. Many business developments have in the past been sited without taking into consideration environmental issues. Clearly the resources for the business should be available, and new ones should not create shortages. Water is very much an issue in many parts of the world. For example there should not only be sufficient water for the businesses, but for the population needed to support them. Further developments should not take place where land is liable to flood. Many areas need to reshape to reduce demand on water resources. Existing businesses should therefore be encouraged to move to areas where there are adequate sources of supply, both for them and housing. The practice of knocking down houses where water is plentiful and wanting to build more houses where there is a substantial lack of water is not sensible.

The more complicated the world becomes the more do businesses need to network with each other. Just like people relying on millions of other people's skills, the private sector relies on thousands of other organisations that contribute to their products. The MH system structure facilitates communication. It also sets up structures to help businesses to be efficient and responsible.

Governments need to know how the private sector operates, so that its regulations are not counterproductive. Complicated laws and regulations take up much valuable time, often of those at the higher levels of the organisations, preventing them from using their time and experience on the real purpose of the business, the production of goods and services. Complicated tax systems with ever varying rates waste a lot of time. The amount of taxation can seriously modify the size for a production line and the capital equipment that could lower the final cost of a product. Varying currency rates and overvalued currencies can completely shutdown factories, built at vast cost. Industry must have stable conditions, one of the reasons for the form of the MH system.

Stable economies and a sound international trading system, including a single trading language, would help the private sector create a much better world for everyone to live in. The private sector collectively have the knowledge required, but will find it very difficult to carry out without the serious co-operation of governments, because it is a government task to allow the sustainable infrastructure to be established. Unfortunately, so many government policies conflict with the requirements for sustainable development. Governments also often make it impossible for highly qualified persons to engage efficiently with senior government officials and Ministers.

CHAPTER 5

GOVERNMENT SECTOR ECONOMY

Already in Chapter 2 the general structure for the MH government sector was outlined, giving the main duties at local district, regional and central government levels.
In this Chapter the structure of government is discussed further.

In Table 119, Volume 2 the following key elements were included:

16	Government
17	Defence
18	Education
19	Health
20	Entertainment

Some of these can now be expanded.

16   Government

Central Government could be divided as follows:

1	Policy
2	Treasury – Central Bank
3	Law
4	Trade
5	Foreign
6	Economics
7	Information
8	Records
9	Standards
10	Infrastructure
11	Museums – National Monuments

17   Defence

Defence could be subdivided as follows:

1	Police
2	Fire Service
3	Emergency Services
4	Military – Army – Navy – Air-force
5	Justice – Judicial Courts

The subdivisions can now be discussed.

16.1 Policy

This would really be Parliament in some form. It would be where central government and top civil servants and ministers and politicians would make democratic political decisions to run and manage the country in accordance with Sustainable economic trading and environmental rules.

16.2 Treasury

In the MH system the role of the Treasury would be to monitor and plan Central Government expenditure and work in conjunction with the Central Bank. The Treasury would also monitor the regions expenditure.

The Central Bank would hold the funds of Central Government and the Nation's reserves. The Bank would also be responsible for overseeing the banking and financial system.

16.3 Law

There appear to thousands of laws that no one can keep up to date with. Many laws could be out of date and unintentionally faulty. The MH system advocates that laws should be kept to a minimum. When mistakes are made they should quickly be corrected.

Many laws should be replaced with codes of practice, and the relevant professional persons and bodies should be responsible for these. They can work in conjunction with the Law Department. Experts and professional persons do not have to follow codes of practice, provided they have sound reasons for not doing so.

16.4 Trade

This department would monitor the trading system and ensure the businesses and organisations followed the trading rules. They would also monitor profits and wage structures to ensure they were complying with the MH system, for both wages and private sector transactions.

The department would also be involved with international trade and sustainable development trade issues.

16.5 Foreign

The Foreign Office or Ministry would lead on all matters for ensuring that the world can be developed on a sustainable basis and in harmony with the environment, assisted by co-opted staff from other pertinent ministries. It would look after its nationals living or working abroad as necessary.

It would help foreign nations with their problems, including emergencies. It would help nations to eliminate crime and conflict, by using sound explainable solutions.

16.6 Economics

This department would be responsible for economic policies, and monitor and co-ordinate the national economy. It would be responsible for the national models of the economy in the MH system format.

The department would work with its regions on national infrastructure and policies. Together regions must maintain a sustainable national economy. The department would be responsible for ensuring the quality and sufficiency of the qualified staff at all levels of the government sector of the economy, from local districts to top advisors in central government.

The department would liase with all other national departments to solve international economic problems and matters concerning the world environment.

16.7 Information

This department would be involved with the establishment of the national and international information system. The object is to have one system as complete as possible, linking information into a sound economic and informative structure as outlined in Volumes 1 and 2. It is visualised both the government sectors and private sectors would jointly fund and provide the system. Users of the system could pay for the service or it could be funded from tax revenues. Individuals, businesses, organisations, institutions and government bodies would supply their information free. However, it then has to be gathered, or interconnected into the national and international network, in a common international language.

There is little point in duplicating systems, as this is more expensive and can waste searchers time. One system uses less human input.

16.8 Records

This department would be responsible for caring for the nation's records like: births and deaths, companies, institutions and other organisations, patents and copyrights, and estate properties, land and natural resources.

16.9 Standards

This department would be responsible for keeping the information on all the national and international standards of practice that apply to the conduct of its country's economy.

It can also be involved with the development of the standards and ensuring that they are really necessary.

16.10 Infrastructure

This department would be involved with national structures that serve all regions and may need to be connected. They could be water, gas, electricity, transport systems, electronic communication systems, buildings and organisations serving the country.

16.11 Museums

Museums and national monuments could be taken as educational and entertainment. However, they are of national and cultural interest and in some countries a massive investment; even if they are not a necessity, they need to be cared for by a responsible body. This would include National Libraries as places of historical record; but local libraries could be a regional responsibility.

17.1 Police

The police force is part of the defence, or security of our economy. They would naturally be working with others security sectors and are joined with them under the security heading.

Customs and Excise department has not been included, as no duties or extra taxes on goods are imposed in the MH system. The only control left is illegal substances and perhaps immigration problems. So they then become more of a special form of policing. They can either be a separate department or be amalgamated with other police duties.

The police force would probably be divided into regional forces. Hopefully with a fairer and more honest society the size of the police force could be reduced.

The prison service too, with the MH system culture, should shrink considerably and like the Customs and Excise department could be amalgamated into the police force.

17.2 Fire Service

The fire service is again a protector of the economy and the environment, by dealing with problems as soon as possible, like putting out fires, making chemical spillages safe and recovering people from all sorts of difficult situations.

16.3 Emergency Services

There are a number of other emergency services that protect or save people. Some of these services are run by charities and others by government departments. They can all be co-ordinated by government

16.4 Military

The Army, Navy and Air Force defend our country. Nowadays they also act as peace forces and emergency forces.

17.5 Justice

This department through legal processes and judicial courts determines whether people have unlawfully been accused or whether a penalty should be paid in some way to compensate for a crime.

18 Education

Education is given in state schools and colleges and managed by governments, but also a considerable amount can be given under the private sector services. Under the MH system the form of education is most important as it relies on people understanding their economy and duties in it.

19 Health

The health service is very important to an economy, but it also needs to be affordable. The MH System optimises the service by trying to reduce costs by a sound education and preventative measures. The service can be private sector, government sector, or both, but must be monitored by the government to ensure a sound sustainable service.

20 Entertainment

This sector covers all our leisure activities. Most entertainment activities would be provided by the private sector. However, visiting museums and national monuments could be both a leisure activity and educational, and could be provided by a government service.

Sporting activities would also be leisure activities, and may well be a cultural activity too.

Central Government Tasks

The foregoing pages of this Chapter have indicated the tasks and duties anticipated in a sustainable form of economy, like proposed using the MH system. Central Government and departments would only be carrying out tasks and running services that could not be carried out at regional and local district level. The tasks of local districts and regions have been outlined in Chapter 2, with reasons for them. As much as possible should be delegated to each level of the economy, but not duties that are a central government's duty.

The use of the MH system reduces the number of government tasks. For example very few laws would be required. The key laws in most countries would be the same. Regions and Local Districts would not have local laws, but only national laws. Therefore, Regions and Local districts do not carry out the duties of Central Government and do not need their powers. Their tasks are for management only.

Political System

Democracies have elected politicians representing their manifesto strategy in government. Parties with majorities, or coalition parties manage the countries economies. Once in power they seek to reshape the economy to suit their economic plan. Generally speaking politicians and the parties' followers are not experts at developing and maintaining complicated economies. Their manifesto can well have unworkable plans. Once in power the civil service is perhaps expected to carry out the impossible. Their own training does not keep up with fast changing economies and laws and management practices needed for sustainable development. Hence world economies are now very distorted.

In principle election of politicians to represent the majorities wishes or aspirations is sound, but the flaw is that the politicians have not the very thorough knowledge needed to create the sustainable economies everyone really would like to have. The MH System is based on a very sound understanding of modern world economies and problems. It is designed to function soundly. It is a tool designed to correct the weaknesses in present management procedures. The persons behind the MH system would be dedicated professional persons with honesty and integrity and backed by their collective detailed knowledge of how the economy is managed and developed to become and remain sustainable. This pool of knowledge is next used to reshape the government structure to aid both the civil servants and politicians in the art of building sustainable economies.

The MH system is a sustainable management structure that can be used by all politicians to shape their political policies. Some policies would be more successful than others. However, its ethical rules should not be changed, but should follow a natural social path that protects human rights.

More use of referendums is needed for major decisions. Politicians and un-elected civil servants should allow citizens to take part in major issues, by not only being allowed to express their views, but by voting on it too. A vote for the party in power does not give the right to go ahead with any important issue affecting peoples lives and the private sector.

As has been previously mentioned, the real purpose of the economy is to serve people. Political parties also serve people and not the private sector. Funding for these parties should come from people and not businesses, and accordingly it would be best for the government to give a reasonable grant for electioneering.

Central Government

The general concept of the government structure does not have to change with the introduction of the MH System. For example, Ministry Departments and Cabinets and a checking establishment like the House of Lords in the U.K. However, with democracy politicians and members the House of Lords should be elected members. All officials in government would need to be completely competent in their task, and have a sound understanding of the sustainable development process outlined in this book.

In due course the sustainable development process will make changes necessary in the size and nature of the work in the departments, but this happens anyway in present governments, as new equipment and ideas are introduced.

Regions and Local Districts

With the introduction of the MH form of sustainable economics, system changes in departments and methods of working and management would also take place. Regions would no longer need much of government from the centre. They would be able to make any necessary changes to keep the economy sustainable, which is their duty. They can create local justifiable local regulations, or codes of practice. A regional economic department would be needed and it would co-ordinate activities with their local districts and the government.

Local Districts would have considerable responsibility for their economy and would need to liase with adjoining local districts and their region on many issues to ensure a sound economy. Instead of just collecting a local tax on property they would be responsible for collecting the flat tax from businesses and the self-employed. They could also make charges for certain services supplied to businesses. They would need to ensure that all local records are kept up to date including the information system. They would have a department for collecting the statistics from businesses and organisations, and monitoring and analysing them. The information would be used to build and up-date the local district economic model. The local district would have an economic development department responsible for ensuring their district was sustainable. It would assist the private sector and individuals concerning work activities and any other economic issues.

Politicians and Senior Civil Servants

For developing sustainable economies it becomes necessary for politicians and senior civil servants to have appropriate training, as their duties are for specialist activities, that presently are not required, as this is left to the private sector, whether or not it is their duty. Governments must have the skills to maintain their economies in a sustainable form, which is not a private sector task, but a government one. Hence, government officials need to know how to maintain and develop their countries and work with other nations to achieve a sustainable environment.

CHAPTER 6

EFFICIENCY OF ECONOMIES

Many people today may believe that the most efficient economies always have high growth rates. However, growth calculations do not take into account whether the economies are efficient. The author's sustainable form of economy does and its approach to efficiency will now be explained.

Efficiency is calculated by using the productivity/master currency unit. This measures the average hours of human effort into producing each product. All products are priced in these units, so whatever is purchased, one knows the hours (or part of an hour) of human input taken in its creation. For example when a small car was manufactured in the late 1930s it represented, say, 1600 hours of human work by the factory workforce, including the supplies of materials and services. Today a similar small car represents 740 hours of work, which also includes a more efficient engine and it is of much higher quality. The efficiency of car manufacturing today only requires 46% of the labour force when compared with the 1930s manufacturing process. Also, one can next take into consideration the running and maintenance costs for the average user, ignoring taxation. The 1930s costs could have been 260 hours work and, today, say 46 hours work to supply the fuel, spare parts and the labour employed in maintenance. Assuming the car has a ten-year life the overall annual cost of the 1930s car was 420 hours and the present day cost is say 120 hours. Therefore, only 28% of the labour force is needed to run a car today compared with the 1930s, because we are using our labour more efficiently. The reasons for the improvement results from the quality of the machines, human aids and materials we have developed, and our understanding of how to use modern technology.

It should be noted that when using the word 'products' it refers to either goods, or services. Services can also include goods. The cost of many services can be wholly, or mainly, labour. For example teaching and cleaning is mainly labour intensive. How we teach or clean affects our efficiency. The better our knowledge of how to teach or clean, including the use of suitable products, the greater is our efficiency. Every process we carry out can be compared in the master currency (productivity/monetary unit). The development process compares previous methods and products with proposed and new ones. One of the necessary comparisons usually involves costs, and the author's method is ideal for this.

The more efficient our economies the higher the standard of living that can be achieved. To increase efficiency in the production of goods and services they have to be produced in less time, or hours of human labour. Modern human knowledge of production and supplying services helps to reduce the time needed to provide the products. It also helps in the selection of human aids of tools, machines and methods of production. Using a trial and error process, or experimenting using different solutions to find the best methods, leads to the most efficient result. Clearly efficiency must also take into consideration affordability and the size of the market, as there is little point in over production that may never be required. Every product produced must be in the right balance for the economy it is serving.

The overall efficiency of an economy is not only dependent on all products being efficiently made, but also on how it is managed. For example, if too many businesses make exactly the same product in a country, and as a result cannot take advantage of economies of scale, which would allow lower costs of production, the economy would be less efficient than possible. Many subsidies are inefficient and often given because elements of the economy are distorted. Subsidies have to be administered by people who organise the distribution of them. And people claiming the subsidies have to spend time justifying entitlement. For example, if the national wage system were fair and sustainable, there would be very few low wage earners, who would need subsidies. Governments could save large sums of taxpayer's money by creating balanced economies, and a nation's economy would become more efficient. Using the author's system, governments can calculate a more efficient balance for the economy. At this point of explanation it can be deduced that free market economies alone cannot create the most efficient and balanced economies. Creating efficient economies is a government duty.

Where present day information systems may reduce our overall hours of work in seeking information, there are too many information systems, incomplete and not co-ordinated. A single more complete information system, properly co-ordinated, would be more efficient, as one would know where to find the information, and whether the information sought exists.

Costs and average human labour productivity are directly linked in the author's system. This is essential if correct comparisons are to be made among nations and when selecting products from other countries. Under-priced products sold in high value currency countries, resulting from imports from low value currency countries, as created by present-day practices, can give the impression that they are cheaper than a product made locally. Many every-day goods are now imported, sometimes from half way around the world, into developed nations whose currencies are overvalued. Many of these products are no longer made by the developed nations, caused by the distorted markets. Even neglecting the wasted skills and assets of the indigenous population, the practice does not use human labour efficiently, as more transport is required than would be when produced nationally. Further, more energy is used and this does not help the problem of global warming. Developing nations, with undervalued currencies, need to pay more than they should for developed nation's products. Many of the advanced products they need must come from the developed countries, some of which would be required to reduce pollution, often affecting the whole world.

Distorted economies are not efficient. As the world develops and we all become better educated, we expect to be treated fairly. Many of the world's problems result from an unfair economic and monetary system, which often creates the conditions of poverty and low wages. Frequently, vast sums are spent on luxury projects, which are really not affordable, except for the rich. Naturally the poorer citizens may also desire them. But is it really sensible to create these expensive luxury items, when so much needs to be done for the essentials of life, the necessary every-day needs? With these distortions crime increases and so does the crime industry. Economies on this basis are not efficient, as crime is destructive and consumes human effort that could be better used. Where crime takes place our quality of life and security are lowered. Governments can cure these problems by creating a sustainable economy, which removes the distortions, and by an education process that explains to all members of the public how our economy should function. People will understand if governments do not subsidise luxury items, or encourage them by creating lotteries and the like to finance them, which should be paid for by the actual users of them.

It is only government bodies that can shape our economies to be efficient and in the right balance, which takes into account quality of life and a sustainable economy. By building models based on the author's monetary and economic system and the correct statistics, governments can reshape economies to be more efficient and better places to live. Clearly, the rate of progress to reshape the economy would be constrained by the country's resources, and the ability of the workforce to adapt to the necessary changes.

As mentioned at the start of this chapter high growth rates do not indicate how efficient an economy is. For example, many services create G.D.P. (gross domestic product) like those that distribute grants, but they do not necessarily increase the standard of living of the citizens. If unwanted services could be removed from the economy, by creating a sustainable economy, less G.D.P could still maintain the same standard of living, and overall the workforce would work fewer hours to achieve it. However, if the public demand a higher standard of living, the economy can be reshaped to allow this to happen.

In Volume 1 Chapter 5, a measure for the standard of living is given as follows:

$$S = \frac{\text{Cost of needs for individual or family} \times 100\ \%}{\text{Average hourly wage based on standard education} \times 1900}$$

This measure is an important one for citizens, as this measure is the one that tells them whether their standard of living has changed for them, year by year. An increase in G.D.P. does not mean that the standard of living has increased; it could have decreased. The increase in G.D.P. could only have benefited business and other institutions, including government bodies.

It is hoped that governments will understand that it is not only the use of human aids and devises that can improve a nation's efficiency, but also the monetary and economic system in use, together with sound management and, of course, an understanding on how economies function, are maintained and developed.

CHAPTER 7

PATENTS, ROYALTIES AND PROFITS

In Volume 2 it was explained that it is very important that profits are kept at affordable levels. This is necessary to maintain the purchasing power of money. It was stated that interest rates should not exceed 4% APR on deposits and the par value of shares, and that profits in businesses should not exceed 10% APR on the added value created by each business. The added value is only created by the labour force and represents the wages paid to them. Businesses should not make a charge for royalties on their own patents as they already make a profit of up to 10% APR and up to 4% APR on their original investment. Shareholders also share the business profit of up to 10% APR. However, where they use other businesses' or people's patents, they can recover the exact cost of royalties paid out. These rules may to some appear restrictive, but are essential.

Royalties on patents and other products should also be maintained at affordable levels, but cannot be on the same basis as business profits, because not every invention is successful. Many inventions and works of art are unsuccessful or maybe only a small percent are successful. The time and expense involved in innovation vary considerably dependent on the nature of a product. Some successful products may have only taken a few hours to develop and many millions products could be sold, whilst others may have involved years of research for a market of only a few thousand. Economies rely on new products to improve our standard of living and quality of life. It is therefore essential to give inventors and artists etc incentives to be creative to allow them to be able to accept the loss of many hours of hard work on unsuccessful products. When successful, the creators will naturally want to cover the cost of their successful products plus a profit, which would help to finance the loss on unsuccessful ones. As world markets grow some successful products could exceed a billion sales, making the owners of a single patent extremely rich from the royalties they receive. Such massive wealth is really not necessary to create incentive and a fair reward. The problem then, for governments, is where to set the cut-off point on profits from patents and royalties. Another problem is the life of a patent, or royalty: should they have a cut-off point, or be permanent? It may be a number of decades before a patent is taken up; should it then end with the life of the inventor, or continue with the family or heir of the inventor?

Looking further at the problem of expenses and profits on patents and royalties, it would appear that inventors, artists and authors etc should keep accurate records of the time they spend, including research, and their expenses. Maybe after extensive modelling by governments they could decide on something like 1100% profit as being affordable and sustainable. Their costs would include their hours of labour, plus expenses and interest, at the rate of 4% APR, if the project exceeds one or more years work. The profits would be based on their successful products, unsuccessful ones would be excluded from the calculations. The royalties would, of course, be based on the master currency, as the profit should not be eroded, as could happen with inflation in the present economies.

Developed nation governments, when modelling and developing their nation into a sustainable economy, should aim for approximately 25% of the value of money being taken as profits to cover incentive in wage differentials, business profits, royalties and interest rates. The real purchasing power of money would then be 75% of money earned, because 25% is transferred as profit during the monetary exchange process.

Developing nation governments may find it necessary to allow overall profits to reach 40%, so businesses can advance the economy more rapidly to reach a sustainable state. These would only be to build up a sustainable infrastructure for the good of all.

The way wealth is distributed, and by how much, is very important to the stability of economies. Clearly businesses need capital to sustain and develop them. Capital is not only available from profits, but can be borrowed from money in savings accounts and pension funds. In sustainable economies there will always be savings and these could be quite considerable in developed countries. Clearly each country needs to check the models of its economy very carefully when setting permissible rates of profit.

The use of profits, after paying shareholders their dividend, where this applies, depends on business policy and the nature of its product/s. Creating limits on profit allows a fairer distribution. Many businesses needing high growth rates to satisfy the market for their product often require considerable more capital than can be raised from profits. Financial institutions would need to understand this and ensure that their lending practices are in the right balance for the needs of the economy. They should liase with local district, regional and national government authorities on the direction of economies to ensure essential projects are funded to maintain sustainable development.

CHAPTER 8

LAWS AND CODES OF PRACTICE

This Chapter is concerned with when we should have regulations and common laws, and when we should have codes of practice to guide us. When laws are created they are interpreted rigidly and not flexibly as would happen when being guided. They in effect are either black, or white. If errors were made in drafting the law and they become law without correction it is a slow process to correct, or repeal them.

Few people can absorb all the laws governing our lives. It can probably be fairly said that the majority of the population are ignorant of the law. Even the well educated can be too. Our lives are so busy that most of us are ignorant until it applies to something we are doing; we could be breaking it and unaware until someone informs us. Many regulations are also acts of parliament, and these too must not be broken. Certain laws govern the trade and professional activities, but how many of them are fully aware of all the laws that apply to their tasks? Most people understand that perhaps they should not be ignorant of the law, but in reality we are. There is probably not a single person in the world that has not broken the law somewhere. When working in Somalia I came across the situation where the laws could be written in any of three languages, Somali, Italian, or English; only some of them were in the three languages! If laws and regulation are important, as they must be, the reason for their existence, why are we not made aware in our education of the ones we must be familiar with? The problem is there are just too many regulations. The majority of the population wish to be law abiding, but there seems to be the problem we do not realise how many laws there are that could apply to our daily activities. When staying in other countries we are supposed to know their laws too! Somehow this situation must be solved, so we are at least aware of the very important laws.

Laws and or regulations guide, give various rights and/or restrictions. Breaking the regulations is an offence, and penalties are submitted on the offenders. Many regulations exist to prevent certain human undesirable actions, prevent accidents, protect health, or other protective purpose. Some laws are to enable land and property to be used by the government, or an essential private enterprise project to be constructed. From some regulations for motorists it would sometimes appear that they are used to increase revenue, like parking tickets. However, the parking problem is not solved. There are so many laws that they cannot be policed or checked. Under the circumstances if the law or regulation cannot be policed, people do not necessarily know they are breaking the law, because they are unaware of it. So one could say as a result of lack of communication the law is ineffective. When laws are ineffective it seems to be human nature not to treat them seriously, and they could also treat important laws similarly.

MH System approach is to have as few common laws as possible, and the ones that there are, are very important, and the right people can be well aware of them as there are not too many laws to know about. There would be laws for the public and others for the private and government sectors. Other regulations would be in the form of codes of practice, and these could be governed by a common law stating they should be used responsibly. There are occasions when parts of codes perhaps should be ignored, for special reasons, like for matters obviously not taken into account when drafting the document, from lack of knowledge or experience. This sort of circumstances can then be judged should there be an accident, or failure of some sort. The laws and codes of practice regulating countries should each be drafted by the relevant experts and be updated at appropriate intervals, depending on how they can be affected as the economy moves forward. With a MH System form of culture, bringing up all children responsibly and an education giving them a sound understanding of the economy and their duties, there should be a considerable reduction in the regulations required.

The Law on Human Rights could well include much of the legislation we should all learn. For example, this law can deal with how we treat/respect each other, the various events which would be treated as crimes including corruption; the right of water, of work and to be properly paid, and to own property; and the right of sound money and a fair, honest trading system, and to have the maximum of freedom within the natural restraints. Clearly laws concerning government and their duties and behaviour are necessary; and the way departments operate could be covered by codes of practice.

When people have rights and those rights are taken from them, it is not unreasonable for them to be properly compensated. For example, like the compulsory purchase of land and property, the compensation should be based on the MH system rules, realistic honest values, not the present-day market forces where prices are manipulated and dishonest. Where theft and damage is caused, people may be fined or go to prison, but often nothing is done to help the victims. If they are uninsured they have no compensation. However, accidents can cause substantial bodily harm. These could be said to be natural events, when even caused by other persons unintentionally. Under these circumstances large sums of money should not be paid in lump sums for life, but financial help given as needed during the rest of their lifespan. When large lump sums are given they are often used up, or mismanaged and lost to others in various ways, and therefore, are then no help to the victims. Sane persons committing the crimes should also pay towards the losses their crimes have caused.

Financial penalties for crimes for poor persons could take a substantial part of their income, yet for a wealthy person, it could be like giving a little gift. It should be noted that a penalty should feel like a penalty. Penalties should be carefully chosen, bearing in mind that financial penalties on a poor family could make the rest of the family suffer more than the offender.

Generally, speaking most people do not wish to cause problems and crimes. When crimes are committed great care should be taken in finding out what has led to the cause of the crime. This could assist in preventing further crimes. The reasons for terrorism should also be carefully checked and the problems sorted out by sound reasoning and not by conflict. Unfairness, resources and oppression are often the reason, and these people should be helped to achieve freedom.

International laws

In a modern world an international language understood by everyone is highly desirable. This does not prevent laws also being translated into the national language. Many of the national laws need to be accepted internationally, because we all rely on a substantial amount of international trade. We are relying on each other's nations to support our modern way of life. We all need the same laws of protection and human rights to create the sustainable environment we all wish to live in. However, nations can also expect to need certain codes of practice special to their country that may never be required in other countries. It also is sensible to make many laws and codes of practice the same throughout the world, making it easier for people to cope internationally.

The present world national economies have much to do before they can harmonise many of their national laws with the rest of the countries in the world. Many countries are oppressed and have dictators, who are abusing their unnatural powers mainly for their own purposes and satisfaction. There is no harm in having heads of state or royal families, where their position does not interfere with people's natural rights: those heads of state in effect form part of a country's culture. However, it is becoming, in the world today, essential to correct the various forms of oppression taking place, by sound reasoning that those causing the problems cannot fail in having to change their approach. It is essential for protecting and supporting people and our world environment. The MH system and its structure are developed to help to achieve this objective. It is a very well thought through system that everyone gains from, but has little to lose.

CHAPTER 9

TAXATION AND PUBLIC SECTOR BORROWING

The reason for taxation is to pay for services given by governments, their departments and local district and regional authorities. In present day economies there are many types of taxation like income tax, which citizens and businesses pay; national insurance and pension contributions; value added tax on goods and services bought; custom and excise taxes; and local authority taxes; capital gains taxes on the sale of assets and death duties on a person's estate, being those taxes commonly charged by government bodies. Many people have insufficient income to pay income tax, because of low pay or unemployment. Some citizens gain considerable profit from their activities and try to avoid taxation, because they believe they are paying more than a fair share. Because taxation is often at high levels, businesses frequently pay a large proportion of all taxation. Business taxation rates vary from country to country and this does not create a level playing field for competition. The author's research has revealed that the redistribution of wealth and the collection of much of the tax revenue all takes place within the business when wages are paid and products are sold. When goods and services are bought the general public indirectly pay the business tax, as they have paid larger profits to the business to cover the cost of their tax. Taxation must be fair for the services given to each individual, or family. The true purpose of the economy is to serve families, and logically they are the ones that should be paying for the nation's general taxation, for the services that only governments can or should provide. The author proposes that sustainable economies should be run on the basis that each employed citizen working in the general economy pays the government taxes and that businesses do not pay any form of taxation, but may be required to collect tax on behalf of government departments. However, economies must be made sustainable and it is also vital that unemployment is eliminated, except for the time needed to retrain or seek new employment.

To build sustainable economies governments must co-ordinate the activities of the non-family economies. The activities need to be guided at local district, regional, national and international levels. Families and each individual should understand how the economy must function, particularly their duties in the economy. Sustainable economies need national and international trading rules, including how wages rates are established. Money too must be defined, as a fixed measure as previously described. Government must also ensure the trading rules are followed so people are properly paid for their work, and profits remain at sustainable levels that do not distort the economy. Nations need a system of defence. Laws and regulations are essential, but the minimum number should be used to ensure they are obeyed. Finally, as the nation moves forward with time our economies must be developed on a sustainable path, which must be carefully guided. Sound education of the public is essential, as this will assist in a smoothly running economy. National and international disasters will also need to be supported by taxation and the environment must be cared for. Many services given by governments could be privatised. However, some services are more economically provided for by government, like the basic pension.

As previously pointed out, businesses and institutions (including the self-employed, and where labour only is supplied) are in an ideal situation to collect taxes for government, on wages and products sold. However, the taxes are collected to provide services for the citizens and, therefore, general taxation should be paid on wages, or personal income only. The author recommends that businesses should not pay tax, which is normally passed on to the public in the prices they pay for the various products, but they should pay for government services specifically for them. These government services could be run as non-profit making businesses, and some may compete with the private sector. Clearly the simplest form of taxation is when it is collected from the wage earnings, and this policy would save both governments and businesses money, and allow them to be more efficient. This would also save governments the problem of how to tax e-commerce. VAT is also no longer charged on goods and services. Under this Flat Tax System, business competition is free of distortion resulting from different tax and VAT rates, as for them taxation is zero. It should be noted that the lower the percentage rate of government taxation, the more that the general public would be willing to accept one form only of tax collection.

Government services should mainly provide for needs, leaving other organisations to provide the wants. On this basis low levels of taxation can be achieved, that should be quite acceptable to the public, who would understand the business sector does not pay tax, because the reasons for this policy had been carefully explained to them. With the MH system business profits are capped, at a level which is sustainable, and this and no inflation maintains the purchasing power of money. Further, with a sustainable wage structure, as describe in Volume 1 Chapter 3, low flat taxes are affordable.

In present-day economies many products have a very high tax element, sometimes more than their actual value. Saying, 'it is imposed to aid the environment, or to prevent certain vices' often defends this practice. However, this defence does not correct the problems that are usually left to continue. Governments should not try and rectify problems by taxation, but instead, they should find other solutions, chiefly through esducation.

In sustainable economies funds from taxation are intended to:

• Protect, manage and guide the economy, the work which cannot be covered by the private sector;
• Provide services like education, health care, basic pensions, roads, transport, water supply, waste disposal and power. Much of this work can also be carried out by the private sector.

In sustainable economies it is best for wants to be provided by the private sector, which would ensure that markets are sufficient, and that over-supply is avoided. Sustainable economies should strive to provide as close as possible the real demands for products.

The level of taxation in any nation should be based on statistics gathered at local district level, and on sound modelling based on the author's sustainable economic system. As the economy moves forward, models would be adjusted to take into consideration the latest conditions and rates of economic development. Clearly the level of taxation must be affordable. People should, under normal conditions, have sufficient earnings to cover their needs and wants, which makes life worthwhile.

Taxation among nations can be expected to be different. Under present world conditions economies are at very different levels of development. Also, each nation has different physical conditions, which can make the cost of living higher, or lower, in comparison with the average, even where the degree of technology used is similar. Some small nations have weaker economies, which may have greater difficulty in recovering from natural disasters, or other shocks to the economy. This can lead to higher taxation rates than the average.

For low levels of taxation, it is important that high employment levels are maintained and people are not retired at too early an age. The right balance needs to be chosen for the level of retraining, and the rate of development must equal the workforce's ability to keep pace with the changes needed.

There is little to be gained by taxing pensioners. If pensioners do not have to pay tax they need to save less for their pension, which makes taxation in their working lives more affordable. For efficient economies governments should carefully study the family lifetime expenditure. With business not paying tax on profits, rents can be lowered to the levels indicated for homes, as Table 12 Volume 1.

An added advantage with a flat tax on wages only and no other forms of taxation and an International Master currency to which all countries join is that trade among nations and prices of goods and services would not be distorted by different national rates of tax and customs and excise duties. It would therefore be much easier to compare the values and the reasons for differences in prices. It would also ensure that goods are not just more competitive resulting from higher taxes on industry in the importing nation and a stronger currency, and this would avoid unnecessary transportation and reduce energy requirements.

Sustainable economies should not run year after year on borrowed money from the private sector of the economy. Money from these sources should only be borrowed, in a 'developing nation situation', or as a result of a very substantial shock, or disaster, to its economy. If a government has borrowed 60% of its Wage GDP and pays 4% per annum it has cost the taxpayers 2.4% of the wage GDP, or 8 % of their taxation would have been paid out for nothing in return. Governments should run their country on a sustainable level of taxation, which can be calculated, based on realistic models of the real economy. They should have reasonable reserves to cover normal contingencies. When unexpected shocks hit their economies, they should not rely on borrowing only, to smooth the rate of taxation to maintain them at affordable levels, but also delay the rate of the less urgent government development projects. Interest paid on borrowed money by the government has to be paid for from taxation, which will need to be justified to the taxpayers, the working public.

Serious shocks to the economy will increase demands for certain products and skills, and in consequence alter the pattern of trade. Money will not solve the problem of shortages of supply of products and labour. Good management and planning to make good the damage created by economic shocks are essential.

When planning taxation levels, governments should take into consideration that the tax rate would not be constant year after year, but vary to take into consideration the ups and downs of an economy caused by natural events. Working population would also vary from year to year. Governments, therefore, need to determine the maximum affordable tax rate for sustainable conditions, and set normal rates below the maximum level, leaving enough margins to cover catastrophic events that may affect their country.

Generally speaking the average hours people would work would amount to 1900 hours per annum. If government did not normally tax income on overtime above the 1900 hours, this would give people incentive to work longer hours. It would also make longer hours for low wage earners far more attractive. Another solution to keeping taxation lower is to increase normal working hours. Suppose working hours were increased by 0.5 hours a day and a normal working day is 8 hours, income would rise by 6.25% and, therefore, tax collected would also rise by that amount and be equivalent to another 1.875% tax rate based on the 30% flat tax rate. It would be better to do this than borrow money. When government spends another 1.875% of the nations normal budget it has created the amount of extra work.

When governments raise taxation on the population's earnings they have a more secure income from the economy. They are then less likely to need to borrow money. Businesses can operate in many different ways, and could run a number of years without making profits, or when working overseas have unprofitable operations, which cancel the home country profits made. Breaking into overseas markets can be expensive. Business cycles are far less stable than family cycles, because their risks are much higher and they are more likely to fail even in sustainable forms of economy.

CHAPTER 10

SHARES, BONDS, CURRENCY AND OTHER MARKETS

In the present day economic system market forces are allowed to drive values of financial products, goods and services. The price is controlled by what people are prepared to pay, or how much people can be squeezed! As should now be clear from reading about the MH system of sustainable development, free markets can considerably distort the economy, leaving people without work, insufficient money to support them, leading to poverty in many countries and allowing other people to become very rich cleptocrats. The MH system is designed as a tool to remove all the distortions in the economies and make it possible for people to understand how their economies need to be managed.

Shares, bonds, currency and other financial markets still would be applicable under the MH trading rules, but the rules set prevent the distortions preventing the sustainable balances needed. To commence, a sound financial system must be based on sound information. The local districts record this information in the single information system. The system records every person, business and institution. If they are not on the system they are not traders. All trade monetary exchanges pass through the current account banking system, which is open to any official, or authorised bodies to view. Therefore, financial services and investors know whom they are lending to, or investing in. It should also be noted that each business or sector of a business would only have one current account. Many of the distortions in the world economies are caused by the financial system, because valuations are floating, as the value of money is based on unsustainable currency market values, which are continually fluctuating.

Present day money is not finite, but growing caused by inflation of prices rising and driven by markets. In the MH system it is finite, in the sense that it is based on the hours of work we are collectively prepared to do, to provide all the goods and services we create to support our living conditions. The hours of work create assets: the goods, service organisations, and national infrastructure. All these have to be maintained and have differing life spans, before being of no further use to us. These can all be valued and are our collective material assets, made by us. The rest of the productive time in our collective work in the economy, whatever it may be, is consumed in the services we have provided, like haircuts, cooking, cleaning, policing, teaching, repairing, managing, entertaining, etc. This is spent labour and not asset making.

In the MH system money is used for two purposes: one as a means of exchange of wages for goods and services, and these always balance; and the other to facilitate the exchange of second hand goods, or infrastructure, like buildings, businesses and their fixed assets, and institutions and their fixed assets. All valuations are on the basis of present values that take into account depreciation caused by use, or aging, or how many hours of work to remake or build using the most modern methods.

The amount of money in our current accounts and cash, belonging to individuals, businesses and other organisations, institutions and government bodies is the liquid money available to be spent: the money supply. All this money is backed by goods and services that are immediately available for sale. This forms part of our wealth. The rest of a nation's wealth is the second hand assets and others assets as discussed in the previous paragraph.

Because we all need savings, and others need money to build their businesses, to carry them through a bad period, or to invest in property, there are methods for lending and making an unearned income, which does not occur when left in the MH current accounts (or very little under present systems). There are safe lending risks like in bank savings accounts and there are other products like bonds, shares and venture capital, the latter being the most risky, as already explained in Volume 2, Chapters 3 and 4. This Chapter is mainly concerned with bonds, shares and other markets, including currencies.

Shares and Bonds

Shares and bonds in the past have usually been in companies and government authorities. In the MH system companies and other organisations must annually revise the true value of their assets and give all the information required as listed in Table 117, Volume 2. Their profits are based on Tables 101 to 110 Volume 2. Bond and share dividends would have to comply with MH rules, that is, not to exceed the limits given. Normally the dividends given would exceed the amount obtainable from bank savings accounts. However, the money invested in them is at risk if the companies fail, as the only security is the remaining assets, following bankruptcy, or liquidation, the equity left; hence the term equities being used for share holdings.

Bonds are usually for periods like 1, 3, or say 5 years with a fixed rate of interest. In the event of a failure, after the state, bondholders would have first call on funds from the liquidation of the assets. Debentures are similar to bonds, and in an event of non-payment of interest could have the right to recover their money. The MH system does not change the present arrangements. It only limits the net rent to being affordable by the economy.

Preference shares like bonds would be at a fixed rate of interest and maybe more than a bond, but not more than the MH rules allow. They would always be paid the intertest due before the profits of other shareholders.

With the MH system, holders of ordinary shares (equities) are entitled to much larger payments, provided they do not exceed the limits set for calculating net rent. The shares in a company are always based on the par value, but with time its assets could grow, making their shares worth more, in proportion to the original capital. Further, if the company employs more people, it can make an additional profit compared with its first years; this too would make the share worth more. However, if a company fails and has to be liquidated, shareholders would have to share what remains, - sometimes nothing.

People buying shares, or bonds etc. should be aware of the company structure and debts, and all other information to make a sound decision on the risk they are taking. Many small investors today do not have this information at the time of purchase.

Various other forms of investment like Unit Trusts, Deferred Capital and Warrants are available, and they are not altered by the MH system, provided its rules are complied with.

Currency markets would be changed very much by the introduction of the MH system. The reason being all money would be pegged to the Master Currency. This has the effect of establishing a single currency throughout the world. No longer would people and business gain or lose money every time they change from one currency to the next. Banks no longer would have to make a charge for the risk they are taking when changing currency, as there is no loss. Hedge funds for this purpose would no longer be required. Speculators will no longer be able to make money out of these markets, by intelligent buying or selling, and playing the markets. For businesses, planning and pricing is much easier and with less risk. The new money would not inflate or deflate, but remain stable. And there would be much more longer term investment, so badly needed in the countries like Brazil. The markets would be a lot less frenetic.

Derivative instruments, hedge funds and funds of hedge funds do not really belong to the MH system. These forms of spreading risk and losing in the tangle of dud companies are unacceptable. Buyers should know exactly what they are buying and no business should be sold for more than it is worth. This does not prevent unit trusts, buying and managing sound stock, but they must not buy and sell shares for more than they are worth. They must choose portfolios carefully. People managing unit trusts and dealing in shares must abide by the MH rules, where they are paid properly for their skill and tasks, and bonuses have to be earned money, not net rents. Fees charged must be calculated and kept within the permissible allowable net rent. All trading must be open and transparent.

Specialist advisors must be very familiar with the true worth of company shares they are advising people on. They should have enough inside knowledge of these companies to make sound decisions. They should really make sure that their clients do understand the risks they are taking, and that they can afford to take the risk. Generally speaking as all shares are properly valued, people should be buying shares below their real worth.

CHAPTER 11

PENSION FUNDING

With the MH system, it is clear that the most economic method for providing the basic safety net pension is from the flat tax collected, that every working person pays. It provides for looking after a small home, and paying for basic expenses. It should be recognised many people seem unable to save and, after all, giving everyone a basic pension is quite fair, as all able people have worked for it. It is not an unsound culture to do so, any more than providing a health service and looking after disabled persons.

Many retired persons want to have more than a basic pension on retirement, and why not, if affordable and they have saved for it, or entered into a separate pension plan, a form of insurance that covers the problem of varying life spans. The other problem for people is the age of retirement, as we now appear to be living longer, but not all of us. Another matter to take into consideration is that it is natural for older members of families to pass on any assets they may have when they die onto their children or relatives. This all helps retired people, provided the state does not claim death duties.

The MH system allows careful long term planning to take place and ensures people are properly paid for their work. It also ensures the type of education that guides them towards intelligent responsibility as far as possible. This means that far less taxation is required and only a simple income tax. There would be no need for governments to tax the rich to transfer funds to the poor. Generally speaking people would not be poor, provided they work reasonable hours to pay for normal expenses of living.

In the modern MH system world there are two ways of saving: money in bank accounts, stored as a promise to pay the hours of work we have kept by for when they are wanted; or to literally have stocks of new goods that can be exchanged, (what had to be done before money was invented). Many of us do have fixed assets like our homes, which could be worth several years work. However, assets have to be maintained and stored. Apart from our homes, as we become older we do not want any more work than we can cope with. The home when we die can be passed on to our relatives and others, or sold to help their finances.

For most people the most convenient means for savings are the monetary form. The monetary form then must be very honest and fair so people cannot loose their savings. The MH monetary and banking system is such a system that allows savings to be safely kept without loss of purchasing power. Money is only lent to people who can maintain its purchasing power. This form for savings is the ideal form of pension funds, because its purchasing power remains safe. However, there must always be enough people to borrow this form of money until pensioners want to use their savings for retirement expenses. Money can be kept secure by understanding the various life cycles of families, businesses and institutions. Population variations must also be understood.

When the balance of the population varies there can be more children, or fewer children and this can lead to situations when there could be a very large retired population. The work of maintaining the economy is then left to a smaller working population and all the economic balances need to change to meet the new situation. Governments and businesses would need to plan for the changes, so the markets will provide for the requirements.

Generally speaking with a sound and well-managed economic system it should not be necessary for the state to provide the second pension. It is up to individuals to plan their own retirement requirements, as they only know the cost of their lifestyle and how and what they would like to leave for relatives and friends, if anything. From a study of the life cycle it is clear, provided work is available, there are likely to be more funds available in the last fifteen years of work, before retirement age. Pension/insurance funds organisations should encourage people to save in this period for their pensions. People should not put all their savings into one organised pension fund, as some could be more successful than others. It would also be prudent to have savings to cover the variations in annual expenditure.

Final-salary forms of pension in a sustainable form of economy are unrealistic, and do not necessarily match our productivity/skills criteria as we reach the end of fulltime employment. For some people their most productive period is at a young age, whilst others in the middle of our careers, or at the end, or perhaps even after we are retired: it all depends on the nature of work we have specialised in. Pension advisors should help people to get the most suitable balance for their particular needs.

Private pension funds are a form of gamble, as contributors to them have to rely on other persons' management skills and luck in the way the funds are invested until paid to the retired persons. Money could be placed just in savings accounts that may pay 2% interest per annum; it could be in bonds paying 4% per annum, or in shares paying 5% to 7% per annum. If share investments fail money could be lost. The fund managers can only place investments where they can sell or buy them, as markets and economies are continually changing. People in the fund may live longer or shorter than expected. These types of pension fund may decide on a fixed sum per annum, or a variable sum until death. All sorts of combinations are possible, but they have to manage the pension rates paid out to pensioners, with the actual money available for distribution each pension year. If they pay out too much the fund could collapse, or pensions would have to be reduced, to balance the books.

There is no doubt pension funds need strict regulation, and companies running their own pension funds must never be allowed to use them in their own business. Pension fund money needs to be carefully spread. The bigger the pension fund the more the investments can be spread to ensure the minimum is lost by unsuccessful investments, which could not be foreseen, or a natural human error.

Most people would not want to be involved with running their main, or second pension fund/s, and would prefer to use a specialist pension company. It is therefore very important that governments have a sound monetary and economic system so that pension funds can provide sound, honest products for pensioners; that do not let them down. Should this happen it is important to have a safety net, to minimise their loss, like an insurance policy.

Other monies for retirement can well be in savings accounts, and it is up to individuals to choose. Some may wish to invest in bonds and shares also, but these would not normally be covered by any safety net. Others might invest in property to let initially and perhaps sell at a later date. These funds could all be treated as people's savings. It is very wrong when governments tax property sales in any way, as they are taking advantage of peope's savings. It is also wrong to tax rent income, as it really is another tax on the tenants. Tax on wealth is also wrong. With the MH system wealth is already fairly distributed and all wage earnings have already been taxed.

Many people after normal retirement age, determined by the state, would still like to work, even if their productivity had fallen to the lowest acceptable level. If these people do not have any form of second pension it would not be unreasonable for them to be exempt from income tax. This could certainly help in situations where there are a large proportion of people in the retired zone of the economy, compared with those normally in the working age workforce. It should be noted that people working after the state chosen retirement age should still be entitled to their state pension. From the modelling in Volume 1 Chapter 9 it can be seen they do require a further income, to maintain a reasonable lifestyle.

CHAPTER 12

REAL WEALTH

Natural wealth is our environment and the universe, which supplies our light and solar energy. Without its resources, we would not be able to create the products and services that enhance our standard of living. Natural wealth is priceless and some is being lost as a result of human exploitation. Such natural wealth is not unlimited and needs to be used sparingly.

Real wealth using the MH system is based on its Master Currency unit, a productivity unit as defined in the other volumes. It can be expressed in hours, or years of productive work, the work-year being based on the time working in the non-family economy. This manmade wealth is the added value to natural wealth. Since our existence we have been reshaping the world. Some of our work has been constructive but also much has been destructive as has been recorded in one way or another. Many structures and ruins thousands of years old still exist.

The wealth elements of our economies are the goods and services we have created, need and want, plus those that still exist but not in real use. This wealth forms our assets. The useful ones that we continually use in developed nations could be equivalent to 10 years wage GDP and other assets not in use are difficult to value without the statistical information. Even today some developing countries wealth may be well below a year's wage GDP and consequently their standard of living and security is poor and many are living in conditions of poverty.

The standard of living certainly cannot be linked to wealth alone, but has to take many other matters into consideration, like human capital, and the products that give quality to life. However, in Chapter 6 a standard of living measure was given as a guide to wealth, and this was the amount of income left for leisure activities and luxuries. National wealth in the infrastructure is very important to the basics of our lives and probably at least two years wage GDP earnings are needed, using modern technology. Naturally the needed investment would vary from country to country, depending on location, topography, and natural resources.

Nations can be very wealthy in assets, but those assets can well be the wrong ones to support the population leaving many people at poverty level. Without the right type of investments in its infrastructure poverty cannot be alleviated, and this needs planning and people with the right skills to carry out the work necessary. Nations need to be properly developed, and this is one of the reasons why the author has developed his sustainable form of economic system.

Because people are different and seek individual paths during their economic lives we do not all need the same amount of wealth for it. This can result in some people carrying out less work in the general economy, as a low income could be all they need to satisfy their lifestyle and pastime occupations. Other people need more income and wealth for their activities.

We are kept alive by the products we make to serve our basic every day requirements. However, our lives are made more pleasurable with artefacts that please us. We like to have buildings, monuments and gardens to serve various activities. Much of our time is also occupied by leisure activities, which again create fixed assets. All these items have to be got into the right balance that is affordable. In soundly run countries this wealth gradually grows. Some families' wealth over a number of generations can become vast.

Economies need wealthy people and businesses so that large projects can be undertaken, from which we can all benefit. Historically, some wealth has come to families from the spoils of conflict or given for favours to powerful tribes, or kings. What has happened in the past is safe to leave in the present world, provided the owners of this wealth are responsible persons. What is important is what people do with their wealth.

Many people abuse their use of wealth and create projects that no one else can enjoy; and they really have too much to enjoy and it is wasted. Many people have marvellous artefacts locked up in safes because they are precious and never really seen or used. Others just buy too much to display or use and this too is abuse of wealth and a waste of resources. This form of wealth use is irresponsible and a form of unnecessary greed. There is a limit to how much wealth a person can really enjoy personally. Beyond that limit one becomes the guardian of that wealth, and a responsible person would either use it soundly to benefit others in the economy, or give it to those needing help. It is like running a business based on the MH system rules.

Many buildings and artefacts we have made in the past are part of our history and culture and we wish to preserve them. However, we can only keep what we can afford to maintain. For many people this is a pastime or hobby, and in many economies they have saved much that would not have been possible otherwise.

The MH system does not prevent the ownership of considerable wealth, as owners are treated as managers of the wealth and must comply with the MH rules and be responsible persons. They must not abuse their wealth, but use their wealth as forming part of the overall national and international economy.

CHAPTER 13

POWER

When establishing economic management structures human nature and how we can act must always be taken into account. People that manage others have a certain amount of power. The more people, the higher up the ladder and the larger the organisation, the more power and authority held. In government there are thousands of top managers and officials, in local, regional and central government and councillors, politicians and ministers. All are public servants and are expected to work honestly, fairly and efficiently, and above any form of corruption or doing wrong. But a position of power at any level can sometimes change people's integrity and balance of mind. Work stress, tiredness, and age can also distort people's ability and judgement. Many posts have guaranteed periods of office. The position allows them to continue in posts using powers wrongly or to their own advantage, or the advantage of certain others. With the MH system people do not enjoy such powers over the direction of the economy. They can be asked to go at any time if they are not performing as intended: confidence in their services is lost and their ability is unsatisfactory for the post held.

In employment people do need a certain amount of security; they cannot normally afford to be without work. Provided one is fit for the post available there is always the right of work; but, in any form of work engaged, one must work properly and conscientiously. One should not be bullied in any way, but helped as necessary.

Politicians, ministers and un-elected senior civil servants have enormous powers. The political party in power tries to fulfil its manifesto and revised additions as they continue in power. However, the general public do not know what is the power that senior civil servants have in the decisions made, and what influence they have on reshaping the manifesto, which could well be unworkable. Clearly the top civil servants will have to be very familiar with all the laws and other regulations and comply with them, whether or not they may be faulty, until they can be corrected. But what sort of other advice do they give and why?

The more sophisticated the government, the more difficult it is to communicate with them, particularly if they do not want to communicate!

The author, an economist and engineer with a lifetime's, very broad experience on how economies need to function and how to develop successful projects, the reason for developing his system, wonders why he cannot find the right people to speak to in government to discuss the economy. If the economies were running smoothly in the world and in harmony with the environment, there would be no real need to communicate. But one can hardly say economies are running very well, as can be understood from reading the three volumes of this book. The whole world is very unstable with considerable hardship for the majority of the world population. So why have his communications with government not produced any results to make the world a better place to live in?

It is only by communication and discussion that one can find out why our economies are failing people so badly. One needs to know whether the government structure is in a system that prevents it from reshaping into a sustainable form, or the skills of both the politicians and senior civil servants include the know-how to develop sustainable economies. If this is not the problem is it because government cannot evaluate the proposed MH system, or is it because powerful organisations are influencing governments?

All governments in the world need to work together to create a world economic structure. The problem is how to determine which powerful forces are holding the present trading system in its present form. Is it the private sector or the government sector? What is needed to convince people or governments to build a sustainable world economy? Which powerful forces are preventing this from happening? The world governments are making little progress on both trade and global warming issues.

What sort of powers are going to be required to build the badly needed sustainable world economic structure? War and armed conflict is certainly not going to succeed. Only very sound arguments, built on a clear understanding of the natural economy and how it functions, can convince everybody that we will all be better off with a sustainable economic structure as outlined in this book. Trust and confidence needs to be established and this is a political process. For the political process to succeed sound explanations on how economies should function are essential, and the persons involved in this process would all need to be well informed. Politicians and senior advisors must all have a sound knowledge of the economic process. Only this form of power is likely to succeed. People expect their elected politicians to carry out this process, but will they? Politicians have the power to create the changes needed to the world economies, but many will need to find the time to understand what is needed, and it is hoped that they will.

If politicians fail to change the way we manage our economies to be sustainable, it is left to the private sector. One of the problems for the private sector is that where the rules necessary for a sustainable economic system conflict with existing laws and regulations, it would not be able to adjust those parts of the economy. The private sector would therefore, have first to build only the parts of the new infrastructure which does not interfere with existing laws, and hope that at a later date governments would make the necessary changes to complete the work started by the private sector

Many professional institutions have rules covering their ethical, fair and honest practice in carrying out their tasks and many institutions support caring for the environment and the sustainable development of the world economies. The private sector has a considerable investment in the world economies, and it is in their interest that economies are sustainable.

The private sector could of course create its own political party, which it could well afford, and its members collectively have all the knowledge required. The power, it could be said, is also in the private sector, to make the world a better place to live in.

CHAPTER 14

EMPLOYMENT CULTURE

The economies of the modern world are changing quickly. We are no longer in a job for life, and many more businesses are working internationally. Work and projects are far more complicated and components can come from a number of countries around the world. Companies want simpler trading rules to assist international exchange. Many would prefer not to be responsible for staff pensions and other benefits. Employees also want greater freedom and to be properly paid for their work. Rapidly changing methods of production and distribution often means employees need new jobs many times during their working lives. Many would also like second jobs to increase their income.

Young employees early in life need income for buying their homes and supporting children, which every nation needs to maintain its population, as can be verified from Table 42 Volume 1. They really do need to be properly paid for their productivity. Many pensioners who have been unable to save sufficiently would often like to work beyond the state pension age.

In Chapter 3 Volume 1, a sustainable basis for negotiating wage rates is given. The basis does not prevent anyone of any age from being paid properly, provided they have the right skills and productivity for the work done. However, the system does not prevent highly skilled persons taking on work, where they may use only some of their skill potential, and they would be paid in accordance with the skills used and their efficiency. Many businesses prevent such persons working for them, because they do not have appropriate work for age and skill. It is felt they could not be offered lower rates of pay; hence the person is left unemployed. The special skill has blighted the person from any form of work. Many people are quite capable of learning news skills and being very proficient in them to late in life, and should not be refused work because of age. We all need work to support ourselves, so we do not feel we are being a burden on others.

Redundancy payments paid in many countries are not necessary, and discourage businesses taking on extra staff. The simpler it is for businesses to engage personnel on daily, weekly or monthly notice basis, the easier it makes it to employ people. With a well-organised economic system finding work would be much easier. Using the MH current account banking system people would be helped to solve financial problems, while their savings would maintain their purchasing power without any loss from inflation.

The MH system business profit structure encourages businesses to employ people, as the more people they employ the larger their permissible profit. Profit in the sustainable economic system can only be made on capital and people employed. Because profits are more fairly distributed within the MH system, businesses would be able to take on more staff to pay for labour intensive work, which they cannot afford under present economic conditions, because profits are being squeezed. Labour intensive work is often for maintenance, much left neglected, for lack of funds.

CHAPTER 15

SUSTAINABLE ENVIRONMENT DEFINED

The three volumes of the book discuss various aspects of present day economies, sustainable development and the environment. For any one element of the economy and the environment to be in a sustainable form, all other elements must be too. Sustainable development must take all matters into consideration, and the economy must readjust the balances needed, as time passes by. Any person specialising in sustainable development of any element of the economy/environment must network to ensure that the proposals and actions taken for that particular element is in harmony with all other elements. That also means that it can be achieved by the manpower and is affordable.

Sustainable solutions are based on a thorough knowledge and understanding of the element, and how nature intends it to operate. That is to say, it must be natural and not forced into an unnatural situation opposing, or preventing the sustainable solution. One could say that balances must be acceptable by nature and by people. Solutions to be used must be achievable at the time of implementation: the right products and skills, and affordable. For many situations, a research, development and modelling process is the only way to produce sustainable solutions.

The trading structure for the sustainable economy must be formed to follow the natural process of exchanging our human labour, and take into account the real productivity used in every skill, and the investment in special skills in trades and professions. The monetary unit for paying for the hours of labour and valuing products must be a constant, so that proper comparisons can be made, people fairly paid, and goods and services sold at prices that are sustainable and that do not distort the economy. The proposed productivity unit based on time, (a Master Currency), and simple trading rules to maintain sustainable profits meets the required criteria.

To manage the world economy and the environment, the world needs to be subdivided into local districts that can be intimately understood by the citizens and managers. Local districts would be responsible for collecting all information. The local districts and regions would co-ordinate their activities with their country and the rest of the world.

The information/knowledge system should be based on a skills/products basis divided into two key sections: Products and Services. These are again subdivided into major sectors of the economy. All the elements of the economy would be listed in this information structure, so that people could then learn where to find all available information that they may need for work, or pleasure activities, and whatever else they may require. The information structure would be like a massive family tree, but with millions of names.

The economic structure serving the sustainable environment would have all the models and tools to manage and guide the whole world environment to be sustainable. The structure would enable people to understand the world they are living in, and what is needed. By using sound measures and development procedures the economy would become more efficient, which would save resources and create sound living conditions for everyone.

Throughout the world, professional persons and governments are monitoring and studying the environment and our economies, both of which need to be kept sustainable to ensure the best conditions for people living in every country. This can only be achieved by creating the right economic structure, where we can all communicate in one international language, trade on the same basis, and co-operate where necessary on matters concerning the stability of every nation. As the world moves on with time the problems caused by instability must be solved and rectified, with solutions that are feasible and sustainable. These solutions need careful planning to ensure both the finance and labour resources are available. The proposed master currency will ensure labour and monetary resources are not distorted.

The developments of the human economies have exhausted many natural resources and cause a considerable amount of pollution, endangering the human economies and reducing and eliminating many species. Conflicts, crimes, wars and poor management have wasted much of the world's resources, including unskilled and skilled labour. Developments have been sited in unsafe locations, and the world financial system has distorted our economies, leaving millions of people with insufficient resources, and others with too many, with some products never used. Sustainable developments can gradually remove the unsound developments, thereby enhancing and bringing back the economy and natural environment into a sustainable form.

We now come to the point of how does one really define a sustainable environment? Clearly the environment covers all that is outside the human economy. For the human race, it also covers the products they have created for their economy. One cannot be considered without the other, but what constitutes a sustainable human economy? None of our assets, generally speaking, are likely to last forever, but with sound technology we can make them last a very long time, and serve us with the minimum of maintenance. However, what is most important to people and families is the quality of life. Firstly, for the vast majority, clearly the elimination of crime and conflicts is very important; secondly the needs of water, food, clothing, housing and furnishings and thirdly good health, time and products for leisure making living worthwhile. An abundance of worldly assets is not essential for happiness, but as much freedom as possible is. The comments just made set the criteria for the quality of life and this needs to be sustained. The condition of the environment must be kept sustainable as it supplies the resources for the economy and the economy must be kept sustainable in order to manage the environment. For the human race both sectors are equally important.

The standard of living must be achievable, and this depends on the hours we are prepared to work in the economy, our collective skills, the natural resources available and the products we have produced. To achieve a sustainable form of economy it has to be managed, and for this a very sound economic structure is necessary. Such a structure needs to take into account that, as time advances, the environment and the economy changes, and the economic structure must also handle this. The economic structure must handle fair trade and for this a sound financial system is vital.

Finally, it is the people in the world that determine whether or not the environment and the economy are sustainable. Collectively they must have the knowledge and skills to manage the level of the achievable standard of living, and each must understand what needs to be done and the part they must play in the economy. We all have duties and obligations and must respect other people's rights and the importance of the environment.

CHAPTER 16

INNOVATION

The present day economies and standard of living have been developed from the millions of innovations that people over the centuries have created. Innovators are people who naturally cannot help thinking of how to improve in some way what we are doing in work and leisure. To a certain extent we are probably all innovators in a very small way. We find ways of making our tasks easier, simpler, or more effective. All sorts of problems and situations can set us into motion to try and improve an operation or object. Innovations are the engines driving the economy forward.

Millions are spent on research and development by both developed and developing nations, to improve, find or create new products. A considerable amount of information is studied and sought: the reason why the MH system seeks to make it more effective and efficient. Ideas have to be developed, and a good information system can help to find vital components to make an idea work.

For complicated innovations one also needs to determine whether they are affordable. Again the MH system has been designed to carry out this important process, by the creation of the Master Currency, linked directly to human productivity. This makes it possible to make comparisons with other similar products or processes.

A good example of millions of innovations is the development of the motorcar discussed in Chapter 6. It has changed considerably since the first ones were made over 100 years ago. They have changed little by little. The engines were small and not very powerful. Then they became more powerful, more efficient, faster, more robust, longer life, requiring less maintenance, self lubricating and made in fewer hours of work by mass production. Millions of little innovations have made this possible. Special metals were developed, manufacturing processes, and management and distribution methods.

Another example on innovation is the manner in how agriculture has been improved, which has resulted in more than half the population working on the land to just 1% or 2% now.

Some innovation results from ideas that only take a little time to develop, whilst others take many years. All sorts of processes take place like, research, designs, and prototype of the innovation, testing, costing, consultation, and marketing. Many innovations are small and are not covered by patents or copyright. New ideas help to develop existing products and improve them, and alone may not be of any use. For example without the hardware of the computer the software would be of little use.

Governments should understand that the more complete an economy, the more likely their population is likely to innovate, as there is a complete cross section of problems to be solved, something for every natural innovator. It should be understood we are different and need our own little slot to fulfil our aspirations.

Wanting to make money, or become very rich rarely motivates innovation; one is more likely to create an improvement, for satisfaction, or achievement. Those that do want to become wealthy are the ones that would promote and market the innovations.

The MH system is a complicated innovation as it is one that is hoped will synchronise the world economies and help people to develop it to be in harmony with the environment; and at more peace with each other, trading on a sustainable and fair basis. It is hoped that it will help governments and managers to understand their tasks and responsibilities better.

CHAPTER 17

POVERTY

There are many causes for the condition of poverty, and they can certainly be caused by natural catastrophe', as most people are aware, and therefore will not be discussed further here. However, most poverty problems are created by our own actions and it is these we must deal with in this Chapter.

The present world economic system and the way we allow our countries to be governed is a major cause of the problem. The economies have evolved over thousands of years, and their form has been dictated by circumstances and people's knowledge, beliefs and practices at that time. Whatever they did, allowed them to progress and create better conditions for themselves, or those in power at the time. They would not necessarily been able to judge then whether their actions were right or wrong: they did not have the knowledge we have today. They survived, even if many others did not.

Since the industrial revolution, we have been able to learn and record much information. Many more people have had the time to study our world and our actions in it, and therefore, begun to realise that we are making grave mistakes. We have had world wars and almost countless conflicts since, all over the world, including terrorism. All this has done serious damage to countries infrastructure, leaving many people feeling very bitter and helpless. People in every country are being exploited in many different ways. There is much corruption and there are dictatorships, with the results that the resources are being used by those that have the power to abuse. All these actions have not made the world a happy place to live in, but only increased poverty and misery.

People, as a result of the modern communication network can very quickly learn what is happening all over the world. We all now have much more knowledge and can understand when our rights are being abused, but millions of people can do little about their situation, particularly where they are suppressed; and many people in the fairer nations have been driven to the attitude, you can't change the system. The cause of poverty needs to be examined in greater detail.

It is likely that poverty exists in every country of the world. Of course poverty can be measured in different ways, as already explained in the volumes of this book. Each country would probably define it differently, based on what they consider it to be, but this does not affect the causes, some of the main ones now being given.

The present economic system is based on a form of free markets (governments prevent it from being completely free) where the amount of profit made (net rent) is not controlled, except by the market. This can allow prices for goods and services to rise to very distorted levels like is happening to real estate all over the world. Further, due to the form of money, the national currencies, it bears no relation to the hours worked for it, because it too is a market value. A developed nation currency can buy considerably more foreign labour than in its own country; see Tables 125 and 126 Volume 2. This situation is bad for both the developed country and the developing country.

For the developed country the distorted value of its currency makes it very much overvalued to perhaps 50 more times than the weakest currency. This results in any goods and services exported having to compete with very low wage costs. Even with the most sophisticated production process many former industries have been forced to close, as production is cheaper in many countries with lower valued currencies. The situation has also lowered the developed nations wage levels to an extent that the minimum wage now set by most governments is insufficient to support them, and many families need subsidies to keep them above poverty level. Pensioners are finding that their pensions each year are falling and are insufficient to cover their basic needs. Taxation has to rise to cover subsidies and this eventually can further affect the ability of many businesses to cope with overseas trade. More goods are imported and more services outsourced abroad, and this will make it more and more difficult for developed countries to be able to pay for the imports.

For developing nations the distorted value of the currencies makes imports of specialist goods and services from developed countries very expensive, and this includes vital medicines and drugs to prevent disease and AIDS spreading. However, many developing nations still with low currency values can now benefit from third world products, provided they have the foreign currency needed to pay for them. The people in developing nations also require to be paid properly for their work, to enable them too to be able to have the benefits of industrialisation, in their own country.

All countries need governments to manage their country democratically and free from any form of dictatorship and corruption. Governments also need honest, dedicated officers with the right training for sustainable development.

Apart from the right form of government and the use of appropriate technology developing countries need a sound basic infrastructure, and an education that is adequate for them to build their country, and understand their rights and duties in it.

The present situation in the developed countries is that governments do not understand how to support people to take themselves out of poverty. They also do not understand it is their policies that have created the problem. For people the only way out of the poverty trap is to get rich somehow. This can lead to over working, and with its consequences, or for example, to overcharging, cheating, stealing and gambling.

The present situation for people in developing nations is to get into positions of power to obtain what they want, or get rich in the other ways already mentioned above and seizing other people's possessions, including land. None of this is sustainable or constructive, but more likely to create more hardship and conflict.

What needs to be done

Using the MH system as a tool, and so creating economic models which make sound comparisons to determine the flaws already mentioned in this Chapter, it is necessary to correct the errors being made in the national and international trading system. Clearly developed nations currencies are overvalued against the developing ones. A proper wage structure is also necessary. These two actions, alone, would go a long way to alleviate poverty, particularly in the developed countries. In the developed countries it would also allow economies to come into better balance, helping to restore export/import financial trading balances.

With much lower rich country currency rates, many developing nations would be getting better value for their imports, so able to buy in what is needed to develop their infrastructure. They would also be able to use more skilled labour to support their own country, instead of subsidising other countries goods and services, by their cheaper labour.

Where countries have unstable and corrupt governments not managing their economies responsibly, it is the duty of truly democratic nations, with the necessary resources, to tackle this problem. If the majority of the world's governments were united in the objectives there would be little difficulty in persuading the minority of unsound governments to change their ways, peacefully. No one really looses with the MH system skilfully applied.

CHAPTER 18

STATISTICS

The MH system monetary unit, being based on productivity and trading rules for all work activities, needs to establish the rates of productivity. The rates are needed for two key purposes, wages and planning. Many readers would pose the question, 'how, or where do we find them, or how do we establish them'. This Chapter deals with this matter and other information on values.

Wages

There are millions of skills used and the MH is concerned with obtaining the average rate. For many operations people of varying productivities could be working under the same roof, but individually. From time and motion studies, built up in trades over many years, the rate for each job carried out can be established. These sorts of operations can be found in publications, which anyone can buy, and in union and business records. Many managers may also have built up their own records of special operations, and these may be recorded, or just held in their memories. Other operations may not have a productivity rate, but just a quality, experience rate for various tasks frequently carried out. Each work discipline has its own natural system. The MH system has also created a calculated means to measure wage differentials, the human capital gained by hours of further study and practice in skilled mental and physical operations. Wage differentials are fully explained, used and discussed in Volume 1. Each business or other institution knows how it uses its staff, for its particular task. Some tasks do not have a productivity rate, but just a time basis, or a varied task basis in a period of time, like working in a shop.

The time statistics using all the different forms of human aids are also recorded, and these cover machines from the smallest to the largest, and the time spent on maintenance operations. Times too are recorded for loading, travelling and unloading operations. Time and motion experts record details of thousands of different operations from the simplest to the most complicated. All this type of information is gathered and available for estimators to forecast costs in all the various productive elements of the economy, and there are millions of them.

Planning and estimating

Apart from the above labour statistics, planners and estimators need other information and statistics.

All the products used in conjunction with the labour activities also need to be valued in the MH units so the total price of a product or service can be given. When the system is fully operational and economies have converted to it, everything would already be sold and priced in the unit. That price would also include the total profit charged, the net rent amounting to approximately 25% of the purchase cost, which helps estimators, who often only want the true labour costs. Before the MH system comes into full operation the MH value of each national

Table 201
Master Currency value in Belgium Francs

Year	1 MH in Belgium Francs
1984	389.8
1985	409.4
1986	426.8
1987	437.2
1988	448.6
1989	472.4
1990	497.8
1991	529.8
1992	559.7
1993	582.3

Table 202
Master Currency value in Danish Kroner

Quarter		1 MH in Kroner
1987	III	141.7
	IV	145.0
1988	I	146.2
	II	148.9
	III	151.5
	IV	153.9
1989	I	154.6
	II	155.5
	III	156.7
	IV	159.4
1990	I	162.3
	II	162.9
	III	164.8
	IV	166.8
1991	I	168.7
	II	171.0
	III	172.5
	IV	173.7
1992	I	175.0
	II	176.4
	III	178.1
	IV	179.3
1993	I	179.9

currency needs to be calculated. An example has already been given on this operation in Chapter 2 and Tables 122 and 123. The statistics have to be obtained from national records, and if these were not available the relevant statistics would have to be gathered as accurately as possible. The Author obtained Central Bank Statistics from Belgium and Denmark and started this process. Table 201 gives figures for the Belgium Francs and Table 202 gives figures for the Danish Kroner, before the Euro was launched.

Sometimes one needs to know the real value of past products. First one needs to calculate the MH value based on the old currency for the year the product was made, and then one can convert it into current values. Old values of products can often be found in old maker's catalogues. They can then be compared with up to date prices. Many historical records can be very useful in determining how long was spent to create past buildings and products. It should be noted that the MH value eliminates inflation making it easier to compare real values.

When every national currency is converted into MH units the real value of products can be compared, and one can discover which ones of the same quality take the fewer hours to make.

In the future if the MH system is widely used, as a single international currency, all products can be valued in MH units, and not in different countries' currencies. All machines and human aids can be priced in these units and this will help the estimating and development process to determine the most efficiently made products, i.e. best value.

Government Statistics

Local district authorities would be the centre responsible for collecting all local information and statistics of its population, businesses, institutions and resources. In Volume 2 Chapter 1 and 2 many of the statistics required to manage the economies are given. The regions and central government would use these to formulate the national statistics.

It is important for government to have real values of all the nations assets in their various categories as, from this, expected maintenance costs can be established. Without a clear picture of the nation's assets it would be difficult to determine the direction for developing the economy. Local district authorities need the information to manage and guide the local economy, and businesses need information on the demands of the local economy and the direction in which it is moving.

It is also important to have detailed information on the workforce and ages of the population, so the shape of the economy would meet the demand requirements. Equally, important to have the details of the state of repair of buildings, infrastructure and the natural environment, and details of the state of brown development sites, and areas subject to flooding.

Government departments would each record statistics concerned with their special duties for example: records of weather conditions, traffic flows, accidents, health problems, crimes, floods etc.

Private Sector Statistics

Businesses would keep key statistics which are required by the government to manage and guide the economy, and to make available to others requiring general statistical information. Many businesses would be able to make available the rates for their standard products.

The use of statistics

Statistics are used in a number of different ways, such as making comparisons, for planning and critical path analysis operations, to check for inflation, to monitor the economy and its stability, and demands for products.

CHAPTER 19

INTERNATIONAL ECONOMY

National economies are very much interdependant as we depend on each others natural resources, including human capital, to ensure collectively we can care for the world environment. We need to be able to communicate, under each others cultures and respect everyone, because we are all equally important as all skills are needed in the collective production of the millions of products, services and ideas exchanged throughout the world.

World economies are in the process of converging, even though each nation has developed to a different standard of living, and our cultures, languages, currencies and laws are only partly international. Many nations are poor or unstable and some are plagued with grave conflicts.

The Master Currency Sustainable Economic System has been developed to help solve world problems and help economies to converge gradually and peacefully, using sound and honest knowledge with fair arguments to solve the variety of problems.

Governments

With hundreds of territories spread over the world and language difficulties, it is not easy to communicate. If there is a lack of good interpreters some unfortunate misunderstandings occur. Countries are governed on different bases, and objectives. How they are governed and trade can upset and cause friction with other countries. All governments have their own ideas on how economies should be managed, and what their duties and responsibilities should be. All this makes it very difficult to manage the world economy and protect its environment.

National laws vary, and tradition and cultures often influence the nature of the law, and how people are treated, when the laws are broken. Historical events sometimes influence the form of law.

International Laws and Agreements

Gradually international laws and agreements are being made to synchronise the manner the world is run and how we trade. However, not all nations are signatories to the laws and agreements made. Agreements are also broken, for various reasons, despite the appearance of well thought through systems, or bases for justifying the terms agreed.

International Organisations

There are many government sponsored international organisations charged with specific international, or regional area duties. Many work quite independently and others co-ordinate similar activities.

Next there are the NGOs and international charities carrying out much important work to make the world a better place for people and to care for the environment. Many are engaged on international relief work, caused by natural events of flooding, tsunamis, earthquakes and droughts, and manmade disasters, of major accidents, pollution and ethnic cleansing.

Sharing World Resources

There are main resources shared in the world, the natural resources and human capital, our very special skills and ideas that improve our quality of life; millions of people have shared this knowledge. However, because of the unnatural structure of the financial system, it has prevented many people in poor countries being able to have vital products they need. The historical manner of the monetary system has been based on markets instead of real exchange of skills, a fairer barter system.

Fresh water is one of the most precious resources for man. Without water we cannot exist and we also need it for our crops and our land environment. Economies are dependant on water. The availability of water determines the sustainable size of the economy. The use of water sources should not interfere with natural river flows along its water course to the sea. Controlling the rate flow is quite acceptable as this can support life as it always has done, for thousands of years. The economic developments must fit in with the rivers minimum average annual capacity. Many rivers pass through many regions and countries and that flow is a natural right for humans and all of nature's other species.

Global warming is already modifying natural water supplies, to an extent that some economies may be starved of fresh water, leaving populations without water. This is an international problem, as people would need to move to where ample water is available.

Forests are being unnecessarily felled and not being re-afforested to maintain a sustainable balance and this is contributing to global warming. The reasons for this should be established and the problems corrected.

Energy is another international source that should be shared. Coal, natural gas and oil are not renewable resources and the consumption of these fuels is also contributing to global warming. The pollution of the atmosphere is also affecting our health. This international problem needs urgent attention.

Drugs and Crime

The reason for drugs and crime need very serious investigation. The market is certainly motivated by money and human weakness, addiction. Most of the drugs come from poor areas of the world. Cut the supply by improving the economy and a sound education process and the problem can be solved. The MH monetary system can make it very difficult to launder money, and a fairer distribution of wealth would make crime less attractive.

Boarders melt with the MH system

The strategy of the MH system binds the trading economies together into a level playing field and a single commercial language. Education teaches us how we are equally important and how much we improve the lives of other people, whom we may never see or meet. Thousands of people have contributed to our economic lives. The arrangement of the economic information system Chapter 7 Volume 1 brings it home to people. We use thousands of items in our daily lives all made by different people. Most people really know little about other people, the reason why it is vital that our trading activities must be honest. It is essential that we can trust each other and most people wish to. People that spend a lot of time with each other are the ones that know their family, friends and colleagues best. They should make sure that they are sound citizens and, if not, help the process to ensure they are. It is one of our many duties essential to creating sound economies.

Transportation

Our transport systems carry vast volumes of products considerable distances and people spend very long hours travelling. Our way of life and economies use vast quantities of energy on travel and transportation, which could be much reduced using a sound financial system and a carefully thought through economy. Early research to study this matter could cut world fuel consumption very quickly and help to reduce global warming to a much safer level. Much more local produce would be used.

Studies for sustainable economies

Studies for sustainable development need to take the whole environment into account, because all resources must be available for changes to be achievable. Projects for sustainable development must be in harmony with each other.

The MH system is designed to manage economies, by first establishing where all the elements of the economy are and explaining how they interact with each other. Once this is known, the state of each element can be determined and how distorted it is, and what is needed to restore it to a sustainable balance. Environmentalists, biologists, scientists and many other experts have already a considerable knowledge of the world problems, and continue with their monitoring of the world species, resources and the condition of the environment.

To achieve sustainable conditions it is necessary to be able to establish the human hours of work required to rectify the problems. We also require the right skills, and need to be able to support the world populations in harmony with the environment. Many studies are necessary to get the balances right, which will also include how to obtain everyone's support throughout the world.

Ones need's an economic structure and a strategy that can accomplish the sustainable use of the environment. The author has produce a skeleton system for this purpose that connects all economies and the environment together. So that all parties working on this massive task can co-ordinate their activities on the same basis, and make sure their solutions are feasible and achievable. Responsible bodies will need to network with each other to help solve each other's problems in managing their part of the economy or special interest.

How to best to help developing nations

The population of developed nations in comparison with developing nations is small. Developed nations do not have the capacity to develop the latter, but they do have much of the technology for the purpose. Developed countries still have much work to make their own economies sustainable, but generally speaking they are not in armed conflict with each other, despite having problems to solve on many serious issues.

Many developing countries need a sustainable form of government before they can create sound living conditions. The purpose of government is to serve everyone, not only government officials, who are abusing their position and the powers of office given to them. This is one of the first problems that other nations must be involved with.

The next duty of developed nations and other stable countries is to establish a world economic system that allows wealth and knowledge to be fairly distributed. Nations need to work together to solve the world's economic problems and eradicate major world conflicts forever.

A fair sustainable economic system as proposed helps considerably poorer countries, as they will be able to buy in technology to develop, and they would be able to obtain affordable loans. Their country being sustainable would attract private capital and know-how. They would also be able to study economic models that would match their own achievable standard of living.

Space research

This is expected to continue, but on an international basis. It is expected to help us to have a better understanding of our role on earth. The resources used for this purpose should be affordable, and could be under the credit created within the MH system by work itself.

CHAPTER 20

PROFESSIONAL AND POLITICAL TASK

The author wishes to stress that to achieve a sustainable environment and human economy all elements of them need to be kept in balance. One cannot have one element sustainable and neglect the others, as they would distort it. Economies have to be understood and guided as they move along and change to meet new conditions. To guide and manage sustainable economies sound measures and structures are needed, that are compatible with world conditions and people's capacity to achieve. Generally all professional persons and those with the required knowledge need to work together to establish the structure for the sustainable environment.

Present day national economies are not well co-ordinated or properly understood: hence all the unsustainable solutions and dissatisfaction. Countries work against each other and seek advantages at others expense. No one person, or body, is in charge of leading the sustainable development process forward. Present national and international laws and practices conflict with what is necessary to create the sustainable environment desired. The structure, personnel, and brief of many institutions, including governments, prevent sustainable development even being considered. Who are really responsible for this process has not been defined. Clearly it should be those with the knowledge and experience to achieve it, and they are professional persons and specialists. Many professional bodies' constitutions have a code of ethics, which includes serving society, being responsible, not being dishonest and involved with fraud, and to strive to maintain integrity and competence in their profession. Therefore, in the author's opinion, the professional persons are the ones that are responsible for leading world economies onto a sustainable path, including setting up the management structure and development process for the desired sustainable environment.

Professional persons and politicians

Professional persons work in all sectors of the economy and all elements of the environment. At their disposal is all the factual knowledge and experience that has been gained in their careers. For assured success all projects need to be properly managed and fit in with the sustainable direction of the economy. Many professional persons work in government departments and have a sound knowledge of how they are presently functioning.

A number of politicians are professional persons and others have other special skills. The general public have voted for them because they believe they will look after their economy and ensure it is run properly. They also expect them to understand how the economy functions.

The professional persons and politicians are the ones that have the power to collectively move forward the process for developing sustainable economies. and caring for the environment.

Religious bodies should also be involved with verifying the concept for a sustainable economic system that cares for people's justifiable human rights, safeguarded peacefully.

Establishing the worthiness of a sustainable economic system

The author over his normal working lifetime has been working on the type of structure and management system needed, and has developed the skeleton and concept required for such a task to fulfil the defined form of sustainable environment outlined in Chapter 15 of this book. The three volumes of this book explain the skeleton of the economic system, and include the key measures, elements and processes needed. The international development project is a massive task that must be developed by a complete team of professional persons in and out of government. Although professional persons alone may have the knowledge and experience, they would lack the massive capital funding required. Therefore major businesses and institutions must also be involved. Governments at the present time are unlikely to start this process, but of course to many people and businesses it is in their interest to have sustainable conditions for their sustainable existence.

Clearly a body needs to be established for this task. It could be a new one or an existing recognised body supporting sustainable economic development of the environment: natural and manmade. This is one of the first tasks to be accomplished and the second is to verify the sustainable economic system and further develop it.

Opposition

With such a massive task there is likely to be quite a lot of opposition. This would have to be fought by sound explanations and convincing people that no one has anything to loose, although in life a give and take process is usually necessary.

It is important to make full use of modern technology and the television services where all sorts of examples can be given on how people will benefit from the system. It would also help to already be establishing the new information system, so people would be able to obtain much more on the internet on how the system works and is used.

There are many sustainable products that the private sector could be developing that are badly needed. For example, the proposed super information system, the Master Currency banking system for national and international trade, sound savings, and pension funds. Courses on sound sustainable development and how it is managed are also very important to prepare for all the future work required. All responsible professional persons really have a duty to move this process forward. We should all be re-examining the nation and international laws and trading practices; the way we are managing our world and what we are teaching the new generations. Are they sustainable, and do people understand the needs of the environment?

What people should clearly understand is that the real cost of any products (goods, services and the maintenance of them and the environment) is the hours of work it takes to produce them: in whichever country they are made. This vital measure of human productivity (Master

Currency) is necessary to work out the real costs of our economic activities and providing for a sustainable environment. It is only people and the hours they are prepared to work, and careful planning and management that can create a sustainable form of economy, together with sound appropriate education, honesty, trust, fairness and an economic system carefully thought through and structured to follow a natural maintenance and development path.

The more people can be involved with the proposals, including politicians, and the more organisations that support the concept, the easier it would become to persuade people to support the new form of economy.

Setting up the new economic system

Once there is the general acceptance that the new economic system is desirable and should be implemented, politicians, with the help of the professions, would need to prepare their manifestos. Referendums could also be used, depending on circumstances.

Many countries belong to different trade areas. It is unlikely that all nations would change at the same time. One or two countries could decide to change, or perhaps a trade area like the European Union, which is having great difficulty with unemployment, pensions and enlarging the number of member nations; and not all the existing members have joined the Euro, because their economies are out of synchronisation with the others. The MH system can be used to guide economies to converge.

The present currency values in MH terms need to be established so people can better understand the differences in their monetary purchasing power from country to country. It is hoped that the international banking industry would establish the currency rates and already offer alternatives means for international trade. This would also assist pension funds and savers to protect them from losses caused by inflation. It would also help people and governments across the Union to understand the advantages of the MH system.

Another project that would help with moving the task forward would be to use the MH system for negotiating wages, and explaining to people why the official state retiring age must be the same for everyone, and not an earlier date for the public sector and a later age for the private sector, for example. Pensions have to be affordable and we are generally speaking living longer. The family models make it quite clear we need to work sufficient hours to be able to afford pensions. Strikes do not alter reality, they just reduce the nations overall productivity, and the nation as a whole is poorer for it, money (productivity) lost that could have been put towards making the economy more stable.

Another use of the MH system could be to make property prices affordable, that is bring them down to real values. However, there is the problem that many people have borrowed on the properties more than they are worth, so really wages should rise. The effect of this would be to right the balance of overvalued properties. The value of the present national currency would then have to fall, or could be made to fall, to correct the currency against other national currencies. Wages paid are also distorted as mentioned in previous chapters, so when wages rates are allowed to increase the low paid could all first be properly paid, and then other wage rates brought closer in line with the MH wage negotiation system People would be quite happy for this to happen and need not necessarily be worse off. Before such a move would take place, careful modelling to determine the balances would have taken place.

Politicians could decide on different solutions to make their economies sustainable. By careful modelling, their ideas can be explained and justified.

In the early days of setting up for change it is important that the professional organisations and specialists set in motion the private sector information so key organisations would support the new economy and allow improvements to start, to give others confidence in the system. Once people start to benefit they would support the proposed changes. The advantage of the MH system is that once the key statistics are gathered, everything can be explained, or justified by modelling and examples.

CHAPTER 21

CHANGING TO A SUSTAINABLE ECONOMY

There are a large number of tasks needed before the world economies can be gently and carefully moulded into a sustainable form that would satisfy most people's requirements and care for maintaining the balance of the natural environment. The following four stages of development are anticipated.

Stage 1

This task is going to be a difficult one. The present trading and monetary system based on free markets is cherished. They are supported by a vast number of influential people and bodies, and the whole economic system is geared to support it. Many organisations have their own agenda and national laws and international agreements holding the system firmly in place. Generally bodies involved with sustainable projects do not take into account the unstable monetary and economic system that is used to finance their proposed remedies to protect the world environment. Without a complete understanding of how economies really should function and be sustained, including the environment, it is not surprising that progress is very slow, and full of obstacles to real co-ordinated and constructive progress.

The problem for the author, having developed a sound strategy, probably the only one that exists, is how does this knowledge get transferred and used to solve the world's economic problems. There is an enormous gap between his strategy and the present economic strategy, in effect held together in a straight jacket. From his research he is aware of apathy and the resistance against change. He knows the objectives for sustainable economies should be a governmental task, but how does one communicate with a sophisticated government? There are few problems with a small country government in a developing nation, as it is easier to communicate. However, when it comes to policy the third world government would seek advice from western governments, international institutions, or consultants. Therefore, any proposed master plan to create a sustainable economy for the world needs to start in the developed nations.

It is clear from previous correspondence with Ministers and government institutions, including the Prime Minister and HM Treasury, that they do not know how to deal with my proposals for the development of sustainable economies. There is probably no legal obligation for any government to act on my proposal, however important it may be to the nation and the world. It is much easier to do nothing active and to just let the matter hopefully slide away. Individuals, who may wish to communicate with the author, under these conditions would be very careful not to risk their reputation. Generally speaking, for the author to communicate with other governments all text concerning developing sustainable economies really should be translated into each nation's language, to ensure good communication, because not all the people involved would speak English. This is a massive task to undertake!

Many politicians have recommended that I should have my work verified to ensure that it is sound and correct. With the way sophisticated modern economies function, most professional persons are specialised in a narrow field, and therefore no sole individual would be prepared to take on the task. A group of persons is required, and not only academics. Who is going to organise such a group and pay their fees? Even if a wealthy individual sponsored the project, who in government is going to be responsible for carrying out the governmental tasks? It is a massive task that is vital to everyone's well being on earth.

The right path for any government on receiving this document is to set up a team to tackle the problem of developing sustainable world economies. I am sure the majority of citizens would not object to government funds being spent on this most important project.

All governments must understand the modern world economy they are living in, whether a dictatorship or any form of democracy. All nations depend on each other for something. The sustainable form of economy is the best to live in and gives security to everyone, even the rich, even benevolent dictators; hardly anyone is threatened.

Let us hope that this document will lead the way to each government carrying out its duty to set up a structure that will allow its economy to become truly sustainable. This would be the first step in making our world a better place.

During this first stage it is anticipated key people in the private sector would become very familiar with the proposed structure for developing sustainable economies and the problems and tasks that will need to be undertaken to make progress. At this stage there will probably be little government involvement. However, there are many products that are useful to the private sector and families, that could be introduced to improve the economy and help people. For some of these projects governments might need to be involved, depending upon national regulations.

Stage 2

In this stage the first national, or international, institution would be set up to drive forward the sustainable development process, and probably funded by the private sector: professional institutions and businesses already involved with sustainable development. This institution would take all matters needed into account for sustainable development, including strategies as proposed in the three volumes of this book.

The institution would study sustainable concepts and structures for developing truly sustainable economies. The basic concepts would be expanded and developed using appropriate statistics that it would have gathered together. From these a document would be produced describing the sustainable economic structure, and its monetary system and trading rules, and how it would be guided. The document would also explain how the new information system would be set up and operated. The key economic models for managing, developing and understanding how economies function would also be included in the document.

The institution, or other related organisations would train personnel in the art of developing economies. Later these persons would be involved in expanding the system nationally and internationally. They would also be involved in the research and decision process that would be required to commence using the system and guide the economy onto a sustainable path.

The implementation of the system would involve the writing of many pamphlets and books to explain to people, businesses and professionals the reasons for the changes and how the economy should function and is guided. The trading process and financial system would be fully explained. The nature of the required educational training would also be explained in great detail. Professional persons and related businesses would commence using the system.

The information and research produced would also be used to explain to national governments why a new system should be established internationally, and why all countries should participate. To create confidence and trust everything must be properly explained, and particularly how sustainable economies would function. Where the national language is not English, everything would need to be translated into the national language, as it would be many years before everyone would have learned the chosen trading language.

During the second stage the trained personnel would also carry out all the necessary activities to implement and set in motion the third stage. This would involve setting up, or modifying existing government departments ready to progress with stage three, including training personnel, and some of this training could be undertaken by universities. Many different specialists would be required.

The activities of the stage two national government institutions would include setting up the International Institutions and how trade would gradually develop into the sustainable form with its international trading partners. These activities are likely to be long term and continue over stage three and into the final stage four where the sustainable economic system would be fully functional.

During stage two governments may well decide to commence to converge their currencies to guide their economies towards a more sustainable form. This action could be taken without the need for business, or the general public, understanding the reasons for them. However, the private sector could be in advance of the government sector and may have already have set up some sustainable trading activities.

Stage 3

At the commencement of this stage the actual institutions and government departments would be set up, or modified, to manage the economies, and the general public and businesses would be informed of the changes taking place. In due course these institutions would give the reasons for the changes and inform the citizens on the direction the economy would be moving. Everyone, or as many as possible, would need to know the part they fulfil in their economy. For the professional persons affected by the changes, training courses would be available in addition to written guidelines. Various means would be used to assist people to understand their economy and the benefits of a sustainable economy.

The education authorities at this point would also be expected to review the educational process to meet our needs and to ensure that their teaching process will ensure the sustainability of our economies. The world population needs to remove all forms of unnecessary conflict, and governments need to explain that all problems must be solved by discussion and understanding on how our world economies should function. People need to understand how much crime and conflicts are costing our economies, and how the same human energy spent on them would enhance our standard of living and quality of life. There is no pleasure in living in fear, or any sense in it, when we can avoid it!

In the latter part of this stage all the necessary statistics would be gathered by the appropriate authorities, and a new information system would be set up ready for use in Stage 4. All the plans for the direction in which the economy would move should take place and be ready, including the plans for implementation of the new monetary and economic system and pegging the existing money to the Master Currency.

By the end of this stage all the managers and key people would understand how economies should converge and would be gradually moved onto a sustainable path, and how it should be maintained.

Stage 4

This stage would only start when sufficient preparation was actually completed. It would commence with the direction set for the development plan and the pegging of the national currency to the master currency. The value of the local currency would be determined and fixed by the government. New laws concerning the local currency, monetary system and wage negotiations would come into force.

Businesses and all other institutions would need to supply vital statistics required for the information system and to help to maintain, plan and develop the economy. Individuals would also need to supply information concerning their skills and degree of competence where possible.

Generally speaking local district authorities would have considerable power and work closely with each other and the regions. It should be noted that although local districts would have considerable power, such power is a collective power of leadership only. The regions would work closely with the government. The tax system would gradually be simplified and locally collected. All information would be obtained from the local districts, which are in very close contact with everyone in their neighbourhood.

The rate of development and the convergence of the economy in this stage would depend on many factors, such as the standard of living, the nature of the local district's economy, and imbalances and distortions in the economy.

The reshaping of the economy could involve some jobs becoming redundant but, being a sustainable form of economy, new jobs would become available replacing the ones lost. Where required for new projects, job retraining would take place, and where possible in advance of the requirements for the skills that would be needed. This would happen because government at local district level would be monitoring the economy and ensuring smooth reshaping of it. There is never a shortage of work as there are always projects waiting to be realised, and often there are more needs waiting than wants.

Governments and Institutions serving a Sustainable Economy

The staff of governments, their ministries, regions and local districts should have the best persons available, particularly for the decisions makers, who are the leaders responsible for moving the economy forward. No one should be in a position of power that cannot be immediately ceased. The decisions in running our economies should be made by the best of individual's abilities and be always honest. When errors are made they must be corrected to ensure everyone's interest in the economy are safe and sound. There should be no secrets in government institutions.

The international institutions responsible for sustaining the world economy would co-ordinate all international matters, including all the key issues to keep our world on a sustainable path. They would be involved in any changes deemed necessary to the structure of the economy and how it trades honestly and fairly.

A country participating in the sustainable world economy may be a Royal Institution as in Britain (and with a King or Queen that heads the Commonwealth) or a dictatorship. However, these persons should not have a position of power that cannot be vetoed. Like any other leader, or head of state, they are generally accepted by the people and may form part of their national culture. The author's system does not propose altering this, or the assets they hold by consent, or agreement as in Britain. However, some dictators have abused their powers and used their nation's resources for their own aims, at the expense of their citizens and donor nations tax payers. This is unsustainable and not permissible.

All governments must take into account the human right to have work and be properly paid for their productivity in the general economy and the right to own assets. Assets should not be stolen to pass on to others, as is taking place in the world today to effect redistribution. The author has taken redistribution problems into consideration with the economic tools he has developed, that generally speaking allows the owners of all existing assets to retain their possession, very necessary to prevent any further destabilising of the world economy (except certain dictators already mentioned). As the world is developed into a sustainable form, the economic balances will change using the author's proposed economic system.

The transition to sustainable economies

Changes must be gradually carried out at a pace people can absorb and manage. Enough time has to be allowed for retraining and this would vary depending on the country and its level of development. Not all countries would start at the same time, and some countries may need considerable help from other nations.

Until the necessary statistics have been gathered and analysed and surveys to determine the problems, it would not be possible to work to a time scale.

During the earlier part of the transition period it would be hoped that existing businesses specialising in information and directories would pool their financial resources and start to form the single information system, on the lines described in Chapters 7 and 8 Volume 1. This is a massive task, and it is visualised that perhaps many universities, and national libraries would like to help with that task.

It is also hoped that the private sector would commence developing new sustainable financial products and value international currencies in Master Currency units, dating back as many years as possible, which, however, could be dependent on national statistics available. This would give great help to the professional developers in their work to steer economies onto a sustainable path.

Financial services and stockbrokers could start the process of valuing and classifying businesses based on the MH business criteria, so buyers and sellers have a better idea of their true worth and the value of their share stock. This information would also help to establish the real worth of national assets and to know more about their condition.

Political parties can also play a crucial role by bringing to the public notice how they could improve the economy. The author has already produced a number of booklets explaining the system as it applies to various sectors of the economy, including one on how wage negotiations are conducted to be honest and fair. There is no reason why sustainable wages cannot already be applied to all government sectors and to all financial and professional services. However, in the developed nations, it would be difficult to raise the underpaid workforce without devaluing the nation's currency. It could be a very good way to stop wage inflation, by freezing it at the MH rate on a particular date!

There is no reason why political parties should not also print their own booklets on the party policy on sustainable economic development and then market them at a low value to raise funds for their party, and those subscribing to the party could receive a free copy. Once members start to read them and take interest, politicians can obtain feedback on their proposals, and this would help to update the party manifesto.

International Government Institutions

There are very many of these covering global economic sectors: banks, health, trade, defence, development, human rights, agriculture, etc. A number of these no doubt would eventually be involved in some way, and national governments would have to decide how.

National governments could elect to set up a new international body to oversee all matters in connection with world sustainable development and the care of the environment.

Use of MH system to solve problems

The MH system can be used as a tool to study all sorts of problems and find reasons for them and to work out solutions, provided the right statistics and other information are used. In the three volumes of this book all sorts of examples have been given for family, business, banking and government purposes.

For example suppose there were 1000 refugees plus their children with a reasonable mix of skills, and there was an abandoned village, or a disused community area with a few shops and some industrial areas that were due for demolishion: this sort of population is like the one used in the model economy as in Tables 33, 34,and 35 in Volume 1. Provided they are given sufficient income to start, guidance and training for missing skills, they could quite quickly have a running economy. They would obviously need to buy in goods and have a market for their surplus production whatever it might be.

When lots of details have been obtained on local district economies there would be many different models, with similar core activities for say 60% of the population and then varied ones depending on the nature of their available exports. Knowing the composition of the refugee skills they could be compared to the local district models and one could be chosen that matched most of their skills. This would save time and allow the project to be set up more quickly. The same process could also be used in developing nations using appropriate technology to raise the standard of living.

Suppose there was a collapse of the banking system. With the MH system the solution would be to reopen all the current accounts immediately and allow all business to continue as normal. As work done = money supply, as soon as wages are paid in the savings would begin to grow again. It must be remembered that the infrastructure and assets are still all intact and money is a promise to pay only.

Global warming is a serious problem. A study needs to be urgently made to examine the amount of fuel being used in long distance transport, purely to bring in goods that could be made or supplied from local sources. The problem is caused by high valued currencies in developed countries. Present currencies there would not be too difficult to lower. The resurgence of local industries would then cut a considerable amount of carbon pollution, and give more time to carry out other measures, which could take many years.

The foregoing examples give an indication how the system can be used. It gives a basis to make sound comparisons to find the most suitable solutions to problems. Without choosing, research, planning and guidance, one cannot expect an economy to be sustainable. We need to put in the right amount of effort and think through all our actions.

CHAPTER 22

THE PURPOSE OF THE MH SYSTEM

Now one has read the three volumes of the book it is hoped it can be clearly understood that the MH system is not a political policy but a tool to manage the world economies in harmony with the environment. The system is a complete management structure, but unfortunately this book has only given the skeleton of it. This is because the proposed layout of the information tree is so large and full of detail that a single person cannot draft it, because it contains millions of parts and will need to be accomplished by a very large team of experts. Each expert would deal with his or her branch. The other major problem is gathering the sound statistics, which is another major task that is a collective responsibility for other professional persons and technicians to do in due course..

The Earth Charter is an excellent document that sets out the policies needed and ones that most professional persons dedicated to sustainable development would agree with. If the world adopts the MH system, it could make the aspirations of Charter happen. The reason is because the MH system takes everything into account and follows nature's natural path and intentions. It takes into account humans and their intelligence and the fact that given the right guidance they are able to judge its significance. However, for their own special benefit, there will always be those that would do their best to prevent it from happening. It is up to the majority to ensure that the human race can do what is right and turn many parts of this world from hell to a form of paradise.

The world is presently managed differently from what is needed for a sustainable form of economy, and the changes involve an education process explaining why changes must take place. People will not want to have to study many volumes of technical data, but they will need to know why the changes need to take place and what they are expected to do in the new form of economy. The author has already written a number of key booklets as examples for this purpose, to guide his intended method of approach forward with the family, business and government sectors, including key specialist sectors of the economy. Many more books will have to be written by a team of authors for all the specialist elements of the economy and each nation will need to translate them into their own language/s, from the chosen international commercial language.

One of the main objects of the MH system is to help people to understand the world we are in, and the big mistakes we have been making, that have caused so much suffering, when it need not have happened. When certain practices have been going on for decades, and some for centuries, it will be difficult to convince some people. The structure of the MH system being based on what is sustainable and works, based on sound measures, gives a good foundation on which to convince those that have any doubts.

One of the past problems is that those managing our economies had no means to understand how an economy really functions. There was no complete pattern that they could examine to see how the different parts of the economy interacted with each other, and because of the pressures for production they had not the vast hours needed to work it out themselves. It has taken the author a lifetime and he has had the advantage of other people's specialist research and articles in their work. His varied career gave him the type of experience needed before carrying out his research, giving him sufficient basic knowledge for the purpose. Working on projects involving large areas of population and having to obtain diverse information for the projects to reach their objective, and to be feasible and affordable, gave him the opportunity to gain experience through a wide range of all the elements that constitute an economy, before commencing his research for sustainable development. This pre-national and international experience on the natural events creating the economies meant he was able to determine which economic theories were valid and which were not. Apart from professional qualifications and various trade skills, he had business, management and production experience, and the experience of communicating and understanding people in all the countries he had worked in. From this background experience he commenced on developing the MH economic system. This has involved a number of economic studies, including one to establish work for the unemployed, but one the government did not want to happen. There has been considerable correspondence with governments including local authorities, central banks and NGOs and a number of companies and unions, many of which were very helpful. These communications have highlighted the support and the problems the system would have to solve. Hence the project has now reached it present situation, where the skeleton of the MH sustainable economic system has been developed and can now be used to make the changes needed to make our economies sustainable and in harmony with the environment.

Now that the foundation has been laid, the MH system, work can commence to establish a sustainable system to manage the world economies. Willing governments and politicians and those supporting sustainable development can start to find the flaws in their economies and know that they can work out the solutions required. Governments, businesses, and people have a direction to go that is positive and beneficial to our standard of living and the environment.

The MH system is intended:

- To give people all the support possible to understand the nature of the world they are living in and what they must do to support their lives and others.
- Fit in with the natural events and constraints of the human economy.
  To give people the greatest amount of freedom compatible in a sustainable form of economy.
- Have respect for the natural environment and to take care of the balances we believe necessary and the ones we should not change.
- To steer people from violence and greed.
- To guide people to be responsible, and respectful.
- To guide people to manage their family economies.
- To guide governments and businesses in their duties and activities.
- To create a sustainable monetary and financial system to honestly and fairly support our trading activities.

Finally it is a system to eliminate as far as possible all forms of violence and destruction that is presently taking place. This can only happen by understanding the causes and humans. Generally speaking early education and the form of it is most important. A child knows little on birth. From this point onwards the child learns what he sees and what he is taught and where his action are restricted and why they must be restricted. Children must be given sound answers to their questions and taught to respect others, with sound reasons. If this process is relaxed or ignored a child's reactions would be, he can do what he wants, and the longer he does it then becomes a right, based on his experience and logic. A child cannot understand the consequences of his action without experience, so cannot be blamed for the wrong conclusion of his rights. It is up to his elders and teachers to ensure he gets the guidance and understands he must follow it, always with sound reasoning. Children can understand from a very early age right and wrong. Children's education is very important and must have enough adult patient attention, preferably from parents, their natural right. Governments need to study this very seriously to get the balances and the priorities right.

CHAPTER 23

RECYCLING

The MH information system treats recycling as a key sector of the economy. It treats the waste as a resource. The system can be used to create sustainable solutions for dealing with all waste and to study ways of reducing waste and pollution.

At the present time not all waste is collected, or taken to collecting points for disposal, but tipped or thrown away anywhere. Some of the litter is collected, but the rest is just left scattered in the towns or countryside as being no-ones duty to remove. Even many landowners in the past have just dumped unwanted items on wasteland, or in woodlands, and there it remains. Sometimes waste has been buried. Visitors to the countryside often leave their litter, and hunters leave their spent cartridges on the ground. Polythene sheeting floats around in the countryside and in streams. Former industrial sites are not always cleared, and toxic waste is left.

Some recycling is now taking place, mainly by local authorities, but unfortunately each authority collects different lines for recycling in different ways. Many items are not collected, and some authorities refuse certain types of waste, like asbestos. Instructions on what is wanted for recycling are poor and vary from place to place. When visiting collecting points, many containers used are so high that steps and platforms are needed for access to them, which one has to mount carrying heavy bags or objects, and for older and even many younger people is a struggle.

Another problem is many people have old furniture and household equipment that they need to get rid of quickly, but no one seems to want it at the time, and it often is broken up, before others with little money know it was available. Recycling warehouses are needed to store these for a reasonable period of time, and where others can have them for free, or for a small charge.

A lot of waste can have toxic elements that the public are not aware of, or could be dangerous in one way or another, and only specialists would be aware of this. Where people are aware of it, but know they have to pay for its disposal, many may well just dump it somewhere and save the cost. One sees plenty of signs promising high fines for dumping, but when it cannot be policed, laws become ineffective.

There is a vast amount of packaging and advertising material delivered to peoples homes that is never read. This should be reduced wherever possible, because it is not only wasting human effort, but wasting all the fuel energy used for its production, delivery, collection and disposal. And just think of the number of trees that are wasted.

Generally speaking in developed countries, liquid waste from domestic properties and farms and factories is being dealt with quite well, but there is always room for improvements.

However, there are other liquid wastes which people do not know how to dispose of safely, without creating pollution.

Some waste has value, like good furniture and equipment and items bought and never used. Many metals too can also be valuable. Waste really needs to be divided into waste of no, or little value, and waste with value.

Waste and recycling policy needs to be very carefully worked out and thought through, taking human nature into account. Whatever the public contribution is to recycling, it must be as simple as possible, a task that everyone can manage, and with rules that are reasonable to follow.

Waste to be recycled needs to be kept as clean as possible and not mixed with wet biodegradable waste, like from kitchens and earth, moss, leaves, twigs and pet waste, from garden areas. These should be separated at source. Where homes use solid fuels like coal and wood, the ash from these again should not be mixed with other forms of waste, but be kept separate.

The rest of domestic waste can be classified as follows: paper, cardboard, cloth, metals, plastics, glass, pottery, wood, small products of mixed materials, electrical equipment, furniture, carpets, liquid materials, rubber, DIY building waste and gardening waste.

Paper

There are many types of paper waste from glossy papers to newspapers. There are magazines stapled together and books with paperbacks to hard covers. There are paper bags, envelopes, letters, posters, pamphlets and wrapping paper. People would want to know whether all these should be treated as paper, or some of it as general rubbish.

Cardboard

There are many types of cardboard from waterproof cartons for drinks and cardboard boxes for cereals and other foods. For non-food products there is a vast range of cardboard packaging using different card products. People would want to know the types of card packaging that should be excluded. Some packaging may have small pieces of plastic or metal used in various ways for particular products and people may wonder whether they might have to be excluded.

Cloth

Clothing and many other products use wool, cotton, silk or manmade fibres, and mixtures of natural and manmade fibres. And there are also various types of sacking. People would want to know what to do with these disused materials. These disused products also use plastic or metal zips, and buttons, and if used for recycling would such items have to be removed?

Metals

The common metals are, zinc, copper, lead, silver, gold, steel, cast iron and aluminium. Then there are alloys like brass and stainless steel, and other items that are protected by galvanising, or chrome and silver plating. Many metals can be valuable, and scrap value payments should be paid for these.

Quite a lot of metal is used for food supplies in the form of cans, lids and bottle caps, and most families could collect these and ensure they are clean. All sorts of other products for disposal are often made from a number of materials, including varying quantities of metal, and these could be saved separately.

Plastic

A considerable amount of polythene and PVC is used, and other forms of plastic. Polythene sheeting is used extensively for all sorts of domestic purposes and for wrapping all sorts of products. It is also used as a damp-proofing membrane and for temporary coverings. Being flexible it is also used in small tubes. Many bags of all sizes are made for various purposes including waste collection bags. PVC is used for many small containers used by most families, and very many building products are made from this material. PVC plumbing is now probably used in most homes and for drainage systems. Plastics are used for all sorts of bottles, tubes and other forms of container, and when emptied, is waste for disposal.

Many plastics can be recycled in various ways and perhaps in a number of ways like a plastic bag: its final use could be as a fuel. However, people need to know which plastics are for recycling.

Glass

Glass is used extensively for windows, bottles, jars and electric light bulbs. Bottles and jars are made in many shapes and sizes. Many other items are made from glass, particularly for domestic use. Little recycling of bottles and jars takes place, before they are treated as waste, and recycled by use in a crushed form or to land fill. It is a pity so many different sizes and shapes of bottles and jars are made, making it more difficult to use them many more times, as is done with milk bottles. If there were fewer sizes and shapes, the bottles and jars could go to the nearest users. Instead of making new bottles and jars just for one short use, studies should be carried out to determine how much energy could be saved by recycling.

Pottery

Pottery in all its various forms for home furnishings, gardens and tiles is not a material, when broken that can be recycled, except for some form of hardcore, or filling material.

Wood

Waste wood can be used for many purposes. Some small pieces can be used for making small products. Other wood can be turned into chips for making chipboards. Sawdust can be used for many purposes. Other wood waste that cannot be found for a better purpose can be used for fuel.

Mixed material products

Many small products are made from a number of different materials that would not be easy for the majority of people to dismantle to separate the materials. These items would need recycling by specialist firms with people trained for this purpose.

Many of these products are electrical, or electronic items, for example cookers, microwave ovens, refrigerators, other kitchen and household equipment, heaters, radios, televisions, telephones, calculators and computer equipment.

To the above can be added the bigger items, like cars and all the other types of machines and equipment that are used outdoors and the mountain of equipment used for transport and by industry.

Furniture

Sound and serviceable furniture should first be recycled for reuse if possible. Furniture that is to be broken up would be recycled dependent on the materials of its construction.

Carpets

Many countries have a considerable amount of fitted carpets that normally have a short life, plus other forms of covering, that cannot be reused. However, where possible a use for this material needs to be found, but it should be a sustainable solution.

Liquid materials

There are many materials, including pastes, that are leftovers and of no use to the owners: for example, paints, liquid tars, oils, resins and hardeners, glues, fertilizers, and acids. Many of these could be toxic and it would be wise for such items to be collected separately.

Rubber

A considerable amount of rubber and synthetic rubbers are used, particularly for vehicle tyres. Much of this is already recycled, but more is still needed.

DIY waste

This form of waste can be quite considerable, but often in very small quantities. Generally, it can be any of the materials used and disposed of by the building industry. Waste disposal systems should take into consideration some people's problems with this waste disposal, when they have no suitable transport.

Garden waste

Many gardens in towns have problems with disposal of their biodegradable garden waste and shrub and tree prunings. Again waste disposal systems should take this into account. Even when owners may have transport many journeys to the tip could be necessary. Leaving containers in streets for this material might be more economic on fuel consumption!

Conclusion

Waste disposal is very complicated. For households it is necessary to make it as simple as possible. It is important for householders to keep their waste clean, as others may have to separate them. Biodegradable items, like kitchen waste, needs to be kept separate. For most people it would be best to restrict waste to: bio-gradable items, paper, cardboard, plastics, metals, mixed material products and non-recyclable waste.

The same disposal system for household waste is needed throughout the country. Office and shop waste could be on the same basis as household waste. Industrial waste needs to be as required for each industry.

Government needs to look into this matter very seriously, and devise a waste system based on adequate research that would result in a very efficient system. It should work with the waste industry and environmentalists. Governments must supply this sector with adequate development funding to ensure a sustainable and achievable waste system is developed.

CHAPTER 24

LAND

Land and its resources are very important to us. Considerable areas of land are farmed and other areas like forests are managed, particularly in the developed countries, where forests are no longer extensive. Much smaller areas are used for habitation and industrial use. There are still vast areas of tropical forests, mountainous regions and deserts that are uninhabited or sparsely inhabited. Other areas are mined for various mineral resources.

Much of the farmed lands have been fashioned over thousands of years by man to suit our needs. This land has to be maintained to remain useful. Fertile land in arid areas is often irrigated where a water source is available. This practice is also used in areas of low annual rainfall. When land becomes disused it can soon return to its previous or another state of little use.

Natural events are continually changing land by erosion, climate warming and plant and animal life. Wind and rain can have a drastic effect on the landscape. Oceans, rivers and streams help to erode land and cause flooding. Man's engineering wonders try to protect land from flooding, and others create lakes and reservoirs to conserve water for our use. Renewable energy, like hydroelectric and wind farms, produces electricity to help serve our modern requirements.

Much of the world's land is in private ownership, but not all of it is managed or cared for. The arable land is farmed to produce food for us and to support farm animals. Many forests are managed to be sustainable and produce sound commercial timber, but others are neglected for lack of long-term finance.

To keep land and forests in good condition, providing what we want from it, it has to be maintained. This involves fences, walls, access, drainage, hedge trimming and, in woodlands, tree pruning. Fields need to be ploughed, or rolled and sometimes re-sown, and weeds have to be removed. All this adds value to the land, and maintains its value. The MH system takes all these matters into account when working out the value of land.

Land would have varying values and would not be all of the same quality. For example land in a river plain could be very fertile and would not require very many hours of work to fashion it for use. Another piece of land could be terraced on a mountainside and need stone walls to support the terrace. Therefore, this land could be three times more expensive. But if this land is a hundred miles from any other arable land it could still be as profitable for the crops produced.

Not all landowners are rich. Many are quite poor, and need to work very hard to keep their land in good order. In some countries people, roaming on private land with or without permission can sue the owner should they come to any harm doing so. Roamers can also cause all sorts of damage, and dump litter, which owners cannot afford to police. Having to insure against such risks of damage, and against possible claims is an unfair extra burden. People ought to understand that they should respect landowners property and the privilege of the right to roam; and they should cover their own risks for unexpected accidents, not caused in any way by the land owner, but more likely a natural event or caused by due lack of care.

Landowners are the caretakers of the land, which many others benefit from. Their farming activities or similar businesses should allow them enough income to look after the land, without subsidies. Woodlands too should render sufficient income to be sustainable.

When a countries currency is so high in comparison with other countries they cannot compete with their products. This leads to the land and woodlands becoming neglected, and prevents a sustainable environment being maintained.

CHAPTER 25

VICE

Addiction whether to drinking, smoking, drugs or gabling is creating serious problems for people, and once addicted it is very difficult for many to give it up. Addictions often start when very young, where children's parents and others around them have the habit. It seems to be a natural thing for children that they should follow. Others start because of peer pressure. For the business sector it is a means of making money, and naturally they would want to encourage it. Mild smoking and drinking for many has allowed them to reach an age of 100 years, and appears to have given them much pleasure, but for the heavy smokers and drinkers it does cause serious health problems. A smoke-filled atmosphere gives secondary affects that harms non-smokers forced to live and work in such conditions. Illegal drugs, where people become addicted ruins their lives, and causes them to do other illegal acts to obtain money to purchase drugs to feed the addiction. Millions of pounds of profit are made by smugglers on the supply of illegal drugs. The drug growers, as a result of the trade in poor countries, are able to enjoy a better life but do not make a fortune on their crops.

Who is to blame for such a situation situation? The problem commenced as a result of our lack of knowledge, when the products first became in general use. Vices can also commence with boredom and depression, caused by economic conditions and stress.

Governments have profited by high rates of taxation on the sale of alcoholic drinks and tobacco products, with the excuse that it will cure the problem, but this just makes the poor poorer, and money needed to support the necessities is cut: children and health suffer, and home living conditions. The resulting illnesses, crime, and the extra health care needed caused by the addictions, have burdened everyone.

Illegal drugs supports the addiction that creates the demand; and the more the criminals get others hooked on it the bigger the market gets for them. There are many programmes to help drug addicts, but this alone will not solve the problem. It is necessary to kill the massive profits of the illegal drug business, yet slowly cut down on the drugs needed by the addicts.

The only workable solution is for governments to buy the drugs needed direct from producers to continue to support the addicts, but with low cost drugs that would result. This would then eliminate the drug addict crimes needed to pay for their addiction. Also more help should be given to support the poor economies where the drugs are grown, so that they can move to other equally profitable products. If the addicts with help programs cannot change, or choose not to, there is little that the state can do, other than to continue the supply. What is extremely important is to cut the present drug culture, by a very active education process, so that the drug barons' trade is killed off.

One might ask what the connection is between vice and the MH system. Firstly, the system uses sound education with explanation to guide people on a sustainable path. Secondly, its financial system only allows money to be paid into current accounts before transfer elsewhere. Money in savings accounts, before transfer to other persons or accounts, would pass into the current account. Each person and business is allowed only one current account. The money in current accounts is in the depositor's ownership and not the bank's. The bank is responsible for overseeing the transactions, and must report on unnatural events of each particular account. Eventually with the MH system very little money would be in circulation and cards would replace money for little transactions. Laundering of money, therefore, will be very difficult, because all transaction can be traced.

With the MH system governments would not tax products with the objective of discouraging people from buying the product. For example, addicts would still continue to buy tobacco and alcoholic products however expensive this is, as they do with illegal drugs. More damage is done to people by this process, as already mentioned. Only a sound education will reduce vice. Where economies and people become unstable the solution with the MH system is to find the cause of the problem and then correct it, where ever possible, and achieve a sustainable economic condition.

CHAPTER 26

CONVERGENCE OF THE ECONOMIES

The standards of living in present day world economies are vastly different, and in spite of most of the world having the opportunity to use the worlds most sophisticated technology and having numerous citizens with the world's most prestigious skills, like in USA, Europe, China and India, we are paid differently for the same skills. The present-day free market system has allowed considerable trade to take place among the nations, with multinational companies trading in all the largest economies. However, the standard of living in these countries ranges from the poorest to the highest: from poverty to billionaires. There is no relationship between currencies and labour costs, so that labour of the same skill can vary up to fifty times more in one country compared with another. Even within a country there can be vast differences for labour of the same task and productivity. The reason for this is values are based on what the market will pay. Wealth distribution, therefore, is so distorted that people have insufficient to live on at the lowest level of pay whilst others become millionaires.

Another effect of the present free market system is that the developed countries generally have highly valued currencies compared with countries like China and India. See Tables 125 and 126, Volume 2. This does not help stability under either situation. Production and manufacture is moving to countries like China and India, so that companies can compete. Labour costs are high in the developed nations and very low in the developing ones for the equivalent skills. The developed countries import vast volumes of products that they could not afford to buy if produced in their own countries. Their countries are becoming richer in material wealth and this process slows the improvements that could be made in countries like China and India. The money gained on the exports to the developed countries buys little in the way of goods and services from them. The greatest advantage for China and India has been inward investment and the latest technology, and an outside market for goods their own people cannot afford to buy.

The vast volume of purchases of goods and services now imported into the developed countries is changing the whole balance of their economies. At one time they had about 40% of their combined workforce in the four key sectors of production, the remaining 60% being in services. Now, in some of these countries as little as 10% to 15% is in production. The changes are taking place so quickly, without any guidance from governments, that unemployment is well above sustainable levels. In the production industries wage levels are falling, and this also has the effect of drawing down the wage levels of unskilled labour in the service sector too. Although most governments have introduced minimum wages, these are insufficient for most families to live on without government subsidies, as is shown by the data in Volume 1.

With cheap imported goods, the standard of living is very high in the rich developed nations. This leads to many immigrants wanting to move to these countries to make money and then to return home; or to stay permanently and enjoy a much higher standard of living. For example, people from Africa, or Eastern Europe. Those with skills can earn good wages in the U.K., live prudently and then use the saved money for big ventures at home. All this action destabilizes the developed nations economies. It also takes away the skills of the lesser-developed countries.

Many developed countries have a surplus of skills and often no work for these persons. Developing nations cannot afford to employ them because they would be too expensive, except for an oil rich country. Developing nations also need to learn many advanced skills that the developed countries have, but with the vast difference in the value of currencies it becomes very expensive for them to learn in the latter's universities.

Most nations want to live in a sustainable form of environment. To achieve this we all have a task in removing pollution from land, rivers and the air. Progress on this matter is slow by all nations, and countries are breaking their promises, or refusing to co-operate. Pollution control and waste recycling is costly, but would be quite affordable if we did not have so many unemployed and people taking early retirement. This is because of bad management by governments, caused by them not understanding how economies should function. People's skills need to match the economies requirements and this will not happen while people in government lack the right skills and knowledge for the process. The MH system is designed to help solve this problem. A lot of dishonest trade is taking place, where people are paid for work not done, or badly done, and other people are suffering. We must all collectively eradicate these practices, encouraged by free market forces devoid of proper trading rules.

Convergence of EU economies

The major issues the Maastricht Treaty tries to solve are:

1 political stability to eliminate conflict among our nations
2 stable money and low interest rates
3 stable economies
4 a common trading system
5 low rates of unemployment
6 elimination of poverty
7 a sound standard of living that is sustainable
8 justice and very low crime rates.

All these issues are inter-related and involve getting all the elements of the economy into general equilibrium. If one of the elements is out of equilibrium it tends to throw others out of balance. We are already finding the criteria set in the Maastricht Treaty are not bringing the economies into equilibrium, and monetary union is only part of the problem as there are also other factors to be addressed. We will now discuss these issues listed above.

1. The first major issue is probably the easiest to accomplish as we are already signing agreements and trying to comply with them. The will for political stability is there in most European nations, and considerable progress has already been made in achieving this objective.

2. Creating stable money is one of the most difficult tasks to achieve because people are very confused concerning the real purpose of money in our economies, particularly the specialists and governments who are maintaining money in its present form. Many people are convinced our present form of money is satisfactory and all that is needed is 'free' markets and plenty of competition. However, as has been explained in this book, that policy alone does not create balanced and sustainable economies. Trading rules and sound money are essential i.e. money that remains a constant value, and based on average human productivity.

   EU interest rates are likely to be below the rates normal in the U.K. However, individual banks may well still charge higher rates than they should, unless the EU central banks place a limit on them. Britain has not joined the first phase of the EU single currency and still has to decide when, or whether it will.

3. Many factors need to be taken into account when examining stable economies, including the eight major issues mentioned concerning the Maastricht Treaty. In fact, all the elements so far discussed in this book (including a sound education on how the trading system needs to operate) need to be thoroughly understood. Economies need to be managed in harmony with the private business/institution sectors.

4. A common trading system is not only essential for Europe but also the rest of the world. At present in the EU our trading rules, taxation system and rates, interest rates, wages and subsidies are all different, and, therefore, our currencies are all different. This varies the competitiveness of our businesses. Britain at present (2006) still has a high pound (£) and this does not help export businesses, or when they are competing against imported goods and services. However, imported goods become cheaper as the £ gains value, and this helps other businesses to become more competitive.

5. None of the EU countries have low rates of unemployment and some are quite high. There are a number of reasons for this situation:
a) the lack of competitiveness of many existing businesses, thus reducing work;
b) higher imports of goods and services due to overvalued currencies, which reduces the values of other currencies, and diminishes EU competitiveness;
c) badly planned economies, creating the wrong businesses and skills to meet the ever changing needs of the businesses and the nation's requirements, leaving the economies out of balance;
d) instabilities caused by sudden changes in wages, currencies, taxation and regulation etc., apart from those caused by natural events, which are sometimes easier to forecast.

6 Many citizens are suffering from poverty, through no fault of their own, but purely resulting from the economic system held in position by governments. This leads to poor rates of pay,

where people are underpaid for their quality of work and productivity, and pensions that do not cover even the basic costs of living. Even if pensioners wanted to work, often no work is available. In a properly run and balanced economy this would not happen.

7 To create a sound and sustainable standard of living in developed countries the economies must be developed, so that each element of them is in proper balance: i.e. skills, wages, pensions, goods, services, businesses and institutions. We should endeavour to produce exactly what we require, within natural capacities. This balance would take longer to develop in third world nations.

8 Poorly run economies and unfair conditions, including exploitation, lead to an increase in crime rates. Sound education, morals, and a balanced economy lead to a reduction in crime. Sometimes people are forced into criminal activities just to survive or support their family. Clearly, for social justice to ensue for the whole community, balanced economies should be created.

The reasons for convergence

It has already been made very clear in this book how dependent we are on each other throughout the world and how badly the economic system and the present trading rules are serving us, thus distorting our economies as already explained in this Chapter. The distortions are making life very difficult for most people. When people do not understand what and why certain things are happening, they will survive and protect themselves in many different ways and not act rationally. Hence, crime, greed and violence, none of which solves the problem, but makes matters far worse by creating bitterness. There is also another problem People are afraid of loosing their jobs and status. Any changes that might be necessary for the good of the majority, is often opposed by those not willing to sacrifice their present positions. These persons are often in a position of power, including considerable wealth.

The reason for the convergence is to create a sustainable environment and economy that satisfies the 8 points issues in this Chapter. The method of convergence must take into account the human problems and a means to achieve an international sustainable economy, the purpose for which the MH system has been produced.

One of the major problems responsible for our distorted economies is the monetary exchange system, which relies on markets valuing products without taking into account human productivity and skills, the only resource we all have to exchange for harvesting the world's natural resources. By changing the monetary system to match nature's natural event, our hours of work process = food and material possessions. This will considerably help to correct the major instabilities in the world economies. Then knowledge and appropriate technology, and sound trading rules and fairness and honesty will maintain and raise our standard of living, until it reaches a maximum point at which nature restrains or does not permit any higher level.

The convergence process

With the MH system it is necessary to value initially all currencies into the Master Currency, as explained and illustrated in previous tables for some of the currencies. To achieve this is a massive task, which requires teams of people to gather the statistics and calculate the new figures, which change continually, caused by wage inflation and other factors that fuel it. However, in this book another approach is going to be used to explain the convergence process.

Under the present world system, economies are out of equilibrium and businesses, sooner or later, should envisage structural changes that will need to take place. Governments realise there are limits on government expenditure, and they are studying ways to reduce it, yet maintaining the security families seek; but they are paying little attention to the other serious structural flaws in our economies. Using models based on average human productivity as recommended in this book, and following through our human transactions, one can discover where the faults in our present economic system lie, and why many families cannot support themselves. My research observations have revealed some of them. Even without government assistance, businesses collectively could negotiate wages around productivity and an average basic rate of £7.50 per hour (or other fixed rates deemed suitable). Businesses could also limit their maximum profits. This would stabilise their economies and allow a more sustainable balance. (Most EU currencies were all locked together in January 1999 with their economies out of equilibrium.) Businesses in EU countries could also adopt the same principal, as just proposed for Britain, by fixing their currencies to the basic productivity unit, but at a rate of 10 euros per hour. Whether Britain is in or out of a single currency, businesses could themselves trade in the euro on the assumption it was fixed to a productivity unit, thereby overcoming some of the competitiveness problems created by the currencies. Careful modelling will help businesses, as the economies converge, or where they remain distorted, to detect problems and work out solutions for their particular circumstances. By understanding the problems, engineered solutions can be provided. Business trade organisations could assist this process, which could also involve the use of import/export agencies to balance trade.

In the first addition of 'Your Business Guide' published in 1998 by the Author he gave a set of currency value figures as in Table 203, but only up to year 1998 the year of publication of the book. The table was given so as to make suggestions as to how the £ Sterling could be converged with the Euro. From this point onwards, excluding the Table which has been updated to 2006, the text is from 'Your Business Guide' updated in 2002.

After Britain came out of the ERM (Exchange-Rate Mechanism) in 1992, and until 1996, its economy became competitive. The value of our labour for a basic unit of productivity in this period amounted to say £7.50 per hour and, using the ecu exchange rate in that period, about 10 ecu per hour, as can be judged by examining the Table. Since 1996 the value of the £ against the ecu has risen steadily, making our labour rates less competitive, as can also be seen from the Table. The value of the basic unit of work of 10 ecu, (or euro after January 1999), per hour is convenient and logical. Industry could have two options from the beginning of 1999

1. peg the £ at £0.75 per euro, or
2. peg £1 to 1 euro.

Under each of these circumstances wages would be negotiated on the basic productivity unit to converge with the euro. If the other EU nations have wage stability problems, as envisaged by the author, and they pegged their wages to the euro, their wages too would converge to common levels against the euro. By Britain leading the way with 10 euros to the basic hourly unit of productivity other nations may well decide on the same route. This would be a most valuable step in converging the economies.

Table 203
The £ Sterling and the Euro

Date	Value of ecu/euro in £	One productivity unit valued in £	One productivity unit in ecu/euro	UK inflation rate
11.1.92	0.72	6.81	9.45	-
9.1.93	0.78	7.21	9.24	5.87
8.1.94	0.75	7.46	9.95	3.47
7.1.95	0.78	7.71	9.88	3.35
8.1.96	0.78	7.91	10.14	2.59
4.1.97	0.73	8.20	11.23	3.67
3.1.98	0.67	8.60	12.84	4.88
2.1.99	0.70	8.95	12.79	4.07
8.1.00	0.63	9.37	14.87	4.69
6.1.01	0.63	9.45	15.00	0.85
4.1.02	0.62	9.77	15.76	3.39
3.1.03	0.64	10.40	16.25	6.45
2.1.04	0.70	10.73	15.33	3.17
7.1.05	0.70	11.22	16.03	4.57
7.1.06	0.69	11.50	16.67	2.50

Note: The ecu values have been based on figures in the 'Economist', as have the euro values from 1st January 1999.

Through British business eliminating inflation in their currency, by carrying out the necessary structural changes, and pegging wages to a productivity unit, there would be no reason for the Bank of England to use high rates of interest. Thus they could follow the EU lower rates, but no higher than 6%.

The author's research and proposals have been carried out very carefully, but within his sole capacity. If the business/private sector assiduously studied the proposals, it is envisaged that they would come to similar conclusions. However, the author would recommend extended gathering of relevant statistics and modelling to ensure utterly sound trading criteria can be established: the research should be properly financed.

The proposed national structural change for sound money, properly paid wages and realistic profits, would mean low wages being increased, in line with the £7.50 (or other chosen or current value) basic productivity unit, and high wages being lowered to remove the distortions. The problem with this solution is the families' borrowed money commitments, particularly home mortgages. For this reason, it is suggested that the second option is to make £1 = to 1 euro. This would result in a 33% inflation in the £, but it is also a 33% devaluation against the euro, when valued at 10 units per basic unit of productivity, which from past experience seems to be about the right balance for the U.K. to remain competitive. Naturally, many models need to be made against various currencies, to check this proposed balance. An added bonus of this solution is that, if we do join the single currency, the British public will not have to learn the value of the euro. We would already have aligned to its correct value. The proposed inflation could take place over say 6 years, bearing in mind the present wage inflation rate is 4.9%, which is not too unacceptable and at a pace the public are used to handling.

Not knowing the path the EU is going, now the euro notes and coins have become available, it is difficult to forecast the euro's proper value against the basic productivity unit, unless the EU also adopts 10 euro to the basic productivity unit (master currency) as proposed in this Chapter. High unemployment, many languages, people's tendency of not wishing to be in a mobile labour force and the international rate of the euro, will perhaps create a slow transition and changes in prices and wage rates. Up to 2002 the majority of the public were still using and comparing values in their familiar currency, as this was the money in circulation. One wonders how much research the EU has carried out concerning how people are to cope with the new situation! It would certainly be very helpful for Britain if a euro benchmark could be given, so that the U.K. economy could gently converge to the correct point, say the proposed 10 euros to the basic productivity unit. If not, the £ would have to be realigned, probably, to a less convenient figure.

In 2006, one is in a position to discuss the present situation in Europe. Businesses, working in the international manufacturing and other producer industries have moved to where wages for the required skills are lowest, in countries like China, India and eastern European countries who have now joined the EU. These businesses are doing well. Other producer industries in manufacturing continue to close or are being re-sited. Farming is still relying on subsidies. Property prices have soared, led by Britain to unsustainable prices, and this is not only in Europe, but is happening throughout the world. In the producer sector of the economy wages have lowered, but these cannot fall below the minimum wage set by most governments, and at this level families need subsidies. Unemployment continues at high levels and the EU has failed to correct this problem, as expected by the author. The service sector continues to do quite well and wage rises in the UK have averaged nearly 4% from 1993 to 2006 as the table indicates.

In Table 2003 the ecu/euro is based on the UK Master Currency value and, therefore, has risen in line with UK wage rates. The wage inflation rate has been different every year in each EU country. For a proper study each EU country needs to calculate its Master Currency rate, based on its wages, as has been calculated by the author for the UK. When this has been done, including the working population, it is possible to calculate the average euro rate. One can then start to work out a smooth convergence of the EU economies.

Had the British Government adopted £1 to 1 euro with 10 euros to the Master Currency (or MH) and taken 6 years for the convergence operation, by 2004 the convergence would have been completed. From this point onwards all inflation would have ceased as this is the point that the existing 15 members could have all converged. The economies would then have all been in a sustainable balance. Inflation would no longer be necessary and the EU members would all be trading on the same basis with the same trade rules, as outlined in the three volumes of this book. As other nations economies continue with inflation their wages would become less competitive. Third world nations would slowly be converging, with the developed ones. It is likely that other developed nations would decide to converge with the EU. Assuming convergence had taken place, then, the present property bubble would not have happened, as doing so would have broken the MH trading rules.

However, Britain did not peg its currency to £1 = 1 euro and 10 euro = 1MH. Now, at the beginning of 2006 1 MH = £11.50. Therefore a new convergent strategy is required. One of the biggest problems in the U.K. is the property bubble that has probably doubled the value of property against the sustainable MH value. Many people too are overpaid, but need that income to cover the massive mortgage on the overvalued property. Property prices need to be frozen and salaries need to conform to the sustainable MH trading system. The author proposes that wages of the underpaid should rise to the sustainable level. It would now appear that the MH should be stabilised at £20 to one MH, because of the property bubble and overpaid salaries. Without the EU statistics it is difficult to know their real value, but it is quite likely that inflation of the first 15 countries has also averaged UK levels, so let us now say 1 MH should also be frozen at 20 euros. All EU countries could then converge to this figure. Wages in all countries need to be adjusted to the MH wage structure to ensure sustainable economies, and in due course a sustainable environment. Convergence needs to take place over a number of years, as in the previous example.

Table 204
MH £ value at different rates of constant inflation

Year	Rate of inflation			
	4%	5%	6%	10%
2006	11.50	11.50	11.50	11.50
2007	11.96	12.08	12.19	12.65
2008	12.43	12.67	12.92	13.92
2009	12.93	13.31	13.70	15.31
2010	13.45	13.98	14.52	16.84
2011	13.99	14.67	15.39	18.52
2012	14.55	15.41	16.31	20.37
2013	15.13	16.18	17.29	
2014	15.74	16.99	18.33	
2015	16.37	17.84	19.43	
2016	17.02	18.73	20.59	
2017	17.70	19.66		
2018	18.41	20.65		

Table 204 shows the £ Sterling inflating at different rates. At the 5% inflation rate it would take 12 years to reach 1 MH = £20 Sterling and even with the 6% inflation rate it would take 10 years. However at the 10% rate of inflation 1 MH = £20 would only take 6 years, which is far more realistic, as it really is necessary to rectify the balance of the economies as soon as possible. With such an inflation rate it would be realistic to adjust wage rates at half yearly intervals.

Low incorrect wages would be raised above the inflation rate chosen by using a higher rate that would allow the wage to be correct at the end of the 6-year period chosen for the convergence. Any overpaid salaries, would be frozen until they reached the correct rate. If for the chosen MH = £20, including correction for the wage differential and productivity, the salary was still lower than the amount paid, this salary would be lowered in equal steps over the 6-year period. At the end of the convergence period all wages would then be in accordance with the fair and sustainable trading rules.

Prices of goods and services would also be adjusted in balance with wages and profits, and where it is too high it would also be reduced to comply with the MH trading rules.

The euro would deflate against other currencies, taking into account the inflation created by the remodelling, and its overvalued amount against all other currencies, but in co-operation with each country outside the EU trading area. Whatever happens the other currencies must also slowly converge towards the MH value so that the world economies can become sustainable.

The reason for convergence

From the foregoing it can be observed that the convergence process is about getting the world economies into a sustainable balance, which also includes natural resources: the environment. By using a natural measure and understanding our world and people the MH system can work out sustainable balances in terms of human mental and physical effort, based on time, human knowledge and technology we have developed.

Before convergence can take place the MH infrastructure must be established, the right statistics gathered and plans made, built on sound economic models for every country. By using the MH system and modelling, the flaws in the unsustainable economy can be located. Solutions can then be established to implement the changes needed to solve the problems. The type of problems would determine the time needed for each convergence operation, and this must take into account people's ability to understand and carry out that change.

The convergence process is not just about changing to a single world currency to create fair trade, but to also solve problems like: family economic problems of work, income, retirement and cultural problems; business strategy, sustainable trading and trading language; government duties and their infrastructure, and damage to the environment and how to care for it.

The convergence process is about making life better for everyone, each process solving a separate, or a number of problems depending on the sector of the economy being tackled by the solution. For example, the MH monetary system and trading rules would create fair trade, give families sustainable incomes, safety net pensions and a sound saving account system that protects its purchasing power. Businesses would be able to operate in stable trading conditions, where old products would be phased out as news ones come into being.

Sound economic conditions would lead to people understanding how trade among millions of people supports their lives. This will help people to understand that fairness and honesty pays dividends of stability, leading to a reduction in stress and more trust in trading activities. This will help all our different cultures to survive peacefully. Caring for each other will lead to any form of crime and conflict being pointless. The convergence process would extend to children's education, with sound explanation, on how to behave in a sustainable modern world economy. Violence and bullying of any form is unacceptable in the MH system, within any culture. Having a single trading language will all help the trusting process, plus the bonus of preventing accidents and misunderstandings due to language problems.

For poor countries, those with very low valued currencies, they would more easily be able to afford the goods from the developed nations with lower valued currencies. As these currencies drop in value during convergence these goods and services would gradually become more affordable. However, the developing countries in real need for vital products and services should be sold these items at Master Currency rates, from the beginning of the convergence operation.

Convergence does not necessarily have to commence only when a country's government decides to adopt the MH system, but can commence as soon as the MH financial products are actually implemented by a private sector business or institution, since they should not conflict with the laws of any country. Charities could use this process to pay for and sell third world products. The system could be used for inter-Commonwealth trade, as that is itself a sovereign body.

Banking institutions could set up savings accounts that save people's savings in MH units with interest rates of up to 4% AER and avoid any losses caused by inflation, and also lend the money in MH units on secured loans. Pension funds could also use these banks for sound investments that would not lose purchasing power. These would all help to converge the economies onto a sustainable basis.

Other institutions could trade internationally in MH units in any country, by keeping in balance exports and imports. Although this might be a more difficult task it would help the convergence process and be able to perhaps increase trade in the production sector and save certain types of business. Using the MH system as a valuation guide a third world country could subsidise some of its products to ensure they would be a competitive export product, or the develop nation manufacturer could set up a factory in the developing nation to cover the cost of imports of their product into that country. By careful balancing both countries could gain in trade and sustainable business.

Private Sector

The private sector of the developed countries, from the above suggestions, could set in motion the convergence process, which governments initially would probably prefer. International banks and the production sector of the economy could save many businesses by developing sustainable trade between developed and developing economies, using the MH system to work out the solutions. Governments could initially help by allowing this process to take place. People in the world could also see the advantage of this form of free trade internationally.

CHAPTER 27

POLITICAL MATTERS

To this point the author's research, observations and recommendations in these three volumes are vastly different from present political thoughts. The difference is broadly due to following the requirements of the natural economy and the way it has allowed the human race to develop its present standard of living. The author's approach removes the man-made distortions from the economy, caused by selfishness, greed, and misunderstandings, many of which form the basis of present political policies in governments. We all have consciences, but when putting down our thoughts and recollections errors occur, or the writings can be misinterpreted by others, unintentionally, sometimes with grave consequences, leading to serious conflicts that destroy the quality of life intended for us.

The present world is governed using thousands of laws, created by governments and dictators, in many languages and not translated into others, and hundreds of international agreements, with various motives behind them and often with a poor understanding of the natural world. The people in the world cannot communicate in a single common language that we are all sufficiently fluent in.

It is clear from my research that people do not realise how reliant we are upon each other throughout the world, for our security and standard of living. Each of our daily lives are supported by efforts of thousands of other people, the majority we have never met, who irrespective of their beliefs have honestly supplied us with the material support we need by trading, using natural resources and specials skills, which have allowed our security and standard of living to rise. Sadly in many parts of the world, mainly due to lack of knowledge, greed and dishonest political policies, people live in appalling conditions, with really little constructive help from the developed nations.

In the past lack of knowledge has been the reason for the nature and form of the economy, plus people who were in powerful situations that only really cared for themselves and their lavish creations. However, many other people gradually learnt to understand the world they were living in and how to develop our economies, perhaps often supported by the wealthy that allowed the world to reach its present form of industrialisation.

Present-day political powers including religious bodies have not found the solutions to properly integrate the world economies and solve the serious conflicts and distortions taking place in the world. World nations cannot trust each other and disputes are extremely difficult to solve under such conditions.

As a very young child up to the second world war, the author at first thought he was being brought up in paradise, but from that point onwards he slowly discovered, how far we were from it. From his business and professional experience, he realised how badly the people managing the world understood how it should function to produce sustainable living conditions, without serious world conflicts: and this approximately thirty years ago led him to commence developing the MH system, of which the skeleton is described in this book.

Having developed the tools to change economies to become sustainable does not mean they can be used or will be used. This is because the policy of the MH system needs to be accepted by people and their governments. Although there may be a number of situations where the system can be used, to be fully effective, it must eventually be accepted by everyone, including governments and religious bodies. To reach this, many policy obstacles to the changes necessary must be overcome.

At present hundreds of government and international organisations exist, having been set up to manage the world economies. Treaties have been signed and laws passed, and very many are not appropriate to the development of sustainable economies. Again, although the MH system is a matter that is a government duty to eventually sanction, which department/s person/s in government has the duty to make the necessary decision? Clearly a political decision is necessary, but when communicating with governments the letters are dealt with by civil servants, who do not keep their ministers informed concerning important information passing to them; they exclude information they may think is inappropriate. When this happens politicians could loose the opportunity to make use of new research.

The MH system covers very many economic disciplines and would be of interest to many government ministries. Each government works differently, so logically one could assume if a letter is addressed to the Prime Minister the letter would end up being studied either by one ministry that is properly equipped with a complete range of experts, as would be necessary for the MH system, or a number of ministerial departments and the central bank. This does not happen. Letters seem to fall into the hands of civil servants that on their own do not want to discuss the MH system concept, whilst the free market concept is generally accepted. They do not appear to want to support radical well thought through systems designed to converge world economies onto a sustainable path. Government officials generally speaking are not the ones managing businesses, particularly the Production Industries that are facing serious problems in the developed countries with high currency values. They are likely to be quite ignorant of their problems, and how important these industries are to developing sustainable economies. The present international currency valuation system and so-called free markets are creating very distorted conditions, making it impossible for economies and the environment to become sustainable.

Generally speaking politicians do not have qualifications sufficient to understand how economies function, are managed and developed. Ministers are often moved from one ministry to another, so how can they be expected to be proficient: surely they have to rely on the civil servants, and therefore should not be responsible for the professional civil servants management errors and practices. When a political party is running a government, its policies are taken over and managed by civil servants. Generally speaking political parties do not have the funds to create sustainable policies to manage complicated modern economies. So is this one of the reasons why modern economies are so unstable?

Most politicians are not economists, but have other general to very specialist skills. The overall skills of politicians would not cover the complete range used in the economy. When in government they are expected to make the right economic decisions on a very wide range of issues. Is this fair and wise, or should there be a more positive method used, where people with the right qualifications for elements of the economy are the ones responsible?

Families and businesses are responsible for the well being of their individual parts of their economy, and not the general economy and on the basis they are law abiding they are not responsible for the remainder of the world economy. The people, however, in democracies are expected to choose political candidates, but this is not normally obligatory, quite rightly, where none of the candidates are acceptable. Frequently people vote for persons or parties that would give them or their occupation an advantage, whether or not it was good for the whole economy. Other persons do not vote in economies that are above average, like in the developed nations, as they believe that whichever political party is in power, it makes little difference to them, or the way the economy functions. In other words, "you can't change the system".

The majority of people working in government work using the skills they have learnt, but they themselves would not know whether the skills they have are necessarily the ones needed by the government. The senior civil servants that decide are well aware of normal past practices, but do not necessarily know whether present day decisions made by governments changing the shape of the economy are really correct. Economists generally gain their knowledge from the past statistics, and they themselves may have little knowledge, on the development process, which is almost entirely in the hands of the private sector.

Successful businesses remain stable or grow, some into massive international organisations. These are all well managed and their activities planned as they move forward. Their activities are not concerned with the stability of the world economy, unless government directs them to take into account sustainable solutions. However, present governments are unable to guide their economies onto a sustainable path, as there is no accepted strategy for this specific purpose. The MH system is a strategy designed to meet this purpose, and to integrate everyone into the system, by sound explanation and reasoning.

Just like the human body, the medical professions have worked internationally to find out more and more how it naturally functions. Governments need to carry out a similar operation for the whole world economy and its environment, so that the management and development of it can be integrated and so that our human activities can move forward in harmony with nature, thereby making our standard of living sustainable, and preventing the destruction of it. The MH system is one of the first steps in this process, as it creates the foundation that integrates all human activities, and explains how to keep the millions of balances needed in harmony with the total environment. It helps people to understand their individual roles from childhood and through their lifespan to death, and how to obtain a more enjoyable and secure standard of living.

All systems and organisations need to be checked and adjusted. People, being human, are not perfect and may not always work logically and correctly, so their performance must also be checked. Economic structures and systems that fit in with nature are everyone's property, once paid for by them. They are a form of code of practice that keeps us living together on a sustainable route. The system guides us in every matter to ensure there are no distortions in our way of life, no major conflicts, people guided to avoid conflicts and accidents, people understanding their tasks to ensure a more or less trouble free life. The majority of people throughout the world are quite capable of making sound decisions given sound guidance and explanations. People are able to respect each other and willingly solve problems democratically. Those with difficulties would be helped. Most people want to have as peaceful a life as possible and, after their work activities in the general economy, be able to enjoy their spare time, without unnecessary stress. All this is possible with the right will and human effort to keep the sustainable economic structure in the right shape; everyone knowing where they are going, and helping those young, or disabled, to reach this goal. However, the right effort in the right places must be made to keep the economy in a sound shape.

A sustainable form of economic system would keep the economies in harmony with the natural environment as it changes shape, because it will be monitoring the effects of the changes and taking the appropriate action, to solve the problems in good time. The sustainable economic system once in place would be in effect self-regulating, with the minimum of national laws needed to keep it secure. People's sound education of the economic system and their duties to maintain it is vital to ensure it functions soundly. Present-day economies are distorted, and frequently dishonest, causing considerable distress in every country, rich or poor. This situation destroys confidence and trust, and leads to conflict and all the other distortions making the majority very insecure.

From the foregoing it seems that the system of government and international co-operation needs to be reformed, to correct the weaknesses causing our global problems, where it is difficult for most to plan a sustainable and realistic future direction for their lives and achievable aspirations. Governments are holding the present economic systems firmly in place. Much of the economies are being changed without sound explanation or consent. Masses of people are unemployed, or underemployed. Essential parts of economies are crumbling and not serving the real needs of the population. People in some parts of the world are starving and not able to have the basics for survival, while in others parts of the world well managed farm products are too expensive and farmers being squeezed into non-active use. Citizens are powerless to prevent this from happening. Clearly sound political decisions are required, but governments seem to be unable to make them! Thousands of laws and armed conflicts do not correct our economies: they only create resentment and bitterness and encourage breaking laws in protest. The only way to correct these serious problems is to understand people and their problems and the natural way we can advance our standard of living. Unnatural constraints and measures held in place by governments are destroying any form of stability. People are also loosing the will to work, or work conscientiously.

So far the author and his close supporters have not yet found the way forward to discuss with the right responsible persons in government or other major organisations how to move his concepts forward. The plan covers a very wide range of professional and practical skills making it difficult for an individual to endorse it. It requires the right panel of professional persons covering all the elements to be ratified. Ideally this panel requires people from all sectors of the economy.

With any product, especially major ones, proof that it works is often required. If the product cannot be used it is difficult to prove that it works. Many thousands of people would be required to prove the system works. The government has not helped the author with such a project, because it appears to only want to support the "free" market system, and is refusing to understand that it is not sustainable. Does it also indicate it has not the people with the experience to verify it? The problem is what comes first is it necessary to verify the MH system before making a political decision, or does one make the political decision and then verify it? When the system follows natural development paths, should there be any reason to verify it? For private enterprise, where it does not conflict with national laws there is no reason why it cannot be used.

The MH system can already offer products, like:

1. The Master Currency, to value a national currency as a sound monetary/productivity measure. This can then be used for all planning activities
2. A negotiating system for fair sustainable wage negotiations.
3. Stable savings and pension funds
4. A means to study the flaws in the world economic system
5. A Master Currency Game, that is also educational.
6. A means to explain to people the purpose of money and the economy.

These are all products that can be used by the private sector of the economy to help businesses and people. People and companies can make their own decision on these. However, without government participation the real benefits of the MH system would not be able to correct the major flaws in the present economies, which continue to harm the lives of millions of people.

Under present circumstances, if government and international government bodies ignore the author's research, how do they intend to make the world economies sustainable?

Fighting terrorism is no simple matter. Even the most modern weaponry does not solve the problems. The only way it can be eliminated is by first locating the reasons, and then finding sound solutions that are fair, honest and realistic. This cannot be achieved until the parties can trust each other. Killing the innocent on both sides in protest against the others reaction does not solve the dispute, only face-to-face serious and constructive discussion and sound practical solutions.

The world is concerned about global warming, pollution, poverty, water, unemployment, failing pensions and dept. How are governments going to solve these? What are governments going to do if global warming forces millions of people to migrate? They are very likely to continue as in the past, not able to solve major problems before they are very serious.

Technology has already allowed many improvements to the world economies, however much of our human energy has been wasted in disputes, caused by greed unfairness, major world conflicts, and various policies, including the unsound monetary system. The management and trading systems create wasted human effort and natural resources. Even too much competition can waste resources. The world now needs to use the available technology to carry out the tasks more efficiently. Using the MH system as an economic tool it can be worked out how we could reduce transportation to save both materials and energy. We can also find the skills required to reshape the economy to become sustainable and improve the standard of living of the deprived nations and the unemployed in the developed countries. By basing economic models of countries on the Master Currency instead of present currencies, migration patterns can be studied. Using the Master Currency badly needed resources would be affordable in the developing nations, making them more stable and increasing business potential, and this would tend to reduce the need to migrate..

The EU could also make models of its members' currency being based on the Master Currency and on the basis the rest of world does too. It would discover that the employment situation could be solved and all the other problems resulting from a single currency. With full employment, countries would become wealthier and pensions affordable and sustainable.

A sound economic system would allow the planners more human resources to create sustainable economies and to look into ways of slowing global warming, by various strategies.

With all changes to economies there are usually winners and losers, but there are considerable advantages when economies can be made stable. More people would gain and overall business turnover would increase, resulting in the increase of people in employment and income. Where unsustainable profits are taken, those businesses would lose, but generally speaking those businesses would be well able to afford the initial losses. Their increase in trade may well make good those losses.

The local district authority is a very important body in the proposed MH system, because they are in real contact with their citizens. It is the body that would help everyone with their problems and information. This authority would hold very complete information of its district and would be the hub of the community. It would be a good idea if the local citizens could elect the department heads of the local district. Councillors would still be required, but mainly to liase and check the work and policy of the local district authority. Regions would oversee the local district authorities and advise the councillors. For very important changes the use of referendums should also be used.

The department heads in both the regions and government, like senior civilservants, should also be elected. The elected councillors could also liase and check the work of their region. Politicians could be elected at regional level, and they would liase with their region and government and check the work carried out by the government. All the elected persons should have the right qualifications for the work they are chosen for.

Central government would need to check the work of the regions and co-ordinate the activities of the country to ensure the economy is sustainable. Where a political party is in power and deciding on policies, another elected body is required to check the new policies to be used. The persons in this other elected body should also be professionally qualified for the work, or law, they are checking and they should have considerable relevant experience. All major issues should also be subject to referendums. It is most important that the elected persons in government have a very sound knowledge on how economies function, are maintained and developed to be sustainable and in harmony with the environment.

The nature of the power politicians and heads of department wield needs to be carefully thought through. Generally speaking people who are good in their jobs stay in their jobs. However, people do change and also sometimes the nature of the work they do. When this happens changes must be possible, i.e. their contract of work can end. This could also apply to a political party in power. Government would of course continue to manage the sustainable economic system with its clear lines of direction.

The major political problem is how to change from the present free market form of economy to a sustainable Master Currency free market economy. When people have little time to study changes proposed for the economy, there is likely to be plenty of opposition, unless the changes can be very well planned, properly explained and moved forward in gentle steps.

In the private sector there are thousands of people wanting to develop sustainable economies, including some politicians. Many businesses and professional bodies are developing the products to help the world change direction. The people supporting and developing sustainable development need to work together, and start to set up the structures that will be required. These people collectively need to lead the way forward, by setting an example. They can start setting up the structures and systems needed, and then themselves use them. Sound sustainable finance is a key to businesses and employees. The MH system opens up trade to every business throughout the world, and for their employees a sound achievable wage structure and pensions. We all have to bank our savings, and such a bank could soon be serving half a million customers in the U.K. The system would soon start to revive the manufacturing production sector of the economy that used to employ more than 20% of our working population.

The production sector, and that is, natural materials, manufacture and construction must be in harmony with nature, and if they do not, their projects fails. They must harness the forces of nature and respect it, and this leads to sustainable products. People working in these industries understand this. Many people working in services are often completely unaware of their problems. People in production are reliant on the environment, need to understand the forces of nature and have to manage people who make their product possible. The years of research and experience in harnessing all these forces and developing the world are vital in understanding how to build sustainable economies, in harmony with the environment. They know when they have failed, because their project then collapses. If people in serving them cannot work together and in harmony, and trust each other there would be many problems. Those that work together under sound leadership and are skilled in their activities can plan activities and keep on schedule.

The service sector of the economy provides the parts of the economy needed by the production sector. If those products are not in harmony with the natural economy, they can prevent the stability of the production sector. The service sector provides the national infrastructure, the government sector, financial system, transport systems and distribution systems, education and care sector. If any of these are distorted and not sustainable, they would undermine the production sector and could even destroy it and yet it is needed for our survival!

The issues that bond the human economies are: trading our human skills, fairness to each other, trust, sharing the natural resources, and a sustainable economic system that is in harmony with the environment.

CHAPTER 28

GLOBAL BODY FOR SUSTAINABLE ECONOMIES AND ENVIRONMENT

At the present time there is no organisation set up to carry out this type of work, and governments are having great difficulty in agreeing on how to solve world problems. There is no agreed world strategy or agreed system method for this process. The purpose of the MH system is to make this possible.

Chapter 27 has highlighted some of the political problems that need to be resolved to make it possible to achieve the objective. The body must be able to co-ordinate the world activities and guide them onto the required path. The system needs to function automatically, just like the human body maintains its balance in each of us; like self-healing and our immune system. People must not have the power to alter the natural system and events.

Using the MH system, or similar system that takes into account that the purpose of the economy is to serve absolutely everyone, the organisation would gradually steer the world onto a sustainable path, taking all the actions necessary. There are many major flaws in the way the world is presently managed. These would need to be corrected by an education and explanation process, and not by armed conflict. The present monetary system and trading rules must be made sustainable, so that wealth is fairly distributed, allowing people to support themselves. Education pays a major role in the system and is needed to guide people on their role in the world and the real purpose of the economy, and why it must be in a sustainable form. The economy must create structures that people understand and which can carry out all the necessary tasks to support the achievable standard of living. The system is a form of world culture that supports and belongs to them, like a language, and cannot be taken away from them, by any dictator or persons in powerful positions: it is their natural sustainable right.

Like the family and business economies, which all have to be planned and managed, the generally economy must be too. The general economy serving all of us without planning and management would never be sustainable. Markets may determine the goods wanted, but they do not keep the economy in a sustainable form. This latter task is the responsibility of governments, and a world co-ordinating body, the one we are discussing in this Chapter. Like governments the co-ordinating body would need to have adequate funding for its tasks. However, initially it may have to be funded by the private sector, like those supporting sustainable development.

The persons managing the Global Body for Sustainable Economy and Environment would all need to be adequately qualified and understand how sustainable economies are managed, developed and maintained. Initially these people may be the only experts in the art of sustainable developments and would have to lead, manage and transfer the knowledge to the rest of the world. They would have to guide existing government officials and explain why trading rules and the present economic system must change.

The new Global Body would work in conjunction with other global institutions where possible, to develop the new sustainable economic strategy. These could be funded by governments, or be other global private enterprise businesses, developing or maintaining sustainable products.

The Global Body would assist governments and private sector organisations to establish the new sustainable world economic system and co-ordinate the economic activities, including adjustments that may be required to the trading rules and international laws. It would be involved with the protection of the environment and the distribution of international resources.

Clearly the body would need to have powers to ensure peoples rights and to maintain a sustainable world economy and environment. However, individuals and employees collectively working for the organisation would not be in a position to dictate policies, without those policies being soundly thought through and accepted, through a democratic process and backed by a respected leadership. No leaders or experts are permanent, but could serve for long periods. The activities of the body would be monitored by governments.

CHAPTER 29

CONCLUDING CHAPTER

The three volumes of this book give the type of concept needed to develop sustainable economies throughout the world. The tasks is a massive one that should be undertaken as soon as possible to right the serious flaws in the world's present economies. Millions of the world population are dying, or suffering from poverty and stress, because of the way present market economies function. It is hoped that the skeleton of proposed sustainable solution given will lead people, and governments, to tackling the problem on a sound and professional basis. The book is only the start of the process needed. Everyone interested and involved in such a project would require different further information. This information would come from many different sources, and experts, including the author.

Not a person has the capacity of providing all the knowledge required. However, the proposed MH system would link together all the information recorded and a structure to manage the world economy onto a sustainable basis at every level, including the trading culture used to exchange the millions of skills that supports each person's personal economy, or standard of living, and the respect for each others peaceful existence.

To create such a sustainable economy is a collective effort of people, private enterprise and governments. This project needs to be led by experienced dedicated leaders. It is hoped that the book's readers will all help in some way to make the sustainable economy reality.

The world project will have to grow organically at a pace that can be managed by the available people and organisations to develop it, and moved it forward. Collectively the world has the right knowledge and technology to manage and build a sustainable economy.

It is hoped that the models and explanation given have clearly indicated that economies must be guided and managed to maintain them on a sustainable path, and that they must have stable trading rules, based on sound measures and criteria. These MH monetary measures must not be based on market values that distort the balance of the economy and the distribution of wealth created by work. In a sustainable form of economy market forces still apply, but they do not distort the economy, and of course they will continue to indicate the demand, or lack of demand for a product, or material need.

Disputes, conflicts and wars in the world never permanently solve problems, as can be learnt from historical events. They certainly can bottle up hatred that sometimes passes from generation to generation. There is only one way to solve disputes and that is by explanation and sound reasoning, or an education process using up-to-date human knowledge, to undo previous beliefs taught that are unsound, or not true.

Building trust among people and governments where long established beliefs have to be changed will be a difficult and slow process. Trust can only be built up by sound and honest explanations and practicing fairness. Where discussions have to be translated great care is needed not to make any errors. For this reason and to prevent accidents the ultimate gaol is for everyone to speak the same trading, or international, language.

Governments must allow the sustainable economic system to be developed and used, by changing laws that prevent it from functioning. They must also allow the right economic trading structure and management system to be established. No doubt private enterprise would fund many of the changes required, once it knows that governments support the sustainable economic concept. However, government must also provide the funding needed to reshape its management of the economy.

Economies run on people working in the economy, which is for their benefit. If they are to support themselves, they must have work and be properly paid for it. The services provided by governments are necessary, as these are the ones they only can provide, or are best provided for by them. The majority of people are quite capable of understanding this, and are most unlikely to oppose paying all government taxation, based on their earnings, as they receive them. Only one single form of tax is required.

Private enterprise, the business and institution sectors do not need to pay any taxation, because any taxation they pay, is in fact paid by the working population. This would save a considerable amount of human effort in collecting taxes from the business sector. It would also eliminate taxation fraud. Industry would then also be competing on the same level throughout the world.

In a well-run economy there would be very low rates of unemployment and government would have a steady flow of income each year. This would assist long term planning.

With a sound sustainable economic system carefully developed, young generations would be able to come into a world where they could learn how to live in harmony with people and their natural environment. Their education would give sound guidance on how they need to behave to maintain a more trouble free existence, and how to avoid problems by understanding the natural restrictions, allowing them to enjoy what the earth offers to suit individual requirements and one's life objectives, or aspirations.

We are really living in a wonderful world, once one has corrected our human behaviour, causing all the distortions, the crimes that could be avoided and our unsustainable economic system. The people of the world have been given by nature all the tools and knowledge to understand what needs to be done to make our lives very enjoyable. The natural resources are all available: all we need to do is to keep within the natural restraints set. We must respect each other, and not exploit each other. We must be honest and not evil. When we overstep what nature has intended we must withdraw and record the constraint so that this knowledge can be passed to others.

It is important to spend enough time with children, so they can have the guidance required by parents and others to ensure they understand life on earth and how to enjoy what it offers.

The conditions on earth are continually changing, making it necessary to readjust our economies to meet the new circumstances, like global warming and earthquakes. We should choose to live where it is safe and the necessary resources are available. People may well need to migrate to other countries and people must understand this is a human right. We need to help one another. We need to plan for these events and sort problems out in good time.

In the present day economies enormous human resources are spent in protection against other people's and state actions; crime, conflicts, terrorism. It is common sense to change our culture through sound education and reasoning, and put these resources to making our world a better place to live in. We should make sure that the few people that wreck our world, cannot, by making sure the culprits understand that their unwanted actions are not permitted. It is everyone's duty to keep an eye on the troublemakers, and ensure they are guided onto the sustainable path.

The Master Currency, the MH productivity unit, is a very important measure, as it is used to measure our average productivity in every skill and with every human aid and machine. By using it we can work out what is achievable and how much human effort is required to produce a product. By using different methods to produce a particular product we can determine the best way to produce it: for example the least cost, least hours of human effort, or for the least energy, or raw materials.

When the new sustainable economic system is finally established, all important information would be available: people's skills and where to find them, products and spares, businesses and where they are situated and what they provide. Because the information system is based on product skills and natural elements, one will know where to look for them, and also to be able to discover what others are available. Time would not be wasted by having to use many different systems that are never complete. The system will also help people to discover all parts of their economy and the skills used in it.

The MH economic system eliminates inflation, making prices stable. All products bought based on the Master Currency indicate the hours of human effort to provide them. This helps everyone to make realistic plans to develop their lifestyle and plan their business operations. It helps governments to develop their economies to be sustainable and care for the environment.

The present world financial system together with free market operations is distorting the earlier developed world economies. Gradually the developing nations are developing modern economies that are using the latest technology. They are also now developing new technology. Because of the way developing nations are improving their national economies, leaving many citizens with low standards of living, their wages and currencies are very much undervalued in comparison with the developed countries, whose currencies have a high purchasing power for the third world countries' products they now have available for export. Many of these products are made specifically for the developed nations. This situation is seriously affecting the competitiveness of not only the whole of the production sector of the developed countries, but also many services. Companies naturally make full use of the lower wages, caused by the overvalued currencies for the same and sometimes better skills in these countries. This is not only distorting the balance of skills in the developed countries, but also creating high unemployment. It is also making it difficult for the EU, as migrants from the low wage sectors of the EU are happy to accept low wages in the rich member countries, as their savings have high purchasing power at present in their home countries. Many producer industries cannot compete and are closing down in the developed countries, because of the unbalanced trading conditions created by the monetary system, and also many very strict production regulations and green issues all adding to the cost of production.

Another problem in the developed countries is that people are living much longer, but have been retiring earlier. As pension ages are being raised people will need to work longer, but work will not be available whilst much of it is being carried out in the developing countries. Therefore, unemployment can be expected to rise.

If the present monetary and economic system is allowed to remain in its present form, unemployment in the developed nations is likely to rise until a point is reached when the only work not outsourced will be jobs that can only be carried out on the spot, like local services. This could reduce the working population down to 60%. The unemployed would have to be supported and taxation would have to rise. The developed nations would have little to export, but would be purchasing many products that were not home produced and the country would be forced into greater and greater debt, and this is unsustainable, because developing countries would sooner or later cut supplies. Gradually over a period of another twenty or thirty years developing nations would have the same standard of living as the developed countries, and no doubt would want to value their currencies at the same rate as the former developed countries. By that time developed nations would be forced to produce all their own everyday goods and services, but would have lost the human skills and the businesses. As a result of the unsound monetary system millions of people will suffer a poor standard of living.

The present form of market economy has not helped the developing nations, but has helped the business sector in the developed countries, particularly the multinationals and its financial sector. The financial markets have gained considerably from the free market as presently operated allowing it to make substantial unearned profits. The developed countries benefited by more material wealth, but are now paying for it with an unsound economy that is unsustainable. Many developing nations have gained by developed nations technology, being transferred by inward investment.

Present world governments generally support the present chaotic free market system or try to use it to their best advantage. However, this does not help the majority of the world population when they have to pay the price of mismanagement, or lack of understanding of sustainable economies. Without economies being guided to become sustainable many developing economies are having a rough time, and unless policies change developed nations will too.

The MH system has been developed to converge existing economies and create sustainable economies. The Master Currency, the MH unit, and the key models and trading rules in this book are the basis for a sustainable form of economy. Using the key models one can compare economies to determine where distortions lie. Economies can be modelled using appropriate technology to raise living standards. Economies can be arranged so that they can create exports to pay for imports, keeping annual payments in general balance. Every nation's currency can be valued in Master Currency units to determine how over or under valued they may be. With the right statistical information one can plan conversion rates to raise or lower existing currency rates that are acceptable and sustainable.

Most people who read this book would probably agree that it is now time to converge the world economies to become sustainable, on the basis that the reasons for doing so can be fully explained, and to prevent all the hardship that most of the world is now facing. The knowledge is available for the task, so why not use it and make our world a much happier world to live in? It is hoped that our politicians and senior civil servants will take on the tasks they should naturally be carrying out, managing the world economies on a sustainable basis, instead of leaving the direction based on the chance that market forces know best.